# WOMEN OF
# RAF TEMPSFORD

# WOMEN OF RAF TEMPSFORD

## Churchill's Agents of Wartime Resistance

BERNARD O'CONNOR

AMBERLEY

First published 2011

Amberley Publishing
The Hill, Stroud
Gloucestershire, GL5 4EP

www.amberleybooks.com

British Library Cataloguing in Publication Data.
A catalogue record for this book is available from the British
Library.

ISBN 978-1-4456-0434-3

Typeset in 10.5pt on 13pt Adobe Caslon Pro.
Typesetting and Origination by Amberley Publishing.
Printed in the UK.

# Contents

# Introduction

Until the last decade or so of the twentieth century, media coverage of the Second World War was largely male-dominated. Consequently, the portrayal of women in wartime in films and books tended to show them in secondary roles. However, the rise of feminism in the 1960s and 1970s produced researchers who set out to investigate what life was really like for women and girls during the war years.

There were women, some of whom who have passed away, who managed to tell their families and friends about their wartime experiences. Some wrote their autobiographies, had their memories written down for them or recorded them in other ways. As the Second World War ended almost seventy years ago, there are still women alive today, now in their 80s, 90s and some in their 100s who have memories of the war years. Talk to them. Encourage them to tell you about their history. Document their stories for your children and your children's children.

My interest in the women of RAF Tempsford, a small airfield in Mid-Bedfordshire, has arisen only recently. I moved from Potton into a bigger house with a garden in Everton in 1990. As a teacher of Humanities at St Neots Community College, I was keen to find out more about my local area. I had researched the 'Potton Iguanodon' and uncovered a fascinating story about a very unusual nineteenth-century industry that involved digging up coprolites, which some thought to be fossilised dinosaur droppings. To find that information I had had to visit libraries, museums and record offices all over southern England. I had to write, email, telephone, fax, knock on doors and talk to people. These were all valuable research skills. I found that women and girls were employed in large numbers in the coprolite industry in Potton. I typed up what I found and, after many years, managed to publish articles and books on the subject.

Looking for another topic to research, wondered about writing up the history of Everton but, with its population of only around 500, I didn't think the book would sell well. Instead I decided to create a website and put my research on that. In fact, I started my research the wrong way round by spending years studying the geology, archaeology and early history of the village. I thought when I first embarked on my mission that I would have a page on the First World War, a page on the interwar period, a page on the Second World War and then bring the history up to date with another on the late twentieth century. By the time I got round to these topics in the mid-1990s, a number of potentially knowledgeable local figures had died. I was too late to hear their experiences of life in the village and local area.

Talking to some of the people in Everton, I eventually discovered that there was much more than a page that could be written on what happened there during the Second

World War. I had seen the war graves in the local parish church and seen the photograph in the village hall of the local man who did not come back, but it was Les and Gwen Dibdin, a local couple, who sparked what has become an ongoing research project. Les told me that he was an aircraft fitter on Tempsford Airfield during the war. I had seen the disued airfield at the bottom of the Greensand Ridge on some of my walks around the village and noticed it on the Ordnance Survey maps I had bought. What intrigued me was that Les was not prepared to give me any details about what work he did there. Why? Because he had signed the Official Secrets Act.

However, the Dibdins were prepared to show me the work of their niece, Susie Scott. It was a piece of GCSE History coursework on Tempsford Airfield which, based on her interviews with some of the pilots, aircrew and passengers, shed fascinating light on what had gone on. She said it had been a secret airfield and the locals were not meant to know what went on. That sparked my interest and I began what has been a sixteen-year investigation into what exactly happened there during the war. The first edition of my book on the airfield was published in 1997 with a print run of only fifty. They were nearly all bought by women, wanting to know what their husband, brother, father, uncle, cousin or grandfather did during the war. They had not been told because of the Official Secrets Act.

Over the years I have added more and more information as my research has uncovered more details. The number of pages has increased more than threefold. The latest edition is *RAF Tempsford: Churchill's Most Secret Airfield*, the story of how the Air Ministry selected this isolated spot and designed it specifically to look as if it was a disused airfield. For all intents and purposes the locals considered it an ordinary airfield, except for the fact that the flights were only a few days every month – on either side of the moon period. It was used by the Special Operations Executive (SOE) in part of Churchill's plan 'to set Europe ablaze' and provide the Resistance with ammunition, supplies and training as part of the Allies' long-term plan to liberate occupied Europe. In a letter to General Hastings, Churchill authorised 'a proper system of espionage and intelligence along the whole coasts, to harass the enemy from behind the lines'.

The book details many of the top-secret SOE missions that the two special squadrons, 138 and 161, flew from Tempsford Airfield. They used Lysanders, Stirlings, Halifaxes, Hudsons and other planes to drop supplies to the Resistance in France, Belgium, Holland, Denmark, Norway, Germany, Austria, Czechoslovakia and Poland. Some went south to North Africa to supply groups in south-eastern Europe. They also infiltrated 1,500 'Joes' or 'Bods', the USAAF and RAF slang for secret agents. These agents included a number of brave women who were flown out on top-secret missions. Sometimes these agents needed bringing back to England. So did stranded air crew, resistance leaders and VIPs. Many were lifted out from behind enemy lines by Tempsford crews.

RAF Tempsford, perhaps a lot more than other Second World War airfields, was very cosmopolitan. Americans, French, Belgians, Dutch, Czechoslovakians, Norwegians and Poles were all stationed there. However, Great Britain's links with the Commonwealth meant that there were also pilots and crews from further afield. Many did not return.

They took part in vital operations such as the destruction of the heavy water plant at Vermork in Norway, the assassination of Heydrich in Prague and the attempts to delay German support reaching Normandy after the D-Day landings. Analysis of the squadrons' records show that between 1942 and 1945 there were 5,634 sorties from Tempsford to France. How many missions there were to Norway, Denmark, the Netherlands, Germany, Austria, Czechoslovakia, Poland, North Africa and elsewhere is unknown. 138 Squadron took 995 agents and dropped an estimated 29,000 containers and 10,000 packages. Seventy of their planes failed to return. 161 Squadron took an estimated 400 agents and lost 49 aircraft.

Exactly how many women agents were taken out from Tempsford is uncertain, but it is estimated that there were at least sixty. Of the estimated 1,400 agents, six were killed either by being dropped too low or by jumping without static lines attached to their parachutes. How many people were lifted out of occupied Europe and safely returned to Tempsford is unknown. Across occupied Western Europe there were about 5,500 dropping grounds, areas jokingly called 'The Field' by those in the know.

Before D-Day the Tempsford planes had dropped an estimated total of 2,151 million propaganda leaflets over the continent. Few, if any, of the pilots and crew recognised the role they played in the Allies' psychological warfare of disinformation and propaganda. Other missions flown from Tempsford included dropping pigeons. The aim of this was that people could open the canister attached to the pigeon's leg, fill in the questionnaire with details about German gun emplacements, troop movements, etc., and then release the bird to fly back to Bletchley Park in Buckinghamshire, where there was a pigeon loft above the Station Commander's garage. The information was then added to that already obtained by the decoders using the Enigma machine. Of the 16,554 birds dropped by the Tempsford squadrons, only 1,842 returned, just an 11 per cent success rate. Perhaps it was still enough to help in vital intelligence gathering. The Germans were reported as saying that these birds tasted nice with peas.

The book investigates what went on in requisitioned local country houses like Hazells Hall, Woodbury Hall, Tetworth Hall, Tempsford Hall and Gaynes Hall. It looks at what links the airfield had with Bletchley Park in Buckinghamshire and the American air base at Harrington, near Kettering, Northamptonshire. It includes extracts from books, memoirs, poems, letters, telephone calls and emails written by agents, pilots, and crewmembers of the RAF (Royal Air Force) and other air forces, the WAAF (Women's Auxiliary Air Force), the FANY (First Aid Nursing Yeomanry), catering staff and local men and women. It includes reminiscences of the social life on the base, in the Officers' Mess, the NAAFI (Navy, Army and Air Force Institute) and local hostelries.

The government restriction on the release of sensitive documents to the National Archives, formerly the Public Record Office in Kew, has meant that secret SOE documents are only gradually becoming available. The release of information has not only shed light on some of the secret work undertaken by the 2,000-plus personnel that served at RAF Tempsford but has also encouraged an increasing number of people to publish their memoirs. The recently launched BBC 'People's War' website has been an attempt to allow anyone with wartime memories to have them transcribed and added to a searchable online database. Some of the contributors have referred to their time at Tempsford. The Imperial War Museum also has taped interviews with a number of people with a connection to Tempsford.

In 2005 I was contacted by the Secretary of Blunham Women's Institute and asked to talk to their members about RAF Tempsford. I suggested that I would try to focus on the role of the women at the airfield and I set about putting together various anecdotes and finding illustrations for them. The talk proved so successful that I was asked to repeat it at Sandy Library. Advertisements in the local press and an interview on Three Counties Radio meant the evening was a sell-out. The interest generated has prompted me to write another book.

I would like to thank Philippa Smalls for editing my initial draft and making valuable suggestions to tie up loose ends. I would also like to acknowledge the following people for their research, publications and reminiscences on the SOE and the Second World War: Mont Bettles, Lucy Bittles, Stuart Black, Bob Body, Bill Bright, John Button, Gordon Dunning, Thomas Ensminger, Beryl Escott, Frank Griffiths, Roly Groom, Maureen Gurney, Steve Harris, David Harrison, Jelle Hoolveld, Eileen Hytch, Keith Janes, Wendy King, Steve Kippax, Bob Large, Tom Lowe, Mrs Park, Juliette Pattinson, Jim Peake, Murray Peden, Edna Phillips, Elsie Riding, Jack and Dorothy Ringlesbach, Geoff Rothwell, Nigel Seamarks, Martin Sugarman, Dorothy Summerhayes, Pierre Tillet, Roger Tobbell, Steve Tomlinson and James Wagland.

The following websites and organisations have also been invaluable sources of background information and illustrations, for which due credit is noted: National Archives; Imperial War Museum; King's College Library, London; Harrington Aviation Museum; Channel 4 – The Real Charlotte Grays; Wikipedia; Spartacus; 64 Baker Street; BBC/ww2peopleswar; escapelines.com; scrapbookpages; sameshield; users.nlc; smithsonianmag; RAF Museum, Hendon; East Anglian Aviation Society; aeroplanemonthly; Jaapteeuwen; Jewish Virtual Library; 2iemeguerre; moviemail-online; Clutch.open; site.voila; nzedge; wereldomroep; specialforcesroh; rafbombercommand; histru.bournemouth; FANY; WAAF; and Steve Kippax's Special Operations Executive user group on Yahoo.com. Full details are provided in the bibliography. Any additions or omissions will be made good in future editions (fquirk202@aol.com).

# 1

# Supplies for the Resistance Movements

One of the purposes of RAF Tempsford was to provide supplies for the resistance units across Europe. While you might be able to guess the most common items that were sent, the range was surprising. It is worth detailing everything: Sten guns; Bren guns; bazookas and PIATs (projector infantry anti-tank guns); .33 Lee Enfield rifles; British Enfield, Webley, Smith & Wesson and captured enemy revolvers and parabellum (automatic pistols). Resistance units were also sent holsters, belts, ammunition, spares, hand grenades, mortar bombs, paraffin incendiaries, eye-shields, plastic and ordinary explosives, limpet bombs, petrol, oil, fire-pots, fog signals, flares, tyre bursters, tyre tearers, instantaneous detonator fuses, safety fuses, wires, trip wires, string, crimpers, detonators, percussion caps, magnets, matches, striker boards, and timing devices.

Because of the nature of these items, these were dropped separately from the containers carrying printing presses, typewriters, printing ink, pencils, glue, adhesive tape, ordinary and miniature Kodak and Bantam cameras and film. Top-quality Swiss watches were supplied to pilots, agents, and the Maquis and *réseaux* (the French terms for resistance groups). Accuracy and precision were vital in secret operations. Folding bicycles, bicycle pumps, bicycle repair kits, flashlights, torches, batteries, bulbs, spare tyres for lorries and bikes, oil and petrol were sent, all with foreign manufacturers' names stamped on them to avoid suspicion.

Small bandage kits, surgical gloves and compact medical and first-aid kits, suitable for units of ten men and upwards, were sent as well as air- and sea-sickness pills and water-purifying tablets. Underwater equipment including amphibian breathing apparatus, 'deep-water, quick-opening' steel containers, buoys, grapnels and several kinds of fishing tackle was packed in separate containers. Sunglasses, goggles, sleighs, skis, ski sticks, snow shoes, ice axes, rope, tents, Coleman stoves and hand grenades were needed in Norway. Even the parts of a Jeep were said to have been parachuted in. Paper and stationery, balloons, newspapers, money, forged documents, soap, needles, first-aid kits, field dressings, Vaseline, medicines, haversacks, regimental panniers, blankets, sleeping bags and toilet paper were carefully packed in bucket bags and placed in 6-foot-long aluminium containers. Splinter-proof windows were supplied so that the agents could build them into their observation posts. Rope ladders, jemmies (crowbars), wire cutters, wood saws, metal saws and 'Giglis' were sent. The Gigli was a very flexible surgical saw of interlaced cutting wire, which could be concealed in a cap badge, an ordinary boot or shoelace. They were vital for evasion, being able to cut through metal bars. Some bicycle pumps had torches specially built into the handle end. Compasses were hidden in specially made fountain pens, shaving brushes, hairbrushes, pipes, golf balls and dominoes. Miniature batteries and miniature cameras were sent. Tiny telescopes, one and a half inches long by half an inch wide (39 x 13 mm), were made to look like cigarette lighters. These were some of the 'Q gadgets' provided by the appropriately named Clothing Department of the Ministry of Supply, headed by Charles Fraser-Smith. In the 'Q War' section of his wartime biography he noted that:

> Food supplies included concentrated blocks of sugar, tea, coffee and dried milk, tins of condensed milk, margarine, sardines, nut oil, biscuits, dried beef, sage and mutton, dried fruit, raisins, boiled sweets, tins of baked beans, bully beef, dried soup, powdered egg, powdered potato, jam, porridge oats and cigarettes. Half a million cigarettes were dropped in Holland for the Dutch resistance to sell on the black market to purchase information and to convert into currency.
>
> Genuine French tobacco had to go into the making of the black cigarettes customarily smoked. Even matches had to be minutely copied in order to perfect the exact type of striking material used on their small boxes. It was entirely different to anything used in this country.
>
> In a storeroom in London's Savile Row (actually under the famous police station there) we kept a mass of equipment of all sorts, besides clothing. Our foreign cigarettes were made for us by the British American Tobacco Company, with no detectable difference from the real thing. They only had one snag. When kept for any length of time, the tobacco used to dry and fall out. We then had to waste time replacing the stock with fresh supplies.
>
> (Fraser-Smith, *The Secret War of Charles Fraser-Smith*, 1991)

Appropriate food for the country of destination was made especially and local cigarettes and matches were provided. Large quantities of coffee, cigarettes and chocolates were dropped in Denmark at the special request of Queen Wilhelmina as a present from her and the Dutch East Indies Company. Supplying British chocolates in occupied territory was a giveaway. French Menier chocolates and Swiss Nestlé chocolates were especially made in Britain to supply agents and the Resistance. Prisoners of war were sent special chocolate. Those who ate the blocks containing up to 45 per cent fat felt it was worth its weight in gold. Some were in the shape of a 'V' for Victory. However, the 'back-room boys' had to be clever. The Germans were using ingenious chemicals to produce *ersatz* confections of all sorts. So, poorer-quality sweets had to be supplied to the agents to avoid the prospect of them being found out.

Because of their delicate nature, portable wireless receivers and transmitters, hand generators, trickle chargers, spare dry batteries, voltmeters, hydrometers, medical supplies, blood plasma and other specialised tools were sent in panniers. These were wire and sacking cages, about 3 feet by 2 feet by 2 feet (1.05 m x 0.74 m x 0.74 m) and reinforced with horsehair, latex and corrugated paper to absorb the impact.

Other unusual items sent were clothes. There was clothing for professional, business and working men and women. Shirts, blouses and handkerchiefs were daubed with the laundry marks of establishments in Paris, Arles or Lille – wherever the agent would be operating. There were large, old, leather suitcases for the professionals and small fibre suitcases for the working classes. Most people are not aware that, during the war, when refugees arrived in this country from France, Germany, Netherlands, Belgium, Russia, Norway, Austria, etc., they were given British clothes. What happened to their old ones? They were collected and sent to Station XV, SOE's camouflage research outfit. It is still called the 'Thatched Barn', a Moat House hotel on the A1 in Borehamwood, North London. Painted in large letters on the wall of one of the workshops was the message, 'Silence is of the Gods … only monkeys chatter.' It was top-secret work. Leather briefcases, suitcases, shoes and gloves were treated to make them look old.

Douglas Everett was transferred to Station XV after working at Station XI, the Frythe, near Welwyn, Hertfordshire. Russell Miller's *Behind the Lines* referred to an interview with Everett in which he described ageing a briefcase. After softening it with lukewarm water, he let it dry, rubbed it first with fine sandpaper, then with Vaseline. What he called 'rotten stone' was then rubbed into the little cracks and crevices and dusted over with it to make it look like an old case. The metal parts were aged by brushing a mixture of methylated spirits and sulphuric acid on them, then wiping it off. Kicking it up and down the workshop a few dozen times to get a few rust scratches on it made it look really old. Suitcases were treated in exactly the same way.

Continental overcoats, hats, ties, shirts, perfumes and aftershave were sorted by country and stored ready to be distributed to the agents leaving from RAF Tempsford and elsewhere. As the only people who wore new suits were German, costume people from the film and theatre world were used to make the clothes look old in a technique known as 'distressing'. It involved wearing the clothes every day for a week, even sleeping in them so they stank to high heaven. Then the rotten stone, Vaseline and sandpaper technique was used. It is said that Station XV could supply sixteen agents a day, with meticulous attention to detail, even ensuring that the word 'Lightning' on zip fasteners was removed with a dentist's drill and 'size seven' dealt with. There was no size seven on the Continent. Although some of these clothes were sent in the containers, most went on the 'Joes'.

Suits, cap comforters, pullovers, trousers, underpants, knickers, vests, boots, dubbin, laces, insoles, soles, leather, heels, nails, socks and a 'housewife' (a small portable sewing kit) were carefully packed into the containers. Special requests for German, Spanish and other national uniforms were also catered for. One unusual request was for new battle dress to be dropped behind the lines for those agents or 'Joes' who wanted to be in full uniform on the day of liberation. There was a factory shop near Oxford Circus where a Jewish refugee from Vienna managed a staff of tailors and seamstresses turning out clothes for each European destination.

David Stafford's *Secret Agent: The True Story of the Special Operations Executive* includes the reminiscences of Claudia Pulver, a Viennese seamstress working for SOE:

We started with shirts; I would imagine we made a hundred or two hundred shirts a week, all by hand and individually. We had all these lovely young men coming. I quite enjoyed all these handsome, dashing officers from France, French Canada, England, from all over the place. They wouldn't say very much, we had to guess a great deal. They came into the show room which was actually in Margaret Street, around the corner from the workroom in Great Titchfield Street. We had to take their measurements. We started making shirts for them in the Continental fashion, which is quite different to anything in England. We got old shirts from the refugees again. We took them apart, we looked at the various collar shapes, looked at the way they were manufactured. We looked at the seams, and there certainly was an enormous difference between the side seams. The shape of the cuffs was different, the position of the buttonhole on the under collar was entirely different, and sometimes the plackets of a shirt were different. The width of the stand underneath the collar was different. I think the Continental were a little slower than the English ones, they were quite high, probably because Continental people have shorter necks than the British. They have their own type of collar, because every man likes a different shape of a collar, but they were allowed to choose from the Continental versions. So we made a lot of cardboard patterns of European shapes so that we would have a library for people to choose from.

Labels were taboo, my goodness, labels were taboo. I remember a pair of gloves went across and the agent came back saying you made a mistake. I turned them inside out and there was a 'Made in England' label in one of the fingers. That's really the only mistake we ever made, because we were terribly careful about the labels.

Claudia's attention to detail must have saved hundreds of lives. By 1944, supplying the Resistance was a vast operation. Steve Kippax's research into the history of the ALM (Air Liaison Movements) of the SOE in the National Archives revealed a great deal about these cylindrical steel containers. They resembled the water cylinder you might expect to see in your airing cupboard, with special padding on the inside, 8 feet long by 18 inches wide (2.96 x 0.55 m). There was a small recess at one end for a folded parachute. A shock-absorbing buffer was attached to the other. They weighed about 300 pounds when loaded, and planes could take between thirteen and eighteen containers, so up to 6 tons of supplies could be taken per mission.

In Michael Foot's chapter on the Polish SOE in his book *SOE: The Special Operations Executive 1940–1946*, he stated that:

The containers used to drop arms and supplies to agents in the field were prone to damage. The 'C' container was 12 inches in diameter and 5 foot 9 inches long with four carry handles and opened along the axis and weighed up to 100 Kg. An un-named Pole redesigned the standard container. Type 'H' consisted of 5 metal drums each with a carrying handle and linked by long metal rods including the end pieces. One end would deaden the shock while the other was used to open the parachute via a static line. Unfortunately, while the design improved usability, they were more prone to impact damage. Poorly packed explosives detonated on impact which resulted in suspicion bomb racks had not been cleared when delivering supplies.

Initially, the containers were packed at Station LXI, Audley End, near Saffron Walden in Essex, before the Poles moved in. From there they were forwarded to a depot at RAF Henlow where the parachutes were attached. From here they were trucked up the A1 to RAF Tempsford. There was concern expressed about security as the SOE men were working behind a screen at one end of the parachute repair workshop with RAF personnel at the other. Due to the distance, the nature of the roads between Audley End and Tempsford, and the availability of a closer centre, this operation was moved in April 1942 to Gaynes Hall, a thirteen-bedroom Georgian mansion set in 23 acres of remote Cambridgeshire countryside in Perry, a small village a few miles west of St Neots and about half an hour's drive from the airfield. The Special Parachute Equipment Section was formed with a staff of thirty, mostly members of the WAAF. According to Rigden's *SOE Syllabus*:

> From May 1942 to January 1945 this section, working in isolation, handled 19,863 packages, made 10,900 parachute harnesses and packed 27,980 parachutes, as well as doing much repair work. The section also became a centre of research into the use of parachutes in special operations.

More light was shed on the operation in William McKenzie's *The Secret History of the SOE*, in which he stated that

> there was a vast packing station at Gaynes Hall, St Neots … Packing became so vast that in October 1943 an outside firm of packers (Messrs. Carpet Trades Ltd. Kidderminster) were employed to pack 'standard loads', so that a reserve supply was built up for the 1944 deliveries, for example in 1941 95 containers were packed.

Ninety-five containers were packed in 1941; 2,176 in 1942; 13,435 in 1943; 56,464 in 1944; and 4,334 in 1945 – a total of 76,504, weighing about 10,000 tons. The record pack for one day, 6 July 1944, was 1,160 containers by a staff of 150, though 96 soldiers from the Pioneer Corps and 100 RAF men were drafted in occasionally to augment the workforce. German prisoners of war were also said to have been drafted in, and some reports suggest that they may have sabotaged some containers.

Locals recall being told that Gaynes Hall was being used for treating tropical diseases, so they kept away from the place. Some tell of seeing people working there wearing white coats. They thought these were medical doctors and never suspected any clandestine activity.

When the Americans joined in these secret operations, they had their own packing base at Area H, Holme Hall. This was close to the main London–Edinburgh railway line near Peterborough and about 28 miles east of Harrington Airfield, Northamptonshire. They employed more than 250 workers. As well as Messrs. Carpet Trades Ltd. (of Kidderminster), two local businesses played an important role in the packaging at Gaynes Hall. R. & H. Wale of Gamlingay supplied the packing, and Havlock of Bedford the latex. Once the containers were ready, they were loaded into the back of Lincoln lorries belonging to the London Brick Company, covered with tarpaulin and driven down to RAF Tempsford. They were offloaded and stored in half a dozen corrugated-roofed Nissen huts in close proximity behind an 8-foot (2.96-m) double-stranded barbed wire fence on the northern outskirts of the airfield. Some reports suggest that guns, ammunition, wireless sets, folding bicycles, etc., were stored there as well as the small parachutes attached to each container. Maybe some were offloaded from those planes forced to return to base without having completed their mission.

One container was reported to have broken open when accidentally dropped on loading, whereupon children's toys spilled onto the runway. They were repacked and no doubt delivered. There was even a personalised shopping service for the agents. One container carrying their 'pay' fell off the bomb rack when it was being loaded and its contents were spilt over the tarmac beneath the plane. A guard was immediately set up around it and each gold sovereign was retrieved and sent in a repaired container. There are claims that many groups in the French resistance demanded gold as it was invaluable for getting supplies on the black market, bribing French and German prison guards, policemen and government officials, and even for paying boat owners and guides to help take people out of the country. Many millions of pounds were sent to the various resistance groups.

After an unsuccessful mission, a pilot jettisoned his plane's containers on the northern outskirts of the airfield before landing. One, marked 'Medical Supplies', burst open on hitting the ground to reveal a variety of groceries, sanitary towels and numerous packets of condoms. Those who found them weren't impressed, realising what hundreds of Special Duties crews were risking their lives for in supplying the Resistance.

Records show that between 1941 and 1945 there were 485 drops in Poland, with the loss of 73 aircraft. 318 parachute drops of personnel were made, including 28 Polish couriers who distributed £35 million in gold and currency to support the Polish Home Army. One wonders what the total cost of all the SOE operations from Tempsford was – probably several hundreds of millions of pounds.

## The Tempsford Personnel

What exactly were the personnel at RAF Tempsford engaged in? Mostly it involved dropping containers and packages by air, dropping agents either by parachute or landing them secretly at night, picking up stranded personnel and VIPs, and dropping leaflets and pigeons. Such work required a considerable task force. How many men and women were there on the airfield? Well, it's difficult to say as numbers must have varied. According to Willis and Hollis' *Military Airfields in the British Isles 1939–1945*, there were 262 RAF officers at Tempsford, 429 SNCOs (Senior Non-Commissioned Officers) and 1,126 ORs (Other Ranks), totalling 1,817 men. Along with 10 WAAF officers, 15 SNCOs and 250 Ors, there were 2,092 stationed there. 275 women therefore amounted to 13 per cent of RAF Tempsford's personnel. Although they were directly involved in the airfield, my investigation covered many other aspects of women's involvement.

My research has uncovered their autobiographies, biographies, personal memoirs and reminiscences which have shed light on not just the WAAF, but also the catering section, the FANY, female SOE agents and many local women and girls. Their wartime experiences complement the otherwise largely male-dominated accounts of RAF Tempsford's history.

### The Catering Section
Exactly how many women were employed in the catering section on Tempsford Airfield is unknown. After one of my talks to a local history society I was told about Ann Seamarks by her grandson, Nigel. He wrote down her reminiscences, which provided

Undated photograph of RAF Tempsford looking east from the London–Edinburgh railway line. (Courtesy of Bill Bright)

details of her life as one of the cooks on the base. She was in the catering section for officers and other senior flying ranks. She got board and lodgings in Everton, near to the Officers' Mess, rather than in the main WAAF camp on Potton Road. Her shifts were either 6 a.m. to 2 p.m., 2 p.m. to 10 p.m., or 10 p.m. to 6 p.m., with normally one day off every two weeks. As she came from North Bedfordshire, she had to catch a bus from Sandy into Bedford and then change to get another one out to her village.

The cookhouses provided welcome sustenance. There were three on the base, segregated by rank, with one for the airmen, another for the sergeants and the third for officers. The Officers' Kitchen had eight black, coal-fired standard house ranges. They were in two sets of four parallel to each other. Electric potato peelers saved time so only the eyes needed poking out. There were also fish boilers. Steam pressure cleaners were used for the washing up and sterilising.

The food Ann served up was the same as civilian rations but there were a few extra perks. Local farmers, butchers, bakers and grocers delivered the rations to the base on a daily basis. Flight crews were allowed sausage, bacon and eggs before their missions and they nearly always asked for an extra egg. When told that there were none left, the cheeky reply was, 'You will find one from somewhere.' They usually did, probably because not all the crews came back. The other perk was Grimsby fish. It used to arrive in wooden crates packed with ice and was often quite pungent. The Catering Officer would tell the girls that it was 'just Grimsby fresh air'. The major event of the year was Christmas dinner – roast turkey with all the trimmings, but with the senior officers waiting on the younger ones and the NCOs.

Ann never really went to the local pubs as she went back to her lodgings or spent time on camp, where there was a common area. Films were shown quite often and dances were held every month. However, there were noticeably fewer social events during the moon period. She mentioned Max Miller, the comedian. He used to visit Tempsford and was particularly enjoyed by the British and Canadians, who were known to mix well. She particularly liked his shows and the dances.

The rule for returning to camp was changed by the girls to a 'two-minute rule'. The official return was 2359 hours but the girls were allowed out until 0001. Throughout her time at Tempsford she never saw a German plane close up over the airfield, but there were rumours going round when they had heard Lord Haw Haw, the pro-German propagandist, describe RAF Cardington, near Bedford, as lots of houses with no chimneys. The top of the hangars had been painted as house rooftops.

Her biggest disappointment was that, towards the end of the war, her squadron was split between Mildenhall and a camp at Haverhill, near Cambridge. The officers had promised the catering girls a flight to the Continent to see the damage done close up. Her best friend went to Mildenhall and was taken on a flight over Germany but Ann's Squadron Leader banned such folly. Although she was jealous, she did get a flight on a Dakota towards the end of the war, but only to Oxfordshire. Afterwards, she was transferred to RAF Hendon to control rations.

In Edna Joyce Phillips' wartime recollections for the BBC's WW2 People's War, Edna said that she started as a NAAFI girl working at RAF Cardington.

We were to serve the WAAFs in their canteen, near to a row of cottages, where we were billeted. Our indoor uniform was a blue overall and cap with a NAAFI logo on. For going out we had khaki tunics and skirt, shirt and tie like the ATS (Auxiliary Territorial Service), felt brimmed hat, or sometimes forage caps. Early morning we made sandwiches and filled rolls, brewed up urns of tea. Cook would make sausage rolls, bread pudding (a favourite with the RAF men), rock buns and jam buns. We were overrun with beetles in the flour and set beer traps. The WAAFs were a mixed lot from all backgrounds and were forever playing Deanna Durbin records.

After a few months, I was sent to Tempsford, Beds. to start a new canteen near fields and woods. Deep muddy tracks led to the building and we had to start with hurricane lamps. We girls had to share one large room, with single beds and a dressing table type chest to keep clothes in. The manageress had her own room.

We got up early to prepare for opening time and a sea of airmen would face us as we pulled up the shutters. We sold chocs, sweets, razor blades, toothpaste and a ration of cigarettes (Woodbines and Players Weights). There were crafty twins in the camp who often queued twice.

Occasionally we had a dance or entertainment and then we served beer and I did not like the smell and our floor was awash with it. I remember Max Miller came telling jokes (all night if he was allowed to), also Evelyn Laye, a singer. The RAF also had their own concert party band called Silverwings.

We had a happy time, made lots of friends and amongst them I met my special airman who was in the fire crew. I used to put extra goodies in his tuck-box for night duty. I had my 21st birthday party in the corporal's bar with fun and games and NAAFI food. Three airmen gave me a blue silk scarf with the RAF badge on it. In 1943 I left to marry my special airman. The girls clubbed together and gave me a lovely eiderdown.

(http://www.bbc.co.uk/ww2peopleswar/stories/17/a4437317.shtml)

The brother of one of the catering staff recalled his sister telling him how, after work one hot summer's day, she had been given half a pound of butter and told to hide it down the front of her dress. The driver of the personnel carrier was in on the joke and instead of dropping her off first in Sandy, dropped her last, by which time the butter had melted all down her front, much to the amusement of the others.

Another website that has provided additional information on the women of Tempsford Airfield is wartimememories.co.uk. On it, Roly Groom posted a note:

My mother, then Sgt Lillian Whitford, served as a mess stewardess at Tempsford during the war. She recalls the visit of the King and Queen and has also relayed stories of a French pilot who always wore silk socks and of a Polish airman who borrowed a flask from the mess to take with him on the promise to return it the following day. Unfortunately he did not return for six months and apparently forgot the flask!

(http://www.wartimememories.co.uk/airfields/tempsford.html#Whitford)

On the same site, Lynne Robinson spoke about her late mother-in-law, Isobel Robinson (née Ogilvie):

She was stationed at RAF Tempsford during the Second World War. Her service number was 204818. She was a Sergeant driver and I understand that she used to drive agents from Tempsford to London for de-briefing. There is a photograph on a similar website of the visit of the then King and Queen, with Issy just behind the Queen. The same photo is also in a book called, 'Agents by Moonlight', page 203. She was mentioned in dispatches and we assume that it was because of her driving the agents through the Blitz to London. She met my father-in-law, I think at Tempsford, although he spent most of the war in Malta.

Dorothy Ringlesbach, the wife of an American airman stationed temporarily at Tempsford, wrote in her book *OSS: Stories That Can Now Be Told* about some of his and his friends' reminiscences. The Office of Strategic Services (OSS) was the United States' military intelligence agency, set up during the Second World War. In a letter home dated 15 September 1943, Colonel Boone wrote to his wife Victoria telling her that he and some others were making soup in their quarters. He asked about the food situation at home, whether meat, milk, eggs and fresh vegetables were scarce and how much they cost. At Tempsford he had well-balanced meals, but not fresh milk, steaks, fruit or vegetables. He then told her about the soup and how his friend Freddie had swiped some onions from someone's patch, another brought a head of cabbage while he himself scrounged some carrots and salt and pepper from the mess hall. They added some 'bouillion' from a pack of K-rations and added tomatoes (where these had originated was not specified). Everything was put in a big tin can and simmered on the stove they had for heat in their quarters. About 2300 hours they had a feast using their mess kits to hold the soup.

Jack Ringlesbach recalled how he used to engage in a bit of barter with the cook in the mess hall. In exchange for a bottle of scotch or some other item, he had been given coffee or other hard-to-get items that could be used as gifts for any young women he might meet.

Not everyone appreciated the NAAFI food. F/Lt Stephens thought it was so terrible that he used to sneak off base and visit one of the nearby farmhouses, where the farmer's wife used to supply some 'heavenly tea and dripping toast'. He thought he had kept this secret rendezvous to himself and was surprised one day to find a group of other officers doing the same thing in her kitchen.

Jack told of being given carrots every day with his meals. The catering staff joked that all the flight crews had to eat them. They were good for the eyes and improved night vision. Although he didn't ask for them, he observed that beans and cabbage were never on the menu for air crews. He presumed it was to improve the atmosphere on board during their long flights. One meal he termed 'chicken ala king' resulted in large-scale runs. The demand on the latrines was so great that the perimeter of the site was decorated the following day with soiled shorts, socks and pants. For the following few days the men only ate cheese and crackers.

# 2
# The WAAF

There were about 275 WAAFs at Tempsford. When the WAAF was formed in June 1939 it came under the administration of the RAF and members were recruited not to fly – that was the men's job – but to fill posts as clerks, kitchen orderlies and drivers in order to release men for front-line duties. However, following the government passing the National Service Act in December 1941, women could be conscripted and those who joined the WAAF were allocated jobs as mechanics, engineers, electricians, aeroplane fitters, telephonists, radio operators and code and cipher interceptors. In Freddie Clark's *Agents by Moonlight*, he included a photograph of WAAF Sergeant Tottie Lintott chalking up details of flights on the operations board in Gibraltar Farm on 10 April 1944. Some WAAFs worked on large tables interpreting aerial photographs, bringing out British and foreign maps and providing weather reports. Others worked in the radar control system department as reporters and plotters.

Although on an equal footing with the men, women were not allowed to fly. The RAF thought it unacceptable to have women pilots flying military aircraft. They were subject to the same military law but received two-thirds of the men's pay.

The uniform the WAAFs were issued with comprised black lace-up flat shoes, grey lisle stockings, two air force blue skirts, tunics, cardigans and underwear, an air force tie, soft-topped blue peaked cap with its winged RAF badge, brown leather gloves, greatcoat and gas mask. This was considered much smarter than the khaki of the Air Transport Service (ATS). Scrambling over aircraft in skirts was one of the reasons why WAAFs were eventually allowed to wear air force blue trousers or slacks. The major complaint was how long it took for clothes and underwear to dry. The WAAFs hung them up over the coal-fired stove in their accommodation block and it often took two days.

The WAAF camp was on the present site of 'The Lawns', a housing estate opposite the recreation ground in Everton. There were about thirty huts erected for over 200 young women, most in their early twenties. Some of the early buildings were 'prefabs' – prefabricated asbestos buildings. Later, Nissen huts of corrugated iron were built on a brick and concrete base. It was about a mile and half's bike ride (2.4 km) from the base. This kept the WAAFs very fit as they had to cycle down the hill to the airfield and back to their camp at least twice a day. According to Les Dibdin of Everton, who worked as a ground engineer on the base, the 'WAAFery' was the only place in the village with a quantity of barbed wire around it 'to keep the chaps out and the girls in'. Maybe this was why some jokingly called it the 'Nunnery'. It was said that many of the young women did their socialising behind hedges as they weren't supposed to be seen going out with men. If they were spotted by their superiors, they would quickly jump behind the nearest hedge.

For weeks before Christmas the girls would collect every piece of silver foil and coloured piece of paper they could find. They hoarded these so they could use them to make bunting to decorate the WAAFery. They wanted to enjoy the festive season, even though there was a war on.

Some of the WAAFs had to be on the base after dusk to deliver agents to Gibraltar Farm. This was the nerve centre of the whole operation. Windows were broken. Roof tiles were taken off and the black Bedfordshire weatherboarding removed to make it look disused. Inside, however, the first floor was removed and a huge map of Europe covered one wall. Several WAAFs worked here, pinning the location of the night's operations on the map, chalking up the details of the night missions and recording successes and losses in the early hours.

In one of the barns, the only remaining evidence of the farm today, the agents were kitted out in their parachute gear before the flight. Other WAAFs were allocated duties picking up aircrews, agents and VIPs when they returned after a mission and driving them on to their accommodation. Bob Body, the nephew of Flight Lieutenant Menzies of 161 Squadron, described their role in his book *Taking the Wings of the Morning*.

For the agents, their journey to the waiting aircraft started when a WAAF driver brought a car to the barn to collect them; she would have been under no illusions regarding the importance of the security that was required. One of these drivers recalled the instructions she had been given regarding the conveyance of the agents to the waiting aircraft. She said that the car was driven up to the barn where she had to wait, eyes facing front whilst the passengers were ushered into the rear of the vehicle. Under no circumstances was she to talk to the passengers or turn around to look at them and the use of the rear mirror was forbidden. As she obeyed these instructions to the letter, to this day she does not know who she ferried out to the waiting aircraft, not even if they were male or female. Once at the aircraft the car had to be reversed up to the door of the aircraft, using only wing mirrors, no use of the rear view mirror or turning around to see out of the back window. A tricky manoeuvre made more difficult by the palpable tension within the vehicle. The rear doors of the car were opened by a waiting crew member and the agents exited the vehicle leaving the driver to return to her station. One WAAF driver recalled that she had been taught to drive every kind of vehicle except a tank but it was not easy. As well as there being no sign posts, street or road signs, the vehicles had the headlights blacked out, leaving only a tiny hole so that over-flying enemy aircraft pilots would not see them. It was worst in winter as the vehicles had no heater. They also had no antifreeze. When the 'Met' Office warned of overnight frost all the water had to be drained out at night and refilled the following morning. She also had the job of fitting the snow chains round the tyres when the driving conditions were icy.

In Frank Griffiths' *Winged Hours*, his autobiography of his years as a pilot in 138 Squadron, he commented that he wasn't sure whether the women he met were hand-picked or not.

… but the Tempsford WAAFs were exceptionally attractive and the Poles flocked round them like flies round a jam pot and I fear that the WAAFs were not lacking in the art of encouraging them. The WAAFs were 'kept' in secluded Waafery in a good defensive position on top of the hill above the camp in Everton village but it didn't prevent the Poles from attempting incursions.

Many of the Poles had aristocratic family backgrounds, were impeccably dressed and considered real gentlemen by the local women and girls as well as the WAAFs. Their dancing skills also gave them the advantage over many of the other nationalities. Some must have had success with Tibbs Turner, Red Humble, Babs Chapman and Audrey Caister.

Elsie Riding, a Tempsford WAAF, felt that she had been hand-picked. After her training she had to wait four weeks before being posted to Tempsford. She was a WAAF corporal there from September 1943 to December 1944 and told me that her job was in the Station Armoury Fitting Room. Her work involved filling boxes with ammunition. Four other young women the same age worked with her and a young boy helped with the heavy lifting. She was Duty NCO when she learnt about D-Day and was more worried that it might delay her getting married at Brighton with only 48 hours' leave. Two other corporals stationed with her were to be her bridesmaids. With a bit of persuasion her Commanding Officer (CO) agreed to increase her leave to a week.

Tempsford WAAFery, Everton, 1943 (now the site of 'The Lawns' housing estate). From left to right: 'Tibbs' Turner, 'Red' Hubble, 'Babs' Chapman and Audrey Caister sitting on top of an air-raid shelter. Another can be seen in the background with the tower of St Mary's church behind. They are all wearing Polish uniforms – presumably the photograph would have been an amusing souvenir for the WAAFs' Polish admirers. (Courtesy of Audrey Caister)

On the Tempsford Squadrons website there is mention of a WAAF, from someone known only as 'Altie's daughter'.

> My mother was a WAAF at Tempsford. She was driving a party of Canadians out to their aircraft at night when another aircraft was taxiing in. She only just saw the lights, threw the Fordson lorry into reverse, and put the back wheels into a ditch. Four of the Canadians helped to get her out, and she was horrified to see the Wing Commander standing in front of her. It had been him in the aircraft! I think she peeled spuds for a week after that, but then she said that you got better food in the kitchens if you had to work in there!!
>
> She also stayed out too late at a party and climbed a fence to get back in, slipped and sprained her ankle. I think she was on kitchen duty for another week after that!
>
> (http://www.tempsford-squadrons.info/Funniesv2p2.htm)

Eileen Hytch recalled an incident when she and the WAAF administration officer went to the CO to ask if the WAAFs could wear slacks on the station. The CO replied by asking, 'What are slacks?'

When Barbara Cartland, the romantic novelist, visited the Everton Women's Institute meeting in the village hall during the war, she caused panic among the WAAF people present. She started her talk by saying, 'You think that these people go out every night on bombing raids but they do nothing of the sort because they are dropping things into Europe.' Where did she get that information from? Almost certainly a quiet but firm word in her ear must have followed, as potentially she had let the cat out of the bag.

# 3
# The FANY

It is said that there were also some FANY (First Aid Nursing Yeomanry) involved with Tempsford, but very few records of their time there have come to light. These young women did an assortment of jobs, including working in the intelligence unit, helping in canteens, guarding prisoners of war, and working as ambulance crew as well as military transport (MT) drivers.

In Margaret Pawley's *In Obedience to Instructions*, she claimed that when Sergeant-Major Baker was injured during General Kitchener's Sudan Campaign, he recognised that

> … no means existed by which men in his position could be given emergency medical treatment and then transported to a place of safety and succour. He conceived a scheme whereby a troop of expert horsewomen, trained in first aid, would ride (side-saddle, of course) on to the battlefield after a skirmish, tend to the wounded and remove them as fast as possible by horse ambulance.
>
> It was not until 1907 that the idea became a reality. The First Aid Nursing Yeomanry in that year became the first of the women's services. Girls who had been brought up with horses, and probably possessed their own, began to join.

The FANY formed part of the Belgian Army during the First World War and, despite being subsequently named the Women's Transport Service, the old term FANY stuck. By 1938 there were over 400 recruits. They were all volunteers with an average age of twenty (the youngest was sixteen and a half). Older women were often married with little children to look after, and any woman over twenty-one was required by the Conscription Acts to sign up and be directed to other war work, often in an armaments factory. Some described the FANY as a 'Cinderella Corps' or 'the Knightsbridge Brigade' as it tended to be made up of wealthy young ladies from middle- and upper-class families who were recruited via advertisements in selected newspapers and magazines. Many were personally recommended by their fathers or relatives.

Eva Stubbs (née Wharton) recalled in an interview transcribed for the BBC's People's War project that:

> I was invited to an official interview at the WTS (FANY) Headquarters at 31 Wilton Place, Hyde Park Corner and had to face several senior officers who asked about my parents, my education and knowledge of French and why I had left school at 15. I

was pleasantly surprised when sometime later I received instructions to report back to London for duty with a group of girls. We were transported to a large country house in Banbury. Here we did training – lectures including Corps history, security, First Aid, mapping, military organisation, censorship and general knowledge – and a very high standard was required.

(http://www.bbc.co.uk/ww2peopleswar/stories/09/a8765409.shtml)

As the war progressed the FANY took on intelligent, experienced women from all walks of life and of all ages – but particularly women who were able to speak a second language. Many were drawn from the Telephone Exchange. The officers tended to speak with upper-class English accents but by early 1944 the 2,000 FANYs included scattered regional accents and much harder vowels. Their friends used to call them the 'Disappearing Brigade' as they seemed to be out of circulation for long periods on end and never said where they were going or what they were doing.

They first got involved with the SOE in mid-1940 when Colonel (later Major General) Colin Gubbins, the then head, rang Phyllis Bingham, a family friend who had recently joined the FANY. He wanted her to send some reliable young women to help pack plastic explosives and detonators into small tin boxes at Aston House, an SOE weapons research laboratory near Stevenage. From there the tins were taken in trucks to Gaynes Hall, near St Neots, to be packed in the containers being sent out from Tempsford. Probably some FANYs drove the trucks.

Phyllis Bingham interviewed all FANY recruits for SOE work at their headquarters in the former vicarage of St Paul's church in Wilton Place, Knightsbridge. She expected them all to be able to turn their hands to anything expected of them and Pawley reported her as saying, 'I want girls who have been taught to do as they are told.' Due to the nature of their work, they had to 'keep mum' about it. According to Pawley:

No word of the existence of a unit, its function or its inhabitants, was to be divulged to anyone. FANYs were not permitted to tell their parents of their exact whereabouts, or, in many cases, especially in the case of radio operators, their function; any connection with long-range communication was very secret. All FANY mail was required to be sent to Room 98, Horse Guards, SW1. Often FANYs did not leave the perimeter of a station for several months, on account of operational security. Secondly, much of the work involved, cooking and orderly duties, was menial and not at that time the province of educated women. It would be boring and repetitive; promotion was rare. Yet on the whole FANYs undertook these roles of domestic administration with dedication and even enthusiasm. They recognised the even greater demands being made of the agents in their care. Thirdly, relationships with the often volatile men in training could be difficult to handle; support and understanding, rather than romantic attachment, were the order of the day.

Working in Aston House with Bingham was Peggy Minchin, who, towards the end of 1941, was requested by SOE to train FANYs as radio operators. According to Des Turner, who researched Aston House:

She had already agreed to train coders to encypher and decypher signals traffic and she had also been a dispatcher of FANY agents who dropped into France. She undertook parachute training with them. Later she went out to Mola, Italy, to become second-in-command of all FANYs in the Mediterranean area.

(D. Turner, *Station XII: Aston House – SOE's Secret Centre*, 2006)

In 1943 their fifteen-day training took place at Overthorpe Hall, an Edwardian stately home near Banbury in Oxfordshire. There were others. A number of what some called the 'Bingham unit' had links with Tempsford. One was Sue Ryder, who founded the homes for the disabled after the war. Her autobiography, *Child of My Love*, provides a fascinating and deeply moving account of her work looking after first the Czech and then the Polish agents. Ryder described going to a training school at Ketteringham, just south-west of Norwich in Norfolk, where

each morning began with drill, at that time taken by a sergeant from the Devonshire Regiment, whose accent made his commands quite difficult to follow. Ethel Boileau, the well-known author, who was the Commanding Officer at Ketteringham, inspected us, paying particular attention to our appearance: hair had to be well above the collar, and our shoes polished vigorously every day – the insteps were expected to be as clean and shiny as the uppers. The Sam-Browne belts, too, had to be polished to resemble a mirror. The course included route marches, training in Army procedure, groups, fire drill, security, respiration and stretcher drill, night vision, mechanics, advanced first aid nursing, convoy driving, night map reading, and driving different types of vehicles ranging from cars to five-ton lorries. Every FANY driver was expected to maintain her vehicle in first-class condition. We later received 11/2d (£0.56) per week. We were addressed by our surnames only.

Once out of basic training, FANYs were engaged in a kind of administrative, teaching and domestic service corps. Some did the washing, cleaning and cooking that servants used to do for the gentry – work they took on in the interests of security to avoid the need to employ 'outsiders' in the seventy-five SOE 'training stations' and 'training schools'. However, some FANYs received instructions in using small arms and signals, as well as ciphering and deciphering secret messages and wireless Morse code transmissions. Some became parachute or explosives packers or helped with producing fake passports, ration cards and other counterfeit work. Some did administrative work, answering and making telephone calls, doing the typing, filing and other routine work around the office. Others escorted the secret agents – 'Joes' or 'Bods', as they were commonly called – throughout their training, often jumping with them on their parachute course. These 'young ladies of good family' were expected to provide company and sympathy but not intimacy. Keeping the line on the back of their stockings straight was considered very important.

The FANYs in SOE helped run training schools, did signals and worked in the operations room. They also drove the agents to Tempsford Airfield once the signal had come through from the occupied country that the reception committee was ready and the weather conditions were favourable. Just before the journey, they had to prepare

Unknown FANY
waiting to open the
door of her car for the
secret agent or agents.
(Courtesy of Bill
Bright)

sandwiches and flasks of coffee – sometimes an agent's last meal – and pack them in
yellow tin 'hay boxes'. Some had a chance to eat these meals themselves. According to
Sue Ryder:

> FANYs too were dropped behind enemy lines by parachute or landed by Lysander
> aircraft. They took part in armed resistance and sabotage and, in the course of their
> everyday duties, travelled many miles carrying information, arms and often wireless
> parts, bluffing their way through enemy posts. The necessity for being constantly on
> the alert in enemy-occupied territory was an appalling strain. During the war a number
> of FANYs were captured, tortured and executed; a few died in concentration camps,
> others were killed in action, some survived.

Becoming a FANY member offered a plausible reason to their family and friends for the
women being away from home, and it allowed them to undergo the specialist training
without any awkward questions.

Many in government and the military establishment did not consider sending women into action the right thing to do. Rules therefore had to be broken to send them out. As women in the armed forces were not allowed to carry weapons and engage in combat, the SOE gave women agents commissions in the FANY as it was a civilian organisation with no such restrictions. Some considered them as 'cap badge FANYs', commissioned into the service as a cover while they were on operations. Should they be captured, they could claim to be an officer in the FANY in an attempt to ensure that they would be treated as prisoners of war according to the Geneva Convention. Non-uniformed agents would normally be expected to be executed if captured. Feedback from people who had managed to escape from German prisons suggested that the Gestapo respected the officer class and kept them alive, whereas lower classes tended to be executed straight away. Hitler's *Führerbefehl*, or Commando Order, issued on 18 October 1942, stated that

> all terrorist and sabotage troops of the British and their accomplices who do not act like soldiers but rather like bandits will be treated as such by the German troops and will be ruthlessly eliminated in battle whenever they appear.

Details of some of these women's experiences of overseas operations are included later. Ryder included an extract from a letter about the FANY written after the war by Colin Gubbins:

> I am left tongue-tied when I try to tell you what the FANYs have meant to the organisation and to me. I say 'to me' because I took the original decision and had the idea to use them to the utmost, and I am personally sufficiently human to be glad to find my judgement proved right. But to the organisation they were everything, as you well know, and without them we just couldn't have done it. In every theatre they have become a household word for efficiency, guts, cheerfulness, persistence, tenacity and comradeship in difficulty, and I am proud to have been the means of their proving their great qualities, and they have been magnificent and valuable. I know that what they have themselves learnt will be of inestimable and permanent value to their country.

Secrecy was vital. All FANYs had to sign the Official Secrets Act – which the girls jokingly called 'The Poison Book' – and were forbidden to talk with anyone about their work – boyfriends, husbands, fathers, mothers, brothers, sisters or friends. 'Anybody who comes here is not expected to ask questions. You will find out what you need to know, but always keep your own mouth shut.' Their cover story was that it was 'a training school for Allied commandoes'. The Military Police were very active, keeping their eyes and ears open. Anyone suspected of leaking secrets was temporarily removed from circulation. Their bed would be empty and blankets folded ready for the next recruit. As has been mentioned, the only address the women could give family and friends was 'Room 98, Horseguards, London SW1'. Their mail was collected and then brought to the stations by despatch riders.

The FANY's outfit was khaki drill – KD as it was known – a lightweight four-pocket jacket and divided skirt, battledress and tin hat. There were two hats, a peaked, khaki service cap with leather strap over the crown and the FANY 'bonnet', a khaki beret with maroon flash and the corps badge on it – a Maltese Cross in a circle. Ryder explained that it meant self-sacrifice to achieve unity and service. Jane Buckland, an eighteen-year-old FANY and trainee radio operator, noted that 'the nicest part of [my] uniform was the most beautiful Sam Brownes, lovely wide belts which we had to polish all the time. It was just like the army – we were in the army, but special'.

On wet and cold days they wore the grey, made-to-measure greatcoat with a double line of buttons up the front, fanning out from the waist to the shoulders, with deep cuffs and scarlet lining. After a certain date in spring, KD had to be worn with the sleeves rolled up above the elbow. Those who were posted overseas stocked up with boot polish and soap and were given an extra allowance of coupons to buy items of uniform. Those in charge wore the round cherry-coloured insignia of a commander on their epaulettes, which signified that they had served during the First World War. They were nicknamed 'raspberry tarts' by the younger members but greatly revered. There were few written rules, but there was a strong *esprit de corps* and discipline among them.

Lucy Redrup, who with her twin sister Gertrude worked at Aston House, recalled in Des Turner's *Station XII* that:

> Another treat came my way when I drove an officer to an airfield, probably RAF Tempsford. He said, 'Have you ever had a flight in a plane?' I said, 'No sir. I haven't.' He said, 'Would you like a trip?' I said, 'Oh, yes, I would!' And it was such a nice experience to fly in this Halifax bomber, I thought am I doing the right thing because it was all unofficial, anyway we came down safely.

Rita Kramer, in her *Flames in the Field*, an account of four female SOE agents, mentioned a Norwegian agent describing the FANYs as 'always amiable – and unapproachable'. A Polish agent commented, 'You couldn't have found a finer type of Englishwoman anywhere. Likeable, cultured and friendly, hard-working and smiling, they created the relaxed happy atmosphere so necessary before the coming adventure.' During the day they would cook, sweep, put the house in order, or chauffeur people around in cars. In the evening, they were said to look exquisite in their long gowns as they danced tangos, foxtrots, waltzes and Polish *obereks* and *kujawiaks*. Despite the women being so prepossessing, the Polish agent claimed that there were no romances. 'Though they were young and attractive, not to say beautiful, we had no heart pangs over them. They remained in our memories as the pleasant and unaffected companions of our last days before the flight.'

# Gaynes Hall

It is said that some of the Tempsford agents had to walk from Sandy station to a tea shop on St Neots Road in Sandy. Their pick-up team would have observed them to ensure they weren't followed and then rendezvoused to take them on their final leg to a safe house before their flight. Most were driven up from briefing or training sessions in London in Wolseys or Rolls-Royces donated to the war effort by owners unable to afford their upkeep. They were taken on a tortuous route round country lanes, often taking up to four hours. The normal journey up the A1 would have taken less than half that time. They were not meant to know where they were flying from. Some were 'kept' at Brockhall in Northamptonshire, not too distant from Tempsford. Others went to Gaynes Hall, near Perry, a large and secluded country house a few miles west of St Neots and about half an hour's drive from the base. It was a three-storey yellow-brick mansion set in 23 acres of parkland, with thirteen bedrooms, nine bathrooms, a ballroom, sitting room and lounge, dining room and library. Before the war it belonged to Millicent Duberly, whose family owned a large estate nearby. The occupants during the war, Lord and Lady Jubilee, moved out when it was requisitioned. Huts were rapidly erected in the grounds for secret operations – packing containers and panniers before they were trucked to Tempsford.

For the owners of the large country houses requisitioned by the government, it had been all but impossible in the first eighteen months of the war to maintain their former lifestyle. There were over a million domestic servants in 1939 and when they were called up, volunteered or were directed into more warlike work, these stately homes were left unoccupied with no one to look after them. Many ladies who had been influential hostesses found it difficult to survive, never having lit a fire, cooked a meal or washed up before. It was therefore a positive advantage to have these large homes requisitioned, to have the furniture put into storage, to be moved out to a smaller house or hotel and to allow the government to look after the leaking roofs and dry rot.

To some, Gaynes Hall was known simply as 'Station 61' and, after the container-packing operation was transferred to Holme Hall, near Peterborough, it was used by the Norwegian section under Major C. S. Hampton. To others, it was a 'hotel' providing a place for liaison and upmarket rest and recreation for agents before the half-hour drive to Tempsford.

According to Michael Foot, the agents' stay there was made 'as delectable as possible. A large number of FANYs, girls in their late teens when recruited, with quick brains and quiet tongues, performed an essential service for SOE.' Oluf Olsen, a Norwegian agent, stayed there prior to being flown out from Tempsford in early 1943 to attack the heavy water plant at Vermork in Norway. The post-war film *Heroes of Telemark* tells their story. In Olsen's book *Two Eggs on My Plate*, he wrote that:

> Late in the afternoon of April 17 we drove into the grounds of an old English country house surrounded by high walls, 'somewhere in England'. Everyone here was sworn to secrecy; every man or woman, from the C.O. down to the washerwoman, was chosen with special care. The same rules applied to all personnel, both ground and flying, at the great airfield half an hour away …
>
> The house contained an extremely cosmopolitan collection of persons who were 'guests of honour' in the place; agents from various European countries. We talked together, ate together, did physical exercises together, but no one knew who any individual was or where he was going. One could only guess from the accent with which he spoke English. No one asked questions; nor did anyone talk about himself.
>
> The thing which perhaps we all remember best about the place, apart from our marvellous entertainment by its young ladies, was the so-called 'Operation Egg'.

Fresh eggs were at that time largely unobtainable by the English public. Only dried eggs from Canada or America were used. At supper-time it might happen that two fine fresh eggs were carefully laid on a plate before a particular person. The person in question, even if he liked eggs better than anything, seemed suddenly to have lost taste for this previously so tempting delicacy which now actually lay before him. His turn had appeared on the programme for the night's operations; a reminder of this, and a last special piece of hospitality, was the 'Operation Egg'.

That evening I was to sit down in a few seconds and look at the two fried eggs on my plate. My appetite was nothing out of the ordinary. There was too much to think about, too many still unanswered questions connected with the coming hours and days.

Knut Haukelid, another of the Norwegian agents involved in the attack on the heavy water plant, had a vivid memory of Gaynes Hall.

The place was very closely guarded. A number of servicewomen kept the place in order, cooked the meals, and gave the men some social life. They belonged to the special section called 'Fannies'. These girls did an uncommonly good job, seeing that everything went as it should and doing their best to prevent the delays from getting on our nerves. And, when the commandant suggested it, they were always willing to come to Cambridge in the evening for a little party … The fannies had their own cars, and very fine ones. When we drove into Cambridge for an evening it was usually to the best restaurant in the city where we would eat and drink at the expense of the War Office; the main thing being to enjoy ourselves as much as possible.

A Mrs Park of Bournemouth submitted her reminiscences of her time as a FANY at Gaynes Hall to the BBC's WW2 People's War website:

I hadn't realised that it was only a section of the FANY that had been drafted into SOE. I went to get my beret and said I was in SC61 and they hadn't heard of them. We were stationed in Gaynes Hall, Buckton [*sic*] nr St Neots and Cambridge. An old hall deep in the heart of the country. This lady who owned it was Mrs Jubilee [*sic*]; she was an elderly lady who had her house requisitioned. We did orderly work, we had a small switchboard, there were two or three cooks there and the food was lovely, because we looked after these BODS very well. We housed and looked after the BODS (secret agents). They had their training and came to us to wait for the RAF to take them in Lysanders on their missions. Sometimes they were brought back if the conditions were not right or if they had received a signal from the ground to abort the mission. We had many different nationalities come through there, Odette [Sansom, one of the women agents] went through Gaynes Hall. You weren't taught to drive and I was unable to drive although I would have liked to. The men would be dropped by parachute and then a canister would be dropped with a parachute also. These canisters would contain all sorts, folding bicycles, dead rats or dung filled with explosives. The RAF would stay at Gaynes Hall also. We used to go out with some of the BODS but we had to go right away from where we were stationed so that we did not draw attention to it. I am sure that some people must have known that something was going on. We were not supposed to get attached to them but we did and when they went on a mission you never saw them again. I remember a man called Trondstad, he was advising the men on the building that contained the heavy water at Vermork that Hitler intended using in atom bombs. He knew this building that they were going to blow up inside out. Many years later I read that this man had been murdered after the war by Nazi followers, it made me feel very sad.

(http://www.bbc.co.uk/ww2peopleswar/stories/66/a4055366.shtml)

The secrecy was under penalty of death. Along with all the other 'country houses', Gaynes Hall was a vital centre of the operation. Writing in an article in the *Hunts Post* about Huntingdonshire being a nerve centre of Allied espionage, Gordon Thomas added that

> … the charwomen were hand-picked. Life at wartime Gaynes Hall was fantastic. It was run on the lines of a luxury holiday camp. There was no shortage of food, drink or entertainment. From the very beginning, the Government had realised that nothing could be too good for the men and women who gambled their lives in the grim game of spying on the Continent.

Gaynes Hall is reported to have been used for briefing the Joes flying into France as well as debriefing the 'passengers' lifted out. When flights were postponed or cancelled due to bad weather, the FANY drove them back in the early hours of the morning. As the weather conditions normally took about six days to improve, it gave a rest to aircrew and agents and a breathing space for the maintenance crew.

During much of the time they waited, the agents went over and over the details of the life of the person they had become, the person named on the identity card and ration books they carried. They had to learn the names of their family members off by heart, what schools they had attended, the names of the streets in their town or village as well as workplace regulations, what was rationed, travel routines, times of curfews, etc.

To distract them, a group of 'very glamorous' young FANYs was on hand as 'entertainers'. Local delivery men were said to have been more than willing to drive into the grounds to catch a glimpse. Local teenage boys used to toboggan on a snow-covered hill in the grounds and loved having these 'dream' girls going down with them. One lady told me that when she was stationed at Gaynes Hall, it was to 'entertain' the agents – not in the modern sense, she stressed – with such activities as ping-pong, cards and dancing. One afternoon after a good lunch, two parachutists attempted to take her around the whole of the ground floor without touching the floorboards. They could use the skirting boards, the picture rails and any available furniture – much to the entertainment of the onlookers. When all three of them were standing on top of one of the old oak mantelpieces, it came away from the wall in one piece, crashed to the floor around them and 'brought the house down!'

Tempsford Hall was another of the 'stately 'omes' where FANYs looked after SOE and other agents (some said SOE stood for 'Stately 'Omes of England'). Tempsford Hall was about a mile away from the airfield, on the western side of the railway line. At the time of writing it is the headquarters of Kier Construction. Mr Kier, the founder, moved his offices to Tempsford after the war and was surprised to find that just over the railway line was the airfield which supplied him and his wife when they were in the Danish resistance. Peter Churchill, one of the agents, referred to his stay there in *Duel of Wits*, the second of his three books about his wartime experiences.

A pleasant car drive took them to Tempsford House, the Holding Camp in Bedfordshire … At the park gates of the camp a sentry took all the particulars from the F.A.N.Y. driver and telephoned the Adjutant's office to have their entry confirmed. They then proceeded up the long drive.

The Holding Camp was no camp at all, but another enchanting country estate with walled gardens and huge lawns … Major (Rose) … took them to the bar … saw to it that they got exactly what they wanted, however deeply it was entrenched behind the counter, and in his usual cheery hospitable manner – just right for such a place – he made them all feel very much at home. The atmosphere was one of gaiety and it never entered the heads of those who were departing to consider what it might be like to stay behind … All they wanted and noticed was whether or not they were given good food, whether or not they were treated with a certain consideration, and in these two matters the personnel of the Holding Camp from the C.O. downwards never failed.

As the days passed arrangements were made for their entertainment. Mixed sports were organised on the running track with members of the F.A.N.Y. Corps taking part. They were good sports and a pleasant atmosphere reigned here, as at Station 17 (Brickendonbury Manor, Hertfordshire – Explosives). Occasionally the girls were transferred from one place to another so as to give them an idea of the sort of work carried on by the other place. These girls kept any and all secrets that came their way just as well, if not better, than the men and their presence in these Schools, just like that of the A.T.S., the W.R.N.S., and the W.A.A.F.s in the other Services, was an all-round success.

As the Commandant of the Holding School had been told to keep the three men occupied to avoid their brooding, there were trees to be felled and all sorts of other activities going on all the time. Of course they had their maps to study as well as their cover stories, and amongst the things kept in store for their operation were French money and compasses. The five days' wait passed all too quickly in the pleasant surroundings of this Bedfordshire estate and every day had brought cloudless skies … After an unforgettable tea in the shade of an old oak, unforgettable for its peaceful setting, so incongruous with what lay but a few hours ahead, the three saboteurs, accompanied by the two Majors and the Commandant, went over to the store room to check over the gear that each man was to carry. Laid out in three neat piles were their khaki parachute overalls with a sharp spade slipped into a special pocket on the leg, a strong jack-knife attached by a cord fitted into another slot. On each pile was a shoulder holster complete with a fully loaded Colt automatic and three spare clips. There were three small bags of pepper, a torch, three money belts with 100,000 francs in each (There were 177 francs to the £ in 1942 and 1,000 francs could buy one kilogramme of real coffee), three parcels of sandwiches, a water flask, a hip flask full of rum, an empty sack and a compass for each man. Against each pile lay a black Sten gun and six spare clips. On a trestle table stood two strong rucksacks, beside which lay the plastic explosives for the operation.

In addition to the two lots of explosives were two tins containing three detonators and three time pencils each. They could not risk attaching the pencils to the plastic before the flight, owing to the danger of their breaking inside and blowing up the aircraft, which would take nearly two hours to reach the target area. On a small table stood three tiny carton pill boxes and in each of these was a lethal tablet.

This was not the same storeroom as the one beside Gibraltar Farm. It was another in the grounds so that agents had the chance to see and touch what they would be taking before their operations commenced.

The five men went over to the bar, the Commandant having tactfully left them together on some pretext. They ordered some drinks and took them out on the lawn. Here they sat in the drowsy atmosphere of the late afternoon and whiled away the last precious moments in these blissful surroundings. Beneath a nearby tree sat Mrs Bingham, the F.A.N.Y. Commandant, reigning handsomely over a graceful gathering of her juniors. They realised that something big was in the air, for they knew what was being guarded in the stores. From time to time they threw a glance in the direction of the five men and scanned the expressions of the three who would be leaving after supper. They admired all of those who went through the camp on a one way ticket and wondered if they would ever know what really happened to any of them once they got over there …

'What would you like for supper, Michel?' asked the F.A.N.Y. Commandant.

'Same as last time, please,' said Michel, perfectly certain that this would be an unfair test to anyone's memory who saw to so many suppers.

'Anne, see to it that Michel gets three fried eggs, bacon, chips, toast and butter, and a pint of Nelson's rum.' …

Supper was now over and the last swallow from their pint tankards alone remained. Michel, who was due away first from the aerodrome at eleven that night, knew that his time had come. It would take quarter of an hour to reach the airfield where another hour would be spent before the aircraft took off. Besides, he had seen the car come round to the front of the house. It must be the car for the aerodrome as its black curtains were drawn by the back seats. Whether this curtain business was to prevent nosey parkers from seeing who was being taken for a ride, or whether to prevent the riders from recognising the airfield, was a question Michel always forgot to ask. At all events, the whole thing struck him as rather ominous …

As the car swept away down the drive, he waved to them all and saw the receding group still waving as they turned the first bend.

They did not talk much during this drive, but Michel was in a pleasant glow thanks to the good fare and the agreeable send-off.

## The FANY's Curse

In Leo Marks's memoirs about his war years as SOE's code maker, he discussed the problem he had in choosing some of his FANY code breakers to be sent to Poundon, Buckinghamshire. As the Americans had joined the war, he had been given the task of providing them with quality code breakers from Grendon Underwood, one of Bletchley Park's sister stations. They recorded wireless and other encoded messages from SOE's agents and other sources and decoded them. There were undoubtedly women at Tempsford – WAAFs and FANYs – who manifested identical problems, so it is worth relating Marks's thoughts.

He admitted being puzzled by the pattern of what he considered unaccountable lapses among the FANYs working for him. The girls had been trained in code breaking and were generally very successful, but occasionally each month there were a few days when they took rather longer to break codes usually broken in hours. He made an appointment to discuss it with Captain Henderson, their personnel officer, known affectionately as 'Mother Hen'. She suggested that it might have something to do with periods. Marks thought she meant moon periods. He had to have explained to him the girls' monthly problems, which led many of them to suffer acute discomfort a few days before their periods began. Not having any sisters, he was obliged to ask for further and better particulars and it took some time for him to realise from the silence that followed that he had blown his cover as a man-about-town.

When it was eventually made clear, he was convinced that the majority of the unbroken coded messages occurred at the onset of their periods, which made the girls tense, erratic and depressed. He had understood that they lived and worked together in very tense and stressful conditions and were under huge pressure to decode thousands of messages a day. His solution was to suggest that he be informed when their periods were so that they could be allocated less arduous tasks like briefing agents about their codes instead.

Captain Henderson had to point out to him that this was a 'most delicate matter' that none of the girls would be willing to discuss. The relevant dates would not be logged on their personal files. The subject had never cropped up during interviews and would never be likely to. She suggested that the regimental doctor might know a few but would not disclose them unless directed by the head of FANY. It was essential to protect the girls' privacy. Marks was totally bemused and is reported saying, 'It's clear to me that once a month even FANY must conduct themselves like ladies – but I just don't understand why they're so shy about discussing it.' 'Few men do, Mr Marks,' was Captain Henderson's reply. Her suggestion was to recruit more girls, increase their rest periods, send them on leave every couple of months and, above all, respect their privacy. Marks realised that, by the time he discovered their dates, they would be too old to have them any more and that more practical measures were called for.

> I decided to tackle the problem cryptographically and made a blanket attack on the girls' forty-eight mistakes to establish a pattern. But even with the inventory in front of me, pinpointing their 'trying times' was like breaking an indecipherable with a misnumbered key-phrase and a dozen hatted columns.
>
> After several hours of total immersion I managed to establish that one thoroughly reliable girl made serious errors during the same four days of every month but at no other time. And that seven others who were equally dependable also made them at monthly intervals, though the dates varied by roughly a week. But in all cases the pattern was unmistakable.

I selected six of these girls for 53c [the American decoding station at Poundon, Buckinghamshire], and completed a list with a mixture of plodders and supervisors whose cycles were predictable. Nick [Marks's superior in the Codes Section at SOE HQ in Baker Street] barely glanced at the names before nodding his approval. I was anxious to tell him how the list had been compiled, but this was clearly the wrong moment to discuss the intricacies of female signals.

I was equally anxious to compare notes with Tiltman [Head of Codes] of Bletchley, but decided to postpone convening a national period conference until I knew what I was talking about, should that time ever come.

I was mercifully unaware of the other 'curses' which would shortly become due …

(L. Marks, *Between Silk and Cyanide*, 1998)

# 4

# Sending Women into Occupied Europe

In Foot's *SOE in France*, he remarked that there are

> plenty of women with marked talents for organisation and operational command, for whom a distinguished future on the staff could be predicted if only the staff could be found broad-minded enough to let them join it. The SOE was such a broad-minded staff.

Known as 'The Organisation', 'The Org', 'The Racket', 'The Outfit', or 'The Firm' by those in the know, the SOE appointed numerous women to its administrative staff. Squadron Leader Beryl Escott, the WAAF historian, reckoned that about 3,200 out of a total staff of 13,200 were female, whereas the Air Ministry only had 300 women. The number of women it took on as agents is uncertain. I estimate about sixty.

Of the thirty-nine women sent to the area of France controlled by what was called 'F' Section, some had previously belonged to the British Auxiliary Services. The SOE organised 'F' Section, the strictly non-political resistance groups under British control. General Charles de Gaulle's Free French Forces organised what was called the RF Section – Republique Française. Some members of the WAAF with particular skills, essentially being able to speak French fluently, were transferred into the SOE and trained as agents to be sent into occupied Europe. Others were given honorary commissions in the WAAF in the hope that, as officers in the regular services, their chances of being treated as prisoners of war would be improved. Although many agents were recruited from the War Office, the Admiralty, Air Ministry, Central Registry and Telegraph Office, others were 'introduced' if it was identified that they had language skills. Other skills that would be useful were patience, emotional self-control and aggression.

Analysis of the SOE records shows that five second officers, six assistant second officers and four flight officers from the WAAF were sent to 'F' Section. Whether any had been at Tempsford beforehand is unknown. Although the Geneva Convention stipulated that women in the Services should not carry weapons, this was not practised by the SOE. Selwyn Jepson, one of the Directorate of Military Intelligence, commented in an interview in 1986 that:

> I was responsible for recruiting women for the work in the face of a good deal of opposition from the powers that be who said that women, under the Geneva Convention, were not allowed to take combatant duties which they regarded resistance

work in France as being … There was a good deal of opposition from various quarters until it went to Churchill.

(S. Jepson (1986) [9331] Imperial War Museum SA)

The taboo of women using arms was abandoned by the SOE when they recognised that women were badly needed in occupied Europe and they needed to be able to defend themselves like any man. Jepson argued that the Geneva Convention did not relate to modern war that called for the wholesale involvement of civilian populations. As he put it, 'Air raid bombs that demolish homes and kill children bring to every woman by every natural law the right to protect, to seek out and destroy the evil behind these bombs by all means possible to her – including the physical and militant.' He subsequently became SOE's recruiting officer, interviewing potential agents at Sanctuary Buildings, in Westminster, London.

All the women agents were therefore given commissions in either the WAAF or the FANY in the hope that they would be treated as prisoners of war under the terms of the Geneva Convention and not be sentenced to death without trial. Of the fifteen in the FANY, there were six volunteers, six ensigns, one lieutenant and two of ordinary rank. Fifteen were given commissions in the WAAF and one in the ATS. The reality was that, if they were caught in civilian clothes and found to be agents, they would in all likelihood be interrogated and tortured to get any useful information out of them, and then executed.

What they did not know was the types of torture they might experience if caught. Juliette Pattinson, lecturer in Modern British History at Strathclyde University and specialising in gender, examined the testimonies of those who survived imprisonment, which showed that they were beaten with implements, kicked about the body, had toenails extracted, toes trampled upon by boots, were chained to furniture, deprived of sleep, forced to stay awake during many hours of interrogation, deprived of light, food and medical treatment for wounds, threatened with mock executions, had their fingers crushed, were immersed in water to the point of drowning, burned with hot pokers, heard others being tortured or shot, were subjected to electric currents passing through their bodies and kept in solitary confinement. Agents reported numerous injuries, including broken ribs, fractured fingers, teeth being knocked out as well as bruises and cuts. Pattinson's interviews with three of the women who were repatriated found that they were all beaten and badly mistreated, with distinct sexist and sexual overtones.

Sue Ryder commented that, 'All the men and women who trained as agents had to be in top mental and physical condition and possess initiative; they were self-reliant and discreet and capable of standing up to rough and arduous training and work.' The women agents were generally much younger than their male counterparts.

Although there was concern expressed about sending women into occupied Europe on dangerous missions, Colonel Gubbins, the then head of SOE, argued that they would be less conspicuous and find it much easier to get accommodation. Lone men were unusual as, from March 1943, the Germans introduced the *Service du Travail Obligitaire*, compulsory work service. All French men had to register their births. Those between nineteen and thirty-two were sent to work on the Atlantic Wall, in factories in

Germany or on the Russian front as many German men were engaged in military duties. Every week, about 20,000 were picked up on the streets of Paris. The Germans expected 500,000 in the first six months.

Forest Yeo-Thomas, a French-speaking British agent sent from Tempsford into France, learned about this compulsory work service and informed London that he feared that the age would be raised to forty-two, then to the middle fifties, resulting in there being no hope ever of forming a Secret Army in France. He suggested that the BBC and SOE use whatever means they could to encourage Frenchmen to avoid conscription by leaving the country or living clandestinely as members of the Resistance. Money needed to be sent, as well as weapons, ammunition, food and forged identity and ration cards so they could survive and defend themselves. He was convinced that these deserters, financed by Britain, armed and trained by SOE agents, would form the nucleus of a Secret Army. The concept of the Maquis was born. The result was that women would be much more visible on the streets than men. It was the ideal opportunity to start sending in women agents. They could invent a hundred cover stories as they could travel extensively and arouse little suspicion. Escott commented that women

> often substituted for a missing husband or brother, as the wage earner of the family. They searched for missing relatives or children. They covered incredible distances hunting for scarce items of fuel or clothing and particularly on a regular search for food to feed their families, with the fierce and protective care that distinguishes a mother for her children. They were to be found on all the roads – in their locality and out of it – most going about their lawful and innocent duties equipped with the legal and correct passes and papers required of every French citizen. A girl on a bike with a carrier was therefore a common sight everywhere and the Germans had such a stereotyped idea of the role of women that it could take a long time before they would suspect one of being an agent. She was therefore more unobtrusive and less liable to be caught. She might also to be able to use more charm and devious wiles that might hoodwink a questioner. Many trainers objected, but they soon discovered that women could be just as skilful and brave as men and this was soon proved in the field, where they had to overcome the extra obstacle of the ingrained prejudice to women of the people in the countries where they worked, no small task in itself. Thus the most unlikely of agents became assets.
>
> (B. Escott, *Mission Improbable: A Salute to the RAF Women of SOE in Wartime France*, 1991)

In Foot's *SOE in France*, he expressed the opinion that:

> By no means all of F Section's women agents had that ordinary, unassuming air which is so precious an asset for a clandestine; several had the stunning good looks and vibrant personality that turn men's heads in the street. This helped to make them noticed; it was counterbalanced, in the section's view, by making it more easy for them to appear to belong to that leisured class, the comings and goings of which only the surliest policeman is ever going to disturb. It was a mistake to forget how surly some of Hitler's or even Petain's policemen could be.

Exactly how many women were sent into occupied Europe is uncertain. There were some sent from Tempsford by the SIS, the Secret Intelligence Service, but their details are scarce. Their records, if any exist at all, are probably still being held by MI6. In Hugh Verity's *We Landed by Moonlight*, he commented that:

> There were a number of different clients, none of whom wanted any of the others to know about their operations. In fact SIS forbade any written matter. Their operations were 'officially inadmissible'.

I have references to over sixty women being sent in. While the majority were flown out from Tempsford, others were sent from Tangmere, Harrington and in one case Waterbeach, near Cambridge. A few were sent by small boats in the middle of the night. Three were sent to Belgium, three to Holland, eleven to the area of France controlled by de Gaulle and, officially, thirty-nine to the area controlled by 'F' Section. The OSS sent two women to France and the Soviets sent two there as well, one to Austria and one to Germany. Unofficially, there were more. Not all were British. The women were of various nationalities, including Americans, Australians, Austrians, Belgians, British, Dutch, French, Mauritian, Swiss and an Indian-Russian. Several were Anglo-French, their British fathers having married French women after the First World War. Many were married, several had children, one was a grandmother and two were sisters. There were two brother and sister teams and one mother and daughter team among those sent by the RF section. The Soviets planned to send one married couple into Prague but they refused to go. Before joining, the women had been told that their chances of survival were about evens, but in fact something like three agents in four survived. Of those sent to France, thirteen paid the ultimate sacrifice.

There were three women organisers, twenty couriers and sixteen radio operators in 'F' Section. They all had to sign the Official Secrets Act. Security was supposed to be watertight. Saying anything about the work to one's boyfriend, parents or friends was strictly forbidden. No one was supposed to know anything about the SOE. In fact, the first hint in the British media of these women's role during the war was not until 11 March 1945. The *Sunday Express* included an article on them by Squadron Leader William Simpson, DFC (Distinguished Flying Cross).

**WAAF girls parachuted into France**
Who are the Waaf officers who parachuted into France to join the Maquis months before D-Day?

This question has plagued Air Ministry officials ever since Sir Archibald Sinclair [Secretary of State for Air] praised Waaf parachutists in the House of Commons last week.

Officially it remains unanswered – for reasons of security. Two only have been named in the press. One Sonia d'Artois (née Butt), is the young daughter of a group captain. She married the French-Canadian officer who jumped with her.

The other, Maureen O'Sullivan, is also young and pretty. She comes from Dublin.

**Demure girls**
The interesting thing about these girls is they are not hearty and horsey young women with masculine chins. They are pretty young girls who would look demure and sweet in

crinolines. Most of them are English girls who speak perfect French. Some were educated in French convents; others attended Swiss finishing schools. A few are French girls who escaped from France and agitated for a chance to go back and work underground. Cool courage, intelligence, and adaptability are their most important attributes. They have to be able to pass themselves off as tough country wenches, and smart Parisiennes.

They were taught parachute jumping in the North of England. They trained with male agents and paratroopers of all nationalities, and leapt with them from fixed balloons and moving aircraft.

But parachuting was a secondary part of their training. They also had to absorb complicated secret details of underground organisation and train the Maquis in radio operating.

After months of intensive training, there often followed weeks of anxious waiting. Then, dressed in the appropriate French civilian clothes of their first role, they were flown by night bomber into moonlit France.

Sometime they dropped 'free' at a pre-determined point. On landing, they fended for themselves; reported to a friendly farmer, then set off at dawn to contact the leader of their resistance group.

Usually however, they landed with arms and food, floating down with the packages and containers. As courier, she went from group to group of the Maquis. It was easier for a girl to pass unnoticed in a France stripped of men by the Germans.

## Great courage

Often she was on the spot when supplies were dropped, and helped to unload and hide the containers.

It sounds easy enough. In fact, it is about the most cold-blooded and creepy task that any young woman could choose.

Death and torture are present realities. Atrocity details are well known. There were traitors in the Maquis itself working to betray. Sometimes they succeeded.

But so great was the courage and spirit of these girls that they could afford to send back humorous messages.

One – behind with routine signals – complained that what with washing and darning, and running around with messages, she had little time for routine work!

Another, who had walked for weeks to return to France, had to jump over Kent – due to engine trouble in the bomber which carried her. As soon as she had collected herself, she asked to be allowed to go on with the job the same night.

Behind the veil of secrecy, not yet raised by the Air Ministry, there are great stories of courage and endurance.

For the agent has no status; no friendly uniform or consul to rely on. With her friends she is outside the law – until it catches up with her.

## Her first aim

There was one girl I met in Vichy France four years ago. Since then, although not in the Waaf, she has been back and forth many times. Acting as courier and radio operator, she has also organised Maquis bands. No doubt she has fought with arms, for her first aim is to kill Germans.

Amongst her perilous adventures are included escapes over the Pyrenees into Spain. And she knows the filth, discomfort and despair of Spanish prison camps. But nothing could dismay her. She went on.

All these unknown young girls of the Waaf have proved one thing for ever. The toughest tests of courage and endurance faced by men can be passed with honour by women.

(*Sunday Express*, 11 March 1945)

After a selection process the agents were sent on a three-week introductory training and assessment course at Wanborough Manor, near Guildford, if they were in the 'F' Section, otherwise at Winterfold, near Cranleigh in Surrey. If they were considered suitable they then were sent on a four- or five-week paramilitary training course in Arisaig, north-west Scotland, where they were taught the art of 'ungentlemanly warfare'. Their trainers' assessment determined whether they would be best used as a radio operator or a courier. The role of an organiser was considered by the SOE to be a man's job.

At the time when SOE first decided to send female agents into occupied Europe, women were banned from carrying weapons in the British armed forces. Special authorisation was needed from Winston Churchill to allow them to be armed. While they underwent the same rigorous training as the men, they soon proved themselves quite capable at subterfuge, using guns, hand grenades, plastic explosives and silent killing.

Apart from those who were going to be sent into the field by boat, all agents had to get their parachute wings. This was done at Ringway Airfield, near Manchester. They stayed either in Dunham House, near Altringham, or in the adjoining estate of Tatton Park. Escott described the training:

They usually did four or five practice jumps, the last one at night and in later years with a leg bag for carrying equipment. Of course the station had its usual complement of airwomen. Having spent about two years at Ringway working on parachutes, 'where most of the time 1,000 troops were dropped day and night', Winifred Smith has clear memories of '… cycling across the tarmac to our section, seeing girls preparing to parachute, complete with lipstick and make-up – otherwise it was hard to tell that they really were girls, what with their parachute suits, crash helmets, and so on. We often watched them waiting to board the plane. It was like follow-my-leader. The girls were towards the back but they were always laughing and we would wave and call good luck. I don't remember more than about three or four together boarding the same plane, in fact often I could only see one.' Trainees sometimes said that they put the girls to jump first out of the aircraft into the grounds of Tatton Park, since they reckoned that the men would not hold back if a woman led the way. As part of her work on modifications to 'chutes and packs, Winifred also went into the training hangar: '… and saw them training on what we called the Fan. They were completely fearless. They were also quick off the mark in getting away afterwards. One had the feeling they didn't expect to come back, so they were living for the moment. When VE Day was over and we could talk more freely, it was agreed by all who had contact with these WAAF, that they had an inner strength and sheer determination which allowed them to do what was asked of them. They were inspired by something greater than the ordinary person.'

Those destined for courier work went to one of eleven secluded country houses in the grounds of Beaulieu, the New Forest. The majority of the women agents trained as couriers. It was thought by the upper echelons of the Dutch section of the SOE as late as 1944 that women were rarely stopped or searched at controls and that they were rarely picked up in mass arrests. That was the case in France early in the war but, as it progressed, most women were stopped and searched as well. What was true was that they made excellent cover while travelling around the country taking messages, papers, money, wireless equipment pretending to be going shopping, foraging for food or visiting friends. It was thought that the Germans wouldn't expect women to be involved in resistance activities. They were expected to be fulfilling the traditional roles of *Kinder, Kirche und Küche* (Children, Church and Kitchen). They were slow to realise that young, attractive women could be politicised and intent of carrying out deadly work. While there were circumstances when a bike was vital for getting around, for long journeys it was recommended that the women travelled first class on the trains as the Germans were less likely to thoroughly search wealthy middle-class passengers than those in third-class compartments. Big businessmen and Germans who travelled in first class didn't want the police to annoy them. The women were taught to hide incriminating items where they would be least likely to be found – in false-bottomed bags, inside bicycle frames or tyres, under dress belts, under the soles of stockings, inside powder compacts or even inside long hair. These methods offered less chance of detection during perfunctory searches. Should a woman's cover story be doubted, she had to expect a full body search.

Women were also thought to be more resourceful and composed than men and could better talk themselves out of tight spots at checkpoints using their feminine charms. They were also more inventive, conjuring ingenious cover stories. Questions they had to be able to answer were 'Where did you get your laundry cleaned?' or 'Where did you get your hair done?'

Unmarried women would probably have been provided with imaginary boyfriends. Those who were married may well have used an imaginary husband in their cover story. There was almost a husband and wife team in SOE. While Marjorie March-Phillips's husband was conducting his 'Small-Scale Raiding Force' on various missions overseas, she was recruited by SOE for operational duties. After working as a conducting officer attached to 'F' Section, she underwent parachute training at Ringway with a view to her being sent into France. However, the situation changed when she discovered that she was SOE's first pregnant parachutist (Howarth 1980, p. 33).

Major Thompson, in his memoirs *The SOE in Belgium*, admitted being an 'accompanying' or 'conducting officer'. With the assistance of a competent secretary, Miss Lee-Graham – later Mrs Koslowska but known only to the agents as 'Mrs Cameron' – he devised ingenious cover stories.

> We considered that most men would look more normal with a little love life and interest, so letters and photographs of girls were provided for men who wished it. The photographs initially provided some difficulty, but one which was solved for us

involuntarily by one of our trainees. Unknown to us at the time, a man on leave in London from one of our schools contrived to insert an advertisement in a Quebec newspaper: 'Lonely Belgium soldier wishes to find girl pen friend.' The resulting replies were intercepted by our Security and of course the man could not be allowed to have them. We were, consequently, put in possession of a vast assortment of letters, most of which enclosed photographs of attractive young French Canadian girls, often signed on the back (and we had others signed ourselves!) Of these many were suitable to provide fictitious girl friends for our men, and they could choose from a selection the girl that they preferred. I do not suppose that many French Canadian girls will ever know how usefully they unwittingly contributed to the allied war effort in their youth!

(http://www.docstoc.com/docs/71981970/NOTES-ON-SOE)

Those destined for wireless training spent a few weeks at Thame Park, Station 52, near Oxford; Grendon Hall, Station 53A, near Aylesbury; or Fawley Court, Station 54A, near Henley-on-Thames. Radio operators were expected to lead a solitary existence, able to keep awake until the transmission time was due and to minimise their use of the equipment to less than twenty minutes. As shall be seen, the Germans used sophisticated detecting equipment which resulted in the life expectancy of radio operators in the field being only six weeks.

They were made familiar with various codes and ciphers that were in use at the time for communication with agents in the field, and with main stations of the Mediterranean Allied Air Force at Massingham in Algiers or Cairo in Egypt. Pawley detailed some of those taught:

In the early days a code called Playfair was taught. It involved putting messages into rectangular 'boxes' on squared paper according to a numbered order of letters determined by the line of a poem (of which some were original and some borrowed) or sentence from a book. The message was encoded by selecting letters from the opposite corners of the rectangle. The code was superseded by a more secure one, named double transposition. Again, it was worked in 'boxes' on squared paper; it placed the letters of a message horizontally under a 'key' word or words which were put in numerical sequence; a fresh selection was made by transposing them vertically, again in numerical order; the final version was read horizontally. The field operator and base coder would be in possession of the identical poem or novel from which the 'key' word or words would be drawn; the page and line would be indicated in figures at the beginning of the message.

Leo Marks, the Jewish head of codes at SOE, introduced an even more secure code he termed the 'One-Time Pad'. Hundreds of lines of code were printed on silk and, once once had been used, it could be cut off and burnt or, if desperate, swallowed.

Great care needed to be taken to include two types of 'checks' in every message, a 'bluff' check, to confuse the enemy, and one 'true' check which it was hoped would not be discovered. Many field operators in the heat of the moment left out their checks when encoding messages. At the base, two possibilities occurred to the coder; was this a genuine lapse or had the set been seized by the enemy and was being worked back by them, as happened on several occasions.

In Marcus Binney's *The Women who Lived for Danger*, he quotes Leslie Fernandez, one of the women's trainers:

> During training we attempted to prepare them physically, building up their stamina by hikes through rough countryside. All were taught close combat, which gave them confidence even if most were not very good at it. These girls weren't commando material. They didn't have the physique though some had tremendous mental stamina. You would not expect well brought up girls to go up behind someone and slit their throats, though if they were grappled, there were several particularly nasty little tricks that we handed on, given us by the Shanghai police.

For many of the women agents, and men for that matter, they had to overcome an instinct instilled in them since birth – they had to look someone important in the face and not tell them the truth. Lying had to become part of their skills while in the field. They had to take on the role of an actor; as in life, some took to the stage much better than others. Escott provided a fitting tribute to them:

> To know what they did and what happened to them can therefore act as a memorial to those who died, and a reminder of the great courage shown by all these remarkable individuals who, in abnormal times, when their world was turned upside down, displayed extraordinary qualities to match their unusual and perilous role.

She went on to say that it was in the spirit of self-sacrifice that most agents undertook this work:

> When deaths occurred it was only for the greater good. On the way, of course, there was excitement, friendship and a gruelling test of the human spirit, but there was also fear, loneliness, hard work and sometimes torture and death.

## Radio Operators

Vital to the success of all these secret missions were the radio operators. A St Neots man recalled how during the war he was posted to Blackpool to run a training course in wireless maintenance and repair in the Winter Gardens. He was struck by one particularly well-behaved group of young women who turned up having just finished a radio operator's course. They spent most of the time discussing their social life, where they were going that night, who with and what they were going to wear. Particularly affectionate, they threw their arms round their trainer on finishing the course, telling him that they had been posted to Tempsford. What a surprise! It was only a few miles south of where he lived. Maybe he would see them some time. He didn't. Radio operators had a dangerous job. It was said that at the beginning of these secret operations, the average life expectancy of a radio operator in the field was only six weeks. Francis Cammaerts, a French resistance leader, said that, 'Without your radio operator, you were a pigeon without wings.'

Those who had been in the Girl Guides fared better as they had some understanding of Morse code. It is worth including a few paragraphs from Pawley's *In Obedience to Instructions* as she provides fascinating detail of exactly what their work entailed:

This knowledge needed to be transferred to operating a special key which represented the dots and dashes in terms of short and long sounds. When proficiency was attained, the mock practice key became part of a B2 radio set which relayed the sounds into the atmosphere and could be captured at a distance on a specified wavelength, previously determined.

… at Fawley Court … a group of twelve girls … sat at a series of wooden tables, practising their morse on a dummy key day after day. As it became possible to speed up, one moved to the next table, with an instructor sitting at the end. Most trainees would stick at one letter and not be able to overcome the resultant pause for a short period. There was a test once a week, when the atmosphere was really tense. Ann Bonsor recalls going to the cinema and quite involuntarily turning the sign EXIT beside the screen into morse. Probably on this account, radio operators, like coders, became obsessional; many FANYs have never lost the skill, only some of the speed, fifty years later.

For the last part of their training radio operators were often posted to Scotland to take part in a scheme called SPARTAN, at Dunbar. FANYs would be based in a mobile signal station, to which agents in training, dispersed throughout the countryside, would work back their sets. Before proceeding overseas, most coders and radio operators received some experience on an operational station, dealing with live traffic from the field. This would be at Station 53A, Grendon Underwood, or Station 53B, at Poundon. Messages came in from Holland, France, Denmark, Norway and so on. During their earlier training radio operators would have become familiar with the Q code and the sending and receiving procedures based on this international method of communication; no other means were allowed, never plain language, though some agents in distress, anger or jubilation, might sometimes resort to it.

A FANY operator on duty at her set would be allocated to what was known as a 'sked' (terminology for an expected message at a previously defined time from an agent), with the appropriate frequency, code name and call sign, by the signal master, or other authorised person. She would listen for the three-letter particular call sign of the out-station which should be calling at intervals of one minute, and then listening for one minute. If contact were established, the home operator would send the call sign, followed by QRK How are you receiving me, plus IMI Question mark. The field would answer QSA Your signal readability is, followed by a number from one to five. If it were over three, and therefore fairly audible, the home operator would wait for the field to send QTC I have a message for you. Field messages were always sent first. With numbers less than three, each group of five letters (the invariable number in which signals were sent) would be repeated. The base operator then took down the message in pencil in block capitals on special forms, and then wait until QRU appeared: I have nothing more. If the base operator had messages, the procedure would be reversed. To ask for repeated groups, or QRS send slower, was not well regarded, unless interference was particularly bad, since it would expose the field operator to danger. At the end of a transmission, the base would send VA close down. In the event of sudden enemy attack, the field could send QUG I am forced to stop transmitting owing to immediate danger, whereupon a FANY operator would report this at once to her senior officer. In the event of gross inaudibility, it was possible to ask for help from a second base operator, but this was an exceptional measure in particular circumstances. 'Listening watches' were set up when a field mission failed to respond at its allotted time according to its signal plan.

A specialised training was given to become a signal planner. A small group of FANYs learnt to provide a signal plan for every mission which went into the field. It included a call sign by which to be recognised by the base station, an allocated frequency, obtained by the supply of the appropriate crystals (two slices of quartz cut to a precise wavelength which determined frequency, about the size of a postage stamp) and specific times on a regular basis at which attempts to transmit to the base station were to be made. Trained signal planners who undertook this skilled technical work were given the rank of Lieutenant.

Another technique in which the FANYS were instructed later in the war was that of 'finger printing', i.e. the recognition of morse-sending methods. All who learnt to send morse developed their own individual style. If an agent in occupied territory were captured, attempts would be made to work the radio back to base in England. A FANY operator who could detect a change in field operator would prevent unwise future communications, drops, or reinforcements to that mission.

Not everyone passed the four-month wireless course. They had to reach at least twenty words a minute, much higher than the peacetime requirements of the Services or Post Office. Those who failed to grasp the hang of it all dropped out, and there were many who were transferred to become coders, registry clerks, copy clerks, signal distributors, and teleprinter or switchboard operators. Ryder mentioned that the men and women who were successful in their training as radio operators included the bravest:

[For] if they were caught with a set they knew they faced death. To escape detection they frequently had to change the place from which they transmitted messages and, to avoid capture, they often had to disguise themselves – sometimes at barely a moment's notice. German radio-telegraphists were on duty at their listening posts twenty-four hours a day. The Gestapo always had a flying squad ready to go into action immediately to hunt and seize these Bods.

An indication of their work in the field was provided in Frank Griffiths' memoirs of his years as a pilot in 138 Squadron:

The resistance units in the occupied countries grew and grew until finally some 1,400 independent units were on the books. Initially an agent and his pianist (radio operator) would be dropped and, in its simplest form, the agent would recruit patriots in small units in various towns and villages. They in turn would select suitable fields for the reception of the drop materials such as guns, ammunition, clothing, money, etc. The agent would, through his pianist, inform London of the place of the reception, give it a code name, a recognition letter and a message which the BBC could broadcast on the day an aircraft was being sent with his supplies. This message would be something in the nature of 'Tartes aux pommes de la tante Helene' repeated twice each time it was broadcast on the BBC transmission. The first time at 1300 hours. The broadcast of the message would indicate merely that the flight was being planned. The 1800 hour transmission confirmed that the flight really would take place – that is, if the aircraft remained serviceable, the weather didn't deteriorate and if the aircraft didn't get lost or shot down on the way. There were lots of 'ifs' even after all the planning was done.

## Preparing for the Drop

Once the agents arrived at Gibraltar Farm their conducting officer escorted them into the barn. Just the same as the men, the women were dressed in a 'striptease' suit – a baggy jumping suit well fitted with spacious pockets into which went a dagger, hard rations, a flashlight, first-aid equipment, wireless parts, secret maps and papers. Their ankles were strapped with bandages to give good support and they were given stout boots with rubber cushions under their heels to further reduce the chances of injury on landing. The RAF Air Liaison Officer in charge would refer to them only by their codename. Their passwords, messages and other information were checked to see that they had learnt them off by heart. Checks were made on their clothes and shoes, specially made in SOE workshops, and their other belongings. No British tags were to be on them, no used bus or train tickets, cigarette packets or matchboxes, no initialled handkerchief, etc. Shoes had not to be new so as to avoid arousing suspicion. Their hair had previously been cut in the appropriate style of the country they were going to and even teeth were checked to ensure that the SOE dentist had replaced fillings with the appropriate gold.

A local lady from Sandy reported having to wash some agents' hair before they left. Presumably she used soap from the country they were going to be dropped in as it had to smell right. Whether the Germans had learned to recognise the smell of Lifebuoy or Wright's Coal Tar soap is undocumented.

The cashier would issue agents with foreign documents, enough foreign currency to run a resistance operation and a collection of loose change for use on arrival. The serial numbers were never consecutive and notes were often trampled on to give them a slightly tattered look. Heavy canvas jumpsuits were provided, suitably camouflaged with patches of green and mustard brown. They had extra wide legs and arms to fit over the agents' ordinary clothes. A harness was fastened over this and a parachute attached. Many were given a Colt revolver and bullets. Other useful equipment included a jackknife to cut through the parachute rigging should it be snagged; a folding shovel to bury the parachute and be used as a splint if bones were broken; a hip flask full of rum, brandy or whisky; a tin of sandwiches for the flight; and their choice of drugs. Terry Crowdy in his *SOE Agent: Churchill's Secret Warriors* mentioned these drugs:

> 'A' tablets for airsickness; (blue) 'B' pills containing Benzedrine (sulphate) for use as a stimulant (the amphetamine Mecrodrin was also issued); the 'E' pill: a quick-working

anaesthetic that would knock a person out for 30 seconds; 'K' pills for inducing sleep and 'L' pills.

'L' pills were lethal cyanide crystals in a thin rubber coating that one could bite through; they were hidden in the top inside part of an agent's jacket, in hollowed-out wine-bottle corks or in tubes of lipstick. If taken, death would follow within fifteen seconds. Agents were told that the Catholic Church had given them a special dispensation to use the pill 'in extremis'. The final thing was being given a good-luck gift. This might be cufflinks, a cigarette case, powder compact or a piece of jewellery – a reminder that SOE was thinking of them. When they ran out of money they were told it could be pawned or sold on the black market.

Some of these smaller items were used to conceal codes, messages and microscopic photographs. Other hiding places included fountain pens, pencils, wallets, bath salts, shaving sticks, toothpaste tubes, talcum powder containers, lipsticks, manicure sets, sponges, penknives, shoe heels and soles, shoulder padding, collar studs, coat buttons, and cigarette lighters. A $2\frac{5}{8}$ by $\frac{5}{8}$ inch aluminium cylinder was developed at Aston House as a rectal/vaginal container. It could be unscrewed in the middle and the message inserted. Understandably, no mention of their use appeared in any of the women's stories.

Sue Ryder, one of the FANYs who accompanied Polish agents to Tempsford, commented that:

> Though the pre-mission hours were naturally very tense, there was also a wonderful sense of humour and cheerfulness among the Bods. I can't remember any false bravado; on the contrary, it was real wit that came through. No written word can recapture the warmth of the atmosphere throughout the station. Whenever the atmosphere was especially tense or a feeling of dread prevailed, someone in the small group would rally the spirits of the others. They had, too, an extraordinary humility and a religious faith which was exemplified in the way they prepared themselves for their missions, such as making their confessions to a priest who would come to the ops station especially for this purpose.

Once on board, it was the job of the despatcher to make the agents comfortable. Wing Commander Pickard was particularly kind to those he called his 'female passengers'. He used to hand over the controls to his co-pilot and go to the back of the plane to sit with them to put them at their ease by chatting. It was often too noisy for lengthy conversations but was appreciated nonetheless.

## Tangmere's Ground Control Interception

161 Squadron's missions to France often started from RAF Tangmere, their forward base close to the south coast, about 4 miles east of Chichester. The proximity to the Continent meant the squadron's range of about 600 miles would take them much deeper into southern France than if they started from Tempsford. Pearl Panton, a WAAF working on Ground Control Interception, recognised immediately when one of Tangmere's special

flights set out across the Channel and then later returned homewards. As recorded by Beryl Escott, Panton said, 'They were given quite a different code, plus a special time for the moon to light their way, and they flew very low.' Like all controllers, she kept mum about her work; she never spoke about it, but in her diary wrote:

> It was a full moon last night, an essential factor for the special mission pilots taking off and returning. At 21.30 hours, I was driven from the Officers' Mess to the 'Happydrome'. The officer of the watch gave me my orders. I was to work on the Skyatron radar. A special mission was going out before midnight, due to return just before dawn.
>
> P for Peter 141 took off at 22.00 hours. One of the girls working the watch was startled as she recognised her husband's voice calling to confirm that he was airborne. She wouldn't have known of this mission, of course. I didn't know her well, but I had met her recently in a nearby café. There she had introduced me to her husband and I remember her delight at a pair of fur-trimmed gloves he had bought her that day. During the night watch she told me she was expecting her first baby.
>
> It was a busy night as usual. P 141 was due to return at 03.00 hours. There was no R.T contact at the scheduled time. I was told to call him and keep calling at regular intervals. He should at least have crossed the French coast. The girl sat next to me, watching the Skyatron, listening intently for her husband's voice. His call would have included a coded message to be passed to Air Ministry. It never came through.

Yvonne George, another WAAF mentioned in Escott's book, said that she liaised between SOE and SIS headquarters, phoning the Intelligence Officer at Tempsford, who – depending on the availability of aircraft and the meteorological report – would decide whether a flight was possible. 'On one occasion I was at Tangmere to see the take off of an aircraft with three agents on board and waited until about 3 am, early morning, for its return. As one of them alighted I caught a strong smell of Guerlain perfume – something we in England had not known for some years!'

Faith Spencer-Chapman, another WAAF, mentioned to Escott that she was in 'Air Ops', which involved dropping agents into Europe, and then in 'Pick up Ops':

> This meant taking agents down to RAF Tangmere and waiting for the Lysander to return with agents who had to be got out of France urgently. Then we had to drive back to London in the early hours and hand them over to be debriefed.

## SOE's Liaison Officers

Kathleen Moore was one of SOE's liaison offers, providing the link between their headquarters in London and RAF Tempsford and RAF Harington. According to her obituary in *The Times*, she was born in 1914, the second child and only daughter of Harold Moore, an Irish journalist, and his wife, Katherine Chapman. They lived in Winnipeg, Canada, and following her younger brother and mother's deaths, she had to manage her father's household while she was still a schoolgirl.

Escape came when she went to the University of Manitoba to read French. Her evident gift for the language won her a scholarship to Paris and to the Sorbonne. She stayed on in Paris through the later 1930s, working at the British Embassy until, with the fall of France in May 1940, she along with the rest of the staff was evacuated to London.

There, with Mary Mundle, with whom she had lived in Paris, and Alison Grant, a Canadian friend whom she had met in Paris, she took a flat at 54a Walton Avenue in Knightsbridge. Known familiarly as the Canada House Annexe, it soon became a notable social hub for those on leave from the Special Operations Executive. Each of the three women had become involved one way or another with the clandestine world of Special Operations and Military Intelligence.

Kay had joined the First Aid Nursing Yeomanry (FANY) immediately on her return, but, with her fluent French, soon found herself directly and deeply involved with the RF section, maintaining contact with the Resistance and the Free French, briefing agents before they were sent to France and debriefing them on their return – if they returned.

She rose eventually to become head of Air Liaison, the section that worked directly with the RAF and the USAAF, telephoning them or sending telegrams to arrange flights for her 'Bods'.

It was through this work, or through the social life that spun around it, that she met her future husband, the young Ernest Gimpel. After the fall of France he had joined the Resistance, had been arrested by the Germans but had managed to escape, and in 1942 was one of the few people spirited to England by submarine.

Codenamed 'Charles Beauchamp', he was sent back to France in November 1943, but was soon captured by the Gestapo, brutally interrogated and then sent successively to Buchenwald, Auschwitz and Flossenburg concentration camps. When the camps were liberated by the Allies in the last weeks of the war, he set about finding Kay.

As it happened, she was already in continental Europe, working in a team repatriating prisoners of war. She and Charles were not only soon reunited but, by the end of August, married and on honeymoon, staying with cousins in Ireland at the start of Charles's long recuperation.

# 5

# Female Agents

Escott referred to about ninety women being selected for training. Not all were successful, though. Details of those who failed their assessment have not come to light. Freddie Clark's *Agents by Moonlight*, a chronological account of 138 and 161 Squadrons' missions, specifically mentions the names of fifteen women who were flown out of Tempsford. While the others may have been flown out of Tangmere, one of the pilots told me that his crew dropped a female agent into France, but she was not referred to in Clark's book. SOE was not the only agency to have recruited women agents.

Two websites, 'Spartacus' and '64 Baker Street', with sections devoted to female SOE agents, mention several other women who were not mentioned by Clark as flying out of Tempsford. If these online sources are accurate, then it is possible that many of the other women were taken by 138 Squadron Lysanders or dropped from 161 Squadron's Halifaxes or Hudsons and just referred to as 'agents'. It is also possible that a number were sent on missions by the SIS, OSS or other agencies.

## Giliana Gerson
The first woman claimed to have been sent in by the SOE was Chilean-born Giliana Gerson, née Balmaceda. A beautiful young actress, she was working in theatres in Paris in the 1930s and married Victor Gerson, a British rug and carpet dealer who had settled in the capital after fighting in the First World War. His first wife had died and his son had been killed in a road accident. Following the German invasion of 1940, Victor and Giliana fled to England, where they both joined the SOE.

In Cookridge's *Inside SOE*, he mentions Victor Gerson suggesting to a Mr Humphreys that he and his wife could help set up an escape route helping get people across the Pyrenees into neutral Spain. Giliana volunteered to use her Chilean passport to return to France, crossing the frontier legally from Spain. Whether she was flown out by one of the Special Duties Squadrons was not documented.

In May 1941 she made her way north to Vichy, where, as well as spying on Petain's government, she collected documents such as ration cards that could be reproduced by the SOE for its undercover agents in France. She also met several Spanish ex-Republicans who were prepared to help with the planned escape route.

In mid-June she left the country and went first to Madrid, presumably visiting a contact in the British Embassy, and then to Gibraltar, from where she was returned to London, bringing back valuable information. A few months after her return, on 6 September 1941, her husband was dropped by parachute near Châteauroux and he went on to set up groups of resisters in the Lyon area and what became known as the 'Vic' escape line.

## 'Anatole'

In Hugh Verity's *We Landed by Moonlight*, he mentions what is thought to be the first female agent to be parachuted into France. Who she was and what she did remain a mystery.

> For operation 'Baccarat' Murphy took off at 2145 on 27 February (1942). He found solid cloud cover over the French coast at 1,000 ft and only 3,000 yards visibility below. Failing to fix his position near Abbeville, he flew north-west until he could get a radio fix from base. Then he found Abbeville and set course for St Saëns where, at midnight, he landed one passenger and picked up two, including Rémy.
>
> The new arrival in France was an unknown young woman called 'Anatole'. Rémy reported: 'She laughs, very happy to be back in France. I understand that she totally vanished.'

However, on Pierre Tillet's list of infiltrations into France he mentions the passengers as G. Renault, aka Rémy, and Pierre Julitte. Freddie Clark did not mention 'Anatole', but added that Murphy carried out 161 Squadron's first Lysander SIS operation. One hopes that one day MI6 will declassify and release their documents of the women they sent into occupied Europe.

## 'Anna Frolova' – Francine Fromont

On 3 March 1942, the first Soviet woman agent was sent out of Tempsford. There had been two other women sent from the Soviet Union as part of a secret agreement between Churchill and Stalin whereby Britain agreed to send their agents, codenamed Pickaxes, into occupied Europe. As German troops occupied much of Eastern Europe, the Soviets were unable to re-establish links with their existing agents in Western Europe. The distance was too far and the chances of their planes being shot down were too great. SOE was given the task of liaising with the NKVD, the Russian secret service, looking after the agents while they were in Britain and negotiating with the Special Duties Squadrons to fly them out.

Thirty-eight-year-old Szyfra Lypszyc arrived with the cover name of Anna Ouspenskaya, but a medical condition meant that she could not be parachuted into France. Special arrangements were made for the Royal Navy to land her by boat on the Normandy coast on 10 January 1942. Rendezvousing with her contacts in Paris, she did not survive long. She was captured with others in her group and executed.

Twenty-eight-year-old Hilde Uxa, using the cover name of Maria Dicksen, was one of a group of five Soviet agents destined for Vienna, but they were all returned to Russia after refusing to go with forged documents they considered to be defective.

Travelling under a French passport, as twenty-five-year-old 'Anna Frolova', the third Soviet woman arrived in Scotland on SS *Arcos* on 8 February 1942, accompanied by two other 'French' citizens, thirty-nine-year-old 'Georges Robigot' and thirty-one-year-old 'Pierre Dandin'. None used their real names. On meeting their Soviet bosses in London, the female agent was provided with papers under the name of 'Annette Fauberge'. Afterwards, 2nd Lieutenant Walsh, their SOE conducting officer, took them to Drokes, one of the country houses on the Beaulieu estate.

Like the other agents, they too had parachute training at Ringway, where they stayed at Dunham House. Major Edwards, the Commandant, reported that:

Fauberge showed good spirit throughout. Could not master the technique of dropping cleanly through the aperture, and would always slide through in a dangerous manner. Continuous practice made her very nervous, and this, combined with her lack of skill made it inadvisable for her to make the first balloon drop with Robigot and Dandin. Nevertheless, she was still anxious to drop, and showed great determination, concentrating on her training, and improving greatly. She was quite calm and collected when taken up for a balloon drop, and showed no hesitation. Her egress was rather bad and might have been dangerous from an aircraft, but her descent and landing were good. Made only one drop …

Fauberge soon became proficient on the trapeze, but could not bring herself to go through the 'mock-up' aperture without a good deal of persuasion. She was so incapable of pushing off, that I could not accept the responsibility of her jumping, and informed H.O. This seemed to give her fresh determination, and she improved considerably next morning, and so I arranged for the balloon to be flown especially for her. This was done and she jumped between two of my instructors …

They were treated as Officer students, but messed separately from the other students in the house.

In order to make things easier for Fauberge the aperture of the balloon cage was closed during the ascent. This, I think, helped her and is a practice that might be followed in certain cases where students are likely to be affected with giddiness. This only applies to the balloon.

(TNA HS 4/342)

A separate mess from the other students was to avoid them discovering that Britain was training Soviet agents. They returned to London on 26 February and stayed at 40 Porchester Court, Bayswater. This had been rented to house Pickaxes and to serve as a meeting place for SOE's Russian section and the NKVD. During this time the agents were provided with cover stories, forged identity cards, demobilisation forms and personal letters. Exact copies of the signature of *le commissaire de police* and accurate official stamps had to be added to ensure they looked authentic. The 500 dollars and 85 Swedish Crowns the three of them had been given were converted to French francs and they were all supplied with appropriate clothing for France.

Annette's cover story was that she was 'Jeanne Claude Garnier' and her report described her as

a good-looking French woman; extremely hard, and it was impossible to find out from her any facts about her former history. Her luggage was carefully examined and from the enclosed photograph, we deduced that she had been 'married' and had produced a small son during the autumn of 1939.

She was a stenographer by trade and had lived in Paris. For some reason which we do not know she left France for Copenhagen in 1940, whence she proceeded to Russia. From her clothes it would appear that she had been well-off and belonged to the bourgeois class.

She would make a good agent and should successfully pass any normal police examination.

The original plan was for three accompanying officers and Miss Jackson, a FANY officer, to take them to Gaynes Hall to wait for their flight from Tempsford. Because of the political sensitivity of Britain sending out Soviet agents, the instructions were for them to be

kept most strictly apart from any others. Those directly concerned should be told that there is a girl in the party; those not directly concerned should be given to understand that the girl is a secretary from H.Q. with Miss Jackson, who will, as far as possible, avoid speaking French to her in the presence of those who are not aware of the fact that she is a passenger.

Circumstances must have changed: on 3 March 1942 the three of them, accompanied by SOE, Foreign Office and NKVD officials, left London at 1530 hours for Tangmere Airfield. The original time of departure was scheduled for 1930 but at 1900 hours it was cancelled. Later, at 1945 hours, this decision was reversed and the agents' dressing was completed by 2015 hours. Having been given their farewell drinks, their general morale was described as 'excellent'. SOE had provided them with a wireless set camouflaged as a suitcase, thought to be tactful as a Soviet wireless set had been destroyed when the plane carrying Pickaxe II crashed on its way to Austria, killing both agents (TNA HS 4/342).

Clark described how Czech Pilot Officer L. M. Anderle, flying Whitley Z9158 on operation RUM, reported in the Squadron logbook that he

Crossed French coast at Port en B. at 2,000 ft., climbed to 6,500 feet in central France to cross mountains, and descended to 600 feet to drop passengers. Aircraft pinpointed Agde (Herault) on the Mediterranean to Lake Thau (this was Bassin de Thau) then north to pinpoint. Dropped three men and two packages. All five parachutes were seen to open. Returned to base. Landed 0536.

Although the pilot reported dropping three men, Clark referred to a letter concerning the three agents for this operation from Lt-Col. R. M. Barry to Capt. Wooler of 138 Squadron, in which he said:

Her name was Anna Frolova, aged 25, her pseudonym was 'Annette Fauberge' and she was the first woman agent to be dropped by parachute into France. The other two agents were Grigory Rodionov, aged 40, who went under the name of 'Georges Ribigot', and Ivan Danilov, aged 31, using 'Pierre Daudin'.

There was no further correspondence in their file until 27 February 1945 when, in a memo from H. A. R. 'Kim' Philby of the Russian section to Miss Bagot of MI5, he commented that, three months after they had landed, the NKVD 'displayed considerable anxiety' that they had heard nothing from them (TNA KV 2/2827). Philby was secretly working for the NKVD.

Two months later, Miss Bagot wrote to Philby telling him that she had shown the French police a photograph of 'Anna Frolova' as they had in their care a woman who called herself Marie-Claude Vallant-Couturier, who had been rescued from Auschwitz concentration camp, and who had excellent command of English. The police did not think it was the same woman, unless her experiences had considerably altered her appearance. The British thought that 'Annette' and her two comrades had been sent to assist the isolated Soviet agents in Lyon and provide communication with Moscow.

In Donal O'Sullivan's *Dealing with the Devil*, he stated that French investigations revealed that 'Garnier', who they knew as Fernande Guyot, was really Francine Fromont and married to 'Robigot', whose real name was Raymond Guyot. The NKVD had reason to conceal their identities as Guyot was a high-ranking official of the Communist Youth International and a prominent French Communist.

> Francine Fromont accompanied him as a radio operator. The Germans eventually caught 26-year-old Fromont in July 1943 and executed her on 5th August 1944 … Guyot and Fromont travel on Fitin's orders to London to get to France illegally. Gave them directives and 6,000 French francs and 1,050 US dollars. After liberation in 1944, the French Communist magazine 'Jeunes Filles de France' ran a story celebrating Francine Fromont's sacrifice, without mentioning her ties to Soviet intelligence. A special brochure published in the post-war years omitted any reference to her stay in the USSR.

After the war, Communist-controlled city councils honoured Francine Fromont by naming streets and schools after her.

## Yvonne Rudellat

SOE records show that the first woman agent they sent into France was forty-five-year-old grandmother Yvonne Rudellat. Colonel Maurice Buckmaster, the head of SOE's 'F' Section, wrote about her in an article published in *Chambers' Journal* after the war. In it, he called her Christiane.

> The revolving-doors of the hotel clicked merrily round. It was a busy hour, and the foyer was full of men in uniform and men who looked as if they wanted to be in uniform: for, in the early months of 1940, permission to fight as a soldier, sailor, or airman for Britain was almost as difficult to obtain as entry to an exclusive club.
>
> Behind the reception-desk Christiane was dealing courteously but firmly with the more obdurate would-be clients, who refused to believe it possible that all the rooms in the hotel were really booked. She was no longer young, and the years behind the reception-desk had brought lines in her forehead and a rather weary stoop to her shoulders. Her steel-rimmed spectacles gave her an old-maidish look, belied only by her strong, straight chin and direct glance.

Christiane was tired; tired of this artificial life of 'No, Madam, I'm afraid the hotel is full until after Easter, or 'Oui, Monsieur, je ferai l'impossible. Demandez de nouveau demain.' There was generally, even in pre-war years, a fairly large French clientele at this London hotel: now, in March 1940, members of French missions thronged the salons and competed for the few available rooms. 'It's a pity the War Office doesn't take the whole hotel over', thought Christiane, as the desire for freedom, the right to express her patriotism in more direct fashion, again overwhelmed her.

Hers was a double patriotism, arising from her parentage: a French father and a British mother had each given her a share of their ardent love for their country. Her own volatile temperament, confined by circumstance into the cramping occupation of hotel receptionist, threatened every now and again to boil over, as it once had when she fell in love with, and married, a young Englishman whom she had met in the 'other war'. She was widowed now and her daughter was expecting to be called up at any moment.

As she answered the persistent ring of the house telephone and the buzzer, Christiane realised with a sigh that she had ambitions which she saw no chance of gratifying. She wanted the active life which lay before her daughter; she wanted the life of any of these hard young men in uniform who were still untried in war, but who promised to give a good account of themselves when the fighting started; she wanted to use her perfect knowledge of French – the thought of clandestine work flitted through her busy brain, but she dismissed it as hopeless; she wanted to break away from the monotony of this drab existence, but she had not the faintest idea how to make the break. She knew many people, some V.I.P.s, but she knew them in her capacity as a hotel receptionist. They would be faintly amused – and the nicer ones more than a little sadly sympathetic – at the whim of an old maid, for such she seemed, seeking to fight for her country, her countries. She was not really tied, since she had put aside, with French frugality, enough to ensure her against hardship in her declining years, and her daughter was capable of earning her living. Yet Christiane felt almost helpless as day followed day and the papers on her desk still had to be dealt with, and the clients became more and more disgruntled.

When summer came, and the disasters in Flanders culminated in the capitulation of France and the armistice which Christiane found shameful she decided that the time had come for drastic measures if she were to retain her self-respect. 'Cela ne peut pas être,' she said to herself of the armistice. 'It just can't be so. At least one Frenchwoman', she thought, 'will refuse this dreadful pact with the enemy.' She sought out the Manager of the hotel and told him she wished to leave. It was not nearly as easy to get away as she had thought, and she was obliged to drag on at her job until a bomb in April 1941, lucky for her, unlucky for some of the guests, solved the problem by partially destroying the hotel.

Calling on a close personal friend of mine, who had often used the hotel in the past when he left his home in Paris for a brief visit to London, Christiane explained her desires to him. He sent her on to me, since he knew, more or less, what I was doing and thought that Christiane might be of help in the office. When I spoke to my friend on the telephone about Christiane, I too thought she would be a good addition to the office staff, and it was for that reason that I fixed up a rendezvous with her.

But Christiane had other ideas. She was a good enough psychologist to let her ideas percolate through to me slowly, to avoid the risk of a curt refusal which it would be difficult to retract. She put out a feeler or two, made light of her age, and finally, with a sincerity which I found completely disarming, begged to be allowed to serve her countries more actively. I had to temporise; there was no other way. We made the usual routine inquiries, we interviewed her several times, and ultimately we agreed to start her training. She was radiant; the years seemed to drop from her shoulders, and she insisted on going through the physically tough courses as well as the purely theoretical ones. She was one of the happiest and most enthusiastic students we ever had, man or woman. Nothing came amiss to her, and she devoted to the acquiring of the finer arts of lock-picking, for instance the same studious attention as she had accorded to the preparations of a client's accounts in her hotel.

(M. Buckmaster, 'They went by Parachute', *Chambers' Journal*, 1946–47)

Her personal file in the National Archives shows that, after passing the assessment course in Wanborough, she went on the paramilitary training course in Arisaig in May 1942, staying at Garramor (STS 25A). Back in London she joined the FANY as an ensign in July 1942 before going to Beaulieu, where she stayed at The Rings (STS 31) with Andrée Borrel, Valentine 'Blanche' Charlet and Marie-Thérèse le Chêne. According to Stella King's biography *'Jacqueline': Pioneer Heroine of the Resistance*, Yvonne was told not to tell anyone that she had been to Arisaig.

To overcome the problem of her not being able to parachute into France, the SOE negotiated a sea passage with a specially trained Royal Navy crew. At the end of July 1942, Flying Officer Thomas Russell of 138 Squadron flew in his Whitley down to Portreath in Cornwall, where he picked up Yvonne and three other agents, Nicholas Bodington, Henri Frager and Harry Despaigne. After refuelling, he flew them down to Gibraltar. From there they were taken secretly by a felucca – a 40-foot-long, narrow-beamed, 20-ton wooden sailing boat – to the south coast of France. Feluccas have been described as having one tattered sail, a malodorous engine, the flags of half a dozen South American republics in the locker, a Polish skipper, some whisky, a revolver, some camouflaged depth charges and as many secret agents as happened to be going their way.

They were landed on the beach at Antibes, near Monaco, on 30 July. Yvonne made her way north to work as a courier for Francis Suttill, for the Anglo-French barrister's Prosper network which covered much of north-western France, but in particular between the Physician and Monkeypuzzle networks in the Île de France. She used a variety of aliases and codenames, including 'Suzanne', 'Jacqueline Viallat', 'Mme. Gauthier (née Cerneau)', 'Soaptree' and 'Leclair'.

Before she was sent into France with a pistol strapped to her leg, she admitted being prepared to kill. According to King, she is reported as saying:

If a German or anyone stops me and tries to search me, there is only one thing to do. I will have to shoot him. I don't want to do that. It would be difficult to bury him. The ground is so hard … If it happens, I hope it is near an asparagus bed where the earth is soft and sandy.

Buckmaster noted that, once Yvonne had found her safe house, she was to search for suitable fields for receiving containers and other agents.

> [To] this end, she acquired a bicycle on the black market and installed herself in an inconspicuous little cottage in the Touraine. Her immediate chief was a French commandant, and through him she was in touch with Prosper, about whom I have already written. I think Christiane was thoroughly happy during this time. She had plenty of scope for action, plenty of excitement, and was in great danger. She enjoyed the affectionate esteem of all those men and women who knew what she was doing, and the amused tolerance of all those others who had not this knowledge.
>
> Only the French Commandant knew that in her bicycle basket, each day as she set off on her excursions, lay a stock of explosives and a hand-grenade, for Christiane always hoped to come across a really worth-while target, and it would have been too provoking to have, say, Hitler's car at her mercy, without the means of destroying it. If anybody at all wondered what was in the bicycle basket, carefully concealed with a scarf or some newspapers, they probably assumed that this eccentric middle-aged lady was engaged in petty black-market deals, buying eggs from the farms, or harmlessly gathering mushrooms in the woods.
>
> To Christiane there was nothing exceptional in trundling about with enough explosive to blow up a house: she was in a war to do a job and she was not going to be content with half-measures. She and her commandant got on together splendidly; they were both single-minded people, whose sole preoccupation was to speed up the task in hand. They didn't worry about non-essentials. The parachute operations which they arranged were admirably carried out, both being invariably careful over details, and their group amassed quite a store of weapons and explosives. Occasionally Christiane would go to Paris to take a message to Prosper from her chief. After such visits Prosper would inform us by radio that Christiane had been in, and we would know all was well.

By March 1943, Yvonne had not only bicycled across hundreds of kilometres of the Loire countryside but also organised parachute drops and took part in various sabotage operations. She helped blow up the 300,000-volt electricity cables of Chaigny power station, south of Orléans, and two locomotives in the goods station at Le Mans.

On 21 June she set off in a car for Beaugency on the Loire, with Pierre Culioli, her organiser, and two recently arrived Canadian agents, who they were to take on the train to Paris. When they drove through the village of Dhuizon in the Sologne they found it full of German troops. Stopped at a check point, Pierre and Yvonne managed to pass inspection. As one of the Canadians' accent was suspiciously Canadian, they were called back for further questioning. Deciding to make a getaway, they were fired on. Yvonne was knocked unconscious by a bullet in the back of her head. According to the Wikipedia entry for Yvonne Rudelatt:

> Pierre saw the amount of blood coming from the wound, and since Yvonne was unresponsive, he decided to kill himself rather than be taken and tortured. He slammed the vehicle into a ditch and then the side of a cottage, but the two woke up in a hospital

at Blois hours later. Yvonne was told that her injury wasn't life threatening, and that the bullet hadn't pierced her brain, but that it would be unsafe to remove it.

The radio set was in the boot. David Harrison's SOE website gives the date as 18 June 1943, while another source gives 21 August.

After a brief time in hospital, Yvonne was taken for interrogation at the Gestapo headquarters and imprisoned at the grey, fortress-like Fresnes Prison, a few miles south of the capital, near what is now Orly airport. The prison was named after the white downy fluff that dropped each spring from the numerous ash trees. According to Andy Forbes's now defunct 64 Baker Street website:

> [She] used the name Jacqueline Gautier, which was whispered to her by a fellow prisoner when she could not remember her own, due to amnesia after her wounds. She was then transferred to Ravensbrück, arriving on 21 April 1944. She was subsequently moved on to Belsen, where she died after contracting typhus on or about 23 April 1945.
> (http://www.64-baker-street.org/agents – accessed October 2008)

Buckmaster's article provided a different ending. He claimed that she recovered from her wounds but was physically in bad shape after a long time in solitary confinement. When the camp commandant found that she was unfit to work,

> he had no compunction in sentencing her to the gas-chamber. It was 'the Führer's will' – and it caused less trouble that way.
> Christiane had no illusions when the wardress ordered her to the baths. She knew what awaited her, but she had no regrets. She knew that her work was well done and that the flame of resistance, lighted by the patriots, would not fade. She was happy that she had done something useful, but she had no inkling of the fact that her name would be forever honoured in France.

Ravensbrück, 50 miles (80 km) north of Berlin, was built in a beauty spot, noted for its lakes and secluded villas for wealthy city-dwellers. Its site was on marshy ground, often infested with malarial mosquitoes. There were enclaves outside the camp for working parties doing factory or heavy agricultural work in the community, as well as a *Jugendlager*, or youth camp, where those too ill or unfit for work were accommodated. Escott gave a long account, which is worth including to provide an idea of the conditions many of the women agents had to endure.

> The main camp surrounded by high walls was built for about 6,000 prisoners. Inside were wooden huts for living quarters containing three tiers of bunks, a few brick buildings for kitchens, showers and a concrete cell block. Cinder paths divided the huts in front of which blossomed flowers in profusion. But there, all semblance of cleanliness and proper conditions stopped. The place was in fact known to the French as L'Enfer des Femmes, the Women's Hell.
> Nearly all the prisoners were civilians, both young and old, from conquered countries either as slave labour or on suspicion of involvement with the resistance,

all being imprisoned without trial, though this did not prevent them being cruelly tortured during questioning in the camp's political department. During the war years over 50,000 women, at the lowest estimate, died in this camp from dirt, disease, overcrowding, squalor, starvation, overwork and ill-treatment, apart from those who were shot or gassed or sent to die elsewhere.

When Cécile Lefort was admitted in 1943, she spent her first days in the quarantine hut, where new arrivals were kept for three weeks to ensure they brought no new infection to the camp. After being checked in, though weary from the long train journey, she had to stand several hours before being admitted to the bathhouse, where she was told to strip and her former clothes were taken away. Here she waited naked in the cold for a further few hours under the tiny hole in the ceiling where the shower worked, and that was only for a few minutes. With a sliver of soap and a pocket handkerchief of a towel she had to clean herself. Again a long wait and then a shock. Two men came in, one to look at her teeth and one to give her a cursory medical examination, which revealed something was wrong.

Then she was issued with prison clothing, thin and inadequate for the advancing winter, and dispatched to the quarantine hut. There, no one was to be allowed outside, though all were awakened well before dawn for bitter acorn coffee. They were crowded at the window watching while the other women lined up five deep in front of their huts, in the freezing cold and rain, the living and the dead together, and stood for the hour-long 'Appells', where they were counted and appointed their work for the day. Some were detailed for gardening, some for sewing or knitting, some for corpse, rubbish or coal collecting, some for road mending, cleaning latrines, tree-felling or potato picking, women being used instead of horses to drag the heavy carts. Work went in shifts of 10 or 11 hours each, day and night, lights out coming at about 9 pm. Food, mainly vegetable soup and half a loaf of bread a day, was not sufficient for such heavy work. This was the life that awaited them when quarantine was finished.

Pattinson mentioned that, while in the camp, Yvonne tried to colour her grey hair with a boiled onion skin that she had found, but her thick hair, which had become brittle from persistent dying, would not change colour. Instead, she had to resort to masking her grey hair by wearing a piece of cloth like a turban.

In Foot's *SOE in France*, he noted that typhoid and dysentery were widespread in the concentration camps:

Unnoticed amongst the hundreds of prisoners suffering from both these diseases at once was a Frenchwoman who called herself Mme Gauthier, who had arrived from another camp six weeks before. Her only close friend in Belsen was separated from her in the middle of March by the iron circumstances of that insensate world; she was then as well as anyone could be amid the prevailing lack of food, fuel, clothing, decency, privacy, what civilised communities call 'the necessities of life'. She 'was not in bad health, she suffered occasionally from loss of memory, but she remained in good morale and she looked neither particularly drawn nor aged'. But she soon fell dangerously ill. When the camp was captured, she was too far gone from her diseases, or too steeped in her own cover story, or both, to mention to a soul what she had been; unnoticed to the last, she died on St George's day or the day after, and her body was huddled with twenty thousand others into one of the huge mass graves. Her name was Yvonne Rudellat.

Yvonne was awarded the Member of the British Empire medal (MBE) by King George and the Croix de Guerre by de Gaulle's new government. Escott mentioned that it was her successes in France that led the SOE to send in more women.

It was not until 1946 that details of what happened to Yvonne and other captured agents started to find their way back to Britain. In some cases, it was not until much later. Vera Atkins, the secretary of 'F' Section, made it her duty to find out what happened to all those she had sent in, particularly the women. She was born Vera Rosenberg and, being Jewish, changed it to Atkins, her Scottish mother's maiden name, when she arrived from Romania in 1937. The *Dictionary of National Biography* describes her as 'a handsome grey-eyed blonde, some 5 feet 9 inches tall'. Given her involvement with SOE, she took it upon herself to see off all those women destined for France. She had made arrangements with them to send already written letters to their families and relatives on designated dates to help lessen their worrying while their loved ones were out of touch. She took charge of the wills that the women made up before they left and ensured their personal possessions were looked after.

There were some nights when her long hours at Baker Street, Portman Place, Tangmere and Tempsford meant that she didn't return to her flat in Bayswater. Her mother, whom she shared the flat with, suspected she was having an affair with a married man. Described as the 'heart and brain' of 'F' Section, with an eagle eye for detail, some suggest that Vera was the model for Ian Fleming's Miss Moneypenny in his James Bond novels and that 'M' was Sir Maurice Buckmaster, her boss.

Vera's role included overseeing all aspects of agents' preparation for entering enemy territory, from the latest work and travel regulations to what clothes they should wear, and what they should carry at different times of the year and in different regions of the country. She even advised them about what they should eat and how they should eat it. Although she didn't accompany them on their training courses, she liaised with their trainers and met up with the women, often at West End restaurants, which allowed them a safety valve to express their anxieties and their hopes for their missions.

It was a particularly difficult task given the secret German policy of disposing of enemy agents in what they called *'Nacht und Nebel'*, in France *'Nuit et Brouillard'* and what Atkins understood as 'Night and Fog'. The parents of those missing must have gone through enormous stress, not knowing what had happened to their sons or daughters but probably fearing the worst. Other sources suggest the date of Yvonne's execution was 24 April.

## Valentine 'Blanche' Charlet

Much of the following detail was not discovered until 1946 and afterwards. Comparatively little detail has emerged about the second woman sent into France. SOE records show that forty-two-year-old Valentine 'Blanche' Charlet was landed in the same way as Yvonne on Rade d'Agay beach, to the south of Antibes, on 1 September 1942. The boat returned with Major Nicholas Bodington (an SOE agent who organised many of the pick-up operations), Andre Gillois, Gillois's wife and two Belgians. Valentine worked as a radio operator with the Detective and Heckler networks in the Lyon area and was known as 'Christianne', 'Sabine Lecomte' and 'Berberis'. According to the SOE records, she was only in operation a month as she was arrested on 1 November. Twenty-two-year-old Brian Stonehouse, the radio operator and – according to Pattinson – one of the few homosexual SOE agents, described what happened in a radio interview held in the Imperial War Museum.

> I'd been at the château on the air for several hours and I'd been spotted by the vans that follow the beam to the transmitter. Château du Hulverent was eight miles outside Lyons, in the country. Monsieur Jourdan had been keeping an eye open for any strange faces in the vicinity and he'd seen someone so he immediately turned off the mains. That was the pre-arranged thing with me if something fishy was going on outside. 'Christiane' was sitting with me when this was turned off. She was feeding me messages, coding or decoding messages, and she said, 'My God, it's the Germans,' and I said, 'What do you mean the Germans?' she said, 'I forgot, I walked past them on the way here.' That was pretty awful, because, if she'd told me when she arrived that she'd passed these Germans, we'd have had plenty of time to pull my aerial down and escape, because the castle wasn't surrounded by then. She wanted to kill herself, she told me, because she felt so awful about that.
>
> I pulled the aerial down, but inadvertently left a little insulating porcelain thing hanging from the ceiling, and hid the transmitter at the bottom of a lift shaft and Monsieur Jourdan put the lift down and jammed it there. 'Christiane' and I tried to get out of the back of the château, which overlooked the garden and the valley of the Rhone. We got out on to the back terrace and sat down pretending to make love, because we'd seen a man come around the far corner of the château. Then another came with a gun and we were caught.
>
> (J. Pattinson, *Behind Enemy Lines*, 2007)

In her debrief after the war, she recollected him being in his dressing gown and they 'sat down and started kissing like mad, pretending we were having a thing'. It didn't work as the Germans found the wireless set. During interrogation, the Gestapo discovered her codename. 'Informant was asked if she really was Christianne. She pretended to faint and, when she recovered, pretended to play the part of a stupid woman who had wanted to play her glorious part in the Resistance but knew nothing about it.'

She was imprisoned at Castres from where, with the help of friendly French guards, she managed to escape with fifty-one inmates on 16 September the following year, but whether she continued her resistance work is not known. Escott said that she only just failed to cross the Pyrenees. Like Yvonne Rudellat, she was awarded the MBE.

### Marie-Lou Blanc

According to Pierre Tillet et al.'s *History of Infiltrations and Exfiltrations into France* (http://www.plan-sussex-1944.net/anglais/pdf/infiltrations_into_france.pdf), during the moon period following Yvonne's arrival, 27 August 1942, Marie-Lou Blanc, codenamed 'Suzanne', parachuted alongside Peter Churchill, Adolphe Rabinovich and Baron de Malval from 138 Squadron F/L Walczak's Halifax (http://www.plan-sussex-1944.net/

anglais/pdf/infiltrations_into_france.pdf). Apart from the fact that their mission was to set up the Spindle network, who Marie-Lou was and what she did remains a mystery as she is not referred to in any of the mainstream SOE literature.

## Lise de Baissac

It was the following moon period when Clark refers to the first FANYs to be flown out of Tempsford. On 23 September 1942, a mission to occupied France was aborted due to the 'wrong reception'. The pilot did not get the correct letter code flashed to him by the people on the ground.

> There was little time wasted in mounting this operation again and the following night, the 24/25th, F/O Wilkin in Whitley Z9428 (NF-W) took off at 20.50 in an endeavour to complete this operation. It was a straight forward trip leaving the UK at Bognor and crossing the French coast at Pte de la Peree at 22.34 hours flying at 2,500 feet. Flying south they pinpointed Orléans and the Loire and made their way down to the target area reaching it at 00.35. They were now flying in low broken cumulus with a ceiling of 500 feet. The DZ was found without trouble but instead of a triangle of red lights, as expected, they were white, but the flashing light was OK. Making two runs over the target at 01.00 hours the drop was made from 500 feet, the despatcher reporting 'agents jumped when told – everything OK'.

One of Flight Officer Wilkin's passengers was petite thirty-seven-year-old Lise de Baissac, a major in the FANY. She was born to French settlers on the island of Mauritius and was thus a British subject. At the outbreak of war she was working in Paris but managed with her brother Claude to get to England via Spain and Portugal. She got an office job in London and Claude joined the SOE. Her language skills attracted her to the SOE and in November 1943 she joined the second all-female training course and was commissioned as a captain in the FANY. One of her colleagues was twenty-two-year-old Andrée Borrel, a member of the French resistance and a lieutenant in the FANY, codenamed 'Denise'.

Given that Lise was the oldest of the second group of women agents to attend the 'finishing school' at Beaulieu, one of her instructors commented that 'she was very much ahead of her fellow students and, had she been with others as mentally mature as herself, she would have been even more capable'. The SOE commandant who prepared agents for clandestine life said she was 'quite imperturbable', a woman who could 'remain cool and collected in any situation'.

They were dropped at Boisrenard, just outside the village of St Laurent Nouain, close to the town of Mer, north of Bordeaux. After they were met by the reception committee, Andrée went north to work in the Prosper network in Paris while Lise, codenamed 'Odile', stayed for a few days before moving south to Poitiers to run a reception réseau for incoming agents with the Artist network. She must have been very brave as the safe house that she lived in and that provided shelter for incoming agents was right next to the Gestapo headquarters in Poitiers. There she played the part of Madame Irene Brisse, a quiet widow who was seeking refuge from the tension of Parisian life. Without a wireless set, she had to make trips to Paris to send and receive messages and receive funds. On other occasions, she went out on her bicycle looking for suitable parachute drop zones while posing as an amateur archaeologist.

Interviewed after the war by Juliette Pattinson, she described how once in a train she asked a German to help put her suitcase on the rack above her head. 'I had things in it. But I mean it was part of ordinary life. It was not important.' What she had inside she didn't specify, but on one occasion Lise was given 250,000 francs (about £1,400) to carry. 'What was needed was cold-blooded efficiency for long, weary months rather than any bursts of heroism.'

Sometimes she went across to Bordeaux, where she met her brother Claude, who had been dropped by a Halifax three months earlier. He was building up the SCIENTIST circuit, which had an estimated 11,000 men, organised sabotage missions and provided reports on submarine and shipping movements to the SOE. Over the next few months Lise acted as liaison officer between the SCIENTIST, PROSPER and BRICKLAYER networks and is reported in her obituary in the *Daily Telegraph* to have taken part in attacks on enemy columns and located suitable fields for parachuting in supplies and landing and picking up agents.

This work entailed her becoming adept at looking the part. She told Pattinson that for her there were not many opportunities to dress up. 'In France, they were wearing very old things. Everybody wore all sorts of things and not particularly elegant. Old clothes were taken out of cupboards. Clothing was in very short supply, rationed and expensive.'

In June 1943, the Gestapo arrested numerous agents involved with the PROSPER network, including Andrée Borrel, but, when word got around, Lise managed to escape. In Maurice Buckmaster's wartime autobiography *They Fought Alone*, he told of one female agent who was arrested when an astute Gestapo agent observed her accidentally looking right before she looked left and stepped into the road. The traffic braked and she unwittingly became the centre of attention.

Lise returned to England with Claude and Major Nicholas Bodington in a Lysander piloted by Hugh Verity on 16/17 August 1943. After being debriefed, she was sent to Ringway to practise parachute jumping with Yvonne Baseden and Violette Szabó. They jumped well but Lise broke her leg. As a result she was not dropped back into France until 9 April 1944. During the enforced wait she acted as a conducting officer. The Lysander was flown by Squadron Leader Hugh Verity, who landed her safely at Villes les Ormes, north-west of Châteauroux, to work with the PIMENTO network in the Rhône-Alpes. Other codenames she was known to have used were 'Marguerite', 'Adele', 'Irene Brisse' and 'Janette Bouville'. She thought the PIMENTO circuit was made up of militant socialists with political aims so she left them to join her brother Claude as second-in-command of his SCIENTIST network in Normandy, reconnoitring large landing grounds that could be held for 48 hours while airborne troops established themselves.

Captain Blackman, the leader of a Special Air Service (SAS) team that parachuted behind enemy lines in July 1944, received lots of help from Lise. He recommended her for an OBE, praising her work during which she risked her life daily. Cycling 60 or 70 kilometres a day carrying compromising material like wireless parts and secret documents meant that she would have been shot without trial if she had been caught.

Another British army officer claimed later that, 'The part she played in aiding the Maquis and the British underground movement in France cannot be too highly stressed and did much to facilitate the Maquis preparations and resistance prior to the American breakthrough in Mayenne.' A note in her SOE file said that, 'She was the inspiration of groups on the Orne and by her initiative caused heavy losses to the Germans with tyre bursters on the roads near St Aubin-le-Desert, St Mars, and as far as Laval, Le Mans and Rennes. She also took part in several armed attacks on enemy columns.' (TNA HS 9/77/1)

Living in constant fear for their lives put pressure on all the agents. Pattinson refers to Lise reminiscing about her experiences to Summerfield after the war. She said, 'You know that you're in danger all the time but you always think that you will go through. I have never been afraid really that I should be caught. It never occurred to me. I think that we're all like that. If you're frightened you can't do anything.' However, she did confess to feeling nervous on a few occasions.

There was another lucky escape when, that summer, Lise was cycling from Normandy to Paris carrying spare parts for wireless sets. They were fastened around her waist under her dress. When she was stopped at a checkpoint, the German guard thoroughly frisked her.

> He searched me very carefully. I knew he could feel the things I was carrying. But he said nothing. Perhaps he was looking for a weapon like a revolver; maybe he thought it was a belt. I do not know … I was very, very frightened. He touched everything and he let us free. That was once when I really was frightened.

Another lucky escape was when the Germans were retreating and they requisitioned her apartment and one of the soldiers was sitting on her sleeping bag, which had been made out of parachute silk. 'I tried to keep my dignity but inside I was very frightened. When I asked the man to get up and let me take my bag, I was really anxious to leave the place.'

There was also a period of nervous tension following her circuit being penetrated by a double agent, which forced her to fly back to Tempsford. 'It is a bit of nerves, you know, will the plane come, will it? As I say, I'm not a nervous person, anxious … It seems to me, it's part of the work, of life.' When she arrived back in France in the early hours of the morning, her reception committee provided her with a bicycle to get to her safe house, but, as she had had an injury during her refresher course, she couldn't keep up.

> I was a right long way back and I had to follow them … they had turned right or left. I couldn't see. Luckily, I turned right and it was there that I found them. Had I turned left I don't know what would have happened to me … But that was really frightening. I still remember that … Perhaps, it's the most difficult moment of all my missions. Should I turn right or left?

After D-Day she and others in her group moved to Orne and in July 1944, dressed in her FANY uniform, she met the Americans. Lise was lifted out of France for the second time on 16/17 August by Squadron Leader Hugh Verity in a Lysander, landing at Tempsford at 0400 hours, despite flak over Caen on the Normandy coast. According to Foot, she was accompanied by her brother Claude and Nicholas Bodington, whom some in the SOE were suspicious about because of his friendship with Henri Déricourt, the air movements officer for the SOE in France. Déricourt was thought to have passed sensitive information to the Abwehr, the military intelligence organisation. Like Yvonne Rudellat and Valentine Charlet, Lise was awarded the MBE and Croix de Guerre.

Following Lise's death in 2004, Jean-Paul Salomé, a French film director, read her obituary in *The Times* and decided to make *Female Agents*, a film released in June 2008 that is loosely based on Lise's wartime experiences. He wanted to pay tribute to the role played by women agents in France.

> When the war was over, General de Gaulle accorded little importance to the role women played. Out of more than 1,000 Liberation Crosses that were awarded, only six went to women … It is this slightly macho view of the Resistance that excluded women.
>
> (http://entertainment.timesonline.co.uk/tol/arts_and_entertainment/film/article4060466.ece)

The reader can decide from what follows whether they think the other women included here deserved similar honours.

### Andrée Borrel

On 24 September 1942, Andrée Borrel, mentioned earlier, parachuted with Lise de Baissac from F/O Wilkin's Whitley into a field near St Laurent Nouan, on the Loire about 20 km south-west of Orléans. She was returning to France after escaping several months earlier and receiving SOE's training.

The daughter of working-class parents, she grew up on the outskirts of Paris and enjoyed bicycling into the countryside, hiking and climbing. She moved to Toulon on the Mediterranean coast when war broke out, trained with the Red Cross and looked after wounded soldiers at St Hippolyte du Fort, a Vichy-government-run internment camp near Nimes. There she met Maurice Dufour, a supervising officer in the camp who had been recruited by Albert Guérisse, a Belgian doctor. He had joined the Royal Navy when he escaped from Dunkirk in 1940, using his Australian friend's name: Pat O'Leary. After being sprung from prison, he was recruited by the SIS and used his contacts and training to establish contacts with London through Switzerland. They provided funds and radio operators for what became known as the PAT line.

Maurice Dufour, an officer in the RF Section who worked with Andrée, thought she was 'a free spirit, this was wartime and inevitably they shared both a bed and a passionate desire to liberate their country' (http://www.timesonline.co.uk/tol/news/uk/article5887620.ece). They became involved in what became known as the PAT line, an escape group which got soldiers out of France. When Gilbert Norman arrived as a radio operator, Andrée became his courier. As the circuit enlarged, Jack Agazarian was parachuted in as another radio operator, with his wife Françine as his courier. Maurice and Andrée established a villa at Canet Plage outside Perpignan, the last safe house before the hard and dangerous route over the Pyrenees into Spain.

Over the next six months they helped numerous SOE agents, Allied airmen shot down over France, Jews and others to escape over the Spanish border into Gibraltar and back to England. When the network was betrayed in December 1941, Andrée and

Maurice were forced to hide in Toulouse. Eventually, they escaped over the Pyrenees themselves and made their way by train and a British diplomat's car to Lisbon in Portugal. Maurice was shipped back to England but Andrée stayed, working at the Free French Propaganda Office at the British Embassy.

Andrée stayed in Portugal until April 1942, when she too went to London. On her arrival she was interrogated at the Royal Patriotic School in Wandsworth. De Gaulle's supporters wanted to determine whether she was a double agent or not. Many immigrants to Britain were said to have spent a few days at the school for 'questioning'. Whether Andréee knew or not is uncertain, but Maurice was suspected by the RF section of being a British agent and was brutally tortured in the converted coal cellar underneath 10 Duke Street, the headquarters of the Free French. According to Dufour's obituary in *The Times*, they had threatened to kidnap and gang rape his lover. After being sent to the Free French camp at Camberley, between Reading and Aldershot, he escaped and made his way to Andree's lodgings. Known to have strong socialist views, Andrée was nevertheless recruited by the SOE in May and became a lieutenant in the FANY, receiving £3 a week in pay. Her training officers considered her tough, self-reliant and absolutely reliable. Buckmaster thought she had the utmost courage and coolness.

Desperately worried that Maurice's escape and his High Court writ would name de Gaulle and others in the RF Section, SOE 'shut him up', put him into a safe house, gave him £2,000 and promised he would be able to stay in Britain. Maurice and Andrée never saw each other again.

Andrée's mission was to make her way north to Paris to work as a courier in thirty-five-year-old Francis Suttill's PROSPER and PHYSICIAN circuits. Tall, athletic and beautiful, she was often to be seen wearing a fur coat and rolling her own cigarettes. With the codename 'Denise' she became more than a messenger, posing as Suttill's sister. 'He let her do the talking, and she played to perfection the harassed country girl taking her farmer brother to the market in the local town' (Buckmaster, 1946–47). She travelled around northern France with him, organising networks and training Resistance members in the use of weapons and explosives supplied by 161 Squadron. She also helped arrange drop zones and the escape of downed aircrew and SOE agents. According to some sources, she was the lover of Gilbert Norman, the radio operator.

Suttill was so impressed with Andrée that, despite her being only twenty-four, he appointed her second-in-command in March 1943. In a note to the SOE, he said that Andrée 'has a perfect understanding of security and an imperturbable calmness … Thank you very much for having sent her to me.' She also worked on the MONKEYPUZZLE network in Brittany and used the codenames 'Monique', 'Whitebeam' and 'Denise Urbain' (http://www.spartacus.schoolnet.co.uk/SOEborrel.htm).

To give an idea of what Andrée was doing, Shrabani Basu, in her book *Spy Princess: The Life of Noor Inayat Khan*, said that in April 1943, Suttill's group had carried out sixty-three acts of sabotage, derailing trains, killing 43 Germans and wounding 110. By June the group covered twelve *départements*, had thirty-three DZs and received 254 containers of supplies. They picked up 190 containers in June alone and more attacks were planned.

However, lax security and betrayal led the Germans to arrest her in Paris on 23 June, along with Suttill and Norman. All three had been inseparable. Kramer's interviews with

Andrée's relatives revealed that she managed to smuggle messages out of prison. Written on cigarette paper, they were folded and hidden in her lingerie and sent to her sister to be washed. Some were laundered in ignorance and it was a sympathetic prison matron who alerted the sister of their existence. Most messages were to reassure her mother and request items like a sweater, notebook and hairpins, ending with lots of kisses. Others indicated that she had been betrayed by Gilbert Norman. Buckmaster said the messages Andrée sent to him were full of courage and the unshaken belief that she would escape. According to Foot, several Germans testified that she never talked at all and treated them with fearless contempt throughout her captivity.

She was then sent to the Natzweiler-Struthof concentration camp in the Vosges mountains, about 50 kilometres south-west of Strasbourg. A month after D-Day, she and three other female SOE agents were executed by phenol injection. Witnesses later told how Andrée was still conscious as she was dragged to the ovens to be cremated. Fighting to the last, she was said to have scratched her executioner's face.

## Mary Lindell

During the moon period following Lise and Andrée's drop, forty-seven-year-old Mary Lindell, codenamed 'Marie-Claire', was Lysandered into France. No details of her or her mission were recorded in the SOE records. The reason why is revealed in Barry Wynne's biography of her, *No Drums, No Trumpets*, and on Christopher Long's Royal Air Force's Escaping Society website. Born in Sutton in Surrey in 1895, Mary was described as 'a very remarkable English woman, impeccably English in upbringing and manner, extremely resourceful, courageous, strong-minded and used to getting her own way' (http://www.christopherlong.co.uk/pub/rafes.html). During the First World War, she served as a nurse but was sent home for hitting a matron with a bedpan brush. Joining the *Secours aux Blessés Militaires*, a division of the French Red Cross, she won medals for gallantry under fire. The last Czar of Russia awarded her the Russian Order of St Anne and the French Prime Minister awarded her the French Croix de Guerre with Star.

After the war she married a French nobleman, Count de Milleville, and settled in Paris on the rue Erlanger. When the Germans invaded France in May 1940, she worked as a nurse, wearing her British ribbons on her Red Cross uniform. As her work allowed her to ferry sick children over the demarcation line into the Unoccupied Zone, she had the requisite passes. With the help of her three children, she hid escaped Allied soldiers who had not managed to get out with the other troops at Dunkirk in her home and then drove them through the night to safety in Limoges.

> Later, Mary, by sheer bluff and boldness, managed to get petrol permits, and permits for herself, a nurse and a mechanic to travel freely on humanitarian missions. These were obtained via the German commander in Paris, General von Stulpnagel, and also Count von Bismark. Earlier, General von Stulpnagel had in fact signed an order, stating that men found helping evaders would be shot and women sent to concentration camps. This order was posted throughout France. He had now given Mary petrol and permits in disobedience of his own orders.
>
> (http://www.christopherlong.co.uk/pub/rafes.html)

One of her daughters had an affair with a German officer, but whether Mary knew about it is unknown. Mary, then in her mid-forties, ensured that many evaders were smuggled to safe houses where they would be met by guides, brave young men and women, who escorted them to Marseille. There they were helped by the Pat O'Leary escape line in crossing the border into Spain and then getting back to England, either via Gibraltar or Lisbon in Portugal. Christopher Long's website records that:

> Despite Mary's success her methods were amateurish and it was only a matter of time before the Gestapo were on to her. Arrested by the Paris Gestapo, Mary was interrogated and kept in solitary confinement for nine months. The Gestapo were now waiting for further instructions to detain Mary, but with the help of a friendly wardress, Mary walked out of Fresnes prison and kept on walking without looking back. Making arrangements for her children first, Mary travelled to a safe house at Ruffec and, disguising herself as an elderly governess, followed the escape line to Spain and England.

A telegram containing news of her escape reached the office of Airey Neave and Jimmy Langley, MI9 officers working in the War Office in London. With the assistance of the SOE, they were supplying escape lines with funds, agents and supplies. They were told of a woman dressed in French Red Cross uniform, with a British passport in the name of Ghita Mary Lindell. Their contact in Barcelona told them that the American Vice Consul in Lyon had obtained her travel visa for her and the Vichy government had issued her with an exit permit after she had informed them that all her money and papers had been stolen.

In Neave's *Saturday at MI9*, he described her arriving at his flat in London dressed in the royal blue uniform of the French Red Cross.

> She had dark brown eyes and chestnut hair, and her face was finely proportioned. Her figure was slight, and her uniform well-cut. She seemed very feminine, but in her expression there was an intensity, a stubbornness which somehow did not fit with her smart appearance.

Although the powers that be would not hear of it, she demanded to be sent back to France. They argued that people known to the Gestapo should not return. It was too great a risk. She argued that she still had many contacts in Ruffec, near Angoulême, who were able and willing to help and, being a long way from Paris, she would not be recognised. Her strong personality eventually prevailed and she was allowed to return. Neave said that she had a crash course in coding and a course in night landing in the little Lysander aeroplane:

> This involved the training of agents in the laying out of flare paths and signals to the pilot. It needed considerable discipline on the part of the 'reception committees', many of whom had only the most primitive equipment. Agents had to be taught how to place the flares correctly and pass on these procedures to others in the field. Since Lysanders were fitted to hold only two passengers, they also had to be trained to warn the pilots of approaching enemy fighters.

> (Ibid.)

Neave gave her a final briefing and drove her down to RAF Tangmere. This was the Special Duties Squadron's forward base. Lysanders flew low by moonlight across the Channel and, avoiding anti-aircraft batteries, used pinpoint navigation to identify their drop zone. Neave gives the date as 21 October 1942 but, checking Freddie Clark's *Agents by Moonlight*, an account of the Tempsford Squadron's operations, there was no mention of her. Eight of the nine missions that night were to France but Mary didn't appear in the records.

In Hugh Verity's autobiography, *We Landed by Moonlight*, he gave a different date of 26/27 October, saying that Mary was flown by Pilot Officer Bridges to Thalamy Airfield, east of Ussel, with Ferdinand Rodriguez, a radio operator. Clark mentions the Flight Officer flying on SIS operation ACHILLES that night but gave no additional details. Officially, pilots weren't meant to know who their passengers were but, according to Neave,

> When we reached Tangmere, the Squadron Commander took us to the briefing room. The reception committee organised by the SOE was at a point sixty miles south-east of Limoges and fifteen from the small town of Ussel. Before take-off, there was a moving incident when she was introduced to the pilot of her aircraft. He was a Canadian, a slight young figure, and a Battle of Britain hero, and with several decorations. He took both her hands and said: 'I just wanted to say thank you for going over there. I can't tell you what we feel about it, but all the boys have tremendous admiration for what you're doing.'

Although MI9 wanted her to have a radio operator, she refused, saying she couldn't work with the person they had chosen. Using her original Red Cross pass and a forged French one and known as Comtese de Moncy, she moved into a room at the Hôtel de France in Ruffec and set up what became known as the Marie-Claire escape line. Not long after her arrival, Mary was said to have been deliberately knocked off her bike by a car thought to have been driven by collaborators. Thinking her to be dead, the patriotic villagers carried her to a remote farmhouse and had begun to dig her grave. A friendly chemist arrived, pronounced her alive and refused to sign the death certificate. She ended up in hospital with five fractured ribs, a serious head wound and injuries to her arm and leg. The Gestapo arrived shortly afterwards, having been informed that there was 'an English agent' there. They searched the wards without success. She had been hidden in a cellar, behind a pile of wood. Although still very ill, she had to move and was taken to Lyon shortly after Christmas 1942. The Christopher Long RAF Escaping Society website states that, in her absence:

> Many more evaders were moved along Marie-Claire line, two of whom were Major C. Hasler and Cpl W. Sparks. This pair were the two survivors of the Operation Frankton raid on shipping in Bordeaux harbour (otherwise known as the Cockleshell Heroes). Lack of a radio operator prevented Mary knowing of the raid. But the commandos, who had to make their way inland to contact an escape line, had been briefed to make for Ruffec and the Café du Paris. This was unusual practice but on this occasion the only way to return was via an escape line. The Café du Paris was not found, however. Both men entered a small café and were helped by the owner, eventually finding themselves

with 'Marie-Claire'. Of the eight Commandos only two survived. The remainder were captured and executed.

It was her youngest son, twelve-year-old Maurice, who took Hasler and Sparks to a safe house in Lyon. When Mary met them there, her first reaction was to hand Hasler a pair of scissors and order him to cut off his magnificent blond moustache. She then lectured him, saying:

> We've only got one rule for Englishmen in our care – NO GIRLS. From past experience we know that once they meet a pretty girl everything goes to hell. So we shall take care to keep you away from them.
>
> (Ibid.)

Before long the Gestapo were back on her trail. Both her sons were arrested to try to find out where their mother was. They didn't talk. Maurice was released after being badly beaten, but Oky was deported to a concentration camp and never heard of again.

Mary spent time out of circulation, recuperating in Switzerland then, despite the pressures, returned to Ruffec and continued her important work, financed with money brought in by agents dropped regularly from Tempsford. Downed aircrews from different parts of France were accompanied in stages to safe houses she had located in Ruffec. Once a group of between five and eight had been gathered, Mary would take them herself to the Pyrenees and hand them over to mountain guides. In early November 1943, she and four 'helpers' took five airmen by train via Toulouse and Foix to Andorra. Before they got to their safe house she learned that the line had been blown, so they all returned to Ruffec. Another route was planned, this time via Limoges, Toulouse, Tarbes, Pau, Oleron and Tardets, and then on foot over the Pyrenees.

> This route proved to be a success and the group crossed the Pyrenees towards the end of November 1943 in winter conditions. On the 25th November 1943 Marie-Claire was waiting to meet a courier called Ginette who was escorting airmen from Ruffec to Pau. The weather was very cold and it was snowing. The train arrived at Pau station without Ginette and the airmen. Marie turned to leave and was confronted by two Gestapo men. Later, after initial interrogation, Marie-Claire was taken by train to Paris. Whilst under escort by two Gestapo guards she feigned sickness, made her way to a toilet, saw an opportunity and threw herself off the train. The guards immediately started firing and she was seriously wounded in the head and neck. She was returned to the train and taken to a German hospital. A German doctor rebuilt her neck and saved her life in a 4½ hour operation. Despite being extremely ill and running a high fever, Marie was deported to Ravensbrück concentration camp. Two things were in her favour and probably saved her life: firstly, she was moved into the hospital at Ravensbrück initially, and secondly, as a trained nurse, she remained in the hospital and survived.
>
> (Ibid.)

After the war, she became the Royal Air Forces Escaping Society's representative in France. A film of her war experiences was made by ITV in 1991; it was called *One Against the Wind* and starred Judy Davis. The story of her life is told in Barry Wynne's book *No Drums, No Trumpets.*

Odette Sansom, another of the lucky few to survive imprisonment at Ravensbrück, told Rita Kramer in an interview after the war about meeting seven other captured women when she was taken to Avenue Foch, the Gestapo headquarters, in an exclusive part of Paris near the Champs-Élysées. Odette recalled one hot day thinking that the building was so beautiful that she might as well enjoy her time there and asked the guards to bring her some English tea. They got it in proper china cups. None of them had seen anything like that in a long time.

They shared one of the girls' lipstick and talked about their experiences of being captured. Several of them, including Odette, believed that they had been betrayed by an informant.

> We were all young, we were all different, but we all had the feeling in the beginning that we were going to be – helpful. That was why we went into it. And to have impressed the people around them as they did is almost enough. They impressed everyone – the Germans, their guards. They behaved extremely well, those women.
>
> (Kramer, *Flames in the Field*, 1995)

After interrogation they were sent to Fresnes Prison. Almost a year later, the Germans transported Odette and several other captured SOE agents – Andrée Borrel, Vera Leigh, Diana Rowden, Sonia Olschanezky, Yolande Beekman, Eliane Plewman and Madeleine Damerment – to the civilian women's prison at Karlsruhe, north-east of Strasbourg. Exactly a month after the D-Day landings, on 6 July 1944, Andrée, Vera, Diana and Sonia were taken to the Natzweiler concentration camp in the Vosges Mountains of Alsace. An eyewitness account was provided by Brian Stonehouse, one of the very few prisoners who survived. The Spartacus website includes his evidence to a military court in the spring of 1946:

> There was one tall girl [Andrée Borrel] with very fair hair. I could see that it was not its natural colour as the roots of her hair were dark. She was wearing a black coat, French wooden-soled shoes and was carrying a fur coat on her arm. Another girl [Sonia Olschanezky] had very black oily hair, and wore stockings, aged about twenty to twenty-five years, was short and was wearing a tweed coat and skirt. A third girl [Diana Rowden] was middle height, rather stocky, with shortish fair hair tied with a multi-coloured ribbon, aged about twenty-eight. She was wearing a grey flannel short 'finger tip' length swagger coat with a grey skirt which I remember thinking looked very English. The fourth woman of the party [Vera Leigh] was wearing a brownish tweed coat and skirt. She was more petite than the blonde in grey and older, having shortish brown hair. None of the four women were wearing make-up and all were looking pale and tired.
>
> (www.spartacus.schoolnet.co.uk/SOEborrel.htm)

The women were taken out, injected with phenol, carbolic acid, and put in the crematorium furnace. Andrée was only twenty-four. After the war she was posthumously awarded the Knight Commander of the British Commonwealth medal (KCBC), the Croix de Guerre and the Medaille Republique Française.

## Andrée de Jongh

Andrée de Jongh was not directly involved with RAF Tempsford, but her work helping Tempsford personnel is worth mentioning here. She helped set up Comète, similar to the Marie-Claire escape line but it operated with SIS help from Belgium. When Belgium's King Leopold capitulated to the occupying German forces three weeks after their invasion in May 1940, twenty-four-year-old Andrée de Jongh ('Dédée') was working as a commercial artist in the Sofina company in Brussels. The director, Baron Jacques Donny, was financing the shelter of escaping British soldiers in various safe houses in the city and Andrée got involved in nursing these men. Along with her sister Suzanne, her father and many other brave Belgians, she helped about four hundred Allied airmen and soldiers get out of the country to safety via neutral countries of Switzerland and Spain.

On several occasions, she accompanied groups across the Pyrenees to give them a second chance to fight the Nazis; some of these groups were flown out of Tempsford. Using a traitor, the Gestapo arrested her father and then her and other colleagues. She was one of the few who survived interrogation and imprisonment at Ravensbrück and after the war was awarded the George Medal by the British, the Medal of Freedom by the Americans, and the Croix de Guerre with palm by the Belgians. She was also created Chevalier of the French Légion d'honneur and awarded the Belgian Order of Leopold. Her biography, *Little Cyclone*, was written by Airey Neave, her SIS controller, who described her as 'one of our greatest agents'. (More details of Andrée and the other women sent to Belgium can be found in my book *Return to Belgium*.)

## Odette Sansom

Odette was one of the few to survive imprisonment. Born in France, she married the son of a British soldier who was billeted with her family during the First World War and moved to London. When her husband joined the Army and was posted overseas, she joined the WAAF as an assistant second officer and responded to an advertisement for translators placed by the 'F' Section of SOE. She later admitted that, during her interview with Selwyn Jepson, the recruiting officer, she had lost her temper when she found out that he had made enquiries about her life in England and France.

> 'Well, what do you mean? Why did you have to make enquiries about me? What do you think I am?' I was told, 'Oh calm down, we're going to explain to you why. We train people here and we send them to the country of their origin, or if they speak a foreign language well we send them to that country where they can use it and be useful for the war effort.' I could see that. I agreed with all that. I said, 'Yes, of course. I can see that.' Then I was told, 'Well, we think women could be useful, too.' 'Yes,' I said. 'I think women are very useful.' And that did it. I was told, 'So glad you think that way because we're going to ask you to do it.'
>
> (Hallowes (Churchill), O. 9478/3; 31578/3 IWMSA)

In Jepson's interview file, also in the Imperial War Museum, he acknowledged that

Odette was a shrewd cookie and she knew at once what it was about. She guessed and said, yes, she wanted to do it. And I said, in effect, 'Wait a minute, what are your domestic circumstances?' she said they wouldn't bother her. She had a husband and a couple of children but the husband didn't come into the matter very much and the children would be looked after by an aunt. When could she start.

I was rather doubtful about her capacity. Although she had perfect French and knew France, her personality was so big that I couldn't quite see her getting away with it. However good the cover story we gave her, I couldn't see her passing unnoticed. I had a little form that I wrote names and addresses on and, for my own guidance, made a comment on the bottom on the question of suitability. I remember very clearly on her piece of paper I wrote, 'God help the Germans if we can ever get her near them, but maybe God help us on the way' – because she has such a huge personality and will dominate everybody she comes in contact with. Not necessarily because she has a dominant nature, but because she just can't help it.

(Jepson, S. (1986) [9331] IWMSA)

She had been separated from her husband, so she arranged for her three daughters, aged seven, nine and ten, to be sent to a convent boarding school in Brentwood and to be looked after during the holidays by her two 'splendid aunts and devoted Uncle' while she was 'working in Scotland'. In an interview after the war by the Imperial War Museum, she said that

I used to say, well, I've got children and they come first. It's easy enough to go on thinking that way. But I was tormented … Am I going to be satisfied to accept this like that, that other people are going to suffer, get killed, die because of this war and trying to get freedom for my own children. Let's face it. So am I supposed to accept all this sacrifice that other people are making without lifting a finger in any way?

(Hallowes (Churchill), O. 9478/3; 31578/3)

In Jerrard Tickell's biography *Odette*, he commented that when she was asked by her instructor how she might handle an assailant, she responded by saying that she would run and, if he pursued and caught her, she would pinch him and pull his hair. The instructor was said to have replied, 'Ladies, it will be my unwelcome and embarrassing duty to teach you other and less refined methods of disabling would-be aggressors … I have never before had to teach such things to ladies.'

Like Yvonne Rudellat, Odette was dropped by a felucca, a 20-tonne Spanish sardine trawler, at Port-Miou, near Marseille on the Mediterranean coast, on 4 November 1942. Whether she flew first out of Tempsford is unknown. Dropped with her were three male SOE agents, an SIS agent and two lieutenants in the FANY: Mary Herbert, who went to work in the SCIENTIST network, and Marie-Thérèse le Chêne, who went to work in the PLANE network.

Tickell detailed how, codenamed 'Lise', Odette acted as a courier in the SPINDLE network on the south-east Mediterranean coast, arranging drops of arms and ammunition to the resistance in the beautiful lake country of the Jura Mountains. Posing as 'Odette Retayer', she and her companion 'Arnaud', Captain A. Rabinovitch, selected drop zones for the containers of arms and other supplies that were delivered by Tempsford crews. Shortly after she arrived, she met Peter Churchill, a British agent operating between Cannes and Marseille, who took to her in a big way and persuaded her to act as his courier.

[He] put her down at about twenty-five. Her name was Lise and from her mop of light-brown hair, swept back to reveal a rounded forehead, down to a pair of discerning eyes, there emanated a distinct aura of challenge that was only intensified by the determined set of her chin below a somewhat colourless face. A fearless look suggested that not even the thought of the prisons held any terrors for this girl; so much so that, in the flash of time he gave to this snap judgment of her, it even occurred to Michel that she might not bother to take all the precautions she should to avoid capture.

But what took and held his gaze above all else were the hands; hands such as he had never seen before in his life. They were long with slim, capable fingers and, as the left one held the wine-glass and the other broke off pieces of cake, he observed the telltale expanse between thumb and forefinger, denoting extravagance, generosity, impetuosity; the ambition in the index fingers; the unusually wide gap between them and the second fingers, showing independence of thought only matched by the independence of action that almost cried out from the gaping valleys that lay between the third and little fingers. At the moment, the second and third fingers of the left hand were overlapped in a shy gesture, as though seeking each other's company – or was it to hide the platinum wedding ring that had not escaped his eagle eye? If the occasion arose he would take a surreptitious look at the lines of her palm and see whether or not they confirmed the already extensive disclosures of the general view.

(Tickell, *Odette*, 1949)

Once Peter managed to get permission from Baker Street that Odette was 'indispensible', he sent her on a mission to Marseille. When she didn't return on time, he arranged for the trains to be watched, eventually replacing the man sent to keep watch at the station himself. He and Arnaud were both in awe of her.

Peter related how one of the rendezvous he had sent her on involved meeting a Dr Bernard, who, concerned about her, found her a room for the night in what he considered the safest house in town – a brothel. She spent a nerve-wracking and sleepless night because the place had been raided by the German Military Police in search of *réfractaires*, men who had avoided being called up to go and work in German factories in France or Germany. The only reason her room wasn't searched was that the madame – a patriot – told the police that her niece was sleeping in that room and that she had got scarlet fever. On another occasion she was stopped by German soldiers after the curfew. When the sergeant called for the duty officer, Odette explained that she was in a desperate hurry to get to Cannes to see her daughter, who she had been told was seriously ill. Adding a few tears worked. When several contacts in the resistance were arrested, Odette and Peter had to make themselves scarce, moving to Arles for the winter. On the train journey there, she astounded her friends by taking a request for two francs for the 'Winter Relief Fund' to a German general sitting in the restaurant car, suggesting that he ought to contribute as it was his army that had caused the distress. To avoid creating a commotion the general paid it, but Peter advised her to keep her exuberance within limits. She didn't, as in his second book, *Duel of Wits*, he recalled that she

> put the cat among the canaries by placing a broom-stick against a German Colonel's door in an occupied hotel where we had once stayed. How she had chuckled when he had opened the door and it had struck him in the face.

While Peter and Odette were there, arms drops were arranged for several thousand poorly armed *réfractaires* camped out on the Plateau de Glières. When Peter's return trip to England was cancelled because the DZ was already being used by the RF, de Gaulle's resistance groups, they moved back to Cannes in the spring. But it was not for long. Following the arrest of two of their close contacts, they moved north into the Jura of the Haute Savoie and stayed in the Hotel de la Poste in the little village of St Jorioz. Odette had an 'authentic' medical certificate stating that she had consumption and needed to stay above 400 metres.

There was a resistance group based 16 kilometres away in Faverges for which they arranged supplies. Arnaud stayed up the mountain and arranged a successful pick-up. Peter left Odette in charge while he went back to England for a debrief and rest. Within a few weeks, Arnaud received a message that Peter was to return on 16 April and, according to Peter, she sent a message back saying she had been visited by 'Henri', identified later as Hugo Bleicher, a sergeant in the Abwehr, the German Security Office. He promised her the release of the two prisoners if she could arrange a Hudson pick-up for them and him to go to England, where he had to try to speed up the end of the war. The message she got back told her to move immediately to the other side of the lake and get Arnaud into another safe house. Henri was 'treacherous'.

The DZ they chose was the snow-covered summit of Mount Semnoz, about 5 kilometres south of Annecy. They had paced out 100 metres to the right and left to ensure there was enough room for a drop and prepared a bonfire the day before. When they heard Flight Officer Legate's 30-ton Halifax bomber approaching, the bonfire was lit with a bottle of petrol and they flashed the letter 'F'. Legate reported that at 0052 hours on 16 April 1943, he dropped the agent at 800 feet at an airspeed of 140 mph, closely followed by five containers.

According to Gibb McCall in his *Flight Most Secret*, Odette did not know that Peter had been ordered not to get in touch with her. She had been compromised. He was singing the Marseillaise, the song of the Resistance, when he landed in her arms. As they came down the snow-covered slopes above Lake Annecy in the pitch dark, she slipped and fell 10 metres down an almost vertical gulley, knocking herself out. X-rays taken after the war show she had shattered her fifth vertebra. Overcoming the pain, she whisked Peter off to a room in the hotel, saying that he was her husband. Within 24 hours, they were both arrested.

According to Peter Churchill, his room was burst into by Henri and a contingent of Alpini, Italian soldiers who were controlling that part of south-east France. Some in the French Resistance say they were still in bed together when they were captured. During the commotion, Odette managed to hide Peter's wallet – containing telephone numbers of some of his contacts and 70,000 francs – and pack some warm clothes. He had previously passed on half a dozen new radio crystals, half a million francs, two Belgian automatics, a Sten gun, 200 blank identity cards and dozens of ration books. Dressed in her one and only dark-grey suit, with silk stockings and square-toed shoes, she managed to share a few moments of conversation with Peter during their train ride to Paris and passed on a tiny crucifix. Even in Fresnes Prison she managed to save the fresh bread she was given, only eating the stale so that she might pass on bits when she saw him on the occasions Henri allowed them to be together. Dr Mark Baldwin, an SOE historian, reported that, to protect Peter, Odette insisted to her interrogators that she was the organiser of the group.

Churchill recalled in his third book, *Spirit in the Cage*, how on one occasion, when their convoy had just arrived back from an interrogation session,

> I found myself in a large open pen where the whole group was herded together under the eye of a guard whilst waiting for the next move. I slipped up close to Odette and as she spoke to me with her back to the sentry, a girl I had never seen before, but who was patently English to her finger tips, stood between me and the guard so that he would not see my mouth moving. Despite my anxiety not to miss a second of this golden opportunity to speak with Odette, I was nevertheless instinctively conscious of this girl's unselfish act which included a delicacy of feeling that made her turn about and face the German so as not to butt in on our privacy. I could not imagine what this refined creature with reddish hair was doing in our midst.
>
> 'Who is she?' I asked Odette.
>
> 'Diana Rowden,' she replied. '… One of us.'

To occupy herself while confined, Odette worked in the sewing-room. While there, as the guards were wearing a new style of Africa Korps cap, in the ones she made, on the piece of cardboard that stiffened the peak, she wrote the words 'Made in England'. She jammed her scissors into the holes of the power point to blow the fuses and cut the electric wires so that she could get the guards to fetch the most hungry prisoners on the pretext that they were electricians and they could be given extra food while 'on the job'. Spare cloth she saved to make children's toys like rabbits and dolls.

Peter and Odette were both incredibly lucky to survive imprisonment, and they returned to England, where they married. In his *Spirit in the Cage*, he said that

> her moral courage and fearlessness were like a fountain of strength upon which I was to draw on many a future occasion of black despair … Odette's morale was sky-high. It was where she had put it and maintained it through her own optimistic personality, and it had devolved on other prisoners and guards alike. I began to understand what Paul Steinert meant by the regard in which he said she was held. But what I did not and could not understand was the principal reason for these words, since neither he, nor Odette, nor Henri ever told me of the sufferings she had undergone, for it was her intention that I should never know and she had sworn those who knew to silence.

In Elizabeth Nicholas' book *Death Be Not Proud*, she claims that Bleicher penetrated a number of the 'F' Section SOE Resistance groups. As a result, not all the drops from

Tempsford went as planned. She believes that the first vital penetration of SOE was in autumn 1941 by Mathilde Carré. Termed affectionately by Bleicher as 'La Chatte' because she often curled up contentedly in large armchairs, Carré was a member of Inter-Allied, a very early Resistance group founded by some Polish groups stranded in France after 1940. She was arrested but, unwilling to accept life in prison, was seduced into becoming Bleicher's mistress. He had her installed in an establishment called 'The Cattery', where she continued to work her wireless, sending German-inspired messages to London.

Rita Kramer's *Flames in the Field* details the penetration and deception, the double and triple crossing that was going on on both sides. She explained how, following the Gestapo's successful penetration of the Dutch resistance, the head of Netherlands Section sent, to the person he thought was his agent, contact details of a PROSPER agent in Paris who would help Dutch agents to escape through France. With this information the Germans were then able to send a double agent to penetrate PROPSER and capture numerous radios and their operators. Those men and women who succumbed to German persuasion allowed the Nazis to play the same game with Baker Street.

Pretending to be the wife of Peter Churchill (who was the nephew of the British Prime Minister), Odette was taken to Fresnes Prison. Tickell claims that, during Odette's interrogation, one of the assistants

> began leisurely to unbutton her blouse. She said, 'I resent your hands on me or on my clothes. If you tell me what to do and release your hands on me, I will do it.' 'As you wish, unbutton your blouse.' Having already been burnt by a hot poker on her spine, she was then told to take off her stockings and her toenails were extracted. 'To be tortured by this clean, soap-smelling, scented Nordic was one thing. To be touched by his hands was another.' Before her fingernails were removed, a higher ranking officer stopped the interrogation, but she was warned, 'If you speak about what has happened to a living soul, you will be brought here again and worse things will happen to you.' [Though] she had kept silent, she was filled with sickness and fear for she had heard of some of the other things that the Gestapo could do to women's bodies.

She was said to have had fourteen interrogations, during which she refused to give any information about her friends.

> I could have told them what they wanted to know, just like that. They wanted to know where our radio operator was; they wanted to know where another British agent who had arrived some time before had been to, and now was. I'm not brave or courageous, I just make up my own mind about certain things, and when this started, this treatment of me, I thought, 'There must be a breaking point.' Even if in your own mind you don't want to break, physically you're bound to break after a certain time. But I thought, 'If I can survive the next minute without breaking, this is another minute of life, and I can feel that way instead of thinking of what's going to happen in half an hour's time, when having torn out my toenails they're going to start on my fingers.

She was then sent to the Ravensbrück concentration camp, 50 miles north of Berlin, on 18 July 1944 to be executed. It was a forced labour camp where medical experiments, like testing gangrene injections, were undertaken. Her cell, where she was kept in solitary confinement, was within earshot of the execution yard. During the hot August days the central heating was on full blast. Depending on the moods of her sadistic guards, she was starved and subjected to extremes of light, dark, heat and cold. Although burnt on her back, she never broke her heroic silence.

> On Armistice day, when I had been in prison since April, at ten o'clock in the evening I was taken out of my cell and taken down to the courtyard of the prison. There was a car waiting with two men in uniform and the man who tortured me, who was not in uniform, said, 'Well, as you are so devoted to your country, I thought you'd like to go to the Arc de Triomphe on 11 November and see the German guard standing there.' We went, believe it or not, round and round the Arc de Triomphe. I said to him, 'You like what you are doing, the job you are doing. You are a sick man. You like doing this.'

To keep up appearances she used margarine as face cream, turned up the hem of her prison skirt an inch every day so as not to let the worn part show, and used rags from her stockings every night to act as rollers in her hair. Interviewed by J. Pattinson about her time in concentration camp, she said, 'I used to put them on every evening religiously in case they would fetch me the next morning to put me to death. I wasn't going to be seen going to my death without my curls.' Machine-gun turrets, search lights, Alsatian dogs and electric wires surrounded the compound, thereby limiting any chance of escape. In Mavis Nicholson's *What Did You Do In The War, Mummy?* Odette admitted that during her solitary confinement she visualised the routine domestic chores undertaken by wives and mothers and imagined making clothes and decorating the rooms of her three daughters.

> I imagined what I wanted them to wear, then I would get the pattern, then the material, lay it out, cut it out and stitch it. Every single stitch I'd sew until it was all finished. Then I would refurnish all the houses of people I'd known, starting with walls, carpets, curtains.

As the Allies approached Berlin, Fritz Sühren, the commandant of the largest women's camp ever known, believing Odette's story that she was the niece by marriage to Winston Churchill and Geneviève de Gaulle was the niece of the French president, drove them in his white limousine as hostages to the American lines to give himself up. Tania Szabó, in her book *Young, Brave and Beautiful*, an account of her mother's life, tells how Geneviève, ill with pleurisy, described Odette as a 'terribly gaunt woman who seemed very old. A few stray hairs had grown again on her shaven head.' Both were still in their twenties.

When Odette told the Americans who Sühren was, he was arrested and, although a physical and nervous wreck, she managed to seize his Walther PPK pistol and returned to England with it. Along with two dolls she made out of scraps of material, it can be seen on display at the Imperial War Museum.

Speaking to the Museum in 1986, Odette described her first night of freedom from the camp.

The first night of my release was unforgettable. It was a glorious night, full of stars and very cold. The Americans wanted to find me a bed for the night but I preferred to sit in the car. It was so long since I had seen the night sky.

(Hallowes (Churchill), O. 9478/3; 31578/3)

She was awarded the George Cross by King George VI and the Chevalier de la Légion d'Honneur by de Gaulle's new government.

## Mary Herbert

At the outbreak of war, Mary, known to her friends as Maureen, worked in the British embassy in Warsaw. When she returned to England, fluent in five languages, she worked in the Air Ministry as a translator and joined the WAAF in September 1941. In fact, she was the first WAAF to volunteer for SOE work in March 1942. After training with Odette Sansom, Lise de Baissac and Jacqueline Nearne at Beaulieu – the second batch of female agents – thirty-nine-year-old Mary was taken by flying boat from Plymouth harbour to Gibraltar. After the felucca didn't appear, she was returned to London to wait. When she went back a few weeks later, it was in a submarine with George Starr, who was to become the organiser of the WHEELWRIGHT network in southern France. They were landed by felucca at Port-Miou, between Marseille and Toulon, from where she had to make her own way by train, bus and bike to Bordeaux. An account of her experiences is given in Escott's *Mission Improbable*.

Using the codename 'Claudine', cover name 'Marie Vernier' and sometimes known as 'Mariel', she worked as a courier, and in December 1941 she met fellow Resistance member Claude de Baissac. Escott commented:

Mary was probably not what Claude had been expecting. She was well educated with training in art and a degree, had travelled widely and like Claude, was of a very good family. She was tall, slim and fair-haired, but at 39, four years older than he. Apart from being highly intelligent and sincerely religious, she had one useful characteristic born from experience, in that she could merge into a crowd without attracting attention, an enormous asset for an agent who always wanted to be inconspicuous. However, her peculiar status in a small mostly male circle, combined with her special closeness to her chief, and being the willing recipient of the compliments and courtesies paid by all true Frenchmen to any female, brought her more vividly to life in the coming year.

As courier for the SCIENTIST network, she carried messages, documents, money and radio parts. She also acted as post box for de Baissac, located safe houses, identified potential recruits and helped escaped prisoners and downed aircrews down the escape line to the Pyrenees. Her network successfully attacked German positions in and around Bordeaux, shattering the radio station at Quatre Pavillions from which Admiral Dönitz communicated with his U-Boat fleets out in the Atlantic. The Luftwaffe airfields near Marignac were crippled and the anti-aircraft batteries and radar establishment at Deux Potteaux were put out of action when the power station at Belin was blown up. The cutting of railway lines, blowing up of road bridges and bringing down of telephone lines made the Gestapo even keener to find and punish the perpetrators.

Mary's travels brought her into contact with her boss's sister, Lise de Baissac, who organised the ARTIST network in Poitiers. Contrary to all the security rules, they became close friends. On one of her visits to Paris, she successfully located Francis Suttill and returned with a replacement transmitter for her organiser.

As the size of the PROSPER and the SCIENTIST networks grew, there was the fear of infiltrators and double agents. In June 1943 the Gestapo swooped. Hundreds were arrested and, under torture, some supplied vital information. When Mary heard about this, she changed her disguise, moved to a new apartment, and started using a new identity card. As she had been in the field for about a year, it was thought she would be Lysandered back with Claude but, as his sister Lise was in great danger of being arrested, she went instead of Mary.

Over time, her relationship with de Baissac had deepened and, as far as my research has revealed, she was the only agent to become pregnant. They dared not marry in case the documents gave them away. Inconsolable at being separated, she was in no fit state to continue her clandestine work. The replacement organiser arranged for her accommodation at a private nursing home in La Valence, a Bordeaux suburb, and provided her with enough money to meet her needs, ensuring she cut all links with the Resistance.

Baby Claudine was born by Caesarean operation in December 1943. Without telling anyone, Mary slipped away and hid in the apartment of her 'sister-in-law' in Poitiers. Although being a mother halted Mary's clandestine activity, it didn't stop the Gestapo arresting her and all the other residents in the building on 18 February 1944. They thought she was Lise de Baissac. Her baby, Claudine, was looked after by French Social Services while she was in prison, where she kept to her cover story that she was visiting from Alexandria in Egypt and didn't know Lise. She was released after two months for lack of evidence. After arguing with the orphanage authorities that she had been wrongly arrested, she was reunited with her daughter and hid in a small country house near Poitiers. Although she survived the war and married Claude in England in November 1944, the relationship did not last. He left her to go to Africa and she lived with her father at Moynes Court, and then in a large country house in the Wye valley.

## Marie Thérèse le Chêne and Madame Petit

Marie Thérèse, codenamed 'Adèle' and also known as 'Marie Thérèse Ragot' and 'Wisteria', worked as a courier between Henri Paul de Chêne's PLANE network and Robert Boiteux's SPRUCE network. When the Germans started to close in, she and nine others were taken to a field north-east of Angers, about one kilometre south-east of the village of Soucelles, where they had to avoid a large herd of bullocks that stampeded past them in the mist when the plane arrived. Marie was safely returned to England on 20 August.

On 28/29 November 1942, Jimmy McCairns returned to Tangmere in his Lysander from Thalamy in the Massif Central with four passengers, the most ever recorded. He was able to add another star to the side of the cockpit to indicate another successful mission. The new arrivals were Max Petit, a member of the Resistance, his wife and their two boys. In gratitude, Madame Petit presented Jimmy with some exquisite lipstick for his mother and a little golden mascot for himself. Hugh Verity's wife was often given little French presents on Hugh's return. At three in the morning one day, he woke her up by emptying a bag of lipsticks for her on the bed (www.plan-sussex-1944.net/anglais/pdf/infiltrations_into_france.pdf; Clark, *Agents by Moonlight*; Verity, *We Landed by Moonlight* ).

## 'Angela'

Sometime in the autumn of 1942, one of 161 Squadron's pilots flew eighteen-year-old Derrick Baynham and a younger FANY radio operator/courier out of Tangmere to a landing strip in the unoccupied zone of France, near Saumur, south of the Loire. Intriguingly, Derrick's name has not appeared in the mainstream SOE literature and neither has that of his accomplice. According to his obituary in the *Daily Telegraph*, he had been awarded the George Medal for bravery when he was only seventeen. Fifty years later, in his short pamphlet-style memoir of his recruitment, training and SOE mission, entitled '*Never Volunteer' Said My Dad*, he referred to her as Angel but admitted towards the end that many names he used were fictitious to protect their identities. They met at Thame Park, one of the SOE's country houses, where they had intensive wireless training courses.

> The previous day a young FANY called Angela had come up to me in a very anxious state saying that she had answered an advert for a bilingual secretary, and was now being trained as a radio operator in Morse, and in various subversive activities. She had no idea of what she was being trained for. I told her that I had no idea either. I did not mention the German Uniforms in the QM Stores …
>
> We were then moved to a similar country house – Chicheley Manor – near Newport Pagnell. Here we had further wireless training, including setting up various Spy sets in the nearby country and transmitting back to base, using one time pad codes …
>
> I was told to choose a Wireless trained courier to go with me. This was because as a man it would be difficult for me to move around without being noticed, and although my French was reasonable, it would not have fooled a French Gendarme for long. I decided to ask Angela, as she had been educated in France, and her morse was brilliant. Also I had grown rather fond of her, which seemed to be mutual. Not a very professional approach, but she readily agreed, and I was given permission to brief her on the details of my mission, or at least the part of it that would affect her.
>
> Later that day I began to have misgivings. She was not eighteen yet and would have been described in my day as 'stunning'. It was certainly a very dangerous mission and the chances of getting back to UK were evens at best. I suggested that she talked it over with the Senior FANY, and postpone her decision until the following day. She said that she would not change her mind, but would do as I said. The following morning the Senior FANY asked to see me in her office. She said that she had told Angela that she would be in good hands, and after all that is what we had been trained for. If she wanted to change her mind, she could be a UK Operator and nobody would ever blame her. She then said that Angela was quite sure of herself, and trusted that I would look after her and not get her into any trouble. I replied that we were both very well trained and would know what to do. She said 'That's not what I meant' and she had the courtesy to blush!!!

I went off to find Angela, and thanked her for her confidence in me. She threw her arms around my neck, kissed me, and said that she was quite sure that we would be lucky. A bit overcome, I said that we should not rely on luck but on our training …

We were to fly in a Westland Lysander by night from RAF Tangmere in a few days time. We were then kitted up in civilian clothes, but something had to be done about Angela's striking good looks. Such treatment was deemed unnecessary for me!! When she reappeared some hours later with a schoolgirl's haircut she looked about fifteen at the most, and would have been classified in the Army as 'Jail Bait'.

(King's College Library, London: GB99 KCLMA Baynham)

Their mission was to report to Baron Philippe de Vomécourt's Ventriloquist network operating around Limoges and find out what had happened to three missing agents; to investigate if a radio operator who had included errors in his messages was being forced to send under duress; to see if there was an informer in the circuit and to eliminate him or to arrange his elimination; to spot new talent in France to be returned to UK by Lysander for training; to 'recce' and report on new small industrial enterprises being relocated from cities to make weapons components; and to plant bogus information to entrap informers.

Things didn't go quite according to plan. When they landed, the expected agent they were supposed to meet had already been arrested.

That night we took it in turns to keep awake with torches at the ready, guns loaded. When my turn to be awake came, around 3am, Angela woke me up. I could see that she had little tears running down her cheeks, she apologised and said that she was cold and frightened. I said cheerfully I hope, 'you need not apologise – I am not too happy myself – so join the club'. I wiped her tears away and stroked her poor shorn hair until she drifted off to sleep. In fact there were a number of options available to us, but I would discuss them with her when we were both awake. I suddenly remembered that we both had a half bottle of Navy rum with our goodies. What better time as I thought it must be the 'Dog Watch'. Life was not so bad after all!!

Despite help from the local farmer and his wife, they didn't manage to make contact with Ventriloquist and only narrowly escaped capture by the Milice, the Vichy government's security police. While Derrick set up his radio in a pigsty, Angela went to the local market with a message. Suddenly,

I heard a noise behind me. I thought that it was Angel – it was a member of the Milice holding a pistol in my direction. I had made an elementary mistake; I could not reach my own weapon! He told me to stand up and keep my hands in the air. Suddenly, there was a loud shot, I thought at first that I had been hit, but it was he who folded up and fell to the ground. Then in tripped Angel as I was about to finish him off. 'Don't fire' she said, 'there is another one and you might alert him'. In fact he was already dead. She appeared to be quite pleased with herself; and told me that I was supposed to be looking after her, and in future she would be my Nanny. She then went on to say that she saw a van arrive, which was parked in the farmyard. There were two Milice in it, one of whom was still sitting in the front reading a paper. The other had gone off to have a look around, first to the copse where we had spent the night and then to the pigsty. She carefully followed him, and when she came to the pigsty, she quickly took in the situation, and shot him through a window.

We had to get rid of the other one. So Angel acted as bait, and lit a small fire, to heat up some water, in full view of the van. The unfortunate occupant had not heard the single shot, and when his accomplice had not appeared back, got out, and looked up on the hillside. He saw Angel about 800 yards away, and set off to investigate. As he approached Angel, I was hidden behind a hedge about 15 yards away and shot him before he had even had time to say anything. All this might seem to be rather cold-blooded, but we could not take prisoners, these were the rules of the game in SOE. We carried him up to the pigsty, and laid him out next to the first victim, I went through their papers and found that their names were those of two of the worst bullying Vichy collaborators in the Town, with a history of arrests and shootings.

When the bodies were found, a search of the surrounding area ensued which discovered the hidden radio set they had brought with them. The locals told them that two men were keeping watch, waiting for their return. Rather than killing these men, Baynham decided to knock them out for twelve hours with an injection. He claimed this had been supplied by the RSPCA and that he had been a fully paid-up member ever since.

I beckoned Angel to come up by my side, and checked that her pistol safety catch was not on. We slid forwards on our stomachs until we were almost up to the spot where I had seen them on my morning recce. I suddenly recognised two bodies lying only a few feet ahead – my heart was pounding – I nudged Angel who was wide eyed with anticipation before the penny dropped. They were both asleep, and their weapons were lying on the grass. I stood up over them gun in hand, and told Angel to quietly wake them, up, but not to shoot unless I did. As they woke up and realised their predicament I made them lie face down, limbs outstretched. They pleaded for their lives as Angel frisked them for any arms – they both had pistols which Angel removed. I was pretty sure that they had been drinking but their panic soon brought them around. I called up the two helpers and supervised the tying up operation which was probably overdone, even to the extent of attaching lines to their feet and wrists between two separate tree trunks so that they could not attempt to untie each other. Angel then injected them in the thighs, we assured them that the jab was just to put them asleep for a few hours until they got relieved. We did not gag them, as we did not know how to do it without risk of suffocation. How to tie up people was not on the syllabus in my SOE training!

The tense circumstances of their mission threw them together in a way which led to the inevitable question as to whether they should develop their relationship.

However, when I woke up at about noon she had put her arms around me, pressed her cheeks which were wet with tears against mine while quietly sobbing. I did not quite know what to do – I just asked her to talk to me. She said that as we approached the Milice she had a fear that almost paralysed her. She had felt that we would most certainly be killed, and we would have died without having shared ourselves with each other when we had the chance. I forget what my responses were, but they were to the effect that when we had got through our mission our time would come, and would be all that more precious for waiting. It's hard for me to explain now – I loved and adored Angel – we both expected that we would be caught eventually to be tortured and executed, but maybe we would get back one day to England, marry and have a little family together. The stakes were too high to risk wrecking our future by giving in to immediate satisfactions, Angel had to be my prize when we had accomplished whatever was required of us.

Not long afterwards they moved to Perigeux, where Angel developed a chest infection. Quite seriously ill, Baynham arranged for her to be looked after by Roman Catholic nuns in a convent, where she stayed until 1945. When he returned to England, he was commissioned into the Royal Signals corps and was wounded by a grenade while serving overseas. He was briefly taken prisoner but escaped and was 'Mentioned in Dispatches', a military award for gallantry. When he returned to England after the war he made enquiries after Angel, only to discover that she had managed to get back, had married and had two children. He kept her identity secret even on his deathbed in 1999.

## Jacqueline Nearne

Twenty-six-year-old, dark-haired Jacqueline Nearne, a volunteer FANY, was, according to Clark, the next SOE agent to be flown out of Tempsford and parachuted into France. Details of her life and wartime experiences were published recently in numerous obituaries. Her Anglo-Spanish family moved to Boulogne-sur-Mer in 1923 and, when war broke out, the family fled to the south coast. Her brother Francis went to England and joined the RAF. When, in November 1942, the Germans took over southern France, Jacqueline and her younger sister Eileen went to live in Grenoble. Desperate to escape German occupation, Jacqueline carefully planned their escape over the Pyrenees, through Portugal and Gibraltar to England. As her brother Francis had by then joined the SOE, the two sisters joined the FANY. Jacqueline was accepted for special duties and sent to work in Buckmaster's 'F' Section as a liaison officer with the French Resistance movement. It wasn't long before she volunteered to train as an agent. Buckmaster started his article 'Travelling Saleswoman', an account of Jacqueline's wartime experiences, with the following:

> In a room in a country-house a girl was sitting alone. The blackout curtains were drawn back, and the only light, that of the moon, nearly full and serene in a clear sky, fell upon her face. It was a young and beautiful face, in which courage and steadfastness showed clearly, but a close observer might have noticed traces of stress.
>
> As on previous occasions, she was spending her leave in this country-house. To her hostess she was just a F.A.N.Y. on leave from the daily round of normal and perhaps monotonous duties. But in the girl's mind thought followed quickly upon thought. 'The moon will be full tomorrow night, and the weather should be clear. Shall we take off, and will the flight be successful this time?' Her thoughts returned to those other flights,

fraught with danger, when she had set out, strung to concert pitch, to fly over France and descend by parachute upon enemy soil, only to suffer the dreadful anticlimax of the return flight because conditions had proved unfavourable for her descent. That long cold wait in the aircraft, that return to another spell of waiting in England; how many more times must I endure them? Thought ran on unceasing.

It was the winter of 1942, and France was occupied by the Germans. The only convenient way for British liaison officers to get there was by parachute. And even this way was not, strictly speaking, 'convenient'.

In the early years of the war few aircraft were assigned to special operations of this type, and the weather, especially in winter, was not often suitable for landings by parachute. Liaison officers might have to wait for weeks possibly months, before their hazardous journey could be undertaken. Even then the pilot might well be unable to find the small field perhaps 400 miles from his base, where the 'reception committee' flashing feeble torches, awaited his passenger.

False alarms, abortive and dangerous flights menaced by enemy night-fighters and 'flak' were even more unnerving for the passenger, who had his mission before him, than for the crew of the aircraft. We used to reckon that three months waiting or two abortive attempts were about as much as an officer could be asked to endure, unless he or she had particularly strong nerves. But Jacqueline, the girl in the moonlit room, certainly had strong nerves. She had to wait from September until December and make several unsuccessful flights before the night arrived on which she made her parachute descent, yet she remained as calm and collected as one could wish …

Jacqueline's name was given to me because of her perfect knowledge of French; after a brief interview she was enrolled in the F.A.N.Y., and seconded to my department for special service. She quickly obtained her commission and started training. But her French education and long residence made difficult to her problems which would have been easy for a girl with English upbringing. She became nervy and depressed; whereas at the first interview she had been confident of her ability to go back to France to live an underground life, now the very complexity of her training shook her self-confidence. She became thinner, and was obviously worrying about her ability to take on the job.

It was at this stage that I saw her for the second time. The training authorities had just issued an unfavourable report on her, and I thought that perhaps I had been over-optimistic about her qualifications. I went to see her at the school. There was no doubt about her being worried; but in the course of half an hour's talk she unburdened herself of her worries, and when I realised that her preoccupation was purely with the mechanics of what she was learning, I had no hesitation in advising her to go on with the course. She worked fantastically hard; she was determined to master the theoretical as well as the practical side of the job. That she succeeded is proved by her magnificent record, which owed much to the high standard of security which she maintained throughout her area of operations.

During the last and successful flight there came again that tense feeling, those speculations upon the immediate and perilous future. Now they were near the place, and she made the final preparations; the green light indicating that she should leave the aircraft showed; a last contact of friendly hands helping her out of the aircraft, and she was falling … She thought: 'I must make a good landing, I hope I don't get caught in a tree. Who will be there to meet me? Have the enemy been warned?' She landed, and as she collected herself perceived a shadowy figure approaching. Was it a German? She drew her pistol and waited.

The figure approached, also with drawn pistol, but all was well, and she was welcomed, and taken to safety for food and rest.

On 25 January 1943, Jacqueline and Squadron Leader Maurice Southgate were dropped about a mile north of Brioude, in the Massif Central, to take over the leadership of a new STATIONER network that stretched from Châteauroux to the foothills of the Pyrenees. Jacqueline must have had her heart in her mouth when, very shortly after landing, Southgate asked a female cyclist the way to Brioude – in English!

Codenamed 'Designer', Jacqueline worked as a radio operator using a suitcase radio and went on to become a courier between several SOE groups operating around Paris. Her cover was that she was a chemist's sales representative. Jacqueline's life as a secret agent was filled with constant danger. The threat of being exposed as an SOE agent or being betrayed by a comrade must have created tremendous tension. Despite this, she travelled on long and arduous train journeys to maintain contact with agents, radio operators and the neighbouring HEADMASTER network run by Sydney Hudson, forming a vital link between several other SOE networks operating in Paris, Clermont-Ferrand, Toulouse, Pau and Poitiers. She also carried spare parts for radios and organised reception committees for newly arrived agents. In Pattinson's book, *Behind Enemy Lines*, she included a transcript from the film in which Jacqueline starred after the war.

CAT     The police were searching luggage at the station.
         They made me open my suitcases.
FELIX   Gosh – what did you do?
CAT     I tried sex appeal.
FELIX   Did it work?
CAT     No, it was a complete flop! I had to open it.
FELIX   What about the WT set?
CAT     I told them with a sweet smile that it was an X-ray machine.
FELIX   It must have been a very sweet smile for them to have swallowed that!

Part of her work included escorting downed British airmen along the escape line south to the Pyrenees. 'Were they pretty glad to see you?' Buckmaster asked her on her return to England. 'Well yes, but of course they had no idea I was English; I didn't tell them who I was' (Buckmaster, 1946–47).

As shall be seen later, her sister Eileen was also dropped into France to work as a radio operator and when Jacqueline learned of her sister's capture, she was told to return to England. Instead, she gave up her seat in the Lysander for a political refugee.

After fifteen months in the field, her life had been one of constant train travel. London eventually became concerned about her health so they arranged for Jacqueline to be picked up by Flight Lieutenant Taylor in a Lysander in April 1944. Chalked on the side were the words 'Jacqueline must come'. She had to leave knowing Eileen was unlikely to get back. Buckmaster told of how,

In the spring of 1944 we received information that the wife of a well known and popular French general (who had escaped to England) was actively being sought by the Gestapo. We ordered Jacqueline to get in touch with her, and arrange to bring her out by a Lysander aircraft which would be sent to fetch her. While these arrangements were being made, we learned that Jacqueline herself and another officer were in imminent danger, owing to the arrest of a member of her organisation. Quick action was essential. The operation was scheduled at once, but the problem of space in the aircraft arose. We knew that Jacqueline would not readily consent to leave her post until 'Madame la Générale' was safe. It was therefore necessary to issue a definite order. The way we did this was to chalk on the side of the aircraft an order of priority for the passengers, which the RAF pilot called the 'batting order'. To our regret we had to leave Madame off the list. But all was well, since Jacqueline had arranged for a safe hiding-place for whichever of the women had to be left behind, and we brought Madame to safety a few weeks later. It was as well we did bring Jacqueline first, for a few days later her Chief was arrested and Jacqueline's photograph figured on the notice boards as: 'Wanted. Reward offered for the capture dead or alive of individual known as Jacqueline or Josette.'

After the liberation of Paris, Buckmaster took Jacqueline, dressed in her FANY uniform, back to her old haunts. When they went into a bistro, her old headquarters,

The manager's face, as he bustled forward to receive the British military visitors, was wreathed in smiles of professional welcome. When he recognised Jacqueline, his surprise was almost pathetic, and although he stoutly protested that he had 'known it all along', his look of incredulous amazement had betrayed him. Jacqueline was immensely popular. Not only has she great beauty and charm, but her sense of comradeship and her kindliness are delightful. She made many friends, whose affection and admiration for Britain are unbounded. The personal example of a girl like her is worth more than the finest political speeches.

Southgate was one of the lucky few to survive imprisonment at Buchenwald. For his work he was posthumously awarded the MBE and the Croix de Guerre.

## Beatrice 'Trix' Terwindt

In Michael Foot's *SOE in the Low Countries*, he mentions three women being sent to Holland and two to Belgium. The first was thirty-one-year-old Beatrice 'Trix' Terwindt. The seventh child of a Belgian mother and a Dutch father who ran a stone quarry, she acquired English, French and some German at an English convent school in Bruges. She worked for some years as an air stewardess for KLM, the Dutch airline, but when Holland was invaded and the Germans closed down civil aviation, she was given a desk-based job.

What sparked her to leave Holland is unknown but it is possible that she had made acquaintance with people involved in the Pat O'Leary escape line, which helped downed Allied pilots, crews and agents get back to England via Belgium, France and then east into the Swiss Alps or south over the Pyrenees into Spain and then Gibraltar.

Accompanied by a young Dutch student, she walked out of Holland, through Belgium and into France in March 1942. While the customs official on the border at St Julian looked the other way, they ran across into Switzerland. Perhaps with the assistance of MI9, the secret organisation supporting the escape routes, she got a flight to Lisbon and from there to England.

There she was introduced to Airey Neave, an intelligence agent with MI9. He had been wounded and arrested at Calais and eventually imprisoned in Colditz Castle. After a daring escape, he managed to get into Switzerland and then along the Comète line through France into Spain and Gibraltar, arriving in England a few months before Trix.

Recognising her potential working with the PAT line, Neave arranged for her to undergo 'F' Section's paramilitary training at Wanborough Manor. After weeks at Beaulieu she underwent parachute training at Ringway. In Neave's autobiography, *Saturday at MI9*, he admitted considering but then rejecting the option of using plastic surgery to reconstruct her facial features. As there were no other volunteers, he escorted her to Tempsford on 13 February 1943, helped her into her parachute harness and handed her some Dutch guilders and forged nurse's identity papers. He also warned her about two collaborators, Poos and Slagter.

Having overcome her fear of flying, Trix was the first female agent to be dropped into Holland, along with several containers, one of which included her wireless set. Codenamed 'Chicory' and also known as 'Felix', she had the mission of helping support the PAT line in getting agents out of the country. Unbeknownst to her or the pilot, the Germans had arranged everything. They had captured a radio operator and their set and coerced them to send messages to London, who did not pick up on the missing security codes. So began the *Englandspiel*, whereby the Germans made arrangements for the SOE to send agents, supplies and money straight into their hands (TNA HS 9/1452/8).

She jarred herself badly when she landed in fields near Steenwijk, a small farming community about 20 kilometres south-west of Groningen, but was helped by the welcome committee, including Poos and Slagter, who, as it was raining, sheltered her in a nearby barn. The collaborators checked her identity papers, suggested they were inadequate and recommended she wait until they could supply her with new ones. As she had been unable to make her first rendezvous with one of the genuine Resistance figures, they managed to coax it out of her. According to Foot, they explained that London was often out of date with its addresses and they could not take responsibility for letting her continue with her mission until they had checked it out for her.

Suddenly, someone threw a blanket over her head. Thinking she was having her nerves tested like when she was rudely awoken at Beaulieu and subjected to brutal interrogation 'practices', she didn't resist as forcefully as she had been trained. She was grabbed from behind and handcuffed before she could manage to get her poison pill into her mouth. Taken to the Abwehr headquarters in Driebergen, she was interrogated without a break for four days. According to Neave, she was surprised at how much more her captors knew about the SOE than she did and was perturbed that the Germans couldn't understand why the British had sent a lone girl who evidently was very poorly briefed about her organisation. Apparently, they didn't realise she was from another covert operations department.

She never knew until much later that the wireless set dropped with her was retrieved and used to send messages back to London. C. J. Smit, her rendezvous, and his friend were arrested at the address she gave them in The Hague. They were shot the following year. The plane that dropped her was shot down on its return journey. Given the amount and density of anti-aircraft artillery in the Low Countries, very few planes returned. Orders were issued to shoot at them on their return flight so their passengers and contents could be dropped safely (TNA HS 9/1452/8).

Nel Lind, a fellow prisoner, said she had got the impression that the Germans wanted to keep Trix alive. They even gave her a wireless with which she could listen to the BBC while she was in solitary confinement for eighteen months, apart from a brief spell during which they unsuccessfully planted a spy in her cell.

Diet Eman, in her book, *Things We Couldn't Say*, recalls her time in prison when she met Trix who, she said,

> wore a tiny piece of fur round her neck that resembled a (pine) marten. She called it 'Freddy' and sometimes spoke to it and stroked it … Her eyes seemed kind of wild and nervous, very sunken, and her facial features were pulled tight. She was very anxious.
>
> That night, after the others had gone to sleep, I stayed awake because something inside me told me that this woman was special. Although I'd never met her before, my instincts told me I could trust her, and I knew there was more to her than the little she'd told us. We sat on the floor against the wall, just the two of us, and we talked the whole night while the others were asleep. She told me her story that night in cell 306.
>
> She was from a very well-to-do family, so rich that she didn't have to have a job. Before the war she had studied at university, but she became bored with going to school, she said. Air travel had just begun at that time, and she became one of the KLM airline's first stewardesses. She said that she flew only to challenge herself: she had been deathly afraid of flying, so she challenged herself to get on an airplane by becoming a stewardess, of all things.
>
> When war broke out, she'd made her way to England and was working for the Dutch intelligence service. When she arrived, Queen Wilhelmina invited Beatrix over for tea! It's difficult for Americans to understand loyalty and love for the crown, but I always loved our royal family. That night, when Beatrix told me that she had had tea with the queen, I was nearly overwhelmed with admiration for her!

Eventually she was transferred to Ravensbrück and then Mauthausen concentration camp in Germany, from where she was eventually liberated by American forces on 5 May 1945. The experience ruined her health. Neave's postscript of her story reads:

> She has never indulged in any recrimination and bitterness. She has treated her nightmarish experience as one of the fortunes of war. It was this quiet faith and serenity of spirit which brought admiration from her captors. Thanks to her refusal to talk, she was one of the few survivors of 'Northpole' who escaped death. As she wrote to me afterwards: 'I was an amateur but in war risks have to be taken. I played a game of cat and mouse with the Gestapo with the only difference that I was caged and the cat was free.'

## 'Yelena Nikitina' and 'Emilya Novikova'

On 24 February 1943, two Soviet women were flown out of Tempsford. They had arrived in Glasgow on HMS *Bulldog* on 28 September the previous year with three other Soviet agents. Travelling on Estonian passports as 'Yelena [sometimes spelt Elena] Nikitina' and 'Emilya Novikova', they were to be sent with a male colleague to Germany and Austria respectively. As the original ship they were sailing in was sunk by German torpedoes, they were lucky to have escaped death. However, their cover documents and wireless sets rested at the bottom of the Arctic Ocean. Given British clothing and issued with food coupons, they were taken by train to London to meet their NKVD masters and accommodated in a flat at Cropthorne Court, Maida Vale.

Documents in their file indicate that Nikitina was thirty-four-year-old Kersti Boska, an unmarried stenographer from Haapsalu whose mission name was TONIC. Novikova was thirty-four-year-old Anna Under, an unmarried governess from Virz-Yarvi whose mission name was SODAWATER. All records of their coming to Britain in their real names and nationality were ordered to be expunged from Immigration, Home Office and National Registration records (TNA HS 4/344).

Having to ensure they had no contact with other SOE agents, they were taken to Alderton Hall Farm, in Loughton, Essex, where they were looked after by Mr and Mrs Chaffe. As well as Group Captain Grierson, their conducting officer, they were also accompanied by Captain Toropchenko, an NKVD minder. While there, they were provided with maps and discussed their separate drop zones. Grierson fed back to London that they were prepared to go to Freiburg-im-Breisgau, Nieusiedler See in Ostmark, and Rostock in Stralsund and asked for photographic plates of these districts to be sent (TNA HS 4/344).

On 27 October, they were taken to Ringway for their parachute training, where they stayed at Dunham House. The Commandant, Major Edwards, reported as follows:

> Anna Unter: Tried hard in all her ground training and had a happy disposition. In her balloon descent she showed slight signs of nervousness, but made a good egress and had soft landing.
>
> Kersti Peska: A very nervous type of person who was frightened in the ground training and also in the balloon descent. She did well to jump at all.
>
> The members of this party had all jumped previously from Douglas aircraft and except in the case of the ladies soon acquired the technique of going through the hole. Miss Unter was slow at learning this but having mastered it she jumped very well from the balloon, and was cheerful throughout. Miss Kruus found the greatest difficulty in going through the hole, and it was feared that she might refuse. She complained of her knees during the ground training, and was obviously very nervous. These two went up in the first car load with Capt. Thornton, F. Lt. Winfield and F/T. Agate, who guided their packs as they jumped. Without this consideration and tactful handling, I do not think Miss Kruus would have jumped. [Miss Kruus was Yelena, married to Juri Kruus, alias Pyetr Kolstov, of the SODAWATER party]

While at Alderton, they had issues with the Chaffes about food and heating. Major Seddon, the head of SOE's Russian section, was informed that the 'guests' had lit coal fires in the dining and sitting room and had electric fires in bedrooms – contrary to orders. They went out for meals at a moment's notice after a meal had been ordered and prepared and

> invaded Mrs. Chaffes kitchen at 11 pm. to make tea or COFFEE for themselves. They go to bed about midnight with the lights and fire going. They have raided the orchard and taken all the pears; they throw the cores of these on the floor when they have finished with them!
>
> (TNA HS 4/344, 3 November 1942)

After only a week in Alderton, they spent the next few months alternating between the Drokes, Cropthorne, Vineyards and Alderton. During this time, they were given additional training in wireless and telegraphy. After seven changes of mind, they finally agreed on their drop zones. The Air Transport Form 6 gave Tonic's as 4 km SSE of Endigen, 5¾ km SSW of Reigel and 15 km NW of Freiburg. Sodawater's was 4½ km E of Wimpassing, 2½ km W of Loretta and 8½ km NNW of Eisenstadt. It was decided that, to increase the chances of a safe delivery, both parties had to be despatched on separate aircraft from Tempsford, and, in accordance with their cover story, on a weekend.

When their radio sets were delivered on 16 December, the final day for handing in their luggage, someone had to locate two appropriate suitcases to hide the sets in and rush them up to Holmewood Hall, Holme, near Peterborough. As the Americans had joined the war by this time, a contingent was attached to help the Special Duties Squadrons. Called the Carpetbaggers, they needed training in night flying and clandestine drops at Tempsford. Gaynes Hall being used more as a 'holding station', the Americans took over the packing operations at Holme. However, there was another problem which caused delays. Among the *Reichmarks* the Soviets had been issued were 5 Mark notes which had long been withdrawn from circulation.

How they celebrated Christmas and New Year at Cropthorne Court was not documented. After a number of cancelled flights, on the night of 24/25 January everything was in place. A plane was available for the Tonic mission to Germany; the weather was okay but Tempsford's Daily Operations Report stated that the flight was postponed because of 'crew difficulty'. The full story of what happened was described by Mary Mundle, their FANY conducting officer:

TONIC's Odyssey

Arrived at Cropthorne Court about 18.30 and found the bods all sitting upright in a row. Engaged the Ogpu [Toropchenko] in light chat while Nikitina collected her belongings and said her farewells. One moment when I expected to be felled with a blow; remarked casually to the Ogpu on the similarity between many Polish and Russian wars. He turned on me with a bound and said: 'Are you Polish'? 'No, no. I'm a good Scot, but I've bumped into a few Polish Communists in my time', I said and hoped that none of the crypto-Fascist slave drivers who are the light of my life would turn up at the aerodrome. The Ogpu relaxed a bit and we set off for Tempsford. Nobody felt much like talking and we drove down in silence apart from a certain amount of sniffing and wheezing from Otto. Arrived at the dressing-huts about 20.30 as expected and settled down to a meal out of a hay box. Tyce, Ellis, W/C Corby and the despatcher were present, along with a couple of FANYs. The Ogpu, having settled how to spell my name and carefully noted my father's profession and the number of my identity card, began to take an interest in the company. Who was the Wing-Commander and what did he do? 'Smith', I said firmly, 'and he is on the ground now'. 'What was the name of the aerodrome?' 'Tempson,' I thought, but wasn't quite sure. The braised ham and two veg being packed away, I turned all the men out into another dressing hut and started to go to town on Nikitina. I mooted the disagreeable prospect of searching her thoroughly and she conceded what I can only call a Russian look, vitriolic but resigned. First, however, she intimated with great dignity, she would like to see the usual offices. Somewhere out in the dark night, the usual offices no doubt existed. I plunged into the blackness and fell over a stone which was strategically placed and fortunately located Tyce. Sent him to investigate. Regret to state that Nikitina's last memory of English sanitation is a sorry one, or would have been if she had ever taken off. Searched her bag and asked her to remove her clothes. With the same quiet dignity, she requested that somebody be posted at the door in case any of the men should try to come in. I assured her that I had squared that one and we started in. I hadn't realised that she was carrying her entire wardrobe on her person. She worked her way into three of everything, a dress, a suit, three jumpers, an overcoat and two hats and by the time they squeezed her into her strip-tease, she looked like a highly distorted version of the Michelin-tyre advertisement. The last straw came when she announced that her handbag must somehow be attached to her person as she couldn't hold it in her hand and somewhere she had to accommodate an extra pair of shoes. The men all trooped back at this point and I discussed it with the despatcher. He recommended that it should be strapped to her chest but, kneeling in front of her, having just strapped up her ankles, he asked in the broadest Gallashiels: 'And what would you be doing with a great baggie like you?' The Ogpu pricked back his ears – this was obviously code – but I eased him up by translating. It was agreed that Otto, who was sitting bolt upright, looking wispier than ever, wearing his crash helmet on top of a grey felt so that the brim stuck out all around, should tuck his shoes inside his strip-tease. The Ogpu whistled at me through his teeth: 'Miss Mundles, they want some poison.' 'Well, have they asked for it? That should have been arranged right at the start.' Yes, yes, they'd asked for it all right. I checked up and told him that 'The Poison' was coming over on a tray at 10 o'clock. When it did come, I dropped the pellets in the Ogpu's palm, carefully explaining Blue for Benzedrine, White were Sleeping Tablets and the big, fat leathery number was lethal. He passed them on to the bods without a word. 'Hadn't you better explain which is which?' I demurred. 'Miss Mundles bespokujetz…' he launched out and they smiled tolerantly. We Russians don't have to be told, I gathered. We piled into the car and made for Tyce's office, where the parachutes were to be harnessed. This was no easy business. Nikitina was so enormous that it seemed doubtful if she'd ever get though the hole and none of the straps would meet round her girth. Eventually, after much pulling, pushing, squeezing, bumping and mashing, they were all tied up and we set out round the track in search of our aircraft. Both Otto and Nikitina looked quietly happy and unperturbed. First of all Tyce drove his car into a quagmire. Then we lost the flarepath. At about 22.20 we found our Halifax and learned with dismay that there was still no crew. We stood around under the machine for twenty minutes and Tyce decided to return to his office and find out if the crew was still alive. He returned about 23.00 with the grievous news that the operation had been postponed at 20.30 but nobody had thought fit to tell him. We drove back to his office and tried to get some ruling on the disposal of the bods. The Ogpu took a great interest in all the maps and operational dope and I spread-eagled myself over Warszawa as much as possible. Passed round hot COFFEE and RUM and felt rather queasy when my turn at the cup came directly after the Ogpu. Rang up Major Barcroft at S.T.S. 61 and asked if it would be possible to segregate three bods, two men and one woman. He rose from his bed of pain and said it couldn't be done. The bods said they would prefer to go back to London. They liked the thought of their own beds, thank you. At midnight, W/C Corby was found and he gave permission for them to return to London. The Ogpu, who had by this time thawed completely, finished his exposition of the spirit of Moscow and the place of the Underground in Modern Europe and led his party back to the car. We reached London about 02.15, parked Otto and Nikitina in Cropthorne and the Ogpu at Notting Hill Gate.

On investigation, I find that the reason for the postponement of the operation was that one member of the crew fell sick and as he couldn't be replaced the operation was scrubbed. The slip-up in contacting was no doubt due to the fact that the a/c [aircraft] was 138 Squadron and the crew borrowed from 161 Squadron.

When news came through that there was a plane arranged for 13 February, 'Yelena' and Gorelov were taken up to Tempsford again. Everything seemed to go according to plan. They were prepared and flown out on schedule. The pilot crossed the Channel and flew over France. However, bad weather meant the pilot had to abort the mission and return to Tempsford after some seven and a half hours in the air. The conducting officer's remark was: 'Passengers quite O.K. The pilot would have been wise not to have dropped his passengers in this strong wind even if he had located the point exactly' (TNA HS 4/344).

Another attempt three days later was abandoned due to cloud cover at the drop zone. On 18/19 February the rescheduled flight was cancelled at the last minute, as 'One of the party sick before take-off. Their Chief called the trip off' (TNA HS 4/344). O'Donnell added that Nikitina ('Annette') was sick at the thought of sharing an aeroplane with Belgians.

The following day SODAWATER's flight was arranged, but the pilot experienced engine trouble south of Stuttgart and aborted the mission. Owing to difficulty in maintaining height, the 'A' type package was jettisoned without parachute in a wood. They landed safely at Tempsford after a round trip of 7 hours 45 minutes.

Another attempt was made to drop SODAWATER on 24/25 February. This time, they were successfully dropped about 50 km south-east of Vienna. TONIC was flown the same evening and they too parachuted safely. The pilot noted that 'The lady was nervous lest they should be dropped on the wrong place. Also slightly airsick, in spite of pills to counteract same' (TNA HS 4/344). Clark has noted that they had logged 17 hours 25 minutes in the air by the time they finally left the aeroplane.

All the time cooped up with their conducting officers provided ideal opportunities for detailed character assessments of the agents to be built up.

Elena NIKITINA (Kersti Poska)

Apparently regarded as the head of the group and certainly possessed the strongest character. Throughout their many trials and tribulations, she maintained a relative calm and only on one occasion – when she was faced with two operational nights running – did events appear to be too much for her. She invariably knew what she wanted and almost as invariably got it. She never allowed her political views be known, indeed she never discussed politics. For most of the men with whom she came into contact, she appeared to exude an ineffable sex appeal, a characteristic which was certainly not based on any misconception of belonging to the weaker sex.

Very little is known of her story; she required a certain amount of alteration to her documents and she was given various additional papers to complete her cover. She, however, did all the filling in herself, as did the other members of both these parties. Towns in which she was interested were Cologne and Berlin, and, amongst other things, she asked to be provided with a wedding ring and a crucifix.

Emilya NOVIKOVA (Anna Under)

A very ordinary woman aged about 35; a somewhat nervous type. Indeed she was the only one to hesitate in jumping. Very much the Hausfrau and indeed she used to prepare, on occasion, a very nice tea for D/P 4. She appears to have been the W/T agent for SODAWATER, and on one occasion evinced great technical knowledge of the subject. She often found it exceedingly difficult to make up her mind on any given occasion of doubt, and several times, inflamed the usually placid E/FC – and many are the stories which he will tell on the subject.

(TNA HS 4/344)

Additional information was provided by research by O'Sullivan, who added that Yelena was

relatively calm and never discussed politics. Nikitina/Polska was in effect German Communist Elsa Noffke, and Gorelov/Ulnoti her colleague Georg Tietze. Noffke had worked in the Communist paper *Rote Fahne* in Berlin until 1933. She had been trained in a special school for agents near Moscow for nine months in 1942 before travelling to Britain. The Gestapo had advance notice of the arrival of 'Tonic', probably through deciphered messages from the Moscow 'Direktor'.

(O'Sullivan, *Dealing With the Devil*, 1997)

Nothing more appeared in their files until 9 August 1943, when the SOE were informed that a Polish/Austrian refugee in Switzerland claimed that English parachutists, dropped near Kaiserstuhl early in 1943, had been captured by local police about Whitsuntide (late June). The W/T set and codes were seized intact. This suggested they were Nikitina and Gorelov. The informant had overheard some German soldiers on a train between Freiburg and Munich saying that a female parachutist had been arrested in Freiburg as a result of a message she sent in English to a friend of hers working in a factory at Mannheim. The message was opened by a German foreman, who reported it to the police, who promptly arrested two 'English parachutists'.

British interrogation of Horst Kopkow, the head of the *Sonderkommando Rote Kapelle*, revealed that the Gestapo had lured 'Anna Müller' across the border from Switzerland and arrested her. She confessed to having worked for the Soviets for twenty years, acting as a courier and organising the escape of agents across the German border into Switzerland by befriending one of the border guards (TNA KV 3/137, 17 January 1947).

Further light on their fate came in May 1945 following the American forces freeing women prisoners from Ravensbrück concentration camp, near Furstenburg in north Germany. A number of female SOE agents captured in France had been imprisoned there, most of whom were executed. One of the survivors, Odette Sansom, was debriefed when she was flown back to England. She stated that she had been very friendly with a woman named Helene Poska, whom she believed was a British agent. The report written up by her interrogator stated that:

> This woman sends greetings to me and asked that, if possible, I would help her to obtain a British, French, Swiss or Spanish passport.
>
> 'Lise' said that Poska had been arrested in February 1943, whilst attempting to make her way to Vienna. The man she was with, who appears to have been Otto ULNOTI, was, according to 'Lise', 'un mauvais type'. Poska when she was arrested took her 'L' tablet, but this was remarked by the Gestapo and she was promptly treated, being given as well a glass of milk. She appears to have been reasonably well treated at Ravensbrück, and never consented to work for the Germans, though these latter tried hard to make her, by means of various third degree methods. She left Ravensbrück for an unknown destination, possibly Berlin, on 10th January, and this was the last that was seen of her. She asked me, via 'Lise', to inform 'her friends' of what had happened to her, so that they might tell her husband.
>
> In the camp also was another German prisoner, who was a great friend of Poska's, a Fräulein FARRE, who was apparently released and was last heard of living in Berlin at an address which 'Lise' is going to give me (Berlin-Dahlem, Falkenreid 30). I was also asked to inform this latter person.
>
> There seems little doubt that this woman is the one whom we referred to usually as Yelena NIKITINA, who was under our care from 29.9.42 to 24.2.43, and who was given the name of Kersti Poska during her stay in England. Should you agree, I propose sending the following telegram to Moscow for further transmission to our colleagues:
>
> 'Woman known as Yelena NIKITINA was for long period prisoner at Ravensbrück camp, whence she was removed 10th January this year for unknown destination. She asked us to inform Soviet colleagues and that they should tell her husband.'
>
> (TNA HS 4/344)

The final note in Tonic and Sodawater's file came from a further interview with Odette. Her report claimed that Yelena was married to Pyotr Koltsov, alias Juri Kruus. He and Emilya Novikova had been picked up by the authorities immediately after landing and it was information they gave which led to the arrest of their colleagues two months later. Before that, they had had wireless contact with 'their friends', but SOE thought this unusual as they had lost all their equipment on landing.

> I gathered the impression from Mlle. Sansom that Nikitina was somewhat jealous of Novikova, and that this latter might conceivably have been the cause of the leakage.
>
> Mlle. Sansom had suggested to Nikitina that a letter be sent to him and they had been on the point of writing this when Nikitina had been taken away. The Kalfaktor or person who was allowed to carry round trays to other prisoners and who did other menial jobs at Ravensbrück, was a certain Frau Hartmann; she informed Mlle. Sansom that she believed Nikitina had been shot. Mlle. Sansom further suggested that she considered Nikitina would have told us anything we wanted to know. She occasionally had a Polish woman planted on her in the prison, according to Mlle. Sansom. While she was in prison in Karlsruhe Nikitina made great friends with a young woman known as 'Lise' who was very well educated and was believed to have worked for the Americans and was actually engaged to an American, who was also in the prison. Apart from this Mlle. Sansom knew little about this other woman, except that she was born in Strasbourg and her mother had been remarried to a lawyer.
>
> (Ibid.)

Additional light on their fate was shed by one of the documents in SOE's Russian file, which included details obtained from 'PW', seemingly a defector from the SS (*Schutzstaffel*), Adolf Hitler's personal armed guard. Dated 24 August 1944, it included the following information on the German counter-intelligence:

> In spring 1943, nr FREIBURG in Breisgau, a farmer found a suitcase attached to a parachute in his field. He was afraid to open it and summoned one of the local boys on furlough. This man called his Bn [*sic*] station in Alsace. The Bn sent an officer over who opened the suitcase. It contained a transmitter. A thorough search of the whole area yielded another suitcase, containing a man's and a woman's clothes.
>
> At the same time a Russian agent was being grilled in VIENNA and under pressure revealed the address of an elderly couple living in FREIBURG. [Kostov was printed in the margin.] The Gestapo thoroughly investigated this couple but could not pin anything on them. As a matter of routine, however, Gestapo agents continued to drop in at the place. On such a routine call, Whitsunday 1943, a youngish woman opened the door when the Gestapo called. [Nikitina was written in the margin beside this line.] The moment she saw them, she put something into her mouth. She was rushed to a hospital and her stomach was pumped. She had tried to poison herself.
>
> Upon interrogation she admitted being a Russian agent. She was the wife of a Hamburg communist and had fled to Russia in 1938. There she had been trained as an agent, mainly in operating a wireless set. The ship which was to take her to Germany sunk and she was rescued and brought to England. Here the British Secret Service tried to buy her out but she had decided to go on with her mission. So the British provided her and her companion with a plane which flew her over Germany. After having been dropped, she could not find her male companion nor the two suitcases. But she went on with her mission and was caught. She confessed that she had

instructions to stay in Germany even after the American army should enter that section of Germany. She had British, French, German, and even American money on her to provide for such an emergency.

(TNA KV 2/2827)

O'Sullivan (2004) suggests that they both chose to collaborate with the Gestapo.

Köhler and Boretzky volunteered information about conditions in the Soviet training school Pionerskaya near Moscow, where they had learned to jump with a parachute. They also disclosed that the NKVD had instructed them not to engage in conversations with their British SOE handlers. According to them, the Soviet guideline was that co-operation between the Allies in intelligence matters should be carefully restricted. Indeed the Gestapo file remark corresponds with the SOE file statement that the leader of 'Tonic' was reluctant to discuss political matters.

Emilya was described as a fashion designer before the war who was trained as a parachutist by the Soviets and jumped in February 1943. She was arrested by the Vienna Gestapo on 31 March (*sic*), fingerprinted, charged with high treason and sent to Ravensbrück concentration camp. In early 1945 she was deported back to Vienna where, in May, she was identified as a traitor by Smersh, the counter-intelligence team, and deported to the Soviet Union where, presumably because of her collaboration, she was sentenced to hard labour in the prison camps (http://en.doew.braintrust.at/db_gestapo_4446.html).

In the 'confession' of the Gestapo's expert on their *Funkspiel* operations, he detailed how operation *'Burgenland'* involved Emilya and Hermann.

In February 1943, a new group of NKVD agents was arrested. It consisted of KOEHLER, alias KNORAD and a woman Emile BORETZKY, who was to operate the W/T set. KOEHLER had been chief organiser of the Communist Party of Austria between 1928 and 1938. He left for France after the Anschluss and from there finally emigrated to Russia.

The two agents of this group had left Russia over Mourmansk for England and had been, later, dropped from England by a RAF plane. (Subject explains that there were two such cases during all his activities with Russian agents). KOEHLER was caught first. He had stored in one leg pocket of his jump clothes a bottle of cognac. The cognac had spilled during the drop and some blood-hounds used by Subject had picked up the trail. Later the parachutes were easily found. Actually the team was caught because of 'apartment trouble' … The Russians needed alternate current to operate their sets and, as there were very few quarters in Vienna which provided with this kind of current, it became relatively easy to supervise these quarters and arrest any suspicious person.

The team were 'persuaded' to cooperate with the Gestapo.

(TNA KV 2/2827)

Faced with the grim choice of execution or collaboration, Emilya handed over her crystals, which provided the correct frequencies for transmitting to and receiving from Moscow, and declared her willingness to take part in *'Burgenland'*. She and Köhler, according to O'Sullivan (2010), provided Thomas Ampletzer, their Gestapo interrogator, with details of

their preparation in the Pionerskaya camp near Moscow, the circumstances of their journey to Britain, and their treatment by SOE, including the farewell drinks at the airfield. Köhler's information led to the Gestapo directly to capture Noffke in Freiburg. Ampletzer forwarded his findings to Kopkow who complied a detailed report to SS boss Heinrich Himmler. From now on, the Gestapo was fully aware of the SOE–NKVD collaboration. In fact, by February 1943, the Gestapo knew more about the Soviet agents than most of the British officers involved in the collaboration. Contrary to earlier assurances, Köhler was murdered in Mauthausen concentration camp in 1945. Boretzsky was sent to Ravensbrück. Her survival did not mean the end of her struggles. When Vienna was liberated by Soviet troops, Boretzsky was arrested by Soviet counter-intelligence Smersh as a traitor and deported to a labor camp.

Kopkow instructed Ampletzer to continue the game and pretend that the two agents had succeeded. Notifying the Moscow 'Director' that Boretzsky had lost her crystals and communication had to be made via Börner, the Germans began an elaborate deception scheme. Soon, Moscow announced the arrival of two agents called 'Nikolaus' and 'Albrecht' near Vienna. They would carry new crystals for Boretzsky. Börner should prepare safe houses for the agents.

## Françine Agazarian

According to SOE records, between 18 March and 17 June 1943, six more women were taken to France by Lysander. Françine Agazarian, a French volunteer FANY, was the first but concerns had been expressed about her in her training. In Pattinson's *Behind Enemy Lines*, she mentioned that one of Françine's instructors didn't think highly of her, reporting her as 'temperamental, might blow the gaff in a fit of jealousy, might be indiscreet in a fit of pique, sometimes exhibited temperament and caprice. Moody, jealous and unattractive to men.' She must have impressed others as she completed her training and went out by Lysander on the night of 18/19 March. She landed south of Poitiers, a few kilometres north of Marnay where, codenamed 'Marguerite' and 'Lamplighter', also known as 'Mme. Cais', she joined her husband Jack, a British agent working in Francis Suttill's PROSPER network. She worked as a courier with this and the PHYSICIAN networks, passing and collecting information and delivering money, forged documents and weapons to members in the Paris area. The Spartacus website includes her post-war comment that:

Although in the same network, my husband and I were not working together; as a radio operator he worked alone and transmitted from different locations every day. I was only responsible to Prosper (Francis Suttill) whom we all called Francois. He liked to use me for special errands because, France being my native land, I could get away from difficulties easily enough, particularly when dealing with officialdom. Francois was an outstanding leader, clear-headed, precise, confident. I liked working on his instructions, and I enjoyed the small challenges he was placing in front of me. For instance calling at town halls in various districts of Paris to exchange the network's expired ration cards (manufactured in London) for genuine new ones. Mainly I was delivering his messages to his helpers: in Paris, in villages, or isolated houses in the countryside. From time to time I was also delivering demolition material received from England. And once, with hand-grenades in my shopping bag, I travelled in a train so full that I had to stand against a German NCO. This odd situation was not new to me. I had already experienced it for the first time on the day of my arrival on French soil, when I had to travel by train from Poitiers to Paris. A very full train also. I sat on my small suitcase in the corridor, a uniformed German standing close against me. But, that first time, tied to my waist, under my clothes, was a wide black cloth belt containing bank-notes for Prosper, a number of blank identity cards and a number of ration cards; while tucked into the sleeves of my coat were crystals for Prosper's radio transmitters; the crystals had been skilfully secured to my sleeves by Vera Atkins herself, before my departure from Orchard Court. My .32 revolver and ammunition were in my suitcase. The ludicrousness of the situation somehow eliminated any thoughts of danger. In any case, I believe none of us in the field ever gave one thought to danger. Germans were everywhere, especially in Paris; one absorbed the sight of them and went on with the job of living as ordinarily as possible and applying oneself to one's work. Because I worked alone, the times I liked best were when we could be together, Prosper (Francis Suttill), Denise (Andrée Borrel), Archambaud (Gilbert Norman), Marcel (Jack Agazarian) and I, sitting round a table, while I was decoding radio messages from London; we were always hoping to read the exciting warning to stand by, which would have meant that the liberating invasion from England was imminent.

(www.spartacus.schoolnet.co.uk/SOEProsper.htm)

Maybe she was involved in the Lysander pick-up east of Tours on 5 April when Charles Besnard, an SOE agent, Mme Besnard and Adher Watt were lifted out and returned to England.

When these networks were broken by the Gestapo, arrangements were made for her and some VIPs to be lifted out on 16/17 June. One was her husband. When the Lysander landed, two women got out, Diana Rowden and Noor Inayat Khan. Françine returned to England safely and her gallantry was 'Mentioned in Dispatches'. Her husband went back, was captured along with Suttill and Borrell, survived six months of interrogation, torture and solitary confinement and was eventually executed alongside Dietrich Bonhoeffer, the Lutheran pastor, at Flossenburg concentration camp.

When Françine learned of her husband's death she was with a group of FANYs stationed at Paradiso, ME 54, the SOE's forward camp near Brindisi in Italy. From here containers were being dropped into northern Italy, Yugoslavia, Albania and Greece. Margaret Pawley, one of the other FANYs, recalled her out in the gardens of the house they shared, kicking the gravel, trying to come to terms with her loss. Just as the boat passed the Scilly Isles on Françine's return to Blighty, she was asked what she was going to do. Her reply was that she was going back to France to see if she could find out who betrayed her husband (Pawley, *In Obedience to Instructions*; www.plan-sussex-1944. net/anglais/pdf/infiltrations_into_france.pdf).

## *Julienne Aisner*

There is confusion in the records over the next women sent into France. Hugh Verity refers to landing twenty-eight-year-old Julienne Aisner in his Lysander in March 1943. She is claimed to have been the French mistress of thirty-three-year-old Henri Déricourt, who recruited her in Paris in November 1941 and gave her the task of finding safe houses for SOE agents. He arranged for her to be Lysandered to England on 16/17 March to be trained to work as a courier in the reformed INVENTOR network. Verity landed her by Lysander at Azay-sur-Cher, near Tours, on 14/15 May. Accompanying her in a double operation was forty-year-old Vera Leigh. Both were described as volunteer FANYs.

On her return, codenamed 'Claire' and also known as 'Jeannette', 'Dominique', 'Eminente', 'Ploye', 'Compositor' and 'Marie Clemence' depending on whom she met, Julienne carried messages between various members of the Resistance in and around Paris. She also worked with Charles Besnard in the FARRIER network west of Paris, with whom she developed a relationship. Whether she was aware of the suspicions about Déricourt being a double or triple agent is not known. Nicholas Bodington, another SOE agent involved with Déricourt, bought a café in Place St Michel for her to run. It was to be used as a contact point for agents seeking to escape from France and also to evacuate RAF pilots or Resistance members who needed taking to England. Noor Inayat Khan transmitted from this café when she was evading capture in Paris in August 1943.

Verity mentions Julienne coming back to England on 15 April 1944 with Besnard, whom she married on the 29th. They returned to Paris after it was liberated. In acknowledgement of her work, she was awarded the King's Medal of Commendation.

Déricourt and Mme Déricourt, according to Verity, were both picked up on 9 February 1944, when he was brought back for questioning by the SOE. She had come on a shopping trip to London and was described as short, plump, having brassy hair and travelling in a very expensive-looking fur coat. Déricourt expected to parachute back with her within the week, despite her having had no training nor taken an active part in the war.

He was returned to France, but not until after the war, to stand trial as being a German agent responsible for the arrest, torture and death of numerous French and British agents. He was released through lack of evidence. It is now acknowledged that he was in fact working for MI6 and used his SOE role as a cover. He claimed at his trial that the SOE allowed agents to be captured to distract the Germans' attention from the Allies' invasion plans. There was a rumour that the Germans had paid him four million francs for his information and that, after the war, the plane he was flying over Laos crashed in mysterious circumstances.

## *Vera Leigh*

According to Wikipedia, Vera Glass was born in Leeds in 1903 and adopted shortly after birth by Eugene Leigh, an American racehorse trainer who raced in the United States and in Europe, where he owned stables at Maisons Laffitte, near Paris. Although she had wanted to become a jockey, after completing her education she worked as a dress designer in Paris. In 1927 she went into partnership with two friends to establish a 'grand maison' known as Rose Valois in the Place Vendôme, When war broke out she joined the Resistance, helping downed Allied airmen to escape over the Pyrenees. When American women in France started being interned in September 1942, she managed to cross into Spain herself but spent several months imprisoned in Miranda de Ebro internment camp. A British embassy official managed to help get her out, into Gibraltar and back to England. There she volunteered to join the SOE, whose trainers described her as 'confident and capable with all weapons … about the best shot in the party' and 'dead keen'.

Flown back into France on 13 May 1943, Vera, codenamed 'Simone' and known as 'Almoner' and 'Suzanne Chavanne', worked as Sidney Jones's courier with the INVENTOR network north-west of Paris, and with DONKEYMAN south-east in the Ardennes. On one occasion she met her brother-in-law, who was running a safe house for Allied airmen as part of the escape line. She helped accompany them through the streets of the capital, openly socialising with Julienne Aisner. Unbeknownst to her, the Germans knew of her activities. She, Sidney and his bodyguard were arrested when they met in Paris on 30 October.

In Foot's *SOE in France*, he reported Bleicher (see pages 80-82) as saying that 'she had lodgings quite near me. For months I would watch her tripping along the pavement in the morning, so busy, so affairée. She was of no interest to me; so long as she kept out of my way; she could play at spies.' Whether this was true, he said, was uncertain but admitted that 'she did choose apartments right on the Gestapo's doorstep. One was right next to the Bony-Lafont underworld gangs; another was close to Bliecher's own apartment.'

After imprisonment, interrogation and torture in Fresnes, she was transferred to 84 Avenue Foch, the headquarters of the Security Police. From there she was sent with other 'F' Section women to Karlsruhe gaol. On 6 July 1944, forty-one-year-old Vera was sent to Natzweiler-Struthof concentration camp, where she was kept in solitary confinement.  A fellow inmate recalled her calling out for a pillow. Shortly after her arrival, she was injected with phenol and placed in the crematorium furnace. A remembrance plaque originally stated that she was murdered, but this was replaced with 'died for her country'. It can be found on the wall of the Holy Trinity church in Maisons Laffitte. Although nominated for the George Cross, the powers that be only awarded her the King's Commendation for Brave Conduct.

## Noor Inayat Khan

The next to be sent in were twenty-seven-year-old Noor Inayat Khan, forty-three-year-old  Cécile Lefort, twenty-eight-year-old Diana Rowden and Charles Skipper in a double Lysander operation. Noor was a particularly beautiful Indian princess whose life story has attracted considerable attention. According to her biographer, Shrabani Basu, her great-great-great-grandfather was Tippoo Sultan, the Tiger of Mysore and last Moghul emperor of southern India. Her father was a popular Sufi mystic who was resident in the Kremlin in Moscow in the early twentieth century and who had married an American woman. Noor's privileged background meant that she travelled widely around Europe and was enrolled at the Sorbonne in Paris.

Her name means 'Light of Womanhood'. However, its burden started when her father died when she was thirteen, which meant Noor had to look after a grieving mother and two younger brothers and a sister. She became a children's storywriter in France and published *The Tales of Jakarta*, stories of the Buddha. When Paris fell to the Germans in 1940, she fled to England with her mother, sister and brother. The bombing and strafing of lines of innocent evacuees convinced her that the German regime needed to be fought against. Calling herself Nora Baker, she joined the WAAF, where she was trained in wireless operation at Harrogate, telegraphy at Edinburgh and signal training at Forth and Medhill before being promoted to Aircraftswoman 1st Class at Abingdon. Despite being described as petite, her training officers were impressed by her quiet determination to be sent back as an agent. A deeply spiritual person, she believed she had to resist Nazism and wanted to be in the front line.

Being fluent in French, she was soon spotted by the SOE. Selwyn Jepson, SOE's interviewer and recruiter, commented afterwards:

> I see her very clearly as she was that first afternoon, sitting in front of me in that dingy little room, in a hard kitchen chair on the other side of a bare wooden table. Indeed of them all, and there were many, who did not return, I find myself constantly remembering her with a curious and very personal vividness which outshines the rest… the small, still features, the dark quiet eyes, the soft voice, and the fine spirit glowing in her.
>
> (http://www.noormemorial.org/noor.php)

In Jepson's interview file in the Imperial War Museum, he acknowledged questioning her about her loyalty.

> She said, 'My first loyalty is to India.' I said, 'I can understand that.' She said, 'If I had to choose between Britain and India I'd choose India.' I said, 'At the moment we have to choose what you feel about the Germans,' to which she said, 'I loathe the Germans, I want to see them lose this war.' So I said, 'Right, would you like to help to that end?' That was the only time when a loyalty was not directly British.
>
> (S. Jepson (1986) [9331] IWMSA)

Early 1943 saw her being posted to the Directorate of Air Intelligence, seconded to the FANY and then sent for SOE training at Wanborough Manor with Yolande Beekman and Cécile Lefort. One instructor commented that she was '*exceptionally reliable and unselfish*'. In Patrick Yarnold's book *Wanborough Manor*, he quotes Lieutenant Tongue describing her as being 'in good physical condition' and Lieutenant Corporal Gordon commenting that 'She is a person for whom I have the greatest admiration … she is not quick, studious rather than clever. Extremely conscientious.'

After paramilitary training at Arisaig in Scotland, instead of parachute training, she was sent to Thame Park, the first woman to attend their course on radio and signals training. By April her Morse speed of 18 wpm (sending) and 22 wpm (receiving) was the fastest of any trainee operator. After that, she attended the intensive course at the Beaulieu 'Finishing School'.

During her time off, Noor visited her mother and her friend Jean Overton Fuller, who went on to write her biography. In Rita Kramer's *Flames in the Field*, Noor's escorting officer is reported as saying that Noor found her mock interrogation during her SOE training 'almost unbearable … she seemed absolutely terrified …. so overwhelmed she nearly lost her voice', and that afterwards, 'she was trembling and quite blanched'.

Foot, in his history of the SOE, quoted one of Beaulieu's staff officer's reports on her that she was 'not overburdened with brains but has worked hard and showed keenness, apart from some dislike of the security side of the course. She has an unstable and temperamental personality and it is very doubtful whether she is really suitable to work in the field.' In the margin beside her report was a note which said she was 'completely unpredictable, too clumsy, too emotional and too scared of handling weapons'.

Buckmaster, the head of SOE's 'F' Section, wrote beside it, 'Nonsense'. As a Sufi Muslim, Noor was a pacifist and it is said that she left her pistol behind when she left.

In Leo Marks's *Between Silk and Cyanide*, he stated that SOE blamed Noor's mystical upbringing for teaching her that the worst sin she could commit was to lie about anything. When she was startled by an unexpected pistol shot she went into a trance, emerging from it to consult the Bible. On one of her exercises while at Beaulieu, she was cycling to a safe house to practise transmitting when a policeman stopped her and asked her what she was doing. She told him that she was training to be a secret agent and showed him her radio to prove it. After a mock interrogation by the Bristol police, the superintendent told her instructor not to waste his time with her. 'If this girl's an agent, I'm Winston Churchill.'

Yvonne Baseden, a fellow trainee, described her as a 'splendid, vague, dreamy creature, far too conspicuous – twice seen, never forgotten', who had 'no sense of security and should never have been sent to France' (Baseden, Y. 6373/2 IWM).

Her friends called her 'Bang Away Lulu' because of the loud clackety-clack of her Morse key tapping – said to be the result of fingers frozen from chilblains. However, Buckmaster was rather taken with her, describing her as a 'sensitive somewhat dreamy girl' whose French would be far more useful to the Resistance in France than it ever could be to the RAF.

SOE records show her as being given a commission as an assistant second officer in the WAAF. Her salary of £350 per year was paid into her bank account quarterly. Squadron records show she was Lysandered out with Jacques Courtard on 21/22 May, but had to return as there was no reception committee (TNA HS 9/836/5). Basu mentions that her file says she was on a 96-hour scheme in Bristol from 19 to 23 May, so the squadron records are out by a few days.

The situation in Paris was increasingly desperate and a new radio operator was needed urgently. So, instead of attending parachute training at Ringway, she, Cécile Lefort and Diana Rowden, other French Section agents, were sent to Chalfont St Giles, probably Roundwood Park, one of SOE's requisitioned country houses near Chorleywood. Here agents had to go over cover stories, check codes, learn maps of the area where they were to be sent, improve radio skills and await instructions. Noor's cover story was that she was twenty-five-year-old Jeanne-Marie Renier, a children's nurse from Blois who was now a governess looking for a job.

Pierre Raynaud, a French agent, recalled coming across Noor, before she left, sitting and poring over a railway timetable. In an interview with Kramer, he told her that Noor had no idea what it was all about, what she was going into. She gave him the impression that she thought that the trains would still be running on the pre-war schedules. In fact, he was convinced that it was intended that she be caught.

On her final visit to her mother, she shocked her by informing her of her engagement to a British officer. The officer was not identified, except it was said that he had a Norwegian mother. Noor had broken an earlier engagement while in France so hoped to marry on her return. Her mother's last words were 'Be Good!'

As she had to wait until the next full moon, she had a session with Marks to improve her coding. In his *Between Silk and Cyanide*, Marks revealed his infatuation with her and how impressed he was with her coding. He insisted she use a transposition key of at least twenty letters. If she used eighteen, he would know that she had been captured.

On 16 June, Vera Atkins drove Noor in what some agents jokingly called 'the hearse', a large station wagon, to RAF Tangmere. According to Basu:

> It was nearly evening by the time they reached Tangmere in Sussex and stopped outside the little ivy-covered cottage just opposite the main gates of the RAF station. It was partly hidden by tall hedges and could hardly be seen from the road. Though it was a summer evening, all the doors and windows were shut and the silence was almost eerie. But as the two women stepped inside, they found the hall was full of smoke and they could hear men's voices.
>
> Tangmere Cottage was a seventeenth-century house with low ceilings and thick walls. One the ground floor were two living rooms and a kitchen. One of the living rooms was used as an operations room for the crew and there was a large map of France on the wall, a table and a map chest. There was an ordinary telephone line and a scrambler 'phone line for confidential conversations. The second living room was used as the dining room and had two long trestle tables where agents and pilots often had their supper before they left. Upstairs there were five bedrooms for the pilots.

According to Verity, after a hearty farewell supper, 'when they were upstairs waiting for the bathroom, she spotted a paperback by a pilot's bed. It was called "Remarkable Women". That book will have to be rewritten after these girls have done their stuff. The only sign of nerves she said was in a slightly trembling cigarette.' As a farewell present, Vera gave her a silver bird brooch from her own jacket lapel to give her luck.

It was a double Lysander mission, piloted by Jimmy McCairns and Bunny Rymills. Vera Atkins waved goodbye to Noor, and forty-three-year-old Cécile Lefort, a courier, in the first and Charles Skepper, the organiser of the MONK circuit, and Diana Rowden, another courier, in the second. Rymills told Verity that 'Cecily looked like a vicar's wife. Her French did not seem to me to be all that hot. Noor Inayat Khan was wearing a green oilskin coat.'

Henri Déricourt was there to welcome them when they landed with their luggage in a field at Le Vieux Briollay, 7 kilometres north-east of Angers, near the confluence of the Sarthe and the Loire. Among the five returning passengers were Françine Agazarian and her husband Jack, and three political figures, Pierre Lejeune, Victor Gerson and Madame Pierre-Bloch, who recalled that while they were waiting they had all had a delicious *poularde à la crème*. Jack Agazarian had been transmitting for twenty-three different agents in Paris and needed to get out before being captured.

It was not as perfect a landing as they had hoped. Raynaud, another SOE agent, commented that a container dropped earlier had exploded on landing, drawing the attention of the authorities to the DZ. The Germans had already captured two Canadian agents and their radio and were playing a radio game back to London that they called 'The Canadian Circuit'. Details of the intrigue, double and triple crossing, can be read in Kramer's *Flames in the Field*.

Skepper and Cécile headed south; Diana headed for Dijon and, codenamed 'Madeleine', Noor first buried the pistol she had been given in case she was attacked on landing and cycled to Angers, the nearest railway station. She was to work with the CINEMA-PHONO resistance group as Henri Garry's much-needed radio operator in Paris and the Le Mans area. When Noor arrived at Garry's apartment – according to Escott – she expected to meet an old lady and made errors with the passwords so that it was some time before they eventually met. It was an intense time as, within ten days of her arrival, the Gestapo made mass arrests in the Paris Resistance groups she was working with.

Basu details how on several occasions Noor was reprimanded by Madame Balachowsky, the wife of a professor at Grignon Agricultural College, for pouring the milk in everybody's teacup the English way, milk last, and openly handing over a map to an agent in the street. However, needs must and she was allowed to transmit from Gilbert Norman's set in one of the greenhouses while the gardener kept watch. On another occasion, he picked up her folder containing her security codes from where she had left it on the hall stand by the front door.

While she was there, two sisters in the resistance, Germaine and Madeleine Tambour, had been arrested. She was probably involved in the negotiations for their release. Suttill offered a million francs to a German colonel, tearing them in half, saying the other half would be handed over when the girls were safe. The women released weren't the Tambour sisters and the Germans demanded a further half million, really annoying Suttill. He was arrested on 21 June, leaving Noor on the run with France Antelme, with whom she developed a romantic relationship.

In her citation for the Croix de Guerre there is reference to her wounding or killing some Germans when they went to search the Balachowskys' house at Grignons, but Basu found no mention of it in her report.

According to the Spartacus website, for five months she was always on the run, having to change houses as part of her mission to help Allied airmen escape and send back vital information about German troop movements. Between July and October, she is said to have sent over twenty messages in extremely difficult conditions, assisted thirty downed pilots to escape and ensured that arms and money were delivered to the right people. She pinpointed positions for parachute drops as well as arranging flights to get agents out. When the SOE eventually realised that the PROSPER, CHESTNUT and BRICKLAYER networks in northern France had completely collapsed, Noor ignored their instruction to return home in the Lysander sent for her.

In August she was the only one of SOE's radio operators still at liberty in Paris with 6,000 francs as expenses from Antelme, 1,000 from Déricourt, 40,000 from Garry as well as 400,000 for Robert Gieules, an administrator at the Compagnie Générale des Conserves. There were descriptions of her posted at all the stations and radio detection units were out to pick up her transmissions. Dyeing her hair red and then blonde and back eventually made it coarse and stiff but, along with wearing dark glasses, helped Noor evade capture, as did carrying her set around with her in a violin case and using numerous safe houses.

General Sir Colin Gubbins, the head of SOE, said that she occupied 'the principal and most dangerous post in France'. When stopped by the Gestapo as she cycled with her wireless in the front basket, she did not tell them the truth. She persuaded them that it was the latest cinematic projector. On another occasion, she managed to get a German soldier who was living in the same apartment building to help her put up the aerial wire in the tree outside without him suspecting her. Luckily for her, she met an old friend who was working for RF Section. He agreed to drive her round in his car so she could continue transmitting.

Knowing the immense risks she was taking, Buckmaster ordered her back to London. She refused until she could be guaranteed a replacement. Three times Déricourt tried to get her on flights during the August and September moons, but each time they were either cancelled or someone else got the seat. When she was assured there was definitely a Lysander coming in the October moon period she agreed, then went off air for ten days.

Raynaud told Kramer that he has evidence he thinks may indicate that she was ready to leave on one of Henri Déricourt's flights but was left behind at the last moment. When she came back on air on 18 October with a new batch of messages, the transposition key was eighteen letters long. She had been betrayed. According to Marks, Renée Garry, the sister of her circuit leader, Henri, was paid 100,000 francs (£560) for giving Noor's address to the Gestapo. This was only a tenth of what they usually offered for information leading to the arrest of British 'terrorists'. Basu suggests Renée had been in love with Antelme who, since he saw Noor, showed no further interest in her.

Although she agreed to be Lysandered out on 14 October, she was finally arrested the day before at an address that had been cancelled as a safe house before she left England. In a post about German radio games on the Special Operations Executive website, it was claimed she went to a rendezvous with, unbeknownst to her, a German agent, Karl Heldorf, who spoke with an American accent. It appears that the Gestapo knew exactly who she was and what she was doing. Whether she evaded those who tailed her, hoping she had led them to other members of the Resistance, is unknown.

Escott says she fought so viscously, biting the wrists and clawing the eyes of the man at the door that, despite his gun, he needed assistance from Gestapo headquarters. Her wireless, codes and notebooks were found in her bedside table, which gave the Germans a list of all her wireless messages sent and received. Kramer wrote that she kept them in a school exercise book 'as a result of a misunderstanding on her part of the phrase in her operational orders instructing her to "be extremely careful with the filing of your messages"'. The Gestapo then used this information to send more false messages to London. Despite Marks suspecting she had been arrested, Buckmaster refused to believe it and the radio game was played for three months. Supplies, agents and money were sent straight into the hands of the Germans, 8,572,000 francs to be exact – but probably counterfeit.

Despite interrogation, the former head of the Gestapo in Paris said that Noor never told them a thing. Escott, in her *Twentieth Century Women of Courage*, claims that they never used torture, finding that kindness drew more out of her, of which she was unaware since directly questioned she would give no information. Her main interrogator considered her utterly unworldly and truly good.

She made one escape attempt by claiming that she needed a bath and then climbing out of the fifth-floor window. Her plan was thwarted when she realised that there was no way down without jumping. A later escape attempt failed when she managed to remove the bars from the ceiling window in her cell and got onto the roof. An RAF air raid alerted the guards, who discovered her escape and caught her before she could get down.

Following this, she was held in chains in solitary confinement as she refused not to make any more escape attempts. After six weeks, on 26 November she was transferred to a prison in Pforzheim, the first British female agent to be sent to Germany. She was given a change of clothes once a week and lived on a meagre diet of potato peel or cabbage soup. After surviving almost a year, she was driven to Karlsruhe, where she met Eliane Plewman, Madeleine Damerment and Yolande Beekman in the Gestapo HQ. The four of them were escorted the following morning, first to Stuttgart, then Munich and then to Dachau. On the journey they were free to chat and reminisce.

Heinrich Himmler, the overseer of the Nazi concentration camp, had decreed that all the Führer's enemies had to die, but only after torture, indignity and interrogation 'had drained from them the last scintilla of evidence which should lead to the arrest of the others'.

Basu thought Noor might have been raped the night before her death. All four were locked in separate cells, perhaps to see if they would talk. According to the scrapbookpages website, 'A.F', a former Dutch prisoner, witnessed her execution on 12 September 1944 by Willhelm Ruppert, a sadistic SS guard.

> The SS undressed the girl and she was terribly beaten by Ruppert all over her body. She did not cry, neither said anything. When Ruppert got tired and the girl was a bloody mess he told her then he would shoot her. She had to kneel and the only word she said, before Ruppert shot her from behind through the head, was 'Liberté'. She was 30 years old.
>
> (http://www.scrapbookpages.com/Natzweiler/SOEagents2.html)

SOE records the date as 13 September. Ruppert was tried for war crimes after the war and executed by the Americans. A square in Noor's home town of Suresnes, Paris, was named in her honour and a blue plaque is placed outside her London residence of 4 Taviton Street. Noor was 'Mentioned in Dispatches', awarded the MBE, the Croix de Guerre and was one of only three wartime women who were given the George Cross. Part of her citation for the honour, quoted on the Spartacus website, reads:

> She refused to abandon what had become the principal and most dangerous post in France, although given the opportunity to return to England, because she did not wish to leave her French comrades without communications, and she hoped also to rebuild her group.

Plans are in place to erect a memorial to Noor in Gordon Square, London, where she used to take a book and sit reading on one of the benches. It was only a few minutes' walk from 4 Taviton Street, where she stayed before being sent on her mission. A bust sculpted by Karen Newman is planned to be erected in the square. It will be the first for an Asian woman in this country and will stand for peace and religious harmony, the principles Noor Inayat Khan believed in (http://www.noormemorial.org).

## Diana Rowden

Also landed with Noor was Diana Rowden, one of the female agents featured in Rita Kramer's *Flames in the Field*. Diana, codename 'Paulette', went to work as a courier with John Starr's Acrobat network in the Jura Mountains of south-east France. Rather stocky, of medium height with red hair, she was a Scot who had been brought up by an English mother on the French Riviera, brought back to boarding school in England and, fluent in Spanish and Italian, enrolled at the Sorbonne like Noor just as war broke out. In the confusion and panic, she volunteered for the ambulance corps of the British Expeditionary Force and remained in unoccupied France after the armistice. During the confusion, she lost contact with her mother and it was not until mid-1941 that she managed to escape over the Pyrenees into Spain and made her way back to England.

Diana promptly enlisted with the WAAF and quickly got promotion before a minor operation meant she was sent to Torquay to recuperate in a convalescent home. Here she met Squadron Leader William Simpson, a pilot shot down over France who had managed to escape. They struck up a friendship and, as he worked in the French Section of SOE, he arranged for Diana to be interviewed. She impressed them, saying she was 'very anxious to return to France and work against the Germans.' Against her mother's wishes, she joined and, although her training report said she wasn't very agile, she had plenty of courage and was physically quite fit. Her grenade throwing was very good, she was a very good shot and did some excellent stalks.

On landing, Diana was met by Henri Déricourt and, using the cover name 'Juliette Rondeau', stayed in a dark back attic room in the Hotel Commerce in Lons-le-Saunier, where the proprietor did not worry about registration. Despite the relatively safe accommodation, Starr thought her accent might give her away so he insisted she moved in with him at Chateau Andelot at St Amour, near Switzerland. She travelled constantly by bicycle up and down mountainous roads and forest tracks, locating dropping grounds and landing strips, assisting in reception committees and delivering instructions and taking messages back to Starr. Occasionally she took the train to rendezvous with agents in Marseille, Lyon, Besançon, Montbéliard and Paris. To avoid a German police check of her forged papers, she locked herself in the toilet on one trip and got away with not being searched.

Some of the plastic explosive delivered from Tempsford to the Acrobat network was used in an attack on the converted Peugeot car factory at Sochaux, near Montbéliard. Harry Rée, known as 'César', worked with Diana, Starr and John Young, their Scottish radio operator, before taking charge of the neighbouring Stockbroker network. The factory was now manufacturing aircraft engine parts for the Luftwaffe and tank turrets, tank engines and tank tracks for the Wehrmacht. It had been targeted by the RAF in mid-July 1943 but many of the bombs fell on the heavily populated residential area near the railway line, killing hundreds of civilians.

Rée suggested to SOE that precision sabotage would be a more efficient and less risky way of putting the works out of operation. Using an inspired tactic, he contacted Rodolphe Peugeot, the boss who was thought to be sympathetic to the Allied cause, and propositioned him. When the RAF attacked again, there was no way of estimating how much damage they would do. Should he co-operate with the Resistance, a well-placed explosion could cripple production but not destroy the plant. To prove his own credentials, Rée arranged through Diana's messages for the BBC to read out a special *avis* or *message personnel*.

It worked and, in Buckmaster's 1992 obituary in *The Daily Telegraph*, it was said he used photographic evidence of Rée's success to convince 'Bomber' Harris at Bomber Command HQ that the SOE were capable of blowing up targets which Harris had maintained were better left to his air crews.

Rée was Lysandered out with Jacqueline Nearne; they both returned safely and starred as SOE agents Felix and Cat in the 1944 RAF film *Now the Story Can Be Told*, which detailed some of their operations in France. There was a plan to go with the propaganda film unit to France but the bad weather meant they had to shoot the action in some fields in Bedfordshire, probably close to the airfield as several shots were of RAF Tempsford. There are also shots of Wanborough Manor, where the agents were trained; Brickendonbury Manor, where industrial sabotage lessons were given; Gibraltar Farm, where the agents got their parachutes and final briefing; and planes on the runway at Tempsford Airfield.

Rée recalled in an interview in the Imperial War Museum that:

> The first sabotage was about the beginning of November and they decided they'd blow up a whole transformer house where all the electricity came into the factory. About five men were involved, Frenchmen who worked in the factory. They had their pistols in the pockets of their overalls and they had their explosives, plastic blocks with room for a detonator, in their pockets too. There was a wonderful carelessness about the whole thing. They were playing football with the German guards outside the transformer house – somebody had forgotten to get the key – and in playing football one of them dropped his plastic block of explosive and one of the German guards who was playing football pointed it out to him. 'You've dropped something, sir, I think.' He put it back in his pocket. That was absolutely typical. The transformer house blew up and after they went on throughout the whole of the rest of the war fixing these magnetic blocks to machines and enormously reducing production. They also arranged for production figures to be produced which we sent back to London.
>
> (Rée, H. 13064, IWM)

Barely a month after Diana's arrival in France, Rée was arrested, betrayed by a double agent. Escott's *Mission Improbable* provides a detailed account of Diana's mission. Knowing that her details would be circulated by the French authorities, she dyed her hair, changed its style, got rid of her old clothes, borrowed more modest clothing, assumed another identity and moved to work in a bistro and shop in Epy, a small hamlet a few miles away. She stayed there for three weeks before joining John Young, the radio operator, in the sawmill of the Chateau of Andelot-les-St-Amour. Her courier work took her to various groups working in south-east France along the Swiss and Italian frontiers. In the middle of November, they got a message from London informing Young that a new agent, codename 'Benoit', was coming. He arrived on the 18th with instructions hidden in a matchbox and a letter from Young's wife. Diana went with him to pick up his suitcase from the dropping ground at Lons-le-Saunier and had a drink at the local Café Strasbourg, one of the network's mail drops. They got back at about six in the evening and the doors were flung open just as dinner was being prepared and the Feldgendamerie, the German military police, stormed in. With no time to react, the agents were handcuffed and taken away for questioning.

The mail drop may have been identified; they could have been followed but the fake 'Benoit' was said to have returned to the house to search for the wireless set and crystals. In Cookridge's *They Came from the Sky*, he claims that Maugenet, one of the agents dropped on 15/16 November, was captured by the Gestapo shortly after he arrived, and he was then impersonated by an English-speaking French agent who successfully identified Diana.

She was taken to Avenue Foch, the Gestapo headquarters in Paris. After being interrogated for two weeks, she was transferred to Fresnes Prison, where she met Odette and other female SOE prisoners. Less than a month before D-Day she was sent to Karlsruhe and, in early July, taken with Vera Leigh, Andrée Borrel and Sonia Olschanezky to the Natzweiler concentration camp. Around 2200 hours on 6 July 1944, she was called out of her cell, escorted towards a large hut by two guards and told to lie down on a bed for a typhus injection. It was not. It was a massive dose of phenol. Her body was then taken to the crematorium and incinerated.

In honour of her work for the Resistance, Diana was awarded the MBE but, according to Escott, it was withdrawn when it was discovered after the war that her death had pre-dated the award. However, she was 'Mentioned in Dispatches'. The French recognised her better, awarding her the Chevallier de la Légion d'Honneur and the Croix de Guerre. Andrée was awarded the MBE and 'Mentioned in Dispatches' as well as being given the King's Commendation for Brave Conduct, the Croix de Guerre and the Medaille de Resistance.

## Sonia Olschanezky

Although not one of the agents sent out from Tempsford, Sonia Olschanezky has been mentioned as one of the women executed alongside some of SOE's agents. The Spartacus website reveals that Sonia was a German Jew, born in Chemnitz on Christmas Day 1923. Her father ran a lingerie shop in Paris during the 1930s, but Sonia did not want such work. Her ambition was to be a dancer, but she had to work as an au pair. When war broke out, aged only nineteen, she joined one of the Resistance groups in the city as an *agent de liaison*. In June 1942 the Vichy government started implementing the Nazi order to round up the Jews in France. Sonia was held at Drancy internment camp with about 2,000 others waiting for transportation to Germany. Her mother managed to obtain her release after providing false papers suggesting that Sonia had 'economically valuable skills' and after paying a to bribe to the appropriate German official.

Codenamed 'Tania' and also known as 'Suzanne Ouvrard', she worked as a courier for the JUGGLER network between Châlons-sur-Marne and their headquarters in the rue Cambon, near the Place de la Concorde. Engaged to Jacques Weil, the second in command, she was promoted to *sous-lieutenant* in November 1943, when the organiser managed to escape into Switzerland. She evaded the round up of contacts in Vhalons-sur-Marne and worked in Paris as well as she could until she was arrested in the Café Soleil d'Or and taken to the Gestapo Headquarters on Avenue Foch on 22 January 1944. After a time in Fresnes, she was taken to Natzweiler, where she was injected with phenol and cremated with the other women on 6 July. She was only twenty-one.

## Cécile Lefort

The only Irish agent sent into France was Cécile Lefort. Born Cécile Mackenzie in London in 1900, she worked as a surgeon's receptionist in Paris in the 1920s. In 1925 she married Monsieur Lefort, a respected Parisian doctor who had a large villa outside the village of St Cast, near Dinard in Brittany. There she enjoyed sailing and became an accomplished yachtswoman. When war broke out, all British nationals in France were advised to leave. Accordingly, she left her husband to his practice and returned to England. Despite being over the age limit, she was accepted by the WAAF as a policewoman but, as with Noor, her knowledge of French brought her to the attention of the SOE and she joined in 1943.

Escott mentioned that, while in training, Cécile told a friend about her villa and the friend in turn told a fellow agent in de Gaulle's RF section who was looking for a safe beach to use as an escape route to England. She gave him her antique Irish ring, telling him to show it to her maid at the villa, who would then let him stay. Thus started what became known as the 'Var' escape line, taking Allied airmen back across the Channel when there was a rising tide on moonless nights, when a rowing boat would land and take the thankful passengers to a waiting fishing boat.

Yarnold mentions Lieutenant Tongue as doubting that Cécile had the ability to achieve much and Lieutenant Gordon commenting that she was 'very ladylike and very English'. Her supreme fitness allowed her to complete her training with ease.

According to Escott, Bunny Rymills, the pilot who flew her across the Channel in a Lysander from Tempsford, accidentally left on his transmitter and the pilot of the following plane could hear his conversation:

Now madame, we are approaching your beautiful country – isn't it lovely in the moonlight? Back came an answer in soft accented tones, 'Yes, I think it is heavenly. What is that town over there?' He replied, and continued pointing out all the local landmarks as they passed over them, a running commentary for which the listening Germans, if there were any, would have been most grateful.

After landing, she made her way south to work as a courier for Francis Cammaerts in the JOCKEY network. Codenamed 'Alice', she worked up and down the Rhône valley.

After a brief trip to Paris with Noor, during which she in all likelihood broke security rules and met up with her husband, she made her way south by train to Montélimar. There she met Cammaerts, who had her accompany him on his visits to organisers and agents in Toulouse, Clermont Ferrand, Agen, Lyon and Digne. Escott commented that she

> carried out her errands conscientiously. She lived every day with the spectre of capture, whether in shelter or on the route, at rest or at work. She knew that any small slip of hers or those around her might give her away. She lived with fear. Timid by nature, she always bore in mind the risks not only to herself, but also those with her and the far wider network of helpers in her own and other circuits. Poor Cécile! How often must she have recalled her comfortable past. Did she ever regret her decision to take on such dangerous work? Was her love for her husband – still out of her reach – a sufficient motive? It was a hard and unforgiving life and at 43 years she was not as young and resilient as most of the others who undertook it. To her organiser she was a rather quiet, secretive, shy person, with a perpetually surprised look about her and to a young man she seemed old.

Cammaert's network, using explosives dropped in containers by 138 Squadron, blew up railway lines, power stations and industrial targets. The attack on the hydro-electric power station on the River Durance near Largentière halted production in the factories making aluminium for German planes. Consequently, there was a search for the saboteurs.

Having only been in France for three months, on 15 September 1943, Cécile was betrayed while she was visiting a 'blown address', a whitewashed villa belonging to Raymond Daujat, a corn merchant and Resistance leader in Montélimar. The constant travelling and nervous strain had made her so exhausted that she was desperate for a comfortable bed for the night. The police arrived early the following morning. Daujat escaped by climbing through a window but, according to Escott, she was caught in the cellar and brutally interrogated at the Gestapo prison in Lyon. In theory she would not have known Cammaert's whereabouts, as he kept tight control over his network's security.

Her arrest and that of the other two women who arrived by Lysander in June made Escott suspect betrayal. All arrangements, she noted, had been made by Henri Déricourt.

> It is also strange that of *all* the WAAF who landed in this way, none survived. Were they betrayed before they landed and were they living on borrowed time before they were taken? Had the Germans first let them go, hoping to be led to more important agents? If so it was a foolish gamble and the German plans must have misfired, as they could not have realised the amount of harm that could be done by leaving the girls on the loose, added to which they almost certainly lost track of each of the girls for some time, although there was always the likelihood that one might later be recognised, as may have happened to Cécile. Noor and Diana were only caught by being betrayed. It shows therefore that either the German intelligence service was remarkably inept, or that the girls had learned their security drill in Britain very thoroughly to stay free for so long.

From Lyon she was transferred to Avenue Foch in Paris and then transported to Ravensbrück. During quarantine, she was diagnosed as having cancer of the stomach, was operated on successfully by the camp doctor and allowed to recuperate in the hospital block on a diet of vegetable soup and a type of porridge. However, following the Allied bombing raids and invasions of Poland and France, the prison staff became more brutal. Sometime in early 1945 she was allocated work duties at the Judenlager, where she was expected to work on a diet of acorn coffee, turnip soup and a little dry bread. Overcrowding meant that there were five or six women to a bed. Clothing and mattresses were infested with lice, and typhoid and dysentery were widespread.

Escott mentioned that Mary Lindell, the former Red Cross nurse and escape line organiser, tried to get Cécile transferred onto a knitting group back in the main camp. Mary signed a form authorising three women's return but, when one refused to go, Cécile stayed behind to persuade her to go. When she went to join the others, they had gone. She was left behind. It is believed, Escott suggests, that she died from an overdose of a white 'sleeping' powder, often issued by a fellow inmate. Otherwise, like many of the others, she was gassed later that month. There was no trace of her body when the camp was overtaken at the end of the war. It was presumed to have been cremated with the others. Afterwards she was 'Mentioned in Dispatches' and awarded the Croix de Guerre.

## Eliane Plewman

There were suspicious circumstances surrounding the dropping of the fifth female agent Clark mentions as having been taken out of Tempsford. On 14 August 1943, Flight Lieutenant Cussen of 161 Squadron flew into the Jura Mountains on operation MESSENGER. On seeing a flashing 'K' to the south-east of Lons-le-Saunier he dropped a package, closely followed by twenty-five-year-old Eliane Plewman, a French SOE agent and member of the Resistance.

Born in Marseille to a Spanish-French mother and British father, Eliane Browne-Batroli was educated in England and Spain and worked in an import company in Leicester when she finished college. She handled business correspondence in Spanish, English, French and German which, when war broke out, allowed her to take up work in the British embassies in Madrid and Lisbon. By 1942 she was working for the Spanish section of the Ministry of Information. That summer she married Tom Plewman, a British army officer, and shortly afterwards was recruited to work in the SOE as a volunteer FANY. Her husband couldn't deter her from undertaking her training and returning to France. Her brother Albert was parachuted into France with Robert Benoist, a retired Grand Prix racing car driver. On her training course she met Bob Maloubier, a French agent, who recalled in an interview with Pattinson that he warned her that:

> If you're too good you'll be taken on as a radio operator. Radio operators usually don't do anything at all. They stay in, in hiding. The others do some type of sabotage, they go round, they form reception committees for parachute. Basically [if you become a radio operator] you'll be in a remote place. It's very dangerous too.

Eliane was driven to Tempsford and flown out, but had to be returned when the pilot aborted the drop. Despite shattered nerves, she was determined to try again. The next flight was more successful. Cussen reported that the reception was laid out about two kilometres south-south-west of the agreed DZ, but that Plewman agreed to be dropped near the package. No wonder. According to Clark, it contained one million francs (£5,600) of SOE money designated for Charles Skepper's Monk circuit. As no one was there to meet her, she found and hid the briefcase. Imagine how she felt when it was later found empty. Codenamed 'Gaby' and sometimes known as 'Eliane Prunier' or 'Dean', she joined Skepper on the Mediterranean coast as his courier, travelling by train or *gamogenetic*, a charcoal-powered Ford truck, between Marseille, St Raphael and Roquebrune, arranging parachute drops and sabotage operations.

As Eliane was already known in this area, she risked encountering old acquaintances as she went on her everyday business. When the network was infiltrated by a woman in the pay of the Gestapo, Skepper was arrested. She and twenty-year-old Arthur Steele, a London music student, tried unsuccessfully to rescue him and were arrested in the attempt on 27 March 1944. After three weeks of physically tough interrogation in Les Baumettes Prison near Marseille, she was transferred to Fresnes Prison. She is said to have had the amazing courage to hint to her German interrogator that, if he took her out for a good dinner, she might be amenable to telling him more about the circuit in which she was employed. Having eaten the dinner, she calmly announced that she had changed her mind. The torture used by the Gestapo included being prodded between the eyes with a very powerful electric current. Steele was hanged at Buchenwald. Skepper was executed in Hamburg.

On 13 May 1944, the Germans transferred her, Yolande Beekman and Madeleine Damerment to a civilian women's prison at Karlsruhe from where, on 10 September, they were transferred to the Gestapo HQ to meet Noor Inayat Khan. The following morning they were transferred to Dachau, where they were locked in separate cells. Within hours of arriving, they were dragged past the barracks, forced to kneel by the crematorium and executed with a single shot to the head. Like many of the other women, Eliane was awarded the MBE, the King's Commendation for Brave Conduct and the Croix de Guerre.

## Beatrice 'Yvonne' Cormeau

On the night of 22 August 1943, Squadron Leader Ratcliff of 161 Squadron took off in his Halifax on a double mission. His first was to drop thirty-three-year-old Beatrice 'Yvonne' Cormeau with eight containers near the village of St Antoine du Queyret in the Gironde, roughly 44 kilometres east of Bordeaux.

Escott's research showed that she was born Yvonne Biesterfeld in 1909 in Shanghai, where her father was a British consular official. The family moved around Belgium, France and Switzerland, where, after completing her education, she worked as a secretary to the legal adviser in the British embassy. She married Charles Cormeau, an army officer, before the war and had a daughter. According to her obituary in *The Times*:

> In the catastrophe of May 1940, her husband was killed in action. Her mother, who stayed in Belgium, was packed off to Ravensbrück, from which she never returned. Yvonne managed to get to England with her two-year-old infant, and decided, on reflection, that it would be better for her child in the long run if she went away to help to defeat Hitler, horrible though the thought of separation was. She joined the WAAF

in the autumn of 1941. She was able to pass for a Frenchwoman, and so moved into the Special Operations Executive a year later. After passing the para military and security schools, she was trained as a wireless-telegraphy operator as well as a parachutist, codenamed 'Annette', and dropped into France on August 22–23, 1943, to work for Colonel George Starr, codenamed 'Hilaire', a principal figure in the Resistance in south-west France.

(www.timesonline.co.uk/tol/comment/obituaries/article3752092.ece)

Her four-year-old daughter Yvette, whom she had to leave behind, was initially sent to a nursery school in Bristol but, when that was disbanded, Yvonne decided that, rather than lose contact with her daughter if the next boarding school was evacuated or closed, she put her in a country convent of Ursuline nuns near Oxford.

Identified early as a potential radio operator, Yvonne was sent to Thame Park in Oxfordshire, another of SOE's large country houses. The sixteen-week course included physical training; using, diagnosing faults in and repairing radios; learning how to encode and decode messages; mastering Morse code; typing at between eighteen and twenty-two words per minute; and memorising all the security checks necessary during transmission. Escott commented that when Yvonne was in the field, she was so accurate, sensible and careful that there was rivalry among the FANY at the home station as to who would get her messages, and the Resistance members would not let her have anything to do with explosives because her fingers were so vital for contacting London.

In an interview recording held at the Imperial War Museum, she revealed her motivation for joining the SOE.

> After my husband was killed I joined the WAAF, the Women's Auxiliary Air Force. Well, going into the forces, one had to fill in a great number of questionnaires and when they asked, 'What have you as special qualities?' I put down my knowledge of German and Spanish and bilingual French. After a while this got through to the Ministry, of course, and then, as they were looking for people for SOE, I was interrogated. I received a telex from London asking that I should come down to town as soon as possible to see a certain Captain Selwyn Jepson. He asked if I was pleased with my work that I was doing and then he spoke about France. France at that time was divided into two parts, the northern part was completely occupied by the enemy and the southern part was so-called unoccupied, so we talked about that and he suddenly asked me if I would return to occupied France. I replied in the affirmative. I thought this was something my husband would have liked me to do, and, as he was no longer there to do it, I thought it was time for me to do it.
>
> (Cormeau, Y. 7385/9; 31572/1 IWM)

The interview went on to shed light on the instruction the SOE provided for women during their training, and on Yvonne's experiences when she landed on French soil again.

> They gave us some ideas about living an operating in France but they said, 'You've got to judge when you're on the spot. Things might change by the time you're there. All we can tell you is that there may be certain days of the week when you can't have certain

drinks or foods in certain cafés, so don't ask, just try and see what is on the menu and advertised for those days. Please don't do too much dyeing of your hair or have very noticeable make-up and things like that because you'll fall foul at some time or other. Try and dress as they do locally as much as possible. If you're going to live in the country, don't have a manicure, don't have this, don't have that …

Slowly but surely my chute opened and I didn't even feel the jerk on my shoulders. It was only three hundred feet so it wasn't a long drop. I took off my jumpsuit immediately and handed it to the French people who were meeting me. I only had a handbag, with my money in, which was strapped behind my back, cushioning the lower vertebrae of the spine so that the shock wouldn't damage anything. I was dressed in what I thought was normal for France: a black coat and skirt with a silk blouse and black shoes. My ankles were bandaged, as I was in shoes and not jump boots.

Her destination was very rural but, as it was the first time an agent had been dropped in that area, many people came out to welcome her, making her very worried that it might attract unwanted attention. As soon as she could, she acquired a bicycle and moved to her safe house to begin transmissions. Before long, she was called to go south to work as a radio operator for George Starr's WHEELWRIGHT circuit. He was a friend of her husband whom she had met in England before the war.

Using the codename 'Annette' and 'Fairy' and 'Sarafan' as aliases, dark-haired, green-eyed Yvonne had her base in a farmhouse in Castelnau sur L'Auvignon, a remote hilltop village in the south-west of France with no electricity and no running water, just a well. Only one of the three radio sets dropped with her was workable, so she had to carry the 20-pound set around with her whenever she wanted to transmit. She followed the instructions never to transmit from the same spot twice, whether indoors or outdoors. Her strict adherence to SOE's rules allowed her to transmit and receive messages for thirteen months with impunity.

Her travels took her to the Dordogne, Gascony and the foothills of the Pyrenees. According to Escott, she had several disguises, such as a district nurse, a children's nurse and, for a very short time, a cow minder. When she went to the Pyrenees she would transmit from the edge of a wood, avoiding the leaves which deadened the transmission. This made it virtually impossible for the German *gonios*, radio detection vans operated by the *Funkhorchdienst*, to pinpoint her.

Starr ran SOE's largest network, for which Yvonne arranged 140 arms and supply drops by 161 Squadron. According to Foot, she broke a cardinal rule by transmitting 400 messages from the same location for thirteen months. Escott suggests otherwise, saying she travelled widely, sometimes up to 60 kilometres a day, carrying her set in a basket on the front of her bicycle covered with vegetables or other items of shopping, and transmitted from bedrooms, the backroom of shops or cafés, in a loft, a barn or an outhouse. She never stayed anywhere more than three days. When she first started transmitting, it was three times a week. During the invasion in June 1944, it was as often as three times a day.

It was her good fortune that instructions were shortly given from London to the effect that the former fixed times and wavelengths of messages that all operators had been instructed to keep and called 'skeds' (schedules) were to be made far more flexible and varied, so that the German detectors would find it harder to focus on any regular pattern of signals. Incoming messages were also grouped at night, a practice that was far safer if more disruptive of sleep. Additionally, agents were instructed not to transmit for longer than 15–20 minutes – shorter if possible and never more than 30 minutes at the maximum. In the early days many operators had been caught beside their sets because of the long, wordy messages upon which their organisers had unwisely insisted. Yvonne had shorter material and she did not start putting it into cipher by the double transposition method until an hour before her call. The key to her cipher was drawn from a sequence of figures, cut from a jumbled assortment printed on a silk handkerchief, which she preferred to use rather than one-time pads, as these were both bulky and difficult to hide and transport. Silk slips and messages were then burned as soon as transmissions were completed, so that nothing remained if she were subsequently discovered. The same went for any incoming traffic, which she promptly decoded and passed to her organiser or gave the instructions to those concerned. She was meticulous about the security of her messages, her set and her location, her care paying dividends.

She was lucky. Such was the success of the *gonios*, the radio detection teams, that the average time before capture of SOE's radio operators was only six weeks. The Germans knew that someone was transmitting in that region but had been unable to locate her. They hoped to attract someone to inform them of her whereabouts with a reward of five million francs, half of that offered for Starr.

During her time in France, Yvonne organised 153 successful drops of arms, explosives and supplies. To assist her she trained two local men, a butcher and a former radio operator in the disbanded French Air Force, but they were not provided with her ciphers or other secret material. Colonel Buckmaster, in his book *Specially Employed*, said of her that 'she was always incredibly precise in her activity. She sent about 400 coded messages under conditions of great strain without a single miscode.' He reported how, in the summer of 1943, the RAF dropped some leaflets near Condom. The following day Yvonne sent a vigorous protest:

ORDERED BY BOCHES TO CLEAN UP LEAFLETS FROM OUR BEST PARACHUTE GROUND. SPENT ALL SUNDAY PICKING UP. LUMBAGO VERY PAINFUL. TELL RAF TO DROP LEAFLETS IN SEA NEXT TIME.

The strain of her work, cycling everywhere, and lack of good food and sleep led to her health declining. Her weight dropped to just over six stone (42 kg) and she suffered from insomnia.

She never carried the pistol she was given, arguing that if she was found with it at a check point, she would be arrested. Carrying a radio would have meant arrest, interrogation and almost certainly torture. 'You had to be very steady. You couldn't afford to feel exhilarated. After I'd come through a difficult check, I would feel washed through. I felt the strain – I couldn't help it.'

Beside her set she had a pair of field glasses through which she could look out over three miles of countryside which was closely guarded by Spanish members of the

Maquis. There was also a contingent of Starr's men based in the village which had been specially trained and were ready for action.

> The identity they gave me, with cards and all that, was quite good, but as soon as I arrived and showed these papers to my boss, he told me, 'Look, the quality of the paper is far too good. I'll get you some new cards.' So those were changed. I went out with ration cards, too, but again the paper was a bit too good. Paper had deteriorated in France.
>
> I'd left my wedding ring and engagement ring in England but my finger was unfortunately marked by the wedding ring after a certain number of years. One very observant woman told me, 'There's a shiny line on your finger.'
>
> I must admit to butterflies floating in my tummy the whole time. You had to be careful. You had to have eyes in the back of your head. The life was totally different to anything I'd experienced previously …
>
> You never knew, man or woman, who was prepared to give information to the Gestapo. Sometimes it was a personal vendetta between two families. Other times it was just for money.
>
> One day I met 'Hilaire'. I'd gone to meet him, to give him messages, instructions from London. And as we got near a very small village, cycling, we saw on the shutters of a house, which served both as the schoolroom and the town hall, two identikit-type drawings of ourselves. So we looked at them, looked at each other, we didn't say anything and we split up. I went back north and he went south.

Despite having to lead a fairly solitary life as a radio operator, she quickly noticed that every local woman wore a necklace, bracelet or other ornament. She duly bought a selection but then discovered that peasant women didn't wear any. In her debrief after returning to England she said, 'I was asked to look after the cows, take them out in morning and bring them back at sunset … Before going, the farmer's wife had told me, "Don't wear a watch. No woman who looks after cows would be able to afford a watch."' Like many British women in the 1940s, Yvonne was a heavy smoker and found it so difficult in Castelnau to find any tobacco – except on the black market at exorbitant prices – that she had to give it up.

Yvonne had an outstanding record, especially when 'Wanted' posters appeared in her neighbourhood with an accurate sketch of her appearance. She even survived being shot in the leg. On one occasion after keeping a rendezvous with Starr, their car was stopped at a road block.

> We'd been told the Germans were coming on the roads to the east and west so we took one due south, hoping to escape them. We hadn't gone fifteen kilometres when we were face to face with a personnel carrier. We were stopped and told to get out of the car, then they put us in a ditch with two soldiers. Both had a pistol, one in my back and one in Hilaire's back. The feldwebel was telling somebody on the radio that he'd stopped a tobacco inspector and a woman, the woman had a district nurse's card on her, what was he to do with them?
>
> My perspiration was coming down and flies were sticking in my perspiration and I couldn't move, because if I'd moved they would have shot me immediately. Waiting,

waiting. Then the crackle came. 'Get in the car' – which we did at once. Suddenly he asked me what was in the case, which had been thrown on to the back seat, which, of course, was my radio set. I opened it. I knelt on the seat and showed it to him. He asked me what it was. I said, 'Radio,' which in German, means X-ray as well as radio-set, and, in view of the fact that I was meant to be a district nurse, he thought it was an X-ray set, he said, 'Go,' and we got out very fast. The engine was already running.

On another occasion, she managed to escape into the countryside, pursued by gunfire, when the Gestapo made an early morning call. Following D-Day, she, Starr and his courier, Anne-Marie Walters (referred to later), had to become much more mobile. She distinguished herself by keeping meticulously to the transmission times, once during a gun battle in which a bullet tore through her skirt. Disguised as a cowgirl, Yvonne managed to escape over the Pyrenees but returned when the pressure was off and accompanied Hilaire to liberate Toulouse.

The occasion was one of great celebration. Escott told how the crowds dropped to the ground when a loud bang rang out from the middle of the procession. It had not been a sniper but the tyre on their car bursting. When the crowd realised, there were laughs and smiles and the car was lifted bodily onto the shoulders of the Resistance, carrying Yvonne and Hilaire into Place Wilson, the main square. According to her obituary in *The Times*, like Hilaire 'she was soon dismissed back to England by a furious General de Gaulle, who could not abide any resisters who were not under his own direct command'.

One of the last messages she received was an instruction to rendezvous with the Chief Test Pilot who had been specially flown in from Farnborough. She had to help him find and bring back to England the black box and a wheel from the latest German Heinkel Bomber. With the help of her contacts, they located the items and she accepted the proffered lift home on 23 September 1944. The *Times* article went on:

> After the war, she and her daughter were reunited, and she settled down to the job of bringing up the girl. She was one of the earliest members of the Special Forces Club, served for many years on its committee, and formed in and around it many new friendships. She became a British citizen, and was appointed MBE. The French were more generous with honours, awarding her both a Croix de Guerre and membership of the Legion of Honour. She was tireless in promoting Anglo-French friendship.
> (www.timesonline.co.uk/tol/comment/obituaries/article3752092.ece )

What it did not mention was that, in November 1944, she accompanied the senior members of SOE's 'F' Section and, over a period of several months, toured the main centres of resistance activity in France, trying to investigate the work and fate of the SOE agents and the French who had helped them. Awards and compensation were arranged and equipment recovered which could be used in the continuing war in the Far East. Escott noted that Yvonne was pleased by the results in her area,

> where from a centre set up there she helped to identify those who had suffered most, and whose distress gifts of money, clothing and, particularly in agricultural areas, farm implements and seed, would serve to alleviate.

## Hilde Meisel and Anne Beyer

Sometime during the September 1944 moon period, two more women were infiltrated into France. There was no mention of them by Clark or Verity. I only discovered their story while researching the story behind the first US-trained OSS agents sent out of Tempsford. Jupp Kappius had escaped from Germany in 1937. For whatever reason he was sent back without a radio set, so two German emigrants, Hilde Meisel and Anne Beyer, were trained and sent out to be his couriers.

An article by Doria Maria Lynch on 'The Labor Branch of the Office of Strategic Services' and the Jupp Kappius website reveal that Hilde was born in 1914, the second daughter of non-orthodox, middle-class Jewish parents in Vienna in 1914. During her childhood she suffered from thyroid problems and often visited Switzerland for treatment. It was during her education in Berlin that her sister Margot introduced her to a social revolutionary youth group called *Schwarzer Haufen* (Black Crowd).

During a visit to London to see her uncle, the renowned composer and conductor Edmund Meisel, she learned more about the activities of the International Socialist Combat League (ISK). Shocked by growing anti-Jewish sentiment in 1930s Germany, which stopped her and other Jewish friends from studying, and by having several friends arrested and held in concentration camps, she decided in 1935 to emigrate to London. Using the name of Hilda Monte, she studied art and then economics at the London School of Economics and mixed with opponents of Hitler's National Socialism.

In 1938, to avoid deportation, she entered a sham marriage with the English caricaturist John Olday, a British citizen, and was then able to publish anti-German articles in *The Vanguard*, the *Socialist Wait*, *Left News* and *The Tribune*. She must have been known to Willi Eichler, the chairman of the ISK and editor of its magazine, *The Spark*. He too had emigrated in the 1930s to England, where he continued his Socialist editorial work.

In Joseph Persico's *Piercing the Reich*, he described her as 'a quiet woman in her early thirties who reflected the resolute simplicity of this Socialist sect. Her brown hair was pulled back in a tight, severe bun. She wore no make up and dressed with no concession to style.'

According to an article in the *Sunday Times* on 1 May 1939, twenty-five-year-old Hilda approached George Russel Strauss, Parliamentary Secretary to the Ministry of Transport and MP for Lambeth North, with a scheme to assassinate Hitler. He had been financing 'Union Time', her secret anti-Nazi organisation, and described Hilda as a heroine of the German underground group. She and a young German, Georg Elser (called 'A' in the article), went back to Germany, supposedly to take news, books and letters. On 8 November, he put some explosives in the central pillar of the famous Bürgerbräu beer cellar in Munich and set a fuse for it to go off at 21.21 hours. Hitler arrived early, fearing an RAF attack timed for his benefit, but left at 21.15, six minutes before the whole middle section of the roof collapsed on the rostrum he had been speaking on.

Seven people were killed and sixty-three injured. Georg was caught and later executed but Hilde was able to make her way to Switzerland, where, shortly before the war broke out, she and three women she knew in the ISK – Anna Beyer, Hanna Bertholet and Aenne Kappius (Jupp's wife) – were invited to the American embassy and told that they were looking for women to train as saboteurs and be sent into Germany. They all rejected the idea.

Hilde returned to England via Portugal in 1939, where her publications, interviews on the BBC and talks she gave in schools on what was happening in German-occupied Europe brought her to the attention of Ministry of Economic Warfare. She was taken on to work in their propaganda department, which broadcast radio messages into Germany and produced pamphlets and newspapers that were taken to RAF Tempsford and RAF Harrington to be dropped by the Special Duties Squadrons.

As early as March 1943, the London Labour Division contemplated sending four agents, two men and two women, to infiltrate the Ruhr, Germany's industrial heartland. Unable at that time to mount clandestine missions into Germany on its own, the OSS proposed that they worked with SOE on a joint venture. The OSS would supply the agents and the finance. The SOE would provide the training and the flights.

Anne Beyer was born in Frankfurt in 1909 and became active in International Socialism in the 1930s. When the pressures on her group became intense, she emigrated first to Belgium, then France and Britain in 1940. Presumably she was in Switzerland when Hilde got out. Whether she accompanied her to England has not come to light; neither has what she did while in England. However, she too was recruited by the OSS in 1944 and, according to Anne Denney of the Jupp Kappius website, was trained in Scotland with Peter Schalmey and Wilhelm Kirchstein.

Willi Eichler pressured George Pratt of the US Labor Department in London to send Anne and Hilda with Jupp Kappius and Willi Drucker, a liberal-thinking German policeman, back into Germany. He was concerned that, should the Allies defeat Germany, his dream of a socialist Europe was in danger of being overtaken by a resurgence in capitalism. Kappius and Drucker could provide strong leadership once the Allied invasion started. Anne and Hilde would be their couriers.

With the Allies' delay in the planned invasion of Germany, the OSS planned the DOWNEND mission, part of what was called the 'Faust Project', a proposal to send about 200 agents into Germany to acquire military and political intelligence. Anne and Hilde were among the first.

The participants in this project were sent on several SOE training courses. Their teachers included members of the American army, some of which were recent German immigrants. In theory, the participants were prepared for the reality of everyday life in National Socialist Germany, which included providing them with accurate copies of the current ration cards and certificates they needed in order to get a job. The conclusion of the course included a trip to Ringway Airfield outside Manchester, where they were provided with parachute training. After three jumps from a stationary balloon basket, they were taken up in a Whitley bomber to do both day and night drops. For reasons of confidentiality, they were forbidden to talk to their family or friends about their impending departure. Throughout the summer of 1944 they were trained in Arisaig, a remote highland area on the north-west coast of Scotland.

Persico reported that Drucker wondered what the refusal of the three others to indulge in alcohol, tobacco and wurst had to do with social justice. He found Kappius tough, intelligent and fiercely committed and he had told him that he was prepared to undergo plastic surgery if necessary. He even refused a salary, accepting only £5 a week for expenses. His mission, agreed by OSS and SOE, was:

To create an underground organisation for the purpose of (1) promoting internal resistance to the Nazi regime; (2) committing acts of sabotage against the war effort; (3) encouraging subversion in all its forms ... you will cause rumours to be spread according to the following directions (1) to create dissension between Wehrmacht troops and all political and semi-political formations e.g. Waffen SS, Gestapo, Hitler, Jugend ... (2) to create financial panic on the German home front and among troops resulting in a run on the banks ... (3) to encourage surrender or desertion.

In late summer 1944, ISK members in Switzerland reported that they had found a safe house in Bochum, but only for one agent. Eichler was adamant that Kappius should go and Pratt agreed. The cover planned for him was to use aspects of his past. His forged identity cards stated that he was 'Wilhelm Leineweber', a structural engineer and section leader of the Todt Organisation, the body responsible for building the Atlantik Wall and other military installations. He had been in France and was returning via Holland to the city of Sögel to try to find his mother, who had lost her house in a bombing raid. From there he would make his way to Bochum, where he had been reassigned. Additional cover included nine forged documents, the *Kennkarte,* his German identity card, food rationing coupons, and blank travel orders to cover any contingency plans.

Thirty-seven-year-old Kappius left from Tempsford on 1/2 September 1944, the first US-trained OSS agent to be parachuted into Germany. His mission was to make his way to Bochum, an iron and steel making centre in the Ruhr, liaise with anti-Nazi sympathisers and collect military and political intelligence about the industrial heartland of Germany. Not being dropped with a radio set, he had to send information via couriers. This was the role of his wife, Aenne, Anne and Hilde.

It was Lieutenant Anthony Turano of the OSS London Air Dispatch Section whose job it was to escort the Anne and Hilde to France and ensure they crossed the border into Switzerland. He picked them up at what Persico described as Area O, an OSS staging facility. This was Grendon Hall, a lovely English country house near Aylesbury, Buckinghamshire, about 50 miles north-west of London, The house was set in a lush, green park and operated by British enlisted personnel screened by MI5 and girls from the countryside who worked in the kitchen and dining room. Overflow agents were said to have been housed around London.

To Turano, the women were foreign in the most elemental sense. Their plainness had a relentless quality to it. They resembled scrubbed nuns in drab, secular dress. Their severe appearance was relieved only by a shy, unaffected manner. The women spoke a precise, German-accented English, but Turano had not the faintest idea what to say to them ...

Arthur Goldberg had come to know Hilde Meisel during his duty in London and had been moved by her simplistic idealism and the serenity with which she faced her mission. He had talked to the woman just before her departure and felt a strange foreboding as he studied her calm face and accepted that OSS was quite possibly sending Hilde Meisel to her death.

(Persico, *Piercing the Reich,* 1979)

When exactly they were flown out is not known, nor where from. Persico states they taken in a C-47 cargo plane, a Dakota, in September 1944. While it could have been from Tempsford, Clark makes no mention of the mission. Their original destination was near Lyon, but, as there was fighting in the vicinity, the pilot flew them on to Thonon-les-Bains, on the south bank of Lake Geneva, and landed them in a meadow which had been used by the SIS as a take-off and landing strip since the beginning of the war.

French peasants drove them in an old open car to a disused tunnel, where they were greeted by an English officer who helped them reach the home of a French professor and his wife in Thonon-les-Bains. There they were prepared a great roast with white bread. Turano noted that the two women declined the meat and quietly ate only the bread. Afterwards, they handed him a roll of film and asked him to have it developed. They had secretly filmed him throughout the flight by using a concealed match-box camera. When he said goodbye the following day, he shook their hands rather than kiss what he called political nuns.

They stayed with the couple for four weeks, until they were picked up by René Bertholet, the organiser of the Swiss ISK, who helped them to cross the Swiss border illegally and get to Zurich. Here they were provided with accommodation and new papers. With Hanna Bertholet, who represented the ISK and German trade unions, Hilde went to Geneva to meet Willem Visser't Hooft, the Dutch theologian who later became President of the World Council of Churches. His house was used for meetings of international socialists. Presumably she met Aenne Kappius, who had escaped to Switzerland and was working as a domestic servant.

Shortly afterwards, Hilde met Anna Beyer and accompanied her into the Ticino Alps to the village of Intragna, where they stayed at 'Al Forno', a safe house managed by the Bertholets for people who had fled from Germany's introduction of slave labour. Codenamed 'Crocus', her mission was to set up an intelligence-gathering network in the Vienna area among fellow radical socialists.

In an attempt to halt cross-border traffic, the Germans had sealed off the German–Swiss border, but, at the end of September, Aenne considered it safe to try. Disguised as a Red Cross nurse, she made the long journey to Bochum to pick up her husband's parcels of information as well as information from other labour resistance members. The material she brought back was given to Bertholet, who arranged for it to be delivered to Willi Eichler in London. He published parts of it in 'Germany speaks and Europe speaks'. According to Persico, it also included a request for a hundred Sten guns, fifty revolvers, fifty grenades and fifty incendiaries to be parachuted to a designated drop zone. He had to listen for the coded message after the BBC news: 'Grandmother has three children.' It didn't come. The RAF decided the site was too close to a Nazi searchlight and anti-aircraft battery. What they didn't know was that he had plans to knock them out.

In mid-January, 1945, Aenne made another trip and brought back a thirteen-page account of the growing cells of resistance building up in the Ruhr as well as debriefing ISK contacts in six other German cities. One startling snippet was that, in a bombing raid on the Gottingen railway station, one in three of the 300 5,000-pound bombs dropped failed to explode. Aenne and her husband survived the war and settled in

Germany afterwards. In essence, Jupp Kappius carried out most of his resistance work out of contact with the Allies.

Sometime in 1945, Hilde escorted Karl Gerold over the border into Austria. He was a left-wing German journalist who, because of his involvement with the Socialist Youth Workers, had been in exile in Switzerland since 1933. He was later to become the editor of the *Frankfurter Rundschau*.

On 17 April 1945, on the way back to Switzerland, she ran into an SS patrol in Feldkirch on the lookout for illegal border crossings. An expert marksman shot her through both legs as she tried to escape. Bleeding profusely, she managed to bite hard on her 'L' pill before the SS guards could reach her. A memorial plaque to Hilde Meisel can be seen at Landhausstrasse 3, Berlin Charlottenburg, where she lived for a time.

## 'Ada', 'Emily' and 'Maria'

American Carpetbagger crews flew three other women into Germany, not from Tempsford but, following the Allied invasion of France, from Lyon. Details of their missions were included in Persico's *Piercing the Reich*, but he admitted to having given them pseudonyms to protect their identities. The SOE had acknowledged that women had certain clear advantages as secret agents:

> A woman did not have to explain why she was not in military service. She did not need the sheaf of passes that a working male or soldier had to carry. That a woman might be involved in secret military intelligence, simply seemed less likely on the face of it. There were always risks, but the odds of exposure were sharply reduced.
>
> (Persico, *Piercing the Reich*)

Peter Viertel, of the Seventh Army OSS Detachment, had recruited three French women, Ada, Emily, and Maria, in the coal mining area near Strasbourg in Alsace. His chief, Henry Hyde, was delighted with the plan to infiltrate them into Germany as couriers.

> Of the three, Ada possessed the purest motivation. She was an Italian circus acrobat, stranded by the war in Strasbourg. She had once been assaulted and repeatedly raped by German soldiers. Her quest for revenge had a deadly coldness which appealed to intelligence professionals.
>
> Emily, a small, pert brunette, had been recommended to OSS by French intelligence, the Deuxieme Bureau. Little more was known of her background beyond her connections with the French.
>
> The third woman, Maria, was young, no more than twenty, and toughened by her early life in a mining town south of Strasbourg. She was an Alsatian prototype, a straw blonde, sturdy, ruddy-cheeked, a seeming milkmaid come to the city.
>
> (Ibid.)

Maria had been recruited from a detention camp where she was being held as a Nazi collaborator. She was reported as being the mistress of a Gestapo officer for three years, having worked in a German mess hall and also a German hospital. The French described her as *cul et chemise*, arse and shirttail, with the Germans.

Maria offered a credible if hardly inspiring answer to the forever nagging question of motivation. Life for a Frenchwoman who had bedded down with the Germans was destined to be hard in liberated France. This unsentimental child of poverty and war was determined to land back on her feet even if she had to start from an American airplane. Maria wanted to get the collaborationist burden off her back and wanted something entered into the records proving that she had aided the Americans.

(Ibid.)

As an Alsatian, Maria spoke German as fluently as French, which meant that she could easily pass as a local east of the Rhine. Once she agreed to work for OSS, she was sent to a mountain retreat outside of Strasbourg where agents were accommodated during training. While there, she was described as 'resilient, confident, and possessed of a native shrewdness'. Her training included elemental instruction in parachuting, communications and lessons in how to identify military units, tanks, aircraft and guns. She was said to have learned quickly, had no fear of parachuting, and seemed a promising prospect to her OSS mentors.

This hard-bitten proletarian also succeeded in scandalizing the American women attached to Henry Hyde's staff. Maria was appealing in a base, available way and not particularly critical in satisfying her physical hungers. Between the Americans and other agents, she was rarely lonely. On February 3 1945, Maria was transferred to the Chateau Gleisol at Lyons to be parachuted near Stuttgart. She was to travel under cover as an army nurse.

Just before takeoff, Maria presented Peter Viertel with a novel problem. She informed the stunned marine that she was pregnant. Why now? Why had she waited until the last possible minute to tell him? Maria made clear that she had no intention of frustrating the mission. But she wanted to strike a bargain. She expected to be gone less than two weeks.

With luck, she would have worked her way back to the American lines by then. After she had thus performed her part of the agreement, she wanted the Americans to arrange an abortion. To Viertel, it was preposterous. To drop the woman from a plane might solve the problem of the unwanted pregnancy, but this hardly seemed an auspicious beginning for a serious intelligence mission. Whose baby was it? he wanted to know. Maria said that her Gestapo lover was the father. Viertel found the ironies more annoying than amusing and recommended that the mission be scrubbed.

A great investment had gone into this operation-in planning it, financing it, gaining the cooperation of Seventh Army and, most difficult, getting the 492nd Bombardment Group to set up the flight. The girl was not that far along. She was willing to go. The decision was made to proceed. Maria was bundled aboard a B-24, practically lost in the billows of her jump suit. Late on the night of February 3, she dropped into Germany.

(Ibid.)

According to Viertel, she did a splendid job. All had gone according to plan. After Maria had landed and disposed of her gear, she successfully used her army nurse's disguise to travel west through various settlements, as she was instructed, to reach the front. As expected, she was overrun by American troops who accepted her password and turned her over to the OSS.

Viertel commented on how sharp-eyed and retentive Maria had been, when debriefed, to be able to report valuable information on the headquarters of German commands, tank parks, and troop deployments. As she had more than fulfilled the expectations of her trainers, she wanted her side of the bargain agreed to.

> Arranging an abortion seemed to fit best under the grab bag of duties assigned to the Seventh Army OSS finance officer, the spirited Peter Sichel. The assignment appealed to Sichel's sense of the absurd, and offered considerable latitude to exercise his talent for invention. Sichel took the girl, whom he referred to as 'the plucky Maria,' to a hospital in Strasbourg and explained to the physician in charge a most delicate matter. This young woman, possessed of a passionate hatred for the Boche, had carried out the most extraordinary act of heroism behind the lines in Germany, a Jeanne d'Arc de la resistance. Her mission inside the Reich had demanded the highest sacrifices of her and, unfortunately, she had become pregnant in the process. The physician indicated complete understanding and told Sichel to leave the girl with him.
>
> Sichel returned several days later to pick up Maria and to square the account with the hospital. The doctor protested vigorously. They did not want a sou. After all, what the girl had done was 'pour La belle France.'
>
> (Ibid.)

Viertel's success with Ada and Emily was nothing like as successful. Five unsuccessful attempts were made to fly Ada, the circus acrobat, into Germany. No details were provided as to why.

> Emily, the petite little thing recommended by the Deuxieme Bureau, carried off a rather ingenious infidelity. She had undergone her training with admirable perseverance. She had mastered the parachute and the radio. After she had landed in Germany, Emily merely substituted the radio crystals provided to her by the Deuxieme Bureau for those given her by OSS and broadcast exclusively for the benefit of the French.
>
> (Ibid.)

## Elyzbieta Zawacka

In David Oliver's *Airborne Espionage*, he mentions Elyzbieta Zawacka, the first and, according to my research, the only female agent sent from Tempsford into Poland. On the night of 9/10 September 1943, Squadron Leader Krol and his Polish crew flew their Halifax and dropped her, two other agents and their stores before returning safely to Tempsford, a round trip of over eight hours. Thirty-four-year-old Elyzbieta was a mathematics teacher in the 1930s and an instructor in the *Przysposobienie Wojskowe Kobiet*, Polish Women's Military Training Organisation. When war broke out, she became a commandant in the Union for Armed Struggle and, codenamed 'Zelma', undertook courier work in Warsaw and became a deputy of Zagroda, the Department of Foreign Communication in the Home Army. In February 1943 she made her way overland across Germany, France and Spain to Gibraltar, from where she was flown to England.

In Ian Valentine's *Station 43: Audley End House and SOE's Polish Section*, he narrates her

taking a suitcase of dollars from Berlin to Silesia in 1942, having to jump from a moving train at night to avoid the Gestapo. Her sister was interrogated and a colleague arrested and beheaded in Katowice in the same year. Under arduous conditions she and other couriers carried information intended for the Polish Commander-in-Chief in London. The information they carried was incredible in their diversity and included intelligence concerning U-boats in the Baltic, German troop movements, V-1 jets and V-2 rockets, Auschwitz, photographs for forged documents, escape routes, German industry, munitions factories, sabotage, information and plans of enemy aircraft and armour, Jewish ghettos, cooperation with the resistance in Hungary and Germany, extermination of Poles and Jews, particularly in the parts annexed by the Reich.

She undertook a training course at Audley End, near Saffron Walden, Essex, sharing a room with Sue Ryder. Having completed that, she underwent parachute training and, codenamed 'Zo', parachuted back into Poland to join her colleagues. She took part in the Warsaw uprising before moving to Krakow to continue her underground activities. In 1945, she joined an anti-communist organisation but quit after the war ended and became a teacher. Her honours include the highest Polish state distinction – the Order of the White Eagle – as well as the British Veterans' Badge.

## Yolande Beekman

According to the SOE records, the next woman sent out was Yolande Beekman, a Swiss citizen. The Nigel Perrin and Spartacus websites state that Yolande Unternahrer was born in Paris on 28 October 1911 and moved shortly afterwards to London. She was educated at Hampstead Heath and later at a finishing school in Switzerland. By the time she had finished her education, she was fluent in English, French and German.

She worked in children's clothing stores in Camden and Highgate but, when war broke out, she joined the WAAF and trained as a radio operator at Thame Park. While there, she gained a reputation as a great sock darner and fell in love with Jaap Beekman, a sergeant in the Dutch Army who was also training there. She was recruited to the SOE in February 1943 and trained at Wanborough with Yvonne Cormeau, Noor Inayat Khan and Cécile Lefort. Their conducting officer was Mrs Jean Sanderson of the FANY.

In Patrick Yarnold's *Wanborough Manor*, he records Lieutenant Colonel Gordon's description of Yolande as 'a nice girl, darned all the men's socks, would make an excellent wife for an unimaginative man, but not much more than that'. He was unaware she was married, as all recruits were given false identities during training. Lieutenant Holland's report at the end of her course stated that 'She shows any amount of determination in mastering the intricacies of W/T.' Nigel Perrin pointed out that:

Her self-assurance and determination soon shone through, as did her cheerfulness and idealism, being motivated by 'the "good of the cause" and devotion to duty.' Her time at SOE's finishing school at Beaulieu underlined the same qualities – popular, practical and dependable, her pace was a deliberate plod rather than a gallop: 'full of common sense and resource … the stolid type.'

In August Yolande began training as a radio operator at Thame Park in Oxfordshire. She found coding and transmitting hard work but she became a great favourite with everyone, not least with a recruit for SOE's Dutch section, Jaap Beekman, who fell in love with her. Their schedules only allowed for a brief engagement, and they married in London later that month. Even as they celebrated plans were underway for Yolande's first mission, and early in September she saw off her husband at King's Cross station, for what would prove to be the last time. Beekman took part in a mission to Holland in August 1944, and returned to England before the end of the war.

(www.nigelperrin.com/yolandebeekman.htm)

Buckmaster (1946–47) acknowledged that a good deal of thought went in to deciding where she was to be sent and who was to be helped.

[We] decided on Yolande, a girl of Swiss extraction sent to us by the W.A.A.F. Her French was perfect; the trace of Swiss accent was a positive advantage, as it diverted attention from her rather typically English appearance. She was quiet and homely – she had gained immense popularity at the wireless school by taking over the unofficial duties of sock-darner for the men – and her unruffled cheerfulness and good humour were great assets. She quickly developed an easy camaraderie with Guy, which promised well for their future activities.

Guy had an amused tolerance for the women engaged in our work, which some might have faintly resented. But Yolande took no offence at his attitude, and her very unaffectedness and simplicity won his esteem and admiration.

The time soon came for the two to leave on their mission, and I went down one November evening to see them off from the special aerodrome which we used. It was fairly rare in November for flying conditions to be good enough to risk a parachute operation involving 'bodies', but that night the moon was nearly full, there was a little cloud, but not too much, and there was no fog forecast. The messages announcing their departure to the waiting 'reception committee' in France had been put on both programmes of the B.B.C: 'Georgette aime les roses,' the French announcer had said in that polite, cool, unemotional voice which he reserved for the 'personal messages'. 'Georgette aime les roses' meant to the listeners who had arranged the message: 'Guy and Yolande are leaving tonight and will be dropped on your ground'. It meant a lot more. It meant: 'And we in England know that you are preparing for your fight to oust the invader. We will help you by sending you the tools, so that you may finish the job. These two British officers have volunteered to make your link-up with the Supreme Command, so that your efforts may be co-ordinated with the general Allied effort'. But we didn't need to tell them that; they knew.

Guy and Yolande were very cheerful as they got into their parachute harness, and watched their packs being stowed away in the bomb-racks of the aircraft. They cracked a joke with the skipper; they embraced, both of them, the F.A.N.Y. driver who had taken them down to the aerodrome; they let themselves be hoisted into the fuselage of the aircraft with much jest and merriment, and they waved a cheery farewell as the pilot taxied off, leaving me standing in the dispersal bay in the deepening dusk.

A month after her marriage, 17 September, thirty-one-year-old Yolande, codenamed 'Mariette', with identity papers in the name of 'Yvonne de Chauvigny', a war widow, landed in France. Buckmaster stated that Guy fell heavily on landing and dislocated his spine, so appointed Yolande to deputise for him.

Verity claims Yolande was landed in a double Lysander mission. Wing Commander Bob Hodges and Jimmy Bathgate of 161 Squadron flew out on 17/18 September, landing her and three others at Le Vieux Briollay, 3.5 kilometres west-north-west of Villeveque, which was north-north-east of Angers. This was the same field that Henri Déricourt arranged for Noor Inayat Khan, Cécile Lefort and Diana Rowden's arrival. According to Perrin:

> Reception organiser Henri Déricourt gave them each a bicycle, which Yolande apparently had trouble riding, and when the morning curfew had lifted he shepherded them into the city. On the way she fell off at her first sight of a German patrol, but they were able to reach the station safely and split up before boarding the first train to Paris. This party was lucky: unknown to them, Déricourt had been helping the Gestapo for some time, and other agents arriving at his landing grounds were followed to their destinations.
>
> The next day they met up briefly with Déricourt at a café near the Arc de Triomphe, before they went their separate ways.

Her contact in Paris gave her a message from Baker Street, cancelling the original plan to work for Captain Trotobas in Lille and telling her to go south to St Quentin in the northern Aisne department. Here, according to the Spartacus website, her unaffectedness and simplicity evoked the esteem and admiration of Gustave Biéler, the Canadian head of the Musician network. The messages she decoded for him included instructions to attack the lock gates at St Quentin, which was at the heart of the French canal system that was being used to carry submarine parts from the factories in Rouen, where they were made, down to the Mediterranean. The Allies didn't want them being used against their forces pushing up Italy towards France. Yolande helped arrange the parachute drops of explosives and other supplies and, on a very dark February night, limpet mines were attached to waiting barges and a timing switch to the lock gates. The operation was a success, closing the canal system for a few months until it could be cleared.

With increased German activity, Yolande still managed to continue her transmissions and, to avoid being recognised, dyed her hair blonde and used different identity papers with a new cover story.

One of the venues she used to meet up with members of several nearby resistance networks was the Moulin Brûlé, a café on the outskirts of St Quentin which she thought was safe. Kramer thought it was the weakest link in the chain of security forged in the early days of clandestine activity. An overenthusiastic conversation was said to have been overheard, which led to the *gonios* successfully locating Yolande's transmissions. Buckmaster (1946–47) narrated how two feldgendarmes rushed in on her before she could draw her revolver, and was taken into custody.

Even when she was beaten into unconsciousness, she resolutely kept her lips closed, and forced her mind to obliviousness of Guy's whereabouts. When they gloatingly told her that he was captured she betrayed no emotion. They did not know whether she believed them or not.

Escott was of the opinion that she hadn't been located by the radio detection teams but either a traitor in the circuit had betrayed her or someone had passed on information during torture. There had previously been literally hundreds of arrests in Francis Suttill's PROSPER network. The arrest of the organiser and radio operator together meant the end of the MUSICIAN network.

Biéler was shot by the SS at Flossenbürg and, following interrogation, Yolande was transferred to Fresnes Prison in Paris. On 13 May 1944 the Germans transported her and seven other captured SOE agents, Eliane Plewman, Madeleine Damerment, Odette Sansom, Diana Rowden, Vera Leigh, Andrée Borrel and Sonya Olschanezky, to a civilian prison for women at Karlsruhe in Germany. She was confined there under horrific conditions until September, when she was suddenly transferred to Dachau concentration camp with fellow agents Madeleine, Noor and Eliane. At dawn on 11 September, the day after their arrival, they were taken to a small courtyard next to the crematorium and forced to kneel. They were then shot through the back of the head and their bodies cremated.

At the end of the war, Yolande Beekman's heroic work was recognised by the French government with the posthumous award of the Croix de Guerre. Yolande's mother referred to her as someone who was gentle and quiet but made with a core of steel and was said to have stated that Yolande was already pregnant at the time she was sent on her mission.

Her gallantry was also 'Mentioned in Dispatches'. She was remembered by her friends as laughing, pretty and unafraid. One wonders about her pregnancy and whether she had the baby. There was no mention of it in Escott's *Mission Improbable*.

## Cecile 'Pearl' Witherington

Five days after Yolande's drop, twenty-nine-year-old Cecile 'Pearl' Witherington, a Flight Officer in the WAAF, was parachuted into France. It was her third attempt in as many days. Imagine her tension. On the first attempt there were no lights from the reception committee, so the pilot aborted the mission and the plane returned to Tempsford. On the second there was still none. The weather was so dreadful they didn't even drop the pigeons. On the third, the Halifax pilot, Flight Sergeant Cole, made a successful drop of fifteen containers and five packages about 30 km south-east of Tours. Sixteen minutes later, he dropped Cecile at a flashing 'D', about 17 km south-south-west of Châteauroux, south-east of Tours. She landed in strong winds between two lakes and was met by Maurice Southgate, the leader of the STATIONER network. The suitcases carrying her equipment were nowhere to be seen but, within a few hours, she was back in the arms of her lover, Henri Cornioley, a French lieutenant whom she had been engaged to before the war. After escaping from a prisoner-of-war camp, he was leading a underground camp of men loyal to de Gaulle.

Born in Paris in 1914 to British parents, Cecile didn't go to school until she was thirteen. She worked as the personal assistant to the air attaché in the British embassy in Paris. Not being a diplomat, she was not evacuated with the consular officials when war broke out, so she moved with her widowed mother and three sisters into the Unoccupied Zone and found accommodation in Marseille. When faced with internment, with the help of the Resistance she managed to escape across Spain and Portugal and eventually reached Britain with her family in July 1941.

Using her connections, she joined the Air Ministry as a personal assistant to the Director of Allied Air Co-operation and Foreign Liaison but, furious at what was happening in France, she was desperate to join the SOE. Her schoolfriend Maurice Southgate was working in the same office and he had successfully applied. She recalled in an interview after the war, 'Deep down inside me I'm a very shy person but I've always had a lot of responsibilities ever since I was quite small.' As her father died when she was sixteen, 'I thought, well, this is something I feel I can do … There's this question of being so mad with the Germans and anyway I didn't like the Germans. Never did. I'm a baby of the 1914–18 war. There is the question of trying to do something useful for the war. But it was also, the biggest part of it was, I think, this fury that I had against the Germans cos I was really mad with them' (Cornioley, C. P. 8689/2; 10447/3 IWM).

Buckmaster (1946–47) claimed that it was Pearl who interviewed him in June 1943 rather than the other way round. In his presumably censored article published after war about some of the agents he sent into France, he commented that:

Pearl struck me as a trifle diffident when I first met her. I know now that she was worried about her family, and perplexed by a most difficult decision: whether to follow her instinct and take the work for which she was suited and which attracted her, or to remain in England doing the dull chores of a household which her genius for organisation alone kept in order. She chose the job which was next to her heart, and never regretted the decision. Once it was made, she was a new person. She had been exacting and a trifle pernickety about the work and what it entailed, but now she threw herself with zest into her training and proved herself an unexpectedly muscular and athletic young woman. Her revolver-shooting was extremely good, and she enjoyed it. I can't help thinking how very much surprised her staid Air Vice-Marshal would have been to see her on the Sten-gun range, or crawling up to 'attack' an electrical sub-station.

All this outdoor life changed her mentally as well as physically. When she joined us, she was pale and tired from office work and the strain of the sleepless nights of the London Blitz. I doubted if she would pass the doctor, she looked so drawn and anaemic. Tall and fair, she had classic features, but she wore a mask of reserve and seemed withdrawn into herself.

When I saw her in action at the school after a few months of training, I could hardly believe my eyes, for here was and outstandingly good-looking young woman, bronzed and sturdy, with the handshake of a backwoodsman. The reserve was gone, the mask dropped. Self-reliance blazed in her eyes, her voice was firm and sure. When she gave an order it was obeyed; she radiated confidence. She was a born leader and the intricate 'schemes' in which she took part gave infinite scope for that blend of intellectual prominence and innate leadership which made up her strong personality.

When her period of training was completed, she came up to London for briefing in her mission, because we took the utmost care to see that the men and women who were selected for liaison work in France received the fullest possible instructions in the methods to be employed, as well as information regarding conditions prevailing in the territory where they were to work.

Pearl worked hard at her briefing; she went into every question in the greatest detail and would not leave it until she was satisfied that she had grasped its smallest implications. She learned much by heart, but, not content with this, she acted her part to herself continuously until it became her nature to adopt it. By the time she was ready, I was convinced that she would make an ideal representative.

Not only had she a perfect command of French and a very good knowledge of the weapons she and her men would be called upon to use, but she grasped with easy competence the full import of a most delicate mission.

After passing the initial assessment, she was said to have missed out the paramilitary training in Scotland and attended a special explosives and weapons course. Such courses were held at Brickendonbury in Hertfordshire. According to her obituary in *The Times*, one instructor expressed doubt about her potential during her training: 'Not the personality to act as a leader … best employed as a subordinate … She is so cautious that she seems to lack initiative and drive. She is loyal but has not the personality to act as a leader, nor is she temperamentally suited to work alone' (www.timesonline.co.uk/tol/news/uk/article3656045.ece).

Not everyone agreed. Juliette Pattinson recorded an interview with Pearl after the war in which she said, 'PT was at half past seven in the morning and they expected me to run … I refused and they said, "What are you going to do if the Germans get you?" and I said, "I'll deal with that when it comes [laughs] but you're not getting me running at 7.30 in the morning." No thank you. [laughs] I couldn't stand it.' Maybe she decided to show just what she was capable of because her final assessment reported that 'this student, although a woman, has got leader's qualities. Cool, resourceful and extremely determined. Very capable, completely brave … An excellent student for the job. Knows what she's in for and anxious to get on with it.' The comment on her demolition work was that she was 'extremely keen on this and would like to specialise'. Her firearms instructor added that she was 'Outstanding. Probably the best shot, male or female, we have yet had.'

Despite this, she was reported in Margaret Rossiter's *Women in the Resistance* as not wanting to engage in any violent acts against the enemy, asserting: 'I don't think it's a woman's role to kill.' Her major weakness was Morse code, so she was pleased she wasn't asked to train as a radio operator.

As she had promised her mother that she would not return to France, to stop her from worrying, Pearl told her a white lie that she had been posted to North Africa. The SOE sent monthly letters enclosing some of her £350 annual salary.

She was codenamed 'Marie' but also used the name 'Pauline'. Her mission was to work as Southgate's courier. Three weeks after she arrived, Southgate was lifted out and taken back to Britain. His expected fortnight stay was extended to three months so Pearl's responsibilities increased, having to liaise with various figures in the Resistance.

Buckmaster (1946–47) narrates how her mission was to persuade a French colonel to accept the requirements of the Allied HQ rather than acting independently. He was won over by her promise of regular parachute drops of supplies.

> It was not an easy assignment for a girl, but I felt sure that Pearl could do it. Where a man would probably have pointed out bluntly that only an officer with the facility of radio contact with London could procure the arms and equipment necessary to turn these maquisards into an efficient fighting force, Pearl secured the same result by tact and charm in half the time and with no hard feelings on either side. When I met the French colonel later on, the obvious devotion in his eyes as he looked at her and the way he told and re-told the story of the battle at Romorantin proved that she was no mean diplomat.

On one occasion she had to take a large sum of money to the leader of a nearby Resistance group but had not been given a password. It took many tense minutes trying to convince 'Roger' that she was from Octave Chantraine's group before she was accepted. The other men were ready to shoot her as a German spy.

In Terry Crowdy's *SOE Agent*, he mentioned that one, Colonel Villiers, who commanded a large Maquis group, was impressed by her successful sabotage of the Michelin factory in Clermont Ferrand. Knowing that Peugeot had been successfully persuaded to have their factory sabotaged instead of bombed by the RAF, Pearl made a similar offer to Michelin's management. Although they agreed initially, they refused to co-operate. On 11 March she wrote to HQ, telling them:

> I regret to inform you that the proposed sabotage of Michelin has completely fallen thro' in spite of repeated attacks. The management, after agreeing to the proposed instructions, refused to collaborate and still do so. Villiers' sabotage leader has been arrested; he tried to set fire to the M. factory by putting thirty incendiaries in one workshop; he did not take into consideration the working of the 'dispositif de sécurité d'incendies'.
>
> I wish to put on record the management's attitude vis-à-vis the sabotage plans. They refuse to believe the R.A.F. will have time to bomb would be too busy to bomb Clermont Ferrand before an Allied landing: in the meantime they are working, turning out material and making money whereas if the sabotage had taken place when proposed they would be doing none of these today. They are playing for time.
>
> If it is decided to destroy Michelin by bombing the factory, the R.A.F. could also bomb Bergougnan where they are turning out material exclusively for the Huns.
>
> There is very little defence around Clermont Ferrand and what there is, is mobile.
>
> I hate to suggest the bombing of M. but Villiers and I think it would give the management a lesson and force Villier's hand if Clermont Ferrand was bombed.

An addendum dated 5 April 1944 pointed out:

Michelin was pinpointed and destruction complete in main factory. People in Clermont say many of the incendiaries were dud. Casualties: about 16 killed and 20 injured. Sanatorium damaged by the blast, no casualties or damaged material.

When she discovered that about 40,000 tyres destined for German military transport vehicles were burnt, she didn't reckon that a great success as she felt more ought to have been destroyed. Whether the Bougourgnan tyre plant was also destroyed is unknown.

Pearl always carried a case of beauty products with her to back up her cover story that she was a sales representative for a cosmetics manufacturer. Having to carry messages between Clermont-Ferrand, Toulouse and Châteauroux, she acquired a first-class season ticket and for the first three months slept on unheated trains often too full of people for her to stretch out. At night there were fewer German and Vichy police checks, so she surrounded herself with pro-German magazines and wore her hair in a plait in German style. In an interview held at the Imperial War Museum, she said that:

> The job of a courier was terribly, terribly, terribly tiring. It was mostly travelling by night. We never wrote and we never phoned. Any messages were taken from A to B and the territory we were working on was really very big, because apart from Paris, we had Châteauroux, Montlucon, down to Toulouse, from Toulouse to Tarbes, up to Poitiers. It meant mostly travelling by night and the trains were unheated.
>
> One of the jobs I did regularly was going from Toulouse to Riom near Clermont-Ferrand. I'd leave Toulouse at seven o'clock at night and get to Riom at eleven o'clock the next morning absolutely frozen stiff to the marrow and having had nothing much to eat. Then I went into the safe house, to the people who received me, where there was no heating either …
>
> I was terribly, terribly careful and very much awake to what was going on around me because you never knew, wherever you were, in a train or a restaurant, if anybody was listening. An occupation is really one of the most awful things because you're just not at home. You have to be careful of everything.
>
> (Cornioley, C. P. 8689/2; 10447/3 IWM)

Sometimes it was arms and explosives she was carrying. Over the next eight months STATIONER network was financed to the tune of about 750,000 francs (£4,200) a month, money dropped by the SOE. Her opposition to killing was evidenced in the same interview:

> I didn't go out and fight with a gun. I don't think it's a woman's job that, you know. We're made to give life, not take it away. I don't think I could have stood up and coldly shot somebody … I didn't actually go in for full blowing-up. I didn't use explosives, neither did I use arms and neither did I kill people … The last thing I felt like was a terrorist.

Shortly after Southgate returned, bursting with new ideas, on 1 May 1944 he walked straight into a trap in Montlucon. He forgot to check for a danger signal and was arrested, interrogated and eventually taken to Buchenwald concentration camp.

Consequently, Pearl had to take over the leadership of the new WRESTLER network in the Valençay–Issoudun–Châteauroux triangle and follow Southgate's new instructions from London. With 150,000 francs for her personal use and the help of Henri Cornioley, she halved the circuit and concentrated on arming and training over 2,700 members of the Resistance. She arranged for them to be supplied by Tempsford's 138 Squadron. Their attacks on the Germans led to, according to one estimate, over 1,000 dead. Desperate to capture her, the Germans offered a million franc reward for her arrest, the equivalent of about £500,000 today.

On one occasion she had to wade waist-deep through a freezing river with her bike slung across her back as a bridge she needed to cross was unexpectedly being guarded. The STATIONER network cut the Paris–Toulouse railway line over 800 times in the Indre district, thus delaying the German reinforcements getting to Normandy after D-Day. The telephone lines her teams cut were not repaired until the Germans left France. Her closest shave came on 11 June 1944 when, holed up with Henri in the attic of the gatehouse to the chateau in Valençay, they were woken by German troops.

According to the 2002 Channel 4 documentary *Behind Enemy Lines: The Real Charlotte Grays*, she and 150 men held off 2,500 enemy troops for fourteen hours before escaping through a cornfield with her group's cash box. She hid there for four hours while the Germans occasionally fired into the field. Twenty-four of her colleagues were shot in the raid, but she and Henri managed to get away and arrange their pick up by one of Tempsford's Lysanders. According to Buckmaster (1946–47):

Commanding her 2,600 men, armed with Bren guns, Sten guns, and hand grenades, she determined to harry the enemy's crossing. The battle raged for the whole of a summer's day. Houses were looted and burned down; men were locked in groups grimly fighting for their lives. Pearl was everywhere, encouraging, ordering, sending up reinforcements, food, and ammunition. When the Germans brought up tanks, it was she who gave the order to let them through and to attack the following column of thin-skinned vehicles from the rear. It was she who watched the ambushes to make sure that fighting was broken off before the enemy could deploy overwhelming force. A great day for Pearl.

It is difficult for us to picture her as she must have been at the end of that great day, when the noise of battle died away and the German troops swarmed like locusts into the little villas of the unfortunate villages that had been in the battle line. Like ghosts the maquisards took to the woods, whence their flying-columns sallied forth again to lay fresh terrors in the path of the Germans advance next morning. There was no sleep for Pearl that night; messages from London had to be read and replies sent. Instructions had come through about the reception of new officers. 'What a bore,' she thought, 'to have new officers now. They'll be too late for everything except the mopping-up – and the victory march.' But there were the orders, and wrenching her weary mind back to her job, she gave instructions for the new arrivals to be received on the parachute ground, safely housed, fed, and sent on their way.

Soon the sweep of General Bradley's army along the Loire came to her relief. 18,000 Germans, caught by the patriots in this area, surrendered to the Americans at Chateauroux, and Pearl, in obedience to her orders, reported back to London. She didn't stop in Paris, because she felt she must first report to her Headquarters; there might be more work for her in Eastern France. When she landed at the English aerodrome, she was just a W.A.A.F. officer, one of thousands travelling on their official duties. She looked no different from any of them; or was there, barely perceptible, a particularly firm tilt to that determined chin, an unusually appraising glance from those fine eyes? I thought so, but then I knew her secret …

The colonel was not the only one to hold Pearl in high esteem. I spent an afternoon in September 1944 at Châteauroux barracks, while she was feted by the officers. It was amusing, yet in a way pathetic. The mess looked like a schoolroom in which the senior boys were celebrating the visit of a very popular master. They had brought out their best fare; there were elaborate table-cloths, fancy cakes (fancy cakes in the France of September 1944 needed 'organising') and of course champagne, much champagne. Pearl was surrounded by the 'boys' all talking at once, recollecting this or that incident, living again the fighting of June and the dangerous, tortuous underground work of the preceding eighteen months. And she was congratulating, praising, promising to come back again, just like an indulgent teacher with a precocious class. But when she said good-bye and they wished her luck, she confessed to me that those were her happiest days.

More details of her time in France are to be found in Escott's *Mission Improbable*:

When we got back to London all the heads of circuits were there; they were all men, and I was the only woman. The head of it all said 'Gentlemen!' And he turned to me and said: 'That applies to you, because you've done a man's job!' I'm the only woman who's ever done such a thing: going from a courier to military commander!

In her debriefing report, Pearl mentioned that her men killed over 1,000 Germans in five months and wounded many more. When she married Henri Cornioley in London in October, the SOE gave her an £8 postal order as a wedding present. Having only completed four parachute jumps rather than the usual five when she was at Ringway, she was refused her wings.

Although recommended for the Military Cross, she was ineligible as she was a woman. Major General Colin Gubbins, the head of SOE, wrote that 'her control over the Maquis group to which she was attached, complicated by political disagreements among the French, was accomplished through her remarkable personality, her courage, steadfastness and tact'. When she was awarded what she termed the 'puny' MBE (Civil), she returned it with a note saying that she did not deserve it as she had done nothing remotely civil.

The work which I undertook was of a purely military nature in enemy occupied country. When the time for open warfare came we planned and executed open attacks on the enemy. I spent a year in the field and had I been caught I would have been shot, or worse still, sent to a concentration camp. I consider it most unjust to be given a civilian decoration. The men received military decorations. Why this discrimination with women when they put the best of themselves into the accomplishment of their duties.

However, she did accept from de Gaulle the Croix de Guerre, the Croix Legion d'Honneur and the Medaille de Resistance. In 2006 she received the insignia of the CBE from the Queen and, two years later, her much more coveted parachute wings. She died in February 2008.

## Madame Berger and Madeleine Lavinfosse

In Hugh Verity's autobiography, *We Landed by Moonlight*, he mentions that on 16 October 1943 he flew a Hudson to a field three kilometres west-north-west of Arbigny, north-north-west of Pont-de-Vaux, to pick up General de Latre de Tassigny and eight other passengers, including a Madame Berger and her baby.

The following night he flew a Lysander to a field two kilometres north-north-east of Vandrimare, east-south-east of Rouen, to pick up Madeleine Fauconnier. He specified that she was a Belgian spy, codenamed 'Claire', who later became Madame Lovinfosse, and that Georges Coeckelbergh, a Belgian radio operator, came back with her. George de Lovinfosse was a Belgian businessman who had a country house near Châteauroux and ran an SOE escape line.

Research by Aubenas, Van Rokeghem and Vercheral-Vervoort (2006) into women in Belgian history revealed that Madeleine was said to have worked with Louise de Lansheere, Ginette Pevtschin and Marie-Louise Hennin in the production and distribution of the clandestine newspaper *La Libre Belge*. Following the arrest and imprisonment in 1942 of the filing clerks, engravers, printers and distributors, Madeleine needed to get out of the country. The praats website (http://www.praats.be/zero.htm), in its section on the Zero network, mentions that she was in Agente Connection and in 1942 was assistant to Albert Hachez, who worked at *La Libre Belge*, and to William Ugeux, the Director-General Information and Action for State Security in London. What work she did back in Britain was not mentioned.

## Elizabeth Devereaux Rochester

SOE records mention Elizabeth Devereaux Rochester and Danielle Reddé as being the last two women agents sent out in 1943. Born in New York in 1917, Elizabeth was educated at Roedean girls' school in England and other schools in France and Austria. When her American mother remarried, Elizabeth was known by some by her stepfather's surname, Reynolds. As an American, she had lived an affluent lifestyle in the 1930s, travelling in style round much of Europe and developing excellent contacts within the European aristocracy. In her autobiography, *Full Moon to France*, she tells how she was on vacation in Greece when war broke out. Rather than return to the United States, she jumped ship at Marseille, lying to the American officer that she was desperate to buy some sanitary towels. Catching the train to Paris, she joined the American Hospital Ambulance Corps.

After the Japanese attack on Pearl Harbor, the United States joined the Allies. As all Americans in France were considered enemy personnel, Elizabeth's mother was interned in Vittel concentration camp. Rather than lose her friends and leave her beloved France, Elizabeth and Bridget, a British girlfriend working with the French Resistance, moved to Chalon-sur-Saône, near the French Alps, helping get Jews, Allied airmen and young French men wanting to avoid forced labour in Germany across the border into Switzerland. Hiding in ditches, avoiding guards in the early hours of the morning, sleeping rough and living simply with sympathetic French peasants was a big change for her.

After reaching Geneva, the American consulate suggested she return to the United States. She refused, expressing an interest in helping in the war effort. Within days she was approached by the British to work for them. They wanted her to return to France and continue working on the escape route. She agreed.

After a few more journeys the local gendarmerie were on to her. The young officer sent to arrest her was successfully bribed with a large bag of oranges she had just brought back. Rather than make things difficult for the peasant family she was staying with, she decided it was time to leave France. In spring 1943, accompanied by Blanc, a fellow resistance worker, she made her way south, first to Carcassonne then to Perpignan. Her mission was to set up a new escape route across the Pyrenees and take important requests to the British consulate in Barcelona, asking for a radio operator, weapons, ammunition, food and blankets for the Maquis.

Having to leave her grey suit and a book by Colette, she wore all her jumpers and her haversack contained only toilet articles, a blouse, some handkerchiefs, pyjamas and a pair of shoes. Using aspirin to counter the effects of an infected wisdom tooth and mumps, she was taken by a Catalan guide over the pass used by the Spanish Republican Army when it escaped into France.

After a month or so working in the British embassy in Barcelona, she got her *salvoconducto* – a cardboard travel pass, new identity cards and a mission to escort nine men to Gibraltar. By early summer 1943 she was back in England. Once debriefed, she joined the Women's Transport Service and was soon identified as a potential agent by the SOE. Having passed her assessment, she was trained at Wanborough, Arisaig, Ringway and Beaulieu.

On 18 October 1943, twenty-seven-year-old Elizabeth was flown out of Tempsford with Richard Heslop, her organiser; Owen D. Johnson, his radio officer; and J. Rosenthal, one of the MARKSMAN resistance leaders. It was Johnnie Affleck's first Hudson mission. He touched down at 0030 hours in a field at Lons-le-Saunier, four kilometres west-south-west of Bletterans, after clipping a belfry tower and ripping the upper branches of some tree tops. This was the same drop zone as Eliane Plewman. In *Full Moon to France*, Elizabeth described what happened:

> We flew an hour or more over the dark and tranquil countryside, the shadow of our plane gliding along to keep us company. Then, when the dispatcher came and took our mugs of coffee, I knew we were almost there.
>
> The pilots who flew these missions, whether in big planes or in tiny Lysanders, were the crack airmen of the RAF. They had to be because setting down their machines in fields lit only by flare paths cast by flashlights or bonfires required the most extraordinary skill. This time, perhaps because the other plane had already landed ahead of us and was taking off as we approached, our pilot missed his landing. Instead we hit the church belfry. The shock was tremendous, sending cases falling all over the place. What it did to the belfry I don't know. Monsieur le Curé would certainly have a lot of explaining to do.

'You'll have to jump. I think my landing gear is jammed.' The impersonal voice came over the long-com.

Suddenly the dispatcher was there, fitting a parachute harness on Paul while the plane veered. I started to feel sick as I drew my rucksack towards me, preparatory to having it strapped to one of my legs. The suitcase would follow later. God only knew where.

Christ! All the Germans in the sector must be on the alert.

'It's all right! She's out. Stand by for landing. Hurry! Hurry!'

And hurry we did. So much so that I sprawled on my face in the mud of France.

Just as well. My mac was too clean anyway.

I returned to France by the moon of October. There was a nip in the air and the sky was studded with stars. It was not a winter sky nor yet a summer one. A farewell and hello one, disputing the mellowness of summer, heralding the sharpness of winter.

The reception committee were said to have been surprised to see a tall, fair-haired young woman with a long aristocratic nose get out of the plane. McCall (1981) said that Elizabeth was accustomed to men's attention.

She looked a typical product of the girls' public school she had attended in southern England. She was in fact American, but showed no trace of her background. Heslop had been reluctant to take her because he felt even the most dim-witted policeman would be unable to mistake her for anything other than British.

Within minutes of landing she learned that Stephen, one of the circuit's leaders, had been arrested. Her initial safe house was a chalet she rented up in the mountains in Albigny, near Lake Annecy, where she hid her suitcase containing plastic explosives in the cellar. Here she prepared for her mission to help arrange the arming of the Maquis of the Ain, the Jura and the Haute Savoie. To give an idea of what it entailed, I include a few extracts from her autobiography.

Back at the house, I clattered down the steps of the cellar, my ski boots ringing against the stones. Behind a heap of empty bottles I found the suitcase. From a separate cardboard box I took the detonators and time pencils, carefully wrapped in cotton. Laying everything out on a board stretched across two barrels, I began to make up my charges, not noticing I hadn't any waterproofing until the primer was wedged in the plastic explosive. Although there was no necessity for the charges to be waterproof, I needed a dark material to wrap them because, once they were clinched by magnets, they would show up lighter than the locomotives. I remembered a navy blue scarf I had. It would be just right …

Much later the four boys turned up, and when they filed in, brushing off the snow and blowing on their chapped hands, I knew I was committed. The thing had to be done.

I drew out Stephen's plans and briefed them step by step. Then I opened the suitcase and handed out the Sten guns. For myself I kept nothing. I was carrying the charges; that was enough.

The next day it snowed till eleven. Afterward the sun came out and everything was crisp and fresh-looking. As I went down the hill, the lake was like a sheet of blue. I had planned the operation for nine, intending to wait in the house of a friend until then. When I hit the road and started towards Annecy, one of the boys tagged along behind. I was precious now. I was carrying the charges.

I left ten minutes before the rendezvous. Everything was quiet in the streets – the dimmed-out lamps casting long shadows on the snow. Only my footsteps made a ringing noise on the frozen sidewalk.

I turned off the secluded street into a busy thoroughfare and a shadow stepped out behind me. In front of the station it and I turned into a dark alley. I was to meet the others in an abandoned warehouse, and as I walked through the cavernous building, I heard the scraping of rats. Once the shadow behind me whispered: 'Careful Mademoiselle! The flooring is bad.'

Through the dirty, broken windows came a glow from the snow-covered station yard … Finally the time came for us to move. My guard went first. I followed some paces behind. As I left the shelter of the warehouse, my back felt nakedly exposed. We walked slowly, stopping only once – when we reached the tracks …

It only took a few minutes to clamp the first charge on the bearing rod. The second was equally easy, but, walking around to the third, I stumbled against a steel girder. The noise was frightful, and to my horror, a flash of light shot up just beyond the snub nose of the locomotive. I stood petrified while behind me my guide slid up and I felt the hard barrel of his Sten gun straining against my thigh. It didn't reassure me at all …

Back in the warehouse I made the boys dismantle their Stens and stow them away in a rucksack. They were feeling so pleased with themselves I feel they would have walked through the streets of Annecy just for the heck of it. The whole operation had taken just fifteen minutes …

I think I made the chalet in record time that night. I know I was puffing when I leaned against the gate. The air was now so clear that I could see down to the lake. I tried to think of anything, anything but three charges wrapped in dark material clamped to a bearing rod. Maybe I'd forgotten to crimp them. It sometimes happens in the excitement of the moment. But no, I'd done it before placing them in the primer. I was close to tears when I thought about my instructors back in England. A hell of a life for an American who happened to have been brought up in France. I should have let the Germans intern me. Time now, I snarled between my teeth, gripping my watch. Yes, time ladies and gentlemen. Time … A vision of beer in pewter mugs and hot, happy faces in the pub. Time. … It must be …

Bang! … It was sharp and clear and sweet music on the cold air.

Grinning, I opened the gate and trudged across the yard. I had my hand on the door when the second charge went off. Almost immediately after, the third exploded. For once I didn't swear when I fumbled with the matches to light the paraffin lamp; later, when I added a few drops of water to the violet, I was very happy.

David Harrison listed her as having worked as a courier for Lieutenant Colonel Richard Heslop, an RF agent in the Marksman circuit in the mountainous region of south-east

France, where she used the codename 'Typist' and the name 'Elizabeth La Grande' (http://soe_french.tripod.com). Her training in 'ungentlemanly warfare' meant that she was as adept with handling explosives as she was with her hockey stick. In whatever situation she found herself, she was said to have

> 'had a dignified bearing, a haughty arrogance which was once the hallmark of the English gentlewoman abroad'.
>
> She became a familiar sight in the Haute-Savoie and Jura, striding along the hilly roads between villages, her rucksack slung across her back, for all the world like an English eccentric on a walking holiday.
>
> Her greatest attribute was a phenomenal memory. She rarely had to carry written messages. She could recite them carefully, memorise them, then repeat them verbatim when she arrived at her destination.
>
> (Rochester, *Full Moon to France*)

Having located landing sites for Dakotas to take Allied personnel back to England, she helped Heslop run what was known by those who used it as the 'Xavier's Air Express Service'. In a comment to George Millar, a former *Daily Express* correspondent and another SOE agent sent to France, she complained that most of the American and British pilots – whom, among her other duties, she helped to repatriate – seemed so common (Howarth 1980). Heslop was very impressed with Elizabeth and commented in his autobiography, *Xavier*, that she

> looked as English as her name – but was American. She was tall, with a prominent nose, and she did not walk, she strode. When you saw her coming towards you in the mountains, you automatically expected to see a couple of Labradors at her heels, and that her first words would be 'Had a bloody good walk, yer know, nothing like it for keeping fit.' I thought SOE were mad to send her to France, as she stuck out like a sore thumb, but when I raised the question they said she was a fully trained operative and knew the Savoie well. I liked her too, and my reluctance to take her was only based on her English looks. She did a fine job, for she had guts and imagination …
>
> I was very fond of Elizabeth, for she seemed so English and appeared my only link with home at that time …
>
> She had worked very gallantly for me and was always on the search for work. She never liked to sit about and if she had to stay in the command post for any length of time she would pester me to give her a task to get her moving again. But as the weeks went by I had more and more discreet and diffident inquiries about her. A person would say: 'Ah, Elizabeth, what a wonderful girl she is and how well she's liked. But doesn't she look English.' …
>
> I didn't want to sack her because of the great assistance she was to me, and anyway I did not have the heart to. I took the coward's way out and asked London to recall her, having explained in my cable the growing concern about her Englishness.
>
> When the cable arrived ordering her to return to SOE, Elizabeth asked me why she had been recalled, but I was evasive and embarrassed and made some poor excuse. She then pleaded to stay, but I told her it would be folly as her mother was under constant

surveillance by the Gestapo and the French police as she was known to be a foreigner. Reluctantly Elizabeth agreed to stay away and finally she left me.

When the Germans sent two divisions to attack the Resistance in the Haute-Savoie, she managed to escape. Had it not been for forgetting her bag and delaying her departure, they would have arrived in a village which was wiped out by the Milice. Skiing through the mountains for two days helped them to escape to safety in Ambérieu.

Sometime later in 1944, Jean Helfer was claimed to have flown his Hudson out from Tempsford on a mission to pick her up from a former Luftwaffe airfield at Ambérieu. Heslop had decided that, as she was 'too conspicuous', he wanted to send her back to England, partly for her own sake and partly for those who were worried about her. She pleaded to be allowed to finish the job but he was adamant. So was she. She was desperate to get to Paris to see her invalid mother before flying back on 29 October. Instead, she was arrested on 20 October at a Swiss friend's apartment where she had left her bicycle, which she needed to get to her safe house in a convent. She wasn't sure if the telephone call she had made had been intercepted or whether she had been betrayed by her friend's friend, who had an Austrian brother-in-law.

A black Citroen took her to Rue des Saussies, where many arrested Resistance members and other criminals were held. In her Canadienne jacket she found a packet of RAF matches and a sixpence. She was being framed. The former she ate and the latter she slipped behind the skirting board.

To avoid her watch being taken she came up with an idea. 'Fortunately it was not too large and fairly flat. If my rectum would take it, it seemed the best place, but even that was no guarantee. I would have liked to smile at the idea of a timepiece playing hookey in my ass, but I didn't. I was just too worried about keeping it in there.' Two pairs of panties helped for a while but it was all in vain as the watch was eventually confiscated when she was put *au secret* – in solitary confinement for trying to escape by removing the bar from her cell window. Despite managing to unscrew the door lock from her cell, she gave up the idea of escape until she was transferred to Fresnes Prison. An iron splinter from the bed didn't draw enough blood when she tried to commit suicide. Her will to live was too strong. Details of her captivity and interrogations can be found in her autobiography.

She stuck to her cover story that she was a US citizen who had only recently returned to France from Switzerland and was eventually one of the very lucky ones to be freed by the prison authorities when the Germans pulled out of Paris. Heslop said of her afterwards that she had done 'a fine job, for she had guts and determination', but blamed London for recruiting someone who looked so un-French. In appreciation of the work she did, she was awarded the Croix de Guerre and the Chevallier Legion d'Honneur.

## Danielle Reddé

Danielle 'Eddie' Reddé, according to the World War Two Escape Lines website (http://www.ww2escapelines.co.uk), was a telephonist who joined the Resistance in Lyon in 1941. When the Australian Tom Groome (Georges de Milleville) was parachuted into France in October the following year to act as Pat O'Leary's radio operator, Danielle worked as his courier, helping to get escapers and evaders into Spain.

In Neave's *Saturday at MI9*, he mentioned her taking his decoded messages to room 202 in the Hotel de Paris at Toulouse at 1430 hours and returning with O'Leary's reply for transmission to London.

On 11 January 1943, she, Tom, and some of the men they were wanting to get out of the country were arrested at a house in Montauban. He had failed to set a look-out while he was transmitting and was caught by German direction-finding equipment. Taken to the Gestapo HQ at Hotel Ours Blancs in Toulouse, Tom jumped out of a window trying to escape. Although he was recaptured, Danielle managed to escape in the commotion and crossed the Pyrenees in March with Nancy Wake, an Australian, and several others involved in the French Resistance. Her codename was 'Camille Fournier'. After arriving in England, she joined the BCRA (Bureau Central de Renseignements et d'Action) on 14 June. This was de Gaulle's Free French Intelligence Bureau on Delphin Square. Using the name Edith Daniel, she was trained by the SOE as a radio operator for RF Section.

Codenamed 'Morroccin'/'Marocain', she was said by Harrison to have been parachuted into France on 1 January 1944 to work in the Lyon area (http://soe_french.tripod.com). Clark says that the winter of 1943 was so severe that many missions had to be cancelled. As there was none from Tempsford that night, it's possible that Danielle was flown in from Massingham, SOE's forward base in Algeria. Whether she had been flown out of Tempsford earlier is unknown. As well as sending radio messages, she acted as a courier and was also known as 'Maria Kermarec'. After the American and French Forces landed on the Mediterranean coast in August 1944, their northern advance eventually overran Danielle's area.

The Mémoire et Espoirs de la Résistance website mentions her arriving back in London on a ship from Calcutta on 3 May 1945. What she was doing in India is unknown but the SOE was active in the Far East at that time. Before long she accepted another mission, this time as Sous-lieutenant Simone Fournier, to work with the SOE in liberating Allied prisoners of war held in Japanese camps in Indochina. On 22 August, this time codenamed 'Edith Fournier', she and Lieutenant Klotz parachuted into Thakhek, Laos, just over the border from Thailand. She was to work as his radio operator. While she was away, de Gaulle awarded her the Médaille du Combattant Volontaire de la Résistance, the Médaille commémorative des services volontaires dans la France Libre, the Croix du Combattant, the Croix de Guerre with Palme and Chevalier de la Légion d'Honneur.

In commending Danielle for the Croix de Guerre des théâtres d'opérations extérieurs avec Etoile d'Argent, Colonel Roos and Capitaine Goudry said that on 14 December 1945 Danielle parachuted with her radio into what they described as a very dangerous part of Laos with no reception committee. Despite being wounded on landing and surrounded by hostile forces, she showed calm and composure. Thanks to her constant efforts and devotion, she saved numerous human lives and participated in the evacuation of all the French from the province where she was working and transmitted vital military and political messages. However, the wound she got on landing resulted in her being hospitalised in Bangkok.

Once recovered from her injury, she was assigned to Saigon on 29 March 1946. This mission involved dealing with all the social problems raised by repatriating the French women and children who had been interned in Shanghai, separate from their husbands. For her work in the Far East, Danielle was awarded a Citation à l'ordre du Corps d'Armée. The British awarded her with the Medal of the British Empire as well as an honorary Colonial Medal. In 1953, she was given the Médaille en Argent du Million d'éléphants (à titre militaire) dans l'Ordre du Règne du Laos, the Médaille militaire and Médaille des Evadés (http://memoresist.org).

## Anne-Marie Walters

The first flight of 1944 from Tempsford was not until 4 January, when Pilot Officer Buchanan flew his Halifax on operation WHEELWRIGHT 50 to France. The Squadron records note that he was suspicious when a twin-engined aircraft was spotted with its navigation lights on near Angoulême. The navigator pinpointed Langon in the Gironde and, 10 km from the target, picked up a Rebecca transmission. He descended in good visibility in the clear moonlit sky to about 700 feet and dropped fifteen containers, four packages and two agents: Claude Arnault, an explosives expert, and twenty-year-old Anne-Marie Walters.

According to her autobiography, it was a marshy field on the edge of a wooded area of the Landes, not far from Condom. While she was sipping acorn coffee in a decrepit farm, deep in straw and manure, a two-oxen cart picked up the packages that were dropped with her (Walters 1946).

With a father who was Oxford don and Deputy Secretary General of the League of Nations, and a French mother, Anne-Marie was raised in Geneva and attended an International school, becoming politicised on hearing about events in the Spanish Civil War. When war was declared, her father drove her, her sister, her mother and their dog in his Humber car to safety in Hendaye, via Narbonne. Several days later they caught a P&O liner at Verdon-sur-Mer which took them to Glasgow. Micky, her dog, had to be left behind at the harbour.

The following year, despite the disapproval of her mother, seventeen-year-old Anne-Marie, like many of the other female agents, joined the WAAF. As an Assistant Second Officer, she worked in the RAF Fighter Command headquarters at Bentley Priory, near Stanmore. Here, as an 'itinerary plotter', she helped plot all enemy raids on wall maps, blackboards and the large 'Ops' table using information provided by WAAFs listening to messages through telephone headsets. Different-coloured counters representing the Luftwaffe formations were moved across the map using magnetic rakes.

Although dismissed for indiscipline, she was taken on by the SOE on 6 July 1943. SOE recognised that her knowledge of French would prove a valuable asset. Her personal file in the National Archives includes comments from the instructor for the Student Assessment Board while she underwent training at Winterfold, near Cranleigh in Surrey. Dated 29 July 1943, the document records her General agent grading as F, Intelligence Rating 9, Aptitude for Morse AVERAGE, Mechanical AVERAGE, with the remark that she was:

A keen, very intelligent girl with a realistic practical sense. Ample courage, determination and a sense of humour. She has marked latent possibilities but is at present immature,

Anne-Marie Walters parachuted into south-west France in January 1944 to work as a courier in George Starr's WHEELWRIGHT network. (*Le Bataillon de Guerilla de l'Armagnac 158ᵉ R.I.* 1997)

inexperienced and not sufficiently in control of herself for subversive work. With maturity she should prove a girl of exceptional qualities.

(TNA HS 9/339/2)

Similar concerns appeared in her instructors' report while she was on the paramilitary training course in Meoble Lodge, Inverness-shire, between 2 August and 13 September. She must have passed her parachute training at Ringway and then went to the SOE's 'Finishing School' at Beaulieu. The instructor there showed a similar awareness of character. His report, dated 26 October, stated that:

She is well-educated, intelligent, quick, practical and cunning. She is active minded, curious and has plenty of imagination. She is keen and, on the whole, worked hard, displaying outstanding initiative. Nevertheless she is erratic and was inclined to be inattentive when she was not particularly interested. She has a very strong character, is domineering, aggressive and self-confident. She is vain and rather self-conceited. She has been badly spoilt and is always 'agin the government'. She is rather an exhibitionist and hates being ignored. She resents discipline or any attempt to thwart her wishes. She is irritable and impatient of the mistakes of others less quick and intelligent than herself. She is inclined to get over-excited and is slightly hysterical. She is rather more immature than the other members of the party, but it was not, on the whole, beneficial. She tended to make them discontented and to distract their attention from their work. It is doubtful whether she is aware of what she is undertaking, especially in its relation to others. She has a strong personality. At times she is charming. All too frequently, however, she is rude and tactless. She is restless and lacking in repose. She would make as many enemies as friends. She will not hesitate to always make use of her physical attractiveness in gaining influence over men. In this respect she is likely to have a disturbing effect in any group of which she is a member. This influence was clearly discernible here. She has the brains, and to some extent, the character to do valuable work. Nevertheless it is doubtful whether she should be employed. As an individual she is likely to be conspicuous. She would almost certainly resent occupying a subordinate position, yet she does not appear to be temperamentally suited to have authority over others. She will probably exercise an unsettling influence upon many with whom she comes into contact. Codes: routine practice only required.

Desperate for more agents, Buckmaster overrode these concerns, and allocated twenty-year-old Anne-Marie a courier role in a quiet, rural area of south-west France. 'She is going to the field with a very limited job which will not endanger the security of any other agents.' On 6 November, she was appointed an assistant senior officer in the FANY, her salary being paid into her bank while she was in the field.

The first attempt to drop her was on 16 December, but the mission was aborted because of the bad weather. The signal letter was flashed but the pilot couldn't make out the red landing lights. Returning to England was traumatic because of dense fog everywhere. Approaching Woodbridge on the Suffolk coast, the pilot communicated with the airfield. The Commanding Officer asked permission of the Commanding Officer of Tempsford to have the passengers bail out. This was refused. On the fourth attempt to land, the Halifax crashed, killing the pilot, navigator and either the engineer or despatcher. The other crew members were wounded, one sustaining broken ribs, another a broken arm and the third a broken leg. According to her personal file, Anne-Marie was lucky. A padded helmet, parachute and padded jumpsuit protected her so that, apart from shock and concussion, she only had a cut on the scalp and a bruise behind the right ear. Claude had an abrasion over his right eye and slight sprains to his ankles. They were driven down to London, where Anne-Marie was provided a safe house with Mrs Winser, 17 Devonshire Close, W1. Both were described as 'in high spirits and expressed a wish to be able to return soon to their jobs'.

The second attempt, on 4 January, was successful. She and Claude landed safely at Créon d'Armagnac, near Gabarret in the Landes, a small village about 40 km east of Mont-de-Marsan. When she left the farmhouse it seemed that everyone knew who she was and where she had come from, welcoming her with wine which she felt it impolite to refuse.

Codenamed 'Colette', Anne-Marie worked as a courier for George Starr's WHEELWRIGHT circuit but used the alias 'Paulette' in her autobiography. Her cover was that she was a Parisian student recovering from pneumonia. Needing the air, she was based in Castelnau-sur-l'Auvignon, a small hilltop community in rural Gascony which was considered safe from German eyes as it had no electricity and no running water. The toilet was the bushes behind the hen house. Yvonne Cormeau was already working there as Starr's radio operator. Escott narrated one of Anne-Marie's first tasks.

> She learned to drive in the hair-raising French style, mainly in vehicles with charcoal powered 'gazo' (for gazogéne) as the French mockingly nicknamed any makeshift power source which they were forced to use for their transport, since only the Germans had petrol for their Citröens. She used cars, trains, her bicycle and crowded buses. She sometimes had to chase far afield after busy members of the circuit to deliver and pick up her messages. She met people of all kinds, shapes, sizes and walks of life who were members of the resistance – a butcher, a spare parts shopkeeper, a womanising spiv, a communist, a second-hand clothes dealer, a wine merchant, a girl whose husband had escaped to England and a Jew.

Her first important mission was to meet twenty-one escapees from the central prison at Eysses, near Toulouse, and accompany them to Fourcés. After a hundred-mile trip in the back of a truck to Tarbes to find guides to escort them over the Pyrenees, she and Starr had to find them safe houses until the weather was right for a crossing. They also had to avoid a detachment of SS troops sent in to get retribution for an attack on some of their numbers. More of her adventures can be read in Escott's book.

> Another escape mission was to accompany a French police inspector to the Pyrenees. He had worked for the resistance in Paris, Grenoble and Agen, but now the Gestapo net was closing around him, so he had to be sent to safety as he was endangering not only himself but also the circuit. On the way to the railway station he confessed to concern over the fact that he carried a gun and two identity cards. One was a false civil card to show the Gestapo, the other was his true police card allowing him to carry arms, which he could use at French controls. In their first train he dozed and all went well, but in the second from Toulouse to Montréjeau, sitting opposite each other in an empty compartment, they were interrupted by a ticket collector. Before looking at their shared ticket he started asking Anne-Marie searching questions and then studied her companion's civil papers. From where she sat Anne-Marie saw the policeman grow pale and she remembered the incriminating revolver. She grabbed her bag and started fumbling in it, drawing the ticket inspector's eyes to her. Still looking at her he handed back her friend's papers and left the compartment without another word. As she relaxed, the policeman warned her to be still and slipped his gun behind the seat. Then two men in turn passed along the corridor, watching them out of the corner of their eyes, a frequent trick of the Gestapo who hoped to catch suspects relaxing and taken off their guard. The police inspector's brother had been caught like this. Nothing more happened, however, the journey was completed, and the policeman was delivered to a safe house ready for onward transmission to the Pyrenees guides.

Other missions included carrying important messages from 'Hilaire', BBC messages, demolition orders, A and B messages (coded orders for before and after D-Day), money and letters between Montrejeau, Mazeres de Neste, Tarbes and Agen in Gers, as well as to places in the Dordogne, Paris and Brittany. Despite her suggesting it, 'Hilaire', did not send her on any risky jobs. In fact, 'The main fighting I did was getting into buses, which was no small enterprise!'

In Jacques Poirier's *Giraffe Has a Long Neck*, he said that on Anne-Marie's first bus journey she made an almost fatal error at the ticket office by saying:

> 'A single to Brive, please.' 'Que dites-vous?' [What did you say?] demanded the woman behind the window. I quickly pulled myself together. 'Un billet pour Brive, s'il vous plait, madame.' And to think I'd just spent nearly six months learning the tradecraft of a secret agent!

In her autobiography, *Moondrop to Gascony*, Anne-Marie admitted feeling like she had 'British agent' written all over her face but, after a while she 'lost the sensation of being an outlaw' and never had a dull moment. When she had to go to large towns she had to modify her appearance. 'I discarded my beret, it was all right in a small town like Condom, but in Agen women wore high, complicated hairstyles and even more complicated ear-rings.' Starr advised her that her hairstyle needed changing as it was inappropriate for rural communities. 'You'd better not do your hair swept up across the back like this. Women in country towns round here wear it very high in front and down at the back … Your clothes are not very suitable for this region either.' He also warned her not to smoke in public as so few women smoked in that area that she would be picked out right away.

It worked, as during her work she brushed sleeves with the Gestapo, arranging for wanted men to leave France, waiting on lonely fields for an incoming plane bringing arms and ammunition and sharing with unflinching bravery the hardships of underground life. While there she became 'romantically involved' with Claude, which also caused concern for Starr. As a present for her twenty-first birthday, he arranged a beautifully decorated cake with twenty-one lighted candles – the latter being impossible to find in occupied France. He had cut some detonating fuse and painted it pink.

After D-Day, having been identified to the Vichy police by an informer, she was ordered to go to Lannemezan. On the morning of 29 June she rendezvoused with US Major Horace Fuller, codenamed 'KANSUL', Captain Guy La Roche and Sub-Lieutenant Martial Siguad, both French. They were the Jedburgh team of Bugatti, parachuted into the Hautes Pyrenees from Blida, in Algiers. The 'Jeds' or 'Jets' were a team of three fully uniformed and trained French, British, American or Canadian officers who were sent into France by parachute on and after D-Day to liaise between the Allies and the Resistance, direct sabotage missions and ascertain the need for supplies, money and ammunition. One of the team was a radio operator who would contact London and arrange parachute drops. They sent a strong message to the local people that the Allies had arrived to help liberate them, a great boost to morale.

In Hewson's postscript to the republished *Moondrop to Gascony*, he quotes from an undated confidential letter Anne-Marie wrote to Buckmaster. In it she told him that, when she returned to Avéron-Bergelle at midnight on 25 July 1944,

I was pushed into a room by Buresie (Hilaire's 'garde de corps' – a Russian ex-legionnaire) and shown a paper declaring textually: prière d'arrêter et d'incarcérer Mademoiselle Colette dès son retour … I was thrown into prison with the captured Miliciens and collaborators (including their fleas and lice) and a guard was ordered to sleep at my side … The whole maquis knew of this and decided I must be a Gestapo double-agent …

The following day she was taken to Hilaire's command post, where he accused her of having an affair with a member of the battalion, spreading scandalous stories about him having relations with another female agent, and of being undisciplined. She vigorously denied his accusations.

I brought KANSUL to HILAIRE who wanted to try and explain the various political entanglements of the region to him. From then on I continued liaison with them, mainly on bicycle.

On July 28th, HILAIRE decided to send me on to LONDON with a report on the various political difficulties in the S.W. He gave me no contact for one of our escape lines, and I am convinced that he had none. KANSUL put me in touch with guides. He also asked me to go on a mission for him to Major Champion, at 1ssU6, Algiers – which I was glad to. Started out on August 1st, lost ourselves four times: left from the Col des Arts, west of Aspet, climbed the Pic du Gard, passed near Boutx and Mollo and arrived well east of Canejan on August 4th …

(TNA HS 9/339/2)

Accompanying her were US Major Fuller, the leader of the Jedburgh BUGATTI team, Captain La Roche, a radio operator and Leslie Brown, a downed RAF pilot who had joined the Maquis and fought bravely with a Bren gun at Castlenau. They were all taken into custody by the Spanish police and transported via Sort to Vielha. After four days behind bars, the British Consul arranged their release and onward journey to Barcelona to meet Colonel General Harold Farquar, described by Hewson as a solid supporter of the SOE.

Under the guise of 'Miss Fitzgerald', Anne-Marie made her way to Madrid, where she had to wait another four days before getting the necessary papers to allow her to get to Algiers with Major Fuller's message.

I was at 1ssU6 Algiers on September 1st; there I saw Major Marten instead of Champion. He suggested that I should go back to France for the Jedburgh section and work with a party under his command. I was to help rounding up the Jeds which I could easily do in the S.W. and help in their debriefing. After that was done, we were to start a new plan of recontacting all the contacts we had (both the F Section and the Jeds) in order to build up, from that very solid basis, new and better post-war relations between the French and the British. We had a long talk with Col. Anstey (?) about it; he agreed to take me on and suggested we should start back to France right away. I was very attracted by this job as I had always been interested in Franco-British relations and because I had worked for seven months and failed to see the conclusion of all our efforts, being away during the big Allied victories. Unfortunately, London refused to allow me on this job and I had to return.

Getting back to England by the end of July 1944, she was upset not to have had three suitcases of luggage forwarded to her and to only be offered a £15 clothing allowance. When she contacted SOE, they told her that the contents of her cases had been bought with SOE funds so didn't actually belong to her.

With the help of US Captain Millet, one of 'F' Section's training officers, she and FANY officer Suzanne Warren managed to get onto another parachute training course at Ringway. Her visit at the end of October caused quite a stir. Sergeant Kenworthy, the External Security Officer at Ringway, commented in his report that she showed complete disregard for personal security during the course.

> The usual precautions taken to hide the sex of FANYs performing parachute descents were put into effect, but from the first they were nullified by her behaviour on the dropping ground at Tatton Park. The following are examples of what happened during the week:–
>
> Immediately on landing, she invariably removed her protective helmet, and shook her hair out, thus advertising the fact that she was a woman to everyone in sight. This happened on at least one occasion when Paratroopers were also on the field. She appeared to make a point of conducting a conversation either on the field or in the air with someone at least fifty yards away ensuring that her voice attracted the attention of anyone who had not previously seen her. Following a descent she and her colleague would remain on the field without their helmets, watching other descents. When spoken to by the Medical Orderly whose duty it was to get them off the field unnoticed, she replied in a rude fashion. In the presence of two M.T. drivers (and I believe among other students) she talked freely of actual operations in which she had taken part. Any effort by her Instructors to make her conform to the Security rules were received with ill-grace; her attitude being that the need for it had passed.
>
> (TNA HS 9/339/2)

Without her knowledge, Starr had sent a message back to 'F' Section saying that he had had to send her back to England because, despite his efforts to train her since her arrival, she was, according to a note in his personal file,

> Undisciplined, Most indiscreet, Man-mad, also disobedient in personal matters, She constitutes a danger to security, not only her own but of everyone. On the other had she does not lack courage, never hesitated to go on any mission. Totally unsuitable for any commission. She should not be sent back to France to work for our organisation.
>
> (TNA HS 9/1407)

Back in England, she got off to a bad start. In a note in her personal file, an RAF pilot training instructor commented on her being somewhat indiscreet. He had noticed her standing on the departure platform for the Manchester train at Euston station. Nothing untoward, but she had caused quite a commotion wearing her blue parachute wings on her FANY uniform. After being spoken to, she resigned her commission. Notes in her file indicate that a planned job working for the Free French fell through, so she made plans to work for *News Chronicle*, one of the British daily papers.

What follows is a transcript of an interview she had with the BBC in early March 1945. The blocked text had to be deleted before transmission.

CUE MATERIAL FOR PARACHUTE GIRL

On March 5th, Sir Archibald Sinclair revealed for the first time in his speech to the Commons that members of the Women's Auxiliary Air Force have been to the fore in helping the Resistance groups in Europe before the landing on D-Day, either as Liaison officers, or couriers or radio operators.

We have in the studio today a girl who was parachuted into France many months before D-Day (and) remained several months after fighting with the Maquis. This WAAF had an English father and a French mother and was brought up in Geneva and she begins this interview with Vera Lindsay by telling how she was chosen for this special work.

[BLOCKED]

PARA.GIRL: Well I was in the WAAFs and as I'd always made quite a lot of noise about being able to speak French and wanted to do some work having to do with the Free French and I had been on the list for transfer of jobs for some time.

LINDSAY: Tell me – how long did you train for this special work and was the training very difficult?

PARA.GIRL: Well I trained quite a long time, and the training was extremely interesting and very useful to me but I'm afraid I cannot talk at all about that right now.

LINDSAY: Were there other women training with you?

PARA.GIRL: Yes, there were a number of other women training with me. Quite a number trained after I left and went later too.

LINDSAY: But were they English girls who spoke French?

PARA.GIRL: Some were French but most of them were English girls speaking absolutely fluent French. Actually French like a native woman.

[BLOCKED]

LINDSAY: But in those days just before you left were you able to see ordinary people? I mean your friends in London?

PARA.GIRL: Well the only people I knew and frequented so to speak were my friends who were doing the same job as I was and my family didn't know anything about it and we had worked out all our stories to the last details. Whenever they came at home they never mentioned anything of the work we were doing. My parents knew I was doing secret work but they didn't know at all, they didn't have any idea what it was. And my friends played up to the game very well.

[BLOCKED]

LINDSAY: And just before the jump – what was the feeling? Were you afraid?

PARA.GIRL: No, I wasn't afraid. In fact it was the only time in all the jumps that I have made that I really wasn't afraid at all. There were so many things to think about and it was our second trip. The pilot had circled some time in the region before being able to contact our people on the ground and we had a horrible moment that we should have to go back once more. And when the pilot declared that he had contacted the people and we were to go to action stations and jump – I felt so relieved at the idea that we wouldn't have to go back again to England it was really quite a pleasure. [BLOCKED]

   LINDSAY: … they've never learned what your work was?
   PARA.GIRL: Oh no, they never found out.
   [BLOCKED]

(TNA HS 9/339/2)

Starr, when he met de Gaulle in Toulouse on 16 September 1944, was given just days to leave the country. The new President of France didn't want a British military figure running affairs. Desperate to get back to France herself, Anne-Marie managed to get appointed as assistant to the American Press Attaché in Toulouse. A report, dated 24 April 1945, reached SOE HQ expressing concerns about 'her justifying herself for her past activities with those with whom she comes into contact'. A message was sent to the Press Attaché in Paris, but whether it affected her employment is not known.

In an interview with the Imperial War Museum, Starr admitted wanting to have her shot. Hewson detailed how she had initiated an investigation into Starr allowing the torture of captured Miliciens to get information out of them. They were put on a salt diet, left in a dark cell and then interrogated under bright lights, given a stool pigeon, someone who encouraged them to talk, and a microphone was installed. There was one case of a prisoner having the bottom part of his leg burned off over a fire. It was found that he was 'never party to, nor did he authorise, approve or condone such ill-treatment or the inflicting of torture' (Starr, G. R. 24613 IWM).

The following year, 1946, Anne-Marie published *Moondrop to Gascony*, an account of her experiences. It provides a vivid portrait of Starr and Arnault, with whom she was romantically involved, and won the John Llewellyn Rhys Prize in 1947. The revised edition, published in 2009, sheds more light onto her experiences.

The report prepared for her OBE stated that: 'She covered the whole region with trips by car, train and bicycle carrying messages for Lt. Col. Starr and his regional organisers. Several days after J day she rejoined the Maquis but continued to conduct different liaisons. She never shrank from any effort to accomplish her missions. Her coolness and profound imagination helped her through her adventures.' Major General Gubbins also added that 'she worked courageously for six months in difficult conditions, and her commanding officer has commented on her personal courage and willingness to undergo any danger'.

What Hewson failed to mention was that Anne-Marie was also awarded the Croix de Guerre and the Médaille de la Reconnaissance Française.

## Marguerite Petitjean

Marguerite Petitjean, codename 'Binette', was recorded by Harrison as parachuting into France on 29/30 January 1944 (http://soe_french.tripod.com). Not mentioned by Clark, it is possible that, like Reddé, she was an RF agent flown in from Algeria. Apart from her being a member of the Corps Auxiliaire Féminin, very little detail about her has come to light. Accompanying her were three men whose mission was to set up an action network with Alexandre Parodi and prepare for D-Day. Codenamed 'Hoe', she acted as their wireless operator until she had to escape the Germans  by crossing the Pyrenees.

## Madeleine Damerment

Clark has detailed how, on 28/29 February 1944, Pilot Officer Caldwell of 161 Squadron took off in his Halifax to complete PHONO 4. Over Ouistreham on the French coast, he flew through a pyrotechnic display of light flak, searchlights and red and orange flares. His navigator pinpointed Angeville, about 40 km south-east of Chartres, and the plane descended to 700 feet to make a DR (dropping run). Three agents, J. F. Anthelme, the leader, Lionel Lee, the radio operator, and twenty-six-year-old Madeleine Damerment, a French captain in the Resistance, were dropped straight into waiting German hands. Unbeknown to the pilot or the agents, the arrangements for their drop had been made by the Germans, who had captured Noor Inayat Khan's wireless set. The flashing code for the circuit was correct but, as the network had been penetrated, Madeleine and her colleagues were caught in a trap. After a brief struggle, they were arrested and taken to Avenue Foch, the Gestapo headquarters in Paris.

According to Foot, she was brave, young and gentle and the least conspicuous of all the available couriers. 'Mlle Damerment's ordre de mission gives the dropping zone as 3km SE Sainville, 31 km ESE of Chartres', some 12 km north-west of Angeville, from where Caldwell made his dropping run. She had two codenames, 'Solonge' and 'Dancer', and separate identity cards which showed her as 'Jacqueline Duchateau' and 'Martine Dassautoy'.

Before the war she lived in Lille, the daughter of the head postmaster, and joined the Resistance with other members of her traditional Catholic family, helping to shepherd downed Allied aircrew and evaders along the PAT escape line through France and into Spain, Portugal and Gibraltar. Her boyfriend, Roland Lepers, was one of the escorts. After a number of arrests in late 1941, Roland got her away from her house before the police arrived and arrested her family. They went south to Tulles to wait until their escape could be organised, crossing the Pyrenees separately in March 1942. She was interned for months by the Spanish until her release was negotiated by the British consulate in Madrid. When she got to England they met up, but Roland refused to marry her. She made friends with members of the Free French Forces and lived for a time with nuns in Hitchin, Hertfordshire.

In October she volunteered to work for the SOE and, despite one instructor's report that she was 'lacking in aggressiveness', was given a commission as ensign in the FANY. Madeleine's mission was to have worked as a courier in the BRICKLAYER network in Chartres, south-west of Paris.

Antelme and Lee were tortured and eventually executed at Gross Rosen prison. After torture and interrogation for four months at Avenue Foch, Madeleine was sent to Karlsruhe civil prison. Kramer interviewed a German woman prisoner with whom she shared a cell and was told that during the heavy RAF raids on Karlsruhe, Madeleine clasped her rosary beads and prayed. Sometimes they sang to keep her spirits up and exchanged stories about their homes and families. Her German cellmate had been imprisoned having been informed on for telling a joke about Hitler in the street.

On 10 September 1944 Madeleine was transferred by train to Munich and then to Dachau with Eliane Plewman, Yolande Beekman and Noor Inayat Khan. At dawn on the 13th all four were taken out for execution. She asked in German for a priest but was told there wasn't one. Holding hands in pairs, they were shot through the back of the neck. Madeleine needed two bullets. All the bodies were then burnt in the crematorium. After the war she was posthumously awarded the KCBC, Croix Legion d'Honneur and the Medaille de Resistance (Kramer, *Flames in the Field*; http://www.conscript-heroes. com).

## Jeanne Bohec

Harrison's records refer to Jeanne Bohec being flown out of Tempsford on 1 March 1944 (http://soe_french.tripod.com). Details of her role were included in Margaret Collins Weitz's *Sisters of the Resistance*. She was another of the French women sent by de Gaulle's RF section. She survived the war and wrote her autobiography, *La Plastiqueuse à bicyclette*. Born into a seafaring family in Brittany, she worked as an assistant chemist in a gunpowder factory before the war. On 18 June 1940, the day the German troops arrived in Brest, the twenty-one-year-old left for England in a tug boat. She had not heard General de Gaulle's call for the French people to resist, but she wanted to. To improve her English she looked after an English couple's baby but wanted to do something more destructive to help France.

On 6 January 1941, she was among the first five women to be accepted into de Gaulle's Corps Féminin, an auxiliary force whose name was quickly changed to the French Women's Volunteers Corps as the double entendre provoked unwanted smirks. The women went to extreme lengths to look presentable for de Gaulle's visit but all he noticed was the absence of bidets in their bathrooms. Trained as a nurse, Jeanne hated the work and insisted on being able to put her knowledge of explosives to good use. Promoted to corporal in the FFL, the Free French Forces, she was eventually posted as a technical secretary to the armaments section in Carlton Gardens, London, an area with many Free French residents.

By spring 1942, she was transferred to the French College's engineering department laboratory researching the best ways of using chemicals bought from a pharmacy as explosives. All her colleagues were hospitalised at one time or another for burns, and their formulas, to this day, remain secret. When Henry Frenay, a leading member of the Resistance, visited the laboratory, she persuaded him to let her use her skills with the BCRA, *Bureau Central de Renseignements et d'Action*, de Gaulle's intelligence service. She undertook to train French agents about to be dropped into France. When she asked why the Resistance could not be taught in France, she was told that no women were sent as agents. But she must have been aware that the SOE had started training and sending female agents into France.

After repeated requests the RF Section changed their minds. As the only woman in a group of seven, she went on the same six-week training courses in sabotage, weapons, theft, silent killing, parachuting and field craft. Collins Weitz reported Jeanne saying how:

The training left me sceptical about my own chances against a strong, determined man, but perhaps someone caught off guard would find it hard to overpower me. In any case, the training gave us confidence in our potential and a combative spirit that would be essential to us.

During her parachute training, she was once more the only woman in the group and, being small, had to have the harness specially adapted. As it was, Jeanne was the first to jump.

The English were fine. The only discrimination came from the men in the BCRA, who initially did not want women involved. I believe this is because France is a Latin country. Even today, it is difficult for women to get equal treatment. Men go to war; women stay home.

When she finished her training, she was promoted to second lieutenant with a mission to train the Galilee network in Brittany in using explosives. On being given her equipment, she crocheted a better secret compartment in the purse she was issued with, threw away her 'ladies' handgun and the 'L' pill, deciding that God would help her keep quiet if she was tortured. Given a codename 'Rateau', meaning rake, she was one of the ten women from the RF section parachuted into France. 'Hoe' was Marguerite Petitjean, her radio operator.

After two flights from Tempsford had to be cancelled due to bad weather, on the night of 20 February 1944 (another source says it was 29 February) Jeanne was dropped in the area of Alençon. One of the reception committee who met her didn't expect such a petite young woman. 'What's going on? They're sending us children now!' After being taken to Paris, she got the train to Brittany in early March and bought a bike. To get around all the Breton departments, she cycled everywhere and by the beginning of April had set up her first 'training school' at Loudéac. Saboteurs were taught the best use of *plastique*, the French term for plastic explosives, for attacking the Germans, and in particular how to frustrate their attempts to thwart the D-Day landings.

There was still time for her to get a suit and dress made. 'Dressing, sleeping, and eating properly are also elements of a clandestine life.' She repeated the explosives training in numerous localities over the next few months and became known as the 'plastiqueuse avec bicycle'. Demonstrating her expertise, she was involved in attacks on the railway between Dinan and Vannes. As the detonators had not been included in the container with the explosives, she made a thirty-minute one herself. She took part in the defence of Saint-Marcel, decoding their instructions from London. When the message came through to keep the German forces from getting to Normandy she co-ordinated several parachute drops, but this team would not allow her to use a machine gun to help force the German troops out of Quimper. Her Maquis companions would have let her. 'I was considered a comrade – one of them. It was the men in uniform, the professional army. They couldn't accept the idea of a woman carrying guns.' However, in appreciation of her assistance, she was named secretary of the regional chief of the Free French Forces in Finistere. When the town was liberated on 8 August, she returned briefly to London before settling in Paris.

## Eileen 'Didi' Nearne

On 2 March 1944, two days after Jeanne's arrival in France, two Lysanders of 161 Squadron left England with young women on board: twenty-three-year-old Eileen 'Didi' Nearne and twenty-nine-year-old Denise Bloch. Didi was from an unusual family in that both she and her elder sister Jacqueline and her brother Francis became SOE agents. The family had been living in Paris, from where they escaped via Spain when war broke out. Didi joined the FANY with Jacqueline as a cadet officer but, being fluent in French and after her sister was sent back to France, she was keen to follow in her elder sister's footsteps. Didi trained first as a cipher clerk at SOE's home station and, using the codename 'Alice Wood', went through paramilitary training in Arisaig and the 'Finishing School' at Beaulieu.

She did not create a good impression while undergoing training. Her assessors commented that:

> She is not very intelligent or practical and is lacking in shrewdness and cunning. She has a bad memory, is inaccurate and scatterbrained. She seems keen but her work was handicapped by lack of the power to concentrate.
>
> In character she is very feminine; and immature; she seems to lack all experience of the world and would probably be easily influenced by others.
>
> She is lively and amusing and has considerable charm and social gifts. She talks a lot and is anxious to draw attention to herself but was generally liked by the other students.
>
> It is doubtful whether this student is suitable for employment in any capacity on account of her lack of experience.
>
> (Report dated January 1944, quoted in *The Independent*, 29 October 2010)

Nevertheless, Buckmaster sent her to Thame Park, where she finished her training as a radio operator. Despite being considered too young by her sister, she was determined to help in the war effort. Although they were not supposed to divulge information about their clandestine training, it became obvious that her sister and brother had also trained as agents. Buckmaster (1946–47) admitted that:

> The way of a radio operator is always hard: when he is being trained to work a morse set in conditions of absolute secrecy, he requires almost more than human perseverance and concentration. The instructors at the school will say, 'So-and-so is not feeling well today; his speed is down to 31'. Men and women in training become moody and disgruntled: there was much bickering and bad-tempered gossip, for the strain was intense. In this school hidden away in the heart of the countryside, there were in the winter of 1943 some fifty or sixty students, who were being trained to be dropped by parachute in occupied countries, whence they would send home by morse those messages which were essential to the carrying out of underground warfare.
>
> In response to messages, aircraft, flying by night from secret bases in England, would take loads of containers slung like bombs, and release them over small fields in the heart of France or Norway, where anxious patriots awaited the distant hum of the aircraft motors before flashing their torches at the western sky. But these parachute operations

could not take place without communications, and radio was the essential link. These solemn students, men and women alike, in this country-house, would become the radio operators who would make these parachute operations possible. They had to learn how to install a set, to fix the aerial so that it attracted the minimum of attention, to remedy minor defects, to tap out their messages at speed, to identify, despite jamming, their distant home station. They had to become familiar with the touch on the key of their partner at the home station, and more important still, they had to acquire an individual technique by which they would themselves be infallibly recognised. They, more than any other officers who were to be sent into occupied countries, had to learn how to live unsuspected and unnoticed. The need for self-sufficiency was great; they had to be prepared to live alone without friends, for months at a time if necessary. The preparation was long and severe; it required much patience to go on tapping day after day without apparent progress. Disheartenment was very frequent and any form of mental anxiety was apt to retard progress in the most spectacular way.

Among the group of pupils in December 1943 was Eileen, her fair curls bent low over her set, patiently practising hour after hour, desperately anxious to pass the test which would permit her to be sent to France, where her sister Jacqueline was already working. Eileen was young, and looked even younger than she was. But the determination to succeed was in her, and she showed all the signs of becoming a really first-class operator.

The day I spent down at the school was the occasion on which the instructor was lecturing on radio-detector vans. He explained that the Germans used harmless-looking delivery vans for the purpose of tracking radio transmitters. The principle was as simple as the apparatus was complex. If the equipment in a van picked up a transmission on a wavelength which was not catalogued, the site of the transmitter was stalked by three vans, each moving in the direction in which the signals became stronger and stronger. By this means a 'fix' was obtained which enabled the detectors to locate the transmitter within an area of twenty or thirty yards square. A police cordon was then thrown round the suspected area, and the flats or houses combed until the set was found and its operator arrested. Eileen's face was grim as she listened to this explanation, but her chin was thrust forward as the means for as the means for avoiding detection were examined and explained. She was determined to remember this complicated business. She felt that Jacqueline would be pleased if she could get through the examinations with credit. Besides, her life might depend upon her remembering. But she found the effort a great strain, and when the time came for her to leave the school and prepare for her departure, she showed by certain signs of emotion that she was not as confident as her ready smile would lead one to believe.

She was chosen by Jean Savy, a French lawyer, to be his 'pianist' in WIZARD, a new circuit he was sent to set up in Paris after the PROSPER circuit had been infiltrated and broken up. As he had a withered arm and could not parachute, he and Didi were landed in a field 2 kilometres north-west of Les Lagnys, about 6 miles (10 km) south of Vatan, not far north of the Châteauroux drop zone. Clark's book sheds no light on the drop, only saying 161 Squadron went on seven sorties that night and 138 Squadron on seventeen. One of the reception committee, according to her obituary in the *Daily Telegraph*, was reported as saying: 'Oh, you're a young girl. Go back. It's too dangerous' (http://www.telegraph.co.uk/news/obituaries/military-obituaries/special-forces-obituaries/8009812/Eileen-Nearne.html).

She stayed and made her way to Paris to rendezvous with 'Louise' in the snow beside the statue of King Henri IV on the Pont Neuf bridge. Provided with a room on Boulevard St Michel and given a wireless set, she began her work. Later she transmitted from a deserted house at Bourg-la-Reine. Codenamed 'Rose', she helped Savy in his mission to arrange for the reception and utilisation of the Jedburgh teams. Using his business contacts, he approached French financiers for money that the Resistance needed. To reassure them that the money would be repaid by the British government, they volunteered a phrase which she transmitted to London. It was then passed to the BBC's French Department, who added it in their *messages personelles* after the evening news. When the message was heard, the money was handed over.

Didi's other codenames were 'Petticoat' and 'Pioneer', and her identity cards showed her as 'Marie Tournier' and 'Mlle. Jacqueline du Tertre'. The first of her 105 messages containing important economic and military details went out on 26 March. It included explosive information that Savy had obtained – details of the Luftwaffe's secret ammunition dump in caves in the stone quarries at Saint Leu d'Esserent, Picardy. Stored inside were about 2,000 V1 rockets ready for shipment to launch sites on the French coast. Within weeks the RAF went in and bombed the quarry and 85 per cent of the town, seriously hampering the Germans.

As Savy was known to the Gestapo, SOE planned a Lysander mission to pick him up and return him to England. Accompanying him would be Mrs Josette Southgate and Didi's sister, Jacqueline, who had been in France fifteen months.

On 10 April 1944, after four days' wait in the open air close to Galèteries farm buildings, 2 kilometres south-south-west of Villers-les-Ormes, north-west of Châteauroux, they were understandably pleased to see Flight Lieutenant Robert Taylor's Lysander appear in the night sky. Lise de Baissac, Philippe de Vomécourt and Arnaud de Vogüé got out and Savy and the two women went back to England.

Prior to D-Day, Didi and another radio operator went to Paris to work for the SPIRITUALIST network which was planning railway sabotage and had urgent need for communications with London for supplies. Afterwards she handled messages about dropping supplies for the MUSICIAN and FARMER circuits, which were attacking railways carrying German troops to the front line in Normandy. In Lilian Jones's *A Quiet Courage*, Didi recalled one occasion when she was sitting in a train compartment with a radio in her suitcase.

> There was this German soldier who kept looking at me and smiling, so I smiled back. Then I was looking through the window and he said, 'Cigarette, Mademoiselle?' And I said, 'No, thank you, I don't smoke.' and my hands, you see, were stained with nicotine. You could make mistakes like that. He was looking at me and he said 'What is in your suitcase?' So I said, 'Oh – c'est un phonographe, savez, de la musique,' and he said, 'Oh, oui' and he was looking at me and I thought Oh la, la, I must get out quickly.

In her debrief once back in England after the war, she admitted that it was a lonely life.

I used to go out a lot and have my meals in restaurants alone. Sometimes I would meet my contact Louise, but all we would do was to pass a note. It was very solitary. I wasn't nervous. In my mind I was never going to be arrested. But of course I was careful. There were Gestapo in plain clothes everywhere. I always looked at my reflection in the shop windows to see if I were being followed.

(TNA HS 9/1089/2)

Buckmaster (1946–47) acknowledged that life in Paris for Eileen was very lonely.

From time to time she had to meet her Organising Officers, the people from whom she received special instructions. These meetings had to take place in streets, trams, trains; a message would be passed and possibly no word spoken, so great was the danger of being observed and discovered. Living in houses from which she had to move constantly, she continued to send and receive messages in code. She knew that discovery meant interrogation by the Gestapo, with possibly torture, the concentration camp, or death.

Her state was made no easier by her inability during her service in France to get in touch with any of her family. How were her father and mother? Her brother? What had happened to her only sister, engaged on such hazardous work? Eileen went for lonely walks, thinking, worrying, passing cafés where the invader lounged at ease. Paris can be lovely in June, but for Eileen the loveliness was encased in nightmare.

And then, one June morning, came disaster.

Other sources state it was on 25 July, two days after Savy was lifted out in a Lysander for the second time and about four months after landing in France, that Didi had just finished transmitting a message for the SPIRITUALIST circuit when the police arrived. The Germans had radio receivers disguised in bread vans which, within twenty minutes, could detect a transmission and send in a hit squad.

She had just enough time to burn her messages in the oven and hide the radio. However, a thorough search of the house uncovered it, her unused one-time pad and her pistol. She was arrested and taken to Avenue Foch for interrogation. In her obituary in the *Guardian*, it was described how, despite the incriminating evidence, she maintained, with considerable sang-froid, that she was an innocent shop assistant called Jacqueline du Tetre who had no idea that the messages she was sending for her boss were being sent to England. She claimed she had met him three months earlier in a coffee shop and he had given her the code pad. It did not take long for the Gestapo to discover that his name and address were false (www.guardian.co.uk/uk/2010/oct/13/eileen-nearne-obituary).

Although subjected to the *baignoire* treatment, a bath of cold water into which prisoners were held down until their lungs almost burst, she kept to her story. Eventually she 'admitted' to a planned meeting with her boss at Gare St Lazare at 1900 hours that evening. She was taken to the rendezvous and won some more time when an air-raid warning went off at 1915. The next day, to avoid more *baignoire* treatment, she offered to take the Gestapo chief to the addresses she had given them. They did not take her up on her offer and transferred her to Fresnes Prison (TNA HS 9/1089/2).

In an interview in 1950 with the *Daily Herald* journalist James Gleeson, she told him that she had created the impression that she had been imprudent and was unaware of the political implications of her involvement with the Resistance, claiming she was 'a bit of a scatterbrain and a tomboy … helping the Resistance for fun and excitement'. Her colleagues made a desperate bid to bribe the German guards to release the Nearne sisters, but it backfired. Two prostitutes were handed over instead.

In Foot's *SOE in France*, he noted that Didi 'put on her act of being a sweet little thing who knew nothing she ought not' and that, consequently, she 'brought off a dextrous bluff, and persuaded the Gestapo she was only a foolish little shop girl who had taken up resistance work because it was exciting'.

Pattinson commented that this gendered strategy was only open to women. Didi had been informed by her training instructors that she was a good liar and found that during interrogations she could improvise plausible explanations and remain calm: 'All sorts of things I pulled from my head. And the more I was lying, the more I wanted to and the more it was easy coming to me.' Her conscious strategy was 'to act confusion and misunderstanding'.

On 15 August, Didi was put in a cattle truck with a batch of suspected English and French girls and spent a week with little food, drink or sleep on the journey to Ravensbrück. The typescript of her debrief details her experiences but names of other prisoners have been blanked out.

I arrived there in September and met [blanked out] and [blanked out], two English girls. We stayed there about 15 days and in October we went to Torgau, where we stayed two months. I met [blanked out] at Torgau, where we all worked in the fields. I knew that [blanked out] wanted to escape, but after that I left the camp and arrived at Abteroda (6 km. from Sisnak) in October. [Blanked out] and [blanked out] stayed in the camp (Torgau) and I worked in the factory. At Abteroda the Commandant S.S. from Torgau came and we heard that he was looking for two English girls who had escaped from Torgau and there were rumours that it was [blanked out] and [blanked out]. They were always with a girl called [blanked out] I did not want to work in the factory so they shaved my head and told me that if I did not work in 20 minutes I would be shot. I then decided to work. I left the camp on the 1st December and went to Markleburg (7 km. from Leipzig). There we worked on the roads for 12 hours per day and one day they told us we would be leaving the camp for a place 80 km away (5 April). Two French girls and I decided to escape and while we were passing a forest I spotted a tree and hid there and then joined the French girls in the forest. [Blanked out] We escaped on the night of 5th April. We stayed in a bombed house for two nights and the next morning walked through Markleburg and slept in the woods. We were arrested by the S.S. who asked us for papers. We told them a story and they let us go. We arrived in Leipzig and at a Church a priest helped us and kept us there for three nights and the next morning we saw white flags and the first Americans arriving and when I said that I was English they put us in a camp.

(TNA HS 9/1089/2)

Buckmaster (1946–47) provided more details of her time in Ravensbrück.

Eileen did her best to adopt the technique of the hunted animal and to merge into her background. At length she tricked the camp guards and got herself included in a working party in a factory. But she had no intention whatever of helping the enemy war machine. She made up her mind to do all the sabotage that her instruments and gauges would allow. Day after day she succeeded in falsifying precision instruments and graphs, and the aero-engine parts she turned out were all rejected by the inspection department. To her delight, it was a long time before they traced the faults to her. As a punishment her long golden hair was shaved, and once more she went through the torments of the icy plunge. She was allowed to return to the factory, and although she now had only limited opportunities for sabotage, she contrived with one wild swoop to wreck a vital machine. She was careless of consequences, and would not yield to force.

The camp authorities decided that she must be punished again, and more severely. Meanwhile Eileen had disappeared among the thousands of French prisoners. By the time she had been found again, trace of her misdemeanour had been lost.

While in this camp she caught diphtheria through drinking filthy water. She recovered eventually, and escaping while in a working-party convoy, reached the American lines.

The 5th Corps of the First US Army reported finding her on 15 April 1945 but, doubting her story, put her in a prison camp with captured Nazi women. Their report, dated 2 May and marked 'SECRET', commented that:

> Subject creates a very unbalanced impression. She is often unable to answer the simplest questions, as though she were impersonating someone else. Her account of what happened to her after landing near Orleans is held to be invented. It is recommended that Subject be put at the disposal of the British Authorities for further investigation and disposition.
>
> (TNA HS 9/1089/2)

She had to withstand further intense interrogation until she was believed. The Americans were worried that she might have been a German agent. Eventually, after a month in captivity, she was identified by a British major and taken to safety.

Liane Jones mentioned that one of the English girls Didi met in prison was Violette Szabó.

> Didi warned Violette that she was passing herself off as French. Violette asked her what the Gestapo had done to her and, when Didi told her about the 'baignoire' in the Rue de Saussaies, she was horrified. She told Didi that neither she nor Lilian nor Denise had been tortured, and she advised Didi to change her story and admit her British nationality. 'She said. "You should have said you were English. English girls are better treated than the French." but I said, "No, I'm sticking to my story."' ... She was wary of being seen with the British women, her alias of Jacqueline du Tetre was important to her as a way of protecting her SOE knowledge and it was as Jacqueline that her fellow prisoners knew her.

Pattinson reported that Maisie McLintock, a FANY coder, had been close friends with Didi during her training, in which she had deliberately disobeyed rules like having baths after hours. When spoken to by her superiors she always 'played the daft lassie' by pretending not to understand.

> She was very clever, I think. It explained a lot when she survived the Germans and that concentration camp using the same method as she had done when she was a FANY. Wide-eyed innocence … One of the first things she said when she was telling me about her experience, she was taken to the Avenue Foch in Paris, that was where she got her preliminary going over, and she said, 'You see, Mac, I did what you said, I played the daft lassie with them' … She was still getting through life somehow, looking innocent and not quite sure why she was there.

In an interview after the war, in response to a question on how she kept alive, she said that it was:

> The will to live. Will power. That's the most important. You should never let yourself go. It seemed that the end would never come, but I have always believed in destiny and I had a hope. If you are a person who is drowning you put all your efforts into trying to swim.

On returning to England on 23 May 1945, Didi was met at the airfield by Buckmaster and Atkins, who could hardly recognise her as the smart, charming girl who had left a year earlier. When they took her to meet her sister Jacqueline in London, she walked jauntily over the threshold, embraced her and then collapsed in tears. She was ill for several months, suffering from nervous exhaustion, but must have been uplifted when she learned that she had been awarded the MBE and the Croix de Guerre for her 'cool efficiency, perseverance and willingness to undergo any risk in order to carry out her work … [She] made possible the successful organisation of her group and the delivery of large quantities of arms and equipment'. (TNA HS 9/1089/2)

In 1997 she agreed to be interviewed for BBC2's *Time Watch*. To protect her identity, she wore a wig, was introduced as Rose and spoke only in French. In fact, she was given the last word in the film: 'When I returned after the war, I, along with lots of others, missed that kind of life. Everything seemed so ordinary.'

Her death in September 2010 provoked such a widespread interest in her wartime exploits and post-war experiences that most British and some foreign newspapers and television companies ran stories on her.

## Denise Bloch

The other woman Lysandered out with Didi during the moon period in early March 1944 was Denise Bloch. According to Nigel Perrin's website, she had joined the Resistance following her parents' arrest during the round-up of French Jews in 1942. She had worked as a courier for Brian Stonehouse, an SOE radio operator in the Detective network in Lyon. This was the centre of the Vichy government during the years of France's occupation and many diplomats and correspondents from around the world were there too. There were times when she accompanied Francis Suttill of the PROSPER network in the Île de France, pretending to be his sister. When Stonehouse was arrested at the end of October, she went south to Marseille and didn't return north until things had cooled down.

Denise was described as a tall, sturdy, broad-shouldered blonde but her SOE photograph shows her as a dark-haired beauty. She dyed it after the police raided her flat in Lyon. Aron, one of her accomplices, was arrested, but she and Henri Sevenet evaded the blue-coated, brown-shirted, blue-bereted *Miliciens,* the Vichy government's police force, and moved from safe house to safe house in St Laurent de Samouchet, Villefranche-sur-mer and Toulouse, where she met up with Maurice Dupont. He helped her to try to escape over the Pyrenees but, as the snow was too deep, they had to return. She then met George Starr, who introduced her to Philippe de Vomécourt, an organiser of the VENTRILOQUIST network in Agen. When their network was broken in April 1943, she successfully accompanied Dupont over the Pyrenees to Spain. From there they made their way safely to Gibraltar and back to England (http://www.nigelperrin.com/denisebloch.htm).

Martin Sugarman, the archivist of the British Association of Jewish Ex-Servicemen and Women, researched Denise's life and on the Jewish Virtual Library website he related how, after her debrief in England, she spent ten months training in Wanborough, Arisaig and Beaulieu, and then on a wireless transmitters' course. One of her instructors commented that she 'was not very fit on arrival and was rather heavy and found the PT and ground training very tiring and also very stiffening' (http://www.jewishvirtuallibrary.org/jsource/ww2/sugar2.html).

With no time for parachute training at Ringway, she was taken to Tempsford on 2 March 1944, from where Flight Officer 'Dinger' Bell flew her and Robert Benoist, this time on his second mission, in one of 161 Squadron's Lysanders to a field one and a half kilometres west of Baudreville, east-south-east of Chartres. Other SOE records state that she landed at Soucelles, 10 kilometres south of Vatun, near Nantes. Codenamed 'Ambroise', she met up with Jean-Pierre Wimille, Benoist's former BUGATTI co-driver to join the 2,000-strong CLERGYMAN circuit as a wireless transmitter. Their mission was to bring down the electricity pylons linking the Pyrenees and Brittany and sabotage the railway system around Nantes. Over a period of three months she sent thirty-one messages back to London and received fifty-two, using Leo Marks's poem as her code.

> Make the most of it
> A coast to coast
> Toast of it
> For what you think
> Has been God-sent to you
> Has only been lent to you.

An indication as to how extensively she travelled on her missions was the number of aliases she used. Harrison recorded them as 'Danielle Williams', 'Claude Rabatal', 'Chantal Baron', 'Katrine Bernard', 'Criniline', 'Micheline' and 'Line' (http://soe_french.tripod.com).

On 19 June, the day after Benoist was arrested, Denise and Mme Wimille were captured by the Gestapo in one of Benoist's chateaux near Rambouillet and taken for interrogation in their headquarters on Avenue Foch. On 24 August she arrived at Ravensbrück prison. From there she was sent to work camps in Targau and Konisburg. In the film *Carve Her Name with Pride*, there is a scene where she tells a fellow inmate that she's made face powder using whitewash from the kitchen wall.

Seriously ill with cold and exposure, she was returned to Ravensbrück and on 27 January 1945 she, Violette Szabó and Cécile Lefort were taken out to a yard, shot in the back of the head and, after the German doctor checked to see if they had were any gold fillings he could remove, she was put in the crematorium furnace. There is no known grave, but her name is proudly carved on four SOE memorials in Britain, France and Germany. Denise was posthumously awarded the King's Commendation for Brave Conduct, Chevalier de la Legion d'Honneur, Croix de Guerre with Palme and the Medaille de la Resistance with Rosette.

## Yvonne Baseden

A fortnight after Denise Bloch's Lysander flight, Flight Lieutenant Downes took off from Tempsford on 18 March and, 40 kilometres away from the intended drop zone, picked up the Eureka beacon of WHEELWRIGHT 64. His passenger was twenty-two-year-old Yvonne Baseden, whose story has been told in several publications. She was born in France to an English father and French mother and had lived in Belgium, Holland, Poland, Italy and Spain before returning to Arachon, where she joined the ice hockey team, enjoyed clay pigeon shooting, and then in England completed secretarial courses in Pitman and Prevost-Delauny. Her attempts to join de Gaulle's Free French were thwarted when they discovered that her father was an English engineer. Instead, she joined the WAAF as a Craft GD (Aircraft General Duties) at Kenley airfield, near London. Here she met and admired the men who flew and the men who worked on the planes. When the Free French pilots formed their own squadron, she was asked to help them with their technical English. A year later, she was commissioned as an Assistant Section Officer in the Intelligence Branch and her special skills eventually got her a position in the Directorate of Allied Air Co-operation. Pearl Witherington was already working there and it was she who mentioned working with the SOE.

After several interviews she started her training in May 1943, a month before Pearl. Over five months she was trained as a radio operator at Thame Park and then sent on a paramilitary course. In an interview after the war, Yvonne commented how

> I had to blow up some railway lines. I was rather fond of explosives and did it effectively. Then there was weapons training. We handled everything from anti-tank guns to Continental automatics. At the end of the course I had developed a great affection and a lot of skill with grenades, the Bren gun, and the Colt .45 revolver. But there was one bad moment for me. The instructor gave me a long, black-handled commando knife. I had to learn how to use it. In a glade among the fir trees were three dummy men, which the instructor manipulated by wires. I had to learn to stab them and kill. 'Stab upwards, stab downwards' was the order repeated over and over again. I hated it. I hated it so much I never did use a knife in France. Then came unarmed combat training with

a tough Commando sergeant-major. By the time I returned to London I had learned a lot of ways of killing.

(Baseden, Y. 6373/2 IWM)

When she was asked by Pattinson whether she had been prepared to shoot someone in the field, she replied abruptly and decisively: 'Oh yes. Yes, absolutely. I don't know whether I would be prepared to knife them because we were trained to do that as well. Oh yes. Certainly I would. It was part of the training and a job to be done.') In a diary entry quoted in Jerrard Tickell's *Moon Squadron*, having almost completed her course, she wrote:

> Another wartime Christmas was over, the Christmas of 1943. It had been a blacked-out Christmas, with no turkey, no ham, no crackers, few carols and even fewer soya-bean sausages. But it had been more than a day in the calendar. It was a day on which one had to pause and look both backwards and forwards … We all knew what the future would hold. There were those among us who wouldn't see another Christmas – or if we did, we would see it through the bars over the window of a cell … I suppose I thought I would be one of the lucky ones who would get away with it. It's somebody else who is run over by a tram … But I said my quiet prayers all the same.

Before being flown out of Tempsford or Tangmere, agents had the opportunity to further practise weapons training in underground shooting galleries in London. They had to be fully prepared for their clandestine mission. Tickell narrated Yvonne's first attempt to be dropped into France with her future organiser, Baron Gonzagues de St Geniés, a very patriotic, brave French nobleman codenamed 'Lucien'.

> Like those who had gone, we made no farewells. We simply faded out. Lucien was wearing an untidy suit of unmistakable French cut. Nobody would look twice at him in a Paris street. I wore a skirt and a blouse, with a loose topcoat and a coloured scarf over my head. I hoped that nobody would look twice at me either.
>
> A car called for us. It was driven by another of those cheerful, healthy F.A.N.Y.s. We went along a winding lane and had to wait a minute or two at some closed railway gates. Beyond it, in the gloom, was a flat expanse of land, with some farm buildings. I asked where we were and realised at once that it was a foolish question. The F.A.N.Y. driver said evasively that it was the place where we took off from. The railway gates opened and we went on. It didn't look like an airfield but now I know it to be Tempsford. We arrived at what I thought vaguely was a cowshed. It turned out to be a Nissen hut and it had been made warm and welcoming with a blazing fire. There we were greeted by an R.A.F. officer who called us by our code names and helped us once again to check all our clothes and belongings. No British labels on the coat; no betraying, forgotten 'bus tickets to Baker Street; and what about this handkerchief with an embroidered initial other than that of the new name I had now assumed? The final check was as thorough as it was necessary. Then I turned out my handbag. Lipstick, comb, powder-puff – all unmistakably French; the silver powder-compact given to me by Colonel Buckmaster. No doubt at all about where that had come from – Paris.

Now for the money. The Nissen hut within the cow-shed was suddenly transformed into a sort of surrealist bank. After the search, I struggled into my jumping suit, pulling on the trousers over my top-coat. A bundle of five hundred thousand franc banknotes was slid, as a sort of cushion, into the small of my back by the obliging cashier in R.A.F. uniform. Lucien was given even more and, over and above these large sums, we were each handed some small change for immediate necessities.

I found it almost impossible to move once my parachute harness was strapped on over my suit. My handbag was on my front, hanging from a string round my neck, inside the suit. All this trussing up business gave me a slightly comic sense of unreality. And then, on a small table, I saw my crystals, my loaded Colt revolver – and my lethal tablet. The sight of this last item wiped the smile from my lips. My instinct was not to take it with me, not even to have it in my possession, and that instinct proved to be abundantly right. There were moments to come when I could have been tempted. So I left it where it was. The other things were stowed in their respective pockets, a protective rubber helmet was put on my head and I was ready to go. Lucien had been similarly trussed up and armed and, there we were, cap-a-pie!

Sitting with her feet dangling out of the Joe hole ready to jump, she didn't see any lights. The reception committee was not there, so the pilot took them back to Tempsford, where they were told to go to London and wait for the next moon period. She and Gonzagues dined around in different restaurants and patronised London shows until the message came through on 18 March 1944 that their flight was arranged.

This time they were dropped successfully in Gabarret, near Auch in the Marmande area of Lot et Garonne, along with fifteen containers and four packages. Their mission was to reorganise the old DIRECTOR network. Codenamed 'Odette', and using the cover story that she was a secretary, she worked her radio set for the SCHOLAR network almost on the Swiss border and was known as 'Marie Bernier' and 'Bursar'. To be as inconspicuous as possible, she dressed like the local women without any make-up. She wore a very casual, plain grey skirt and a blue blouse and did her hair so as not to attract attention in her cover as a shorthand typist. She still had some intense moments, which she revealed in an interview with Juliette Pattinson.

We had to go from where we were, which was near Auch, which is north of the Pyrenees, to Marseille by bus and take the train from Marseille to Dijon and Dôle where we were going … Naturally very anxious to get on with things … I had my crystals on me and my ciphers … First we went by coach … That was quite worrying in a way because it was the first time one travelled on public [transport] in occupied France and because it was a coach there was no other way out except the front door. Anyway, there was no trouble. We were stopped once or twice. They just glanced at the papers as we walked out and walked back into the coach … Marseille was terrible of course because there were several hours to wait there. I think I waited about four hours on a bench and of course I was on my own … It was very difficult because there were patrols in the station. Anyway, I got on the train and it's quite a long way to Lyon … I got off at Lyon without much trouble and got into Dôle. It took a day and a half.

In the grey morning of Sunday 26 June 1944, she played a major role in a huge daylight drop to her circuit. Over 400 containers were dropped by thirty-six Flying Fortresses of the American Eighth Air Force in operation CADILLAC. In an interview with Pattinson she recalled that she 'found a sort of culvert where I could be in with my radio, yet open in the field and so I sat there with my radio and established contact with England and to guide the planes in … It was incredible. I was jumping around, waving madly to them!'

Probably in the exuberance, there had been some careless talk and the Germans' successful radio detection led to her circuit being penetrated. She and Lucien were arrested on 28 June. Foot, in his *SOE in France*, describes how:

> Two days after Cadillac, the first mass daylight drop by the USAAF, the inner circle of SCHOLAR dined together at their best safe-house, a cheese factory near Dôle, to celebrate the safe stowing of thirty-six Fortress-loads of arms. A sub-agent in his middle teens was caught nearby carrying a transmitter, and the Germans raided the factory. They found the caretaker's wife, wringing her hands beside a table laid for eight, and an atmosphere of alarm. An NCO, impressing on her that he meant business, fired a random burst of bullets through the ceiling, and so shot through the head of de St Geniès who was hiding in the loft. The bloodstain was at once noticed, and Yvonne Baseden and several companions were found and arrested.

Lucien almost certainly swallowed the 'L' pill he had been issued with at Gibraltar Barn. Pattinson says Yvonne was caught having a meal with her friends in the regional Resistance and not with her wireless set, so she was able to keep to her cover story of being a shorthand typist who had unknowingly become involved with them. She said that, 'In all fairness I wasn't put to any form of distress, if you like, till someone who had been arrested said I was a radio operator and probably come from England.' Those captured were taken initially to the military barracks in Dôle, and then to Gestapo HQ in Dijon. There, despite being questioned in English, being shown photographs of HQ staff of various British organisations, having her bare toes stamped on by guards in army boots and a mock execution being staged to try to make her send a transmission to England, she kept to her cover story. At one point, she told Pattinson that she thought she was going to be raped.

> I felt a threat once … I was in solitary confinement at the time and somehow or other I had a feeling that there was something afoot to possibly try to get me down into the cellars by two or three of the guards. But this is something I vaguely understood through their shouting and things like that. Certainly nothing like that happened. I wasn't raped.

The Germans were unable to prove her to be a British agent, like Denise Bloch, and so Yvonne was kept in an underground cell, beaten, starved and tortured. Eventually, she was put on a train and taken to a concentration camp in Saarbrucken in Germany. Her experiences are recorded in Escott's *Mission Improbable*. On the journey she saw Violette, Denise and Lilian.

I thought it's incredible, they've got the whole of SOE. I hesitated about speaking to them and they naturally reacted in the same way until I realised it was safe to speak with Violet and I thought I would love to be with them, if only I could get into their group. But fortunately, as circumstances worked out, it was just as well that I was not able to do this. I saw them just to see that they were OK and they were on their way before us.

In her interview with Pattinson, she said she met up with Violette, Denise and Lilian at Saarbrucken.

They were all going off on a transport … in another part of Germany and I thought I must try and get in with them, which was crazy of course and thank goodness I didn't achieve that. They were not particularly keen. They could see both sides of me going with them.

On one occasion a feather from a pillow she was unloading from a truck landed on the uniform of one of her guards. He immediately raised his truncheon to hit her, but one of her fellow inmates pushed her out of the way and received the blow herself on the thigh, an action which she was severely beaten for. Who her anonymous helper was, she never knew.

Later, Yvonne was transferred to Ravensbrück, where she was given a red pleated skirt and sailor boy's shirt, just enough to cover herself. As number 62,947 she worked under armed guard on agricultural work as inconspicuously as she could until she developed tuberculosis in February. 'I was just part of a group of French women, which probably saved me in the end.' Like the others, she was forced to wear a red triangle on her baggy prison dress with a black F in it and the words *Politischer Franzose* in black. If it had been an E for 'Englander', she would have been shot like many of her compatriots.

Her planned transfer to Belsen was thwarted when she was diagnosed with tuberculosis and transferred to the hospital wing. Stafford reported that, by some miracle, she met Mary Lindell, a fellow prisoner and escape-line worker whom she had already met in Dijon and who was also a qualified Red Cross nurse. Her name was removed from the list to be executed. Like Didi Nearne, she kept to her cover story that she was French. It was the timely intervention of the Swedish Red Cross in April 1945 that saved her from the fate of her other colleagues. Once back in Britain, she spent several months in hospital being nursed back to health before reporting back to work at the Air Ministry. Escott said that Yvonne had been one of the fortunate ones who had done something few had achieved. She had been to hell and come back. After the war she was awarded the MBE and the Croix de Guerre.

## Yvonne Fontaine

On 21 March 1944 Yvonne Fontaine, a British FANY, and Virginia Hall, the second American agent, were landed by a gunboat at Beg-an-Fry on the south coast of Brittany. This was Yvonne's return trip to France. She had earlier worked with Pierre Mulsant's Tinker network south-east of Paris but, as the Gestapo closed in, she, Pierre and Dennis Barrett, the radio operator, were lifted out by a Hudson flown out of Tempsford on

16 November 1943 and brought back to Britain. One of the other passengers was Francois Mitterand, the future President of France; another was Francis Cammaerts, the head of the JOCKEY circuit.

Her personal file details how, four months later, Yvonne was returned to France after undertaking SOE training. Some comments in her report suggest she didn't create a good impression on some of her instructors.

> She is egocentric, spoilt, stubborn, impatient, conceited and anxious to draw attention to herself … hair worn loose in rather unbecoming disarray, liable to frequent alteration no doubt … very large goggly eyes. She likes a great deal of attention from those whom she is pleased to call les boys!
>
> (NA HS 9/457/6)

She passed, though. Codenamed 'Mimi' and also using the names 'Yvonne Dumont', 'Yvette Fauge', 'Yvonne Fernande Cholet', 'Nenette' and 'Florist', she rejoined Mulsant and Barrett, who had been dropped elsewhere to create the MINISTER network. In Marcus Binney's *Secret War Heroes*, he mentions her acting as Ben Cowburn's courier in the revived SPIRITUALIST network around the Seine-et-Marne department to the east and south-east of Paris. He described her as

> an ardent patriot, quite fearless and ready for anything. She worked in a laundry, and for her SOE work he paid her 2,000 francs a month. Thanks to Nenette, Cowburn did not feel in need of a woman courier from London ... Nenette had found a 'nice, safe restaurant where they could get meals without tickets, ironically named the Paul l'Allemand, opposite the town theatre.'

She helped organise five drops over two months which provided her group with a total of sixty containers packed with Sten guns, rifles, grenades and explosives. Following Cowburn's successful sabotage of the rail transport around the important junction town of Troyes, the ensuing clampdown by the Gestapo made her lie low. When a fleet of Flying Fortresses flew over Troyes on their return from bombing Stuttgart, seven of them were shot down. Of the thirty American crew who baled out, eighteen were rescued by local people and Yvonne helped make arrangements for them to escape into Switzerland.

Enquiries about her private life were made with a local doctor, a member of the Resistance, so she kept out of circulation until shortly after D-Day, when she accompanied a Resistance group to help a uniformed party of SAS troops trapped in the forest of Fontainebleau. Yvonne managed to evade capture but two of her comrades were caught and died in Buchenwald.

Back in England, prior to her debrief in which she had to write up a report, she met up with two other female agents, Odette Wilen and Anne-Marie Walters. Their night chatting about their experiences caused concern to someone in the SOE.

> I saw these ladies this morning. They are all staying at the same hotel and I found them this morning for different reasons in a highly excitable and appeared to me, unsatisfactory, frame of mind.

Mme FUAGE. This agent, I think, has probably performed her duties well. Her present nervous condition is largely due to the fact that she blames the organisation for the arrest of her two friends GUERIN AND STEPHANE. Apparently uniformed party was dropped into the Foret de Fontainbleu, which was already being used for two other receptions organised by GUERIN. The result was a thorough search of the woods in which GUERIN AND STEPHANE were caught. I am not anxious to go into details, but I think it is only right to notify the slightly unsatisfactory frame of mind in which she finds herself at present.

… I was very seriously shocked by the attitude of these three ladies, who had spent the night in exchanging confidences in the hotel. For one thing they were talking freely of the arrests of a great number of our agents, the facts of which they had no reason to be informed. I pointed out particularly that in the case of GARDE, we did not wish the news of his arrest to be spread since his wife had been seriously ill and we had been unable to inform her of this bad piece of news.

(TNA HS 9/339/2)

After the war, de Gaulle awarded her the Medaille de la Resistance.

## Virginia Hall

Virginia Hall was the next woman to go out. Denis Rake, one of SOE's radio operators, stated after the war in his book *Rake's Progress* that 'Virginia Hall in my opinion – and there are many others who share it – was one of the greatest women agents of the war.'

Born in 1906 into a wealthy family in Baltimore, she attended the best schools and colleges and then finished her education in France, Germany and Austria, becoming fluent in French, German and Italian. In the early 1930s she worked in the American embassy in Warsaw in Poland, Tallinn in Estonia, Vienna in Austria and Izmir in Turkey, but her hopes of a long career in the diplomatic service were dashed when she had to have her lower left leg amputated after a hunting accident. The aluminium leg made for her she called 'Cuthbert'.

Peter Churchill, one of numerous SOE agents who were helped by her, reported in his autobiography, *Of Their Own Choice*, how surprised he was when she showed him a little opening in its heel. She told him that she was able to hide various documents in her 'aluminium puppy'. His response to her was that it was 'A walking ground-floor letter-box that nobody would ever find. Hermes has nothing on you…'

Although she resigned her job in 1939, it did not deter her. She got a job in the Ambulance Service in Paris but, following the German occupation of the city, she caught a train out and happened to chat with someone who told her about the SOE. When she managed to escape to England, she found work as a code clerk for the Military Attaché in the American embassy. Fluent in French and German, knowledgeable about France and having an American passport, she was reckoned by Vera Atkins to be a potentially valuable agent. An interview with Jepson was arranged, during which she volunteered her services to Baker Street.

After specialist training at several SOE schools, they had her sent back to Vichy-controlled France on 23 August 1941. Unable to be parachuted back in, she is thought to have flown from Tangmere to Gibraltar. From there a felucca took her to the south coast. Codenamed 'Philomène' and using the pseudonym 'Marion Monin', she worked under the cover of an accredited Vichy correspondent for the *New York Post*.

In Patrick Howarth's *Undercover*, he mentioned that one of Virginia's services was to find Rake, one of the radio operators, lodgings with a prostitute. 'Being an undeviating homosexual, Rake had to explain his predicament to the girl, but it was accepted in good part, and, so far as security was concerned, the arrangement was an excellent one.'

In early 1942 she was relocated to Lyon, the main centre of the Vichy government, to work with those who refused to collaborate. Apart from Giliana Gerson, who only spent three weeks in France, Virginia was SOE's first permanent agent. While there, she sent important messages back to London. In Dennis Casey's biography of Virginia on the now defunct 64 Baker Street website, he states that:

> She described Vichy as a small town increasingly beset with shortages and deteriorating living conditions including the absence of butter and milk. By early 1942 her reports indicated that people were near starvation which curiously occurred simultaneously with the tightening of German control.
>
> (http://www.64-baker-street.org/agents – accessed October 2008)

Sometimes she included a personalised shopping list. As well as the usual requests for arms and ammunition from the Resistance, she regularly ordered Elizabeth Arden cosmetics with details of her skin texture, lipstick colour, powder shade and scent. She even gave them the address of the suppliers for a new stump sock for 'Cuthbert'. Thanks to the Tempsford 'Moon Squadrons', she got them all delivered to her safe house.

From her apartment she helped arrange the return to England of downed American aircrews and escaped prisoners. While doing this she continued to write newspaper stories, but when the United States entered the war she became an enemy alien and had to conduct business clandestinely from restaurants and cafés, constantly vigilant of plain-clothed Vichy and Gestapo officers.

Following the Allies' invasion of North Africa, in November 1942 the Germans took over the Free Zone in Southern France. In time they became suspicious of Virginia, so her minders in Victor Gerson's escape line helped her get out. A Spanish guide took her, a Belgian army captain and two Frenchmen over the mountains. In Judith Pearson's 2006 Clement Lecture on Virginia Hall, she told how:

> In the SOE, she learned coding, hand to hand combat, and weaponry... Since America had not yet entered the war, Virginia returned to France as a journalist, with the secret mission of setting up networks. Stationed in unoccupied Lyons, every British resistance fighter who came to France in that first year came by Virginia's apartment. By the time the Allies made their advance into Nazi territory in November of 1942, the Nazis were on the lookout for 'the most dangerous Allied spy', a woman with a limp. Virginia was forced to flee over the Pyrenees to Spain, in the dead of winter, on her very painful artificial leg.
>
> (A. Hoffman, 'Judith Pearson delivers a talk on Spy Virginia Hall',
> *The Trinity Tripod*, 4 April 2006)

Cate Lineberry, writing about 'The Limping Lady' for the *Smithsonian*, added an amusing related snippet:

> As her guide led her across the frozen landscape in mid-winter, she transmitted a message to SOE headquarters in London saying she was having trouble with her leg. The reply: 'If Cuthbert is giving you difficulty, have him eliminated.'
> (http://www.smithsonianmag.com/history-archaeology/hall.html)

Having escaped into Spain, she was captured and imprisoned by the Spanish civil guard and needed the help of the American consul. She spent a few months doing SOE work under the cover of being a reporter for the *Chicago Times* in Madrid before returning to England. She taught herself Morse privately so the SOE would take her on as a radio operator. Her contribution to the war effort was acknowledged by King George VI when he awarded her the Order of the British Empire in 1943.

To assist her future work, she was trained as a radio operator. In Pearson's account, she pointed out that:

> Returning from Spain, Virginia was recruited by the new American Office of Strategic Services (OSS), headed by 'Wild' Bill Donovan. Donovan, whose recruits included contortionists and safe crackers, found a way for Virginia to return to France and the resistance without being recognized. Since the Nazis were still looking for the woman with a limp, Virginia disguised herself as a French peasant, with padded, rustic clothing, grey hair dye, and the shuffling gait of an old woman.

On 21 March 1944, she was landed by motorboat at Beg-an-Fry Cape, 3 km north of Guimaec, north-east of Morlaix on the Finistère coast (www.plan-sussex-1944.net/anglais/pdf/infiltrations_into_france.pdf). From there Virginia made her way to the Haute-Loire, where she chose suitable drop zones for Allied parachute supplies and trained Resistance fighters to blow up railway lines, engines and train depots and capture supply caravans.

Virginia was also responsible for a great deal of the wireless transmission that would be so valuable in the Allied attack on D-Day. She and her Resistance compatriots continued to provide false information to the retreating Germans and destroyed their lines of communication. On one occasion, she had to cycle all day to deliver a vital message but got so desperate to go to the toilet that she deliberately wet herself rather than getting off the bike. She said she would never have got on again if she had got off. On another occasion she is said to have thrown a grenade into a restaurant where a group of Gestapo officers were eating. She met Jedburgh's team 'Jeremy' when they dropped from Tempsford into Le Chambon-sur-Lignon on 24 August 1944 and liaised between them and de Gaulle's FFI, the Free French Forces of the Interior.

Lineberry's article provided more detail about Virginia's work.

> By staying on the move, camping out in barns and attics, she was able to avoid the Germans who were desperately trying to track her radio signals.

D-Day loomed. Everyone, including the Germans, knew an Allied landing was imminent, but they didn't know when or where it would take place. Hall armed and trained three battalions of French resistance fighters for sabotage missions against the retreating Germans. As part of the resistance circuit, Hall was ready to put her team into action at any moment. In her final report to headquarters, Hall stated that her team had destroyed four bridges, derailed freight trains, severed a key rail line in multiple places and downed telephone lines. They were also credited with killing some 150 Germans and capturing 500 more.

After the war she returned to America, where she was awarded the Distinguished Service Cross, the second highest US military award for bravery. The British gave her the OBE. Although the French government did not honour her, Jacques Chirac, the French President, claimed that 'Virginia Hall is a true hero of the French Resistance'.

## Patricia 'Paddy' O'Sullivan

On 22 March 1944, twenty-six-year-old, Dublin-born Patricia 'Paddy' O'Sullivan, a second officer in the WAAF, was flown out of Tempsford and dropped at Angoulême, south-west France. Clark was unsure whether the plane was flown by Pilot Officer Smith, of 161 Squadron, on Operation John 72 or by Pilot Officer Pick, of 138 Squadron, on Operation John 59. Both dropped one agent that night.

After her training at Inverie House (STS 24) and time at Beaulieu, she was sent for additional radio training. SOE was desperate to get another agent into the field, so she was ordered from her course to a meeting in Baker Street and asked if she would be prepared to go into the field on the next moon. Although she hadn't finished the training, she said yes. This so annoyed Percy Mayer, her conducting officer, that he commented that:

> Miss O'Sullivan spent six weeks in Scotland on demolition and weapon training. I suggest that this time could have been more profitably spent at a security and radio school, or simply learning to ride a cycle. The requirements for a radio operator are not that she should be able to shoot straight or even shoot at all, but that she should know how to use a W/T set properly. Her means of defence should be to know how to baffle the Gestapo rather than to know how to shoot them.
>
> (TNA HS 6/585)

Over the next few weeks she had to learn her cover story, study the maps of the region she would be sent to, and learn the codes for her radio transmissions. Paddy was waiting at Gaynes Hall to see when her name would appear on the blackboard. According to Escott, when it did:

> Quietly and hardly noticed, she slipped away from the other expectant groups to join the car which whisked her away in the darkness to a hut on Tempsford airfield … then she joined her aircraft, looming in the dark like a gigantic bird, bade farewell to her escorting officer and the engines began to throb, pulsing along the cold floor where she squatted, senses alert, ready for her journey to France. Soon she was airborne and the

heavy aircraft droned its way to a dropping zone in Maurice Southgate's great Stationer circuit in the middle of France. The flares were there and the Morse signal flashed to confirm that the reception was ready.

Paddy leapt out into the night sky, feeling that at long last she was starting on her great adventure, a feeling that soon evaporated when she realised that although she had done all that she had been taught, her parachute cords had become tangled and her parachute would not open properly. This was the great fear of all parachutists, as falling from such a height was almost always fatal. Her descent became swifter and she was almost losing consciousness as she struggled with the lines trailing above her. Now, short of an unexpectedly soft landing, she was doomed before she had begun. Seconds became hours, when suddenly her fall was halted by a great jerk, as her parachute flowered out high above her.

With the ground only a short way below, it had opened just in time. Even so, she made an awkward heavy landing, rolling as the ground met her, suffering a bad shaking and bruising as her parachute dragged her along, working now when she had no need of it.

She landed so heavily she wondered if she had broken her neck. When she recovered consciousness, she felt hot breath on her face – a friendly cow. She felt sure the two million francs (£11,200) strapped to her back cushioned her fall. Twenty containers, two packages of personal belongings and two radios were collected by the waiting reception committee and, after a big meal, she slept for twenty hours.

In Russell Miller's *Behind the Lines*, he reported an interview he had with Claudia Pulver, one of the seamstresses at SOE's clothes section at the Thatched Barn in Hertfordshire. She recalled dressing a wild Irish girl called Paddy who told her that she carried her radio with her in her bike's saddlebag. When the Germans stopped her and asked her what she had in her bag, she jokingly suggested that it was a radio. She got away with it and survived the war. Claudia also mentioned providing dresses for a pregnant French countess who came to England in a rowing boat and another girl who had to have the most unusual and very elegant clothes, a riding outfit and an evening dress. Who these women were remains a mystery.

Paddy's codename was 'Simonet' and she worked as a radio operator with the Mayer brothers in the Fireman network around Angoulême. Edmund Mayer, codenamed 'Barthelemy', was advised that Paddy's smoking might expose her. Pattinson referred to her debriefing file, which said that:

Informant is a very heavy smoker and most French girls do not smoke, or if they do, they could not afford to keep packets of cigarettes which were a terrible price in France. It would have looked very suspicious if informant had smoked too much in public places and was told not to by Bartelmy [*sic*].

Her other codenames included 'Josette', 'Marie-Claire', 'Stenographer' and 'Stocking'. She was a valuable asset, being able to speak French, English, Dutch, Flemish and some German, but had to be taught how to ride a bike. She was also described as hot-tempered. On one occasion, when the hated Milice searched her bag, they missed her coding sheet, which was hidden in a false side. In Beryl Escott's *Mission Improbable*, she narrates how Paddy was cycling down a country lane with her radio set in her bicycle basket when she saw two German soldiers at a checkpoint ahead of her. As there were hedges on both sides, she could not avoid them.

> Putting on her most sunny and beguiling smile, she rode boldly up to the two men, one of whom, who liked the look of her, advanced some way up the road to meet her. She stopped and leaning on her bike, chatted animatedly with him. Flattered by her friendly attitude, he asked her to meet him for a drink … the other German awaited her, and while he examined her papers, she laid herself out to be just as delightful to him, consequently so bemusing him also that he completely forgot to examine her case, while excited by the notion of making his own assignation with her for the same evening … It had been a very close shave, only carried off by consummate acting and the brazen use of her charms.
>
> All the girls would have found it difficult to carry out their missions unless they had been consummate actresses, studying each new person that they were to become and slipping into it like a character on the stage.

In spite of numerous arrests and extensive searches by the Germans, Paddy managed to evade arrest. The squalid conditions of her lodgings were outweighed by its safety. Heavily overworked, she transmitted over 300 messages and still managed to train two operators and act as a courier. Her circuit was overrun by the Allies after D-Day and, suffering from ill-health, she was glad to be returned to England in August 1944. After the war, she was awarded the MBE and the Croix de Guerre and received a lot of media attention following a *Daily Mail* article, which noted that '"Paddy the Rebel"… until the invasion crawled through hedges and ditches watching the movements of German troops'.

### Lucie Aubrac

Lucie Aubrac and her husband Raymond endured trauma during the war. Details of the couple's background were provided in Margaret Collins Weitz's *Sisters in the Resistance*. Lucie was a teacher in Strasbourg in the late 1930s, but the war and falling in love and marrying Raymond Samuel, a Jewish engineer, stopped her from taking up a scholarship in the United States. Shortly after her husband was called up, he was captured. Lucie helped him escape from a POW camp and they settled in Lyon, where they helped set up Libération-Sud, a resistance network. Using 'Catherine' as her codename, she did liaison work and helped publish and distribute *Libération*, a clandestine journal. Raymond changed his name to Valmont, then Aubrac, in order to disguise his Jewish identity following anti-Semitic legislation. His cover name was 'Clause Ermelin'. Their first baby was born in 1941 and, to allow them both to continue their fight, they placed their son in a children's home.

In 1943 Lucie joined a hit squad that rescued *résistants* from Vichy and German prisons, but when one of the members was captured, the group was betrayed and nearly thirty were arrested, including Raymond. Lucie went directly to the district prosecutor's home and threatened him with reprisals from London unless he released her husband, the then leader of the Lyon resistance. It worked. However, less than a month later he was arrested again, this time by the Germans, and was tortured by Klaus Barbie, the chief of the Gestapo in Lyon. Margaret Collins Weitz says how:

> After careful reflection, Lucie decided upon a daring and dangerous plan to get Raymond out of Barbie's clutches by staging an armed attack while he was being transported somewhere. Lucie went to Gestapo headquarters and met a sympathetic German officer particularly appreciative of her gifts – Cognac, Champagne, silks and stockings. Posing as the aristocratic 'Guillaine de Barbentane' seduced by 'Claude Ermelin', Lucie, who was indeed pregnant, begged an SS lieutenant introduced to her by the officer to arrange a marriage before 'Ermelin' (Aubrac) was executed. She claimed not to care for him – all the more so now that he had been 'exposed' as a 'terrorist' – but she was adamant that her unborn child be legal. French law permits marriage in extremis to regularize such situations. She came from a conservative, Catholic, military family, and, she insisted, honour was at stake.

While planning Raymond's escape, Lucie managed to rescue two wounded comrades from St Étienne's hospital, but nearly had a miscarriage. She circulated the wards dressed in a doctor's smock and carried a stethoscope, which allowed her to memorise agents' medical charts and make arrangements to free them. The plan was to inject some sweets with typhus and give them to her husband in prison. Seriously ill, he would have to be transferred to a clinic and be rescued on the way. However, there would be a guard in the back of the armoured car carrying him, so they needed a silencer if he was not to be alerted. To get one she had to cross over the border into Switzerland. Twenty minutes later she was back in France, but the timing of the attack went wrong. Another mission had to be planned. This time, they did get 'married' and on the way back to prison the 'party' was attacked, three German guards were killed, thirteen prisoners were released, but Raymond was wounded.

The Gestapo was now after both of them. They had also learned the whereabouts of their three-year-old son, so a quick escape was vital. The boy was rescued an hour before the Germans arrived. When Lucie, then eight months pregnant, found him in the back of the truck, he was playing with a live grenade. Somehow the agents must have left it. She managed to get him to put down the lethal 'toy' before she fainted. In her memoirs, *Outwitting the Gestapo*, she said that:

> The resistance leaders decided that the three of us had to go to London. We went into hiding in central France to await the low-flying British plane [Lysander from RAF Tempsford] that was to take us to England and safety. All the peasants and the villagers in the area were aware of our situation. They were extraordinary and took us from one home to another. Because of the unfavourable atmospheric conditions, two full moons passed. We were transferred to the Jura area. The farmers – who had little enough themselves – treated us (and a downed British aviator now with us) royally. I think of the peasant woman who cut up her precious blankets to make diapers for the baby I was expecting. We learned then that some of our family – including Raymond's parents – had been betrayed and captured. In preparation for the next landing, we were taken

to stay with three elderly sisters – fiercely patriotic. Finally, on the evening of February 8th, 1944, a plane managed to land.

Freddie Clark related how RAF Tempsford had been sent information that the Gestapo in France were about to go in and pick up seven people in the Resistance. Operation BLUDGEON was set up. On the evening of 8 February 1944, Flight Lieutenant Johnnie Affleck piloted his Hudson on yet another mission to France. At 0300 hours the following morning he landed in a small field in Bletterans, France, and turned ready for take-off, but once the seven were safely on board he couldn't get his plane off the ground. The port wheel was stuck in the glutinous mud. The reception committee mustered about 200 local men and women who came to the rescue. With sheer guts and determination and, after fervent cries of 'Allez-oop' and much heaving and pushing, they managed to free the wheel only to discover the tail wheel bogged. Through bitterly cold wind and driving snow, they struggled until some farmers harnessed a team of six horses and twelve oxen. Once ruts were dug for the wheels, the plane was able to make its getaway two and a half tense hours later.

On their arrival at Tempsford at 0640 hours, Lucie was rushed to Queen Charlotte's Hospital in London to have her second child – a daughter. She had told her friends that if her baby was a boy he would have Maquis as one of his names. Catherine Mitraillette was named after a little machine gun. The Tempsford ground crew had the task of cleaning the red mud off the undercarriage of the Hudson. It was said to have looked like a tank. To put the Germans and anyone else off the scent, the disinformation put out was that this French family had been taken by train to Spain concealed beneath a railway carriage. Affleck got his DFC (Distinguished Flying Cross) a few days later and, after liberation, Lucie returned to France, where she was appointed the first French female parliamentarian.

### Alix d'Unienville

The next woman to be flown out was Alix d'Unienville. According to the French l'Independant website, she was born in Mauritius in 1919 and moved to Brittany with her family in 1926. When war broke out, the family moved to London in June 1940. When her brother joined de Gaulle's Free French Forces, she joined the French Corps Auxiliaire Féminin and got a job in the French Secret Service HQ on Duke Street, London, producing radio broadcasts to be transmitted to France. She then worked as secretary to Alexandre Parodi, the executive director of the Committee of National Liberation, and Roland Pre, one of de Gaulle's deputies in the northern zone, and specialised in producing the propaganda leaflets that the Tempsford squadrons dropped over occupied France.

After she trained at Beaulieu in summer 1943, her cover story was that she was born on the island of Réunion in 1922 and moved to France in 1938 to study and was married to a prisoner of war. On 31 March 1944, she and another agent, codenamed 'Lace', were parachuted from a Halifax near to Saint Aignan in the Loire-et-Cher region. The reception committee had heard the *message personelle* on the BBC, 'Two angels will make lace tonight.' Accompanying her was another agent, numerous containers and two suitcases, one containing important documents, the other 40 million francs for the

Resistance. She landed in a tree and had to extricate herself from the parachute with a knife.

Using codenames 'Myrtil' and 'Marie-France' and an alias of 'Aline Bavelan', she made her way to Paris and worked as a radio operator, arranging drops for RF forces loyal to de Gaulle. Her mission was named ORONTES – Meadow Brown.

On D-Day she was with a small group including Pierre-Henri Tietgen, a future French Minister, which was arrested by the Gestapo. She underwent lengthy interrogation at Fresnes Prison, during which her apartment was searched and a large quantity of money found. After several unsuccessful attempts to escape and desperate to avoid death, Alix feigned madness, which led to her being transferred to Saint Anne's psychiatric hospital. When the Gestapo determined she was sane, she was sent to La Pitié, a place renowned for brutal atrocities.

On 15 August, she was one of 665 women and 1,650 men put in cattle trucks on the 'death train' destined for Buchenwald concentration camp. When it was attacked by the RAF, the passengers had to walk along the track, and at Méry-sur-Marne she managed to escape. After being treated by a doctor and hidden by a local policeman at Thouvenot Saaây-sur-Marne, she was eventually taken back to Paris by American troops. After the war she worked for several newspapers and was a war correspondent for American Forces in the Far East. She received an MBE for her work and a Croix de Legion d'Honneur.

## Violette Szabó

Three days after Alix's drop, perhaps the most well known of female agents flew out of Tempsford. Violette Bushell, the daughter of an English taxi driver and a French mother, spent part of her youth in Paris and part in the Pas de Calais with her Aunt Marguerite. In *Young, Brave and Beautiful*, a biography of her written by her daughter Tania, there is a suggestion that, during the 'phoney war' in 1939 and 1940, Violette had helped her Aunt in clandestine resistance work when she visited her in the summers, sheltering downed Allied aircrew and spiriting them across the Belgium–France border and onto the escape line through France, into Spain and safety.

When in London, she worked on the perfume counter in the Brixton branch of Bonmarché and later as a sales assistant in various shops, including Woolworths on Oxford Street. She joined the Land Army in 1940 when she was only nineteen, and on Bastille Day that year her mother sent her to find someone French to invite back home to celebrate. She returned with Etienne Szabó, a thirty-year-old Czech officer in the French Foreign Legion They fell in love and within a month were married. She joined the Auxiliary Territorial Service and served competently in an anti-aircraft unit until a few days before her twenty-first birthday. She gave birth to a daughter, Tania, who never saw her father. He was fighting with General Koenig's French Force at Bir Hakeim and was killed at El Alamein in October 1942.

George Clement, an SOE agent, reported how he met her in some swanky London clubs, where she had mentioned a willingness to do something useful in France. A check was done on her and she was invited to an interview with Captain Jepson and Vera Atkins, the deputy intelligence officer of SOE, and was reported as saying, 'My husband has been killed by the Germans and I'm going to get my own back.' She took up the offer of clandestine activities in France with great determination, using the codename

Violette Szabó was sent into France twice in 1944. She was captured and executed at Ravensbrück concentration camp in January 1945. (Courtesy of Harrington Aviation Museum)

'Vicky Taylor'. During parachute training at Ringway, she sprained her ankle and had to spend time convalescing in Bournemouth in a wheelchair. So determined was she to continue that as soon as she was considered fit, she went down to Beaulieu to continue her training. Revenge was said to have been her prime motivation.

One of her instructors commented in a film about her, *Carve Her Name with Pride*, that 'it takes time to turn a pretty girl into a killer'. Tania reported how Violette and the other trainees, including Nancy Wake and Sonia Butt,

> had all learned survival skills like silent killing, the use of codes and wireless transmitters, parachuting at night or in the day, rowing boats, the use of many kinds of plastic explosives and detonators along with grenades, guns, rifles and pistols. Physical training was important and weeks spent on learning various cover stories and withstanding interrogation under fairly harsh conditions such as sleep deprivation, to break those same stories and intelligence they had been given to learn. Cycling, swimming, and other physical training was given. Violette was exemplary in them all. She annoyed

her instructors as amply described in her reports for not taking it all seriously enough. However, she did not fail any of these 'exams', so under her sparkling fun-loving attitudes was a steel-like determination to succeed, plus the inherent abilities to do so.

In Maurice Buckmaster's book *Specially Employed*, he devoted a whole chapter to Violette. He considered her really beautiful, 'dark-haired and olive-skinned, with that kind of porcelain clarity of face and purity of bone that one finds occasionally in the women of the south-west of France'. He described her as *'nerveuse'* in the French sense, having a 'wholly admirable tension of the mind and senses which causes people to overcome fear and hardship when there is a tough job to do'. She so impressed Leo Marks, the head of SOE code room, that he gave her the following romantic code:

> The life that I have is all that I have,
> And the life that I have is yours.
> The love that I have,
> Of the life that I have,
> Is yours and yours and yours.
>
> A sleep I shall have,
> A rest I shall have,
> Yet death will be but a pause,
> For the peace of my years
> In the long green grass,
> Will be yours and yours and yours.

He thought her a 'stunning-looking slip of mischief'. Prior to being sent out, she was taken to Station XV, the Thatched Barn, a requisitioned hotel on the A1 at Barnet, to provide her with some French outfits. Claudia Pulver, who worked there, thought she was 'probably the most beautiful girl I'd ever seen. I remember making black underwear for her – God knows why she wanted black underwear – among other things.'

Although strongly discouraged to undertake secret work overseas as she would be leaving her one-year-old daughter behind, Violette insisted, ensuring Tania was cared for by a friend in Mill Hill. She flew on two missions, both said to have been from Tempsford, but there are discrepancies in SOE literature about the date of the first, the plane, the pilot and whether she was landed or jumped by parachute. It is possible some historians conflated the two. According to Clark:

> Cookridge says they [Violette and Philippe Liewer] landed by Lysander on the 15th April but there were no Lysander operations that night. Minney, Violette Szabo's biographer, says the Lysander which took off from Tempsford was spotted by a German fighter (this sounds fictitious) near the landing field between Chartres and Orléans.
>   F/Lt Taylor and F/Lt Whitaker both flying Lysanders took off from Tempsford (returning to Tangmere) each taking two agents on operation UMPIRE, both landing in a field 1.5km ENE Azay-sur-Cher some 7km ESE Tours. Verity names three of the passengers, the 161 Squadron diary records that Lt Hysing-Dahl took three agents with

4 packages on operation LILAC. Verity says the field was 1.5km W Baudreville some 30km ESE Chartres but does not mention that passengers were taken out. It could be possible that the Norwegian, Hysing-Dahl flew them in, the landing field was certainly between Chartres and Orléans, and a train to Paris could have been caught at nearby Angerville.

M R D Foot says they were parachuted in, it is questionable if they were included in the Tempsford parachute operations that night which were, as it can be seen, way to the south and Szabo and Liewer were going to Rouen. However, Vera Atkins, the intelligence officer who worked closely with the women of 'F' Section, SOE, was recently kind enough to clarify this mystery by saying that she remembered escorting Violette Szabo to an awaiting Carpetbagger B-24 sent to collect her from Tempsford.

Their flight was on Wednesday 5 April 1944 in a converted USAAF Liberator. They parachuted into a field near Rouen, east of Le Havre. This was in the *zone interdite* – an area heavily guarded by Germans within 25 kilometres of the Channel coast. Violette's codename was 'Seamstress' and her cover was as a professional secretary from Le Havre called Corinne Leroy on holiday with a task of trying to find an uncle missing after an Allied air raid. Her real mission was to find out how much the Salesman *réseau* had been broken, distribute money to families who had suffered financially when the breadwinner was arrested, gather information about the German V1 rocket installations and organise whoever was left to blow up the Barentin viaduct. To help, she had been given 250,000 counterfeit francs. According to Tania, Philippe had instructed her

> to have a substantial sum on her at all times, the larger part of it well-concealed in her worn-looking leather shoulder-bag with a cleverly disguised double lining and base. Perhaps some in her jacket. More in her money belt. Once she was on her own, which could be at any moment, she might need the extra cash for travelling (first class) by train, for bribes, buying various clothes, getting and paying for forged ration cards or even new forged identity cards, maybe even buying a car, truck or bike – with or without motor. Everything had to be considered.

Rouen, where German soldiers, the Gestapo and the Milice had just broken a Resistance group and were watching known contacts, was a very difficult place for Violette to move around. Using a borrowed bike, she managed to meet a number of women who had been involved and succeeded in completing her mission, even getting close enough to the concrete bases hidden in the woods near Saint-Leu-d'Esserent from where the V1 flying bombs were to be launched.

Unable to re-establish contact with the agents of the penetrated *réseau*, she rendezvoused with Philippe in Paris, where she learned that she was to be brought back to England on the evening of 30 April. He informed her that the viaduct had been brought down. Pleased with the success of her mission, she decided to reward herself. A display in the shop window of Molyneux, a top Paris fashion house, caught her attention. According to Tania, the bill for a black crêpe de chine evening dress, a crimson and deep-blue plaid dress, a floral silk dress and yellow jersey was for 37,475 leftover counterfeit SOE francs – the equivalent of £21,300 today. A pair of wedged-heel, sling-back, peep-toe sandals bought the next day were perfect with the dresses. Three Maigret novels, red earrings, a silk dress for her daughter, Worth's Je Reviens perfume, silk-lined kid gloves, Bourjois rouge, silk ties, ivory fan, silk scarf, linen handkerchiefs, a Meccano set for her family and an unusual bead brooch for Vera Atkins were additional purchases.

A train journey of a few hours to Issouden, near Châteauroux, and a short car journey took Violette and Phlippe to a small farm near the disused Le Fay airfield, at Ségry, near St Aubin. It was a double Lysander pick-up by Flight Lieutenant Bob Large and Flight Officer J. P. Alcock. Within minutes of the three agents arriving, Philippe was strapped into one of the Lysanders, Violette in the other with her suitcase and packages containing all her presents.

The flight back to England, according to Large, was not without incident. They were attacked by enemy fighters near Châteaudun airfield. Flak burst all round the plane, holing the propeller, but Large flung his Lysander around the sky to escape the danger zone, knowing there was a female agent in the back whom he had to save. It was a very bumpy landing at Tangmere. The plane tipped over, sliding along on a wing, causing Violette to bang her head. One of the tyres was in shreds, having been punctured by a piece of flak, and Large said it did a 'ground loop'. He got out and went to help out the passenger and was greeted by an angry tirade in rapid French and an assault with an umbrella. He was pleased she did not have a gun. She was said to have been more shaken by the fact that her intercom had become unplugged and she had thought they had landed in enemy territory. It being too dark to recognise the pilot's uniform, she presumed that he was a German who had come to arrest her.

Unable to understand her screaming and shouting, Large tried to placate her by calling for a car to fetch them. When the mix-up was sorted out, a broad smile appeared on her face. *'Vous est le pilot!'* she exclaimed, flung her arms round his neck and kissed him. He felt it was all worth it just for that one kiss.

Dressed in the uniform of a military nurse, the common disguise for female agents back home, she spent a few days with her family during the hottest summer of the war, celebrating her promotion to lieutenant and impressing onlookers with her stunning French outfits. Tania reports her spending time with Nancy Wake and Sonia Butt, other female agents whom she had trained with.

On the afternoon of Monday 5 June, Violette and her new team, nineteen-year-old Jean Claude Guiet, twenty-year-old Bob Maloubier and thirty-two-year-old Philippe Liewer were driven in a black Humber out of London, up the A1 to Hasells Hall, a few miles south-east of Tempsford. Like Gaynes Hall, it was a handsome red-brick Georgian mansion belonging to the Pym family, situated on the crest of the Greensand Ridge. It was set in beautiful grounds, landscaped by Humphrey Repton, with arbours, paths and follies. Tania described it being used as

sleeping quarters and clubhouse for agents and flyers leaving for France on so many undercover missions. Woods and fine grounds surrounded the house. It was a good and peaceful place to try to relax and keep things in perspective while waiting for the right weather conditions or pilots and aircraft to wing them away to danger.

The RAF had requisitioned this already decaying but lovely house so amenities were sparse but adequate, there was, however, plenty to drink in the way of alcoholic beverages, much brought over from occupied countries. Reasonably good food was on offer. All at the government's expense. There was just enough hot water for showering or shallow baths, the bedrooms were clean and basically comfortable. Unfortunately, perhaps, the wooden floors kept naughty activities to a minimum as they creaked and groaned at the slightest step or …

A FANY driver arrived at dusk in a blacked-out car to take them the few miles down the hill to the airfield. When their preparations at Gibraltar Farm were complete, Vera Atkins sent them off with the traditional salute, '*Merde!*' As the Halifax was taxiing to the runway, the pilot suddenly brought it to a standstill. One of the ground crew gesticulated with his arms to abort the flight. The operation was cancelled due to stormy weather. There were 66-mile-an-hour gales reported over the south coast, thunder, lightning and very heavy rain.

Imagine the tension that had built up prior to their departure and the disappointment and anti-climax when it did not happen. Her team were taken back to Hasells Hall. Nancy Robert, Violette's conducting officer, said she had had to get her ready and

make sure she had everything and say goodbye, and then it didn't happen. And then we just had to wait. I will never forget it. Ever. Where we were, it was beautifully sunny and there was Violette sitting on the lawn with this Polish young man who was going too. They were laughing and chatting and playing a gramophone record over and over and over again. I can still hear it: 'I want to buy a paper doll I can call my own.'

When the flight was postponed, Violette is said to have remained calm and enjoyed the trip to Cambridge the following day, despite the low clouds and strong winds. A punt on the Cam, a pleasant lunch of bangers and mash in an olde worlde pub and a stroll around the city was lightened by lots of laughing and joking and singing of their team's song, 'I'll Be Around'. When they got back to Hasells, she relaxed in the company of two SAS officers, Lieutenant Richard Crisp and twenty-two-year-old Captain John Tonkin. In a letter Tonkin sent to his mother, quoted in Helm's biography of Vera Atkins, he described Hasells as the

'last resting place' for all agents to enemy countries. We were very well looked after by the ATS [Auxiliary Territorial Service]. The only operational people there were Richard and I and the Jedburgh team for Operation Bulbasket, two of our officers for Houndsworth, two for Titanic, and four agents, of whom two were surprisingly beautiful girls. We had checked and rechecked everything and packed our enormous rucksacks about fifty times. Finally, there was nothing more to do, so we spent the time very profitably with the girls, doing jigsaw puzzles.

That evening, Violette and her team were driven down to the airfield. Checks were carried out. Equipment was issued. Goodbyes were said and the Halifax took off. They settled down to coffee and sandwiches and prepared for the drop. Three hours later the pilot reported no lights from the reception committee, so the operation was aborted. Playing blackjack in the back, they were unaware on their return to Tempsford of the enormous operation that was going on beneath them in the English Channel off the Normandy coast. It was 6 June – D-Day.

Three hours after getting back to Hasells, Violette woke up her team members with the news of the landings. Annoyed at having been rudely awoken by 'that Bloody woman', Bob went back to sleep. She sat around talking about what would be happening from now on. They were very annoyed not to have been told by the pilot as it would have been a wonderful sight, watching the invasion through the Joe hole.

That day was dominated by games of ping-pong and cards, Violette surprising Vera Atkins by her calm. That night, according to Tania, Captain Nancy Frazer Campbell drove one of two Humbers the 45 miles to Harrington, USAAF 36 Bomber Squadron's base. Mike Fenster's Liberator B-24 was waiting to pick up Violette and the other three agents. Her escort officer commented that 'in a group of heavily armed and equipped men waiting to take off from the same airfield, Violette was smiling and debonair. She wore a flowered frock, white sandals and earrings which she had bought in Paris during her first mission.' She insisted on kissing each member of the crew, the pilot and the co-pilot.

The day before her baby daughter Tania's second birthday, Viollette and her team were dropped by parachute at Saint-Gilles-les-Forêts, hilly farmland near Limoges, central France, at 0149 hours. Twenty-two containers containing machine guns, hand grenades, ammunition, explosives, clothes, food and medicine were dropped with them. While some of the reception committee disposed of the supplies, she was taken to Sussac and provided with a room over the grocer's shop opposite the church. She was to be known as 'Carine Leroy' and 'Louise', and her mission was to take messages to various units of the Resistance. The 600 Maquis and 200 gendarmes who had joined them following D-Day needed co-ordinating and instructing. Armed saboteurs cut electricity supplies for the submarine base at Rochefort and blew up the railway lines between Limoges and Paris, and between Bordeaux and Toulouse. Maloubier claimed to have blown up seven bridges in one day. The group claimed to have held back the 2nd Panzer Division, which was being rushed from the south of France to Normandy to strengthen the German resistance to the Allied landings. In revenge for an attack in Tulle, just south of Limoges, in which 137 Germans were killed, 97 men were rounded up and hung from the lampposts.

According to Robin Mackness' research into the massacre at Oradour, German General Lammerding was in charge of getting the 2nd Panzer Division from its base in Montauban up the Rhone valley. One of his majors had been kidnapped on his way to Tulle and his empty car was found near Oradour-sur-Glane. Added to Lammerding's problems was the fact that he was said to have had secretly amassed 600 kilos of gold, about half a ton, while on operations. As he couldn't leave it in Montauban, he had it crated and labelled as the division's records. His plan was to have it trucked with his papers back to Germany. On the way, however, the convoy was ambushed and the gold taken. The only SS survivor said that it happened near Oradour-sur-Glane, which prompted widespread patrols in the area Violette was sent to (R. Mackness, *Oradour: Massacre and Aftermath*, 1988).

Shortly after landing, Violette met up with Anastasie, a Maquis leader, and another Resistance fighter with the mission of alerting the other Maquis in the Dordogne area.

A plastic-explosive bomb sat between her feet on the floor of their black Citroën. As they drove towards Salon La Tour, they were intercepted by a party of SS troops. The car was fired on. It stopped and, running for safety through a wheat field, she was shot in the arm, stumbled through rutted furrows, fell and twisted her ankle. The film *Carve Her Name with Pride* shows her telling Anastasie to go on without her and providing him with covering fire as he swam across a river until she ran out of ammunition. Tania tells of her hiding behind an apple tree, firing at the advancing enemy. However, historian Howard Tuck's investigations suggest there was only one Sten gun in the car and she did not use it.

During her training, she is reported to have said that 'I only want to have some Germans to fight and I should die happy if I could take some of them with me.' The film shows her shooting five soldiers before she gets wounded and another afterwards. A high-ranking officer congratulates her on her performance: 'You put up a good fight Mademoiselle. Cigarette?'

After being captured and imprisoned at Maison D'Arret in Limoges, she was taken daily for interrogation at the nearby Gestapo headquarters on Rue Louvrier de Lajolais. There, she was said to have been tortured. Hugette Desire, a member of the French Resistance, recalled in a BBC programme, *Secret Agent: The True Story of Violette Szabó*, that Violette had told her that an SS man had put his pistol into her neck, said he could kill her tomorrow if he so wished and then raped her. Bob Maloubier planned a rescue attempt but, hours beforehand, she was transferred to Paris.

On the same day that Violette was captured, the same SS division carried out another savage reprisal, one of the worst atrocities of the war. Troops arrived in Oradour-sur-Glane, a 20-minute drive north-west of Limoges, and instructed all the men, women and children to gather in the main square. The women and children were locked up in the church while 200 men were herded into barns. The men were gunned down and the barns set alight. Then the 400 women and children were shot and the church set ablaze, by detonating a box of explosives sat upon the altar, along with all remaining buildings in the village. Women from nearby villages who came to pick their children up from school were shot. Only one eight year-old boy survived. He managed to evade the bullets as he ran away. The following morning, soldiers disposed of the bodies to prevent identification.

In Paris, Violette then suffered weeks of interrogation at Avenue Foch, the Gestapo HQ, and then imprisonment at Block Five in Fresnes Prison along with many other captured SOE agents. It is claimed in Joe Saward's *The Grand Prix Saboteurs* that the details of a safe house in Paris were extricated from her, which led to the arrest and death of several other SOE agents.

Following the instructions given to every captured prisoner to try to escape, she began working loose one of the bars in the roof light of her cell. She had become so thin that one bar forced a few inches to one side would allow her to squeeze through. Before she managed it, though, there were orders to assemble for a mass transfer. The Germans were retreating following the Allies' push towards the city and sent many of their prisoners by train to concentration camps.

The date of her departure has been given by Madame Rosier, an inmate at Ravensbrück, as 8 August, eight weeks after her arrival. Ironically, the cattle truck Violette was in was strafed by the RAF at Compiègne. Unable to escape without being shot by the guards, Violette, still chained to Denise Bloch, got hold of a tin cup and crawled to the adjoining compartment to give water from the lavatory to the men. In Bruce Marshall's *White Rabbit*, he narrates how SOE agent Yeo-Thomas was picked up by a Lysander and returned:

> 'We all felt deeply ashamed when we saw Violette Szabo, while the raid was still on, come crawling along the corridor towards us with a jug of water which she had filled from the lavatory. She handed it to us through the iron bars. With her, crawling too, came the girl to whose ankle she was chained.
>
> 'This act of mercy made an unforgettable impression on all. She spoke words of comfort, jested, went back with the jug to fill it again and again.
>
> 'My God that girl had guts,' says Yeo-Thomas. 'I shall never forget that moment,' says Harry Peulevé [an old friend and fellow SOE agent], 'I feel very proud that I knew her. She looked so pretty, despite her shabby clothes and her lack of make-up – and she was full of good cheer. I have never under any circumstances known her to be depressed or moody.'

Buckmaster said that one of the other prisoners who escaped death in the camps told him that Violette gave him half a bottle of wine abandoned by the guards, saying, '*Bon courage. Les alliés sont aux portes de Paris. Rassure-toi.*' She and Denise were hit with rifle butts when the guards returned. On reaching Metz, the prisoners were 'billeted' in stables where she met Harry Peulevé, an old friend and SOE agent who Tania was convinced was in love with her mother. Tania reported it as being extremely crowded:

> They were there for about two days with little food but adequate water. So much so that Violette was able to wash out her white blouse and underwear. Other women undoubtedly did likewise. Yvonne Baseden particularly remembers as she told the author on a visit to her flat, seeing Violette washing her blouse in a bowl on what seemed to be a stack of crates … Harry had this to say:
>
> 'Violette and I talked all through the night. Her voice, as always, was so sweet and soothing, one could listen to it for hours. We spoke of old times and we told each other our experiences in France. Bit by bit everything was unfolded – her life in Fresnes, her interviews at Avenue Foch. But either through modesty or a sense of delicacy, since some of the tortures were too intimate in their application, or perhaps because she did not wish to live again through the pain of it, she spoke hardly at all about the tortures she had been made to suffer. She was in a cheerful mood. Her spirits were high. She was confident of victory and was resolved on escaping no matter where they took her.'

After being separated from the men, the women were taken first to the Gestapo headquarters in Strasbourg and then to Saarbrücken, a transit camp and finally Ravensbrück concentration camp in the third week of August. In Nigel Perrin's *Spirit of Resistance*, he mentions that Harry Peulevé in his unpublished memoirs, admits to having fallen in love with Violette while in London and that, having managed to escape from concentration with Yeo-Thomas's help, he captured two SS guards. On them he found photographs of nude female prisoners, Violette among them. Perrin doubted the veracity of Harry's memory. Tania writes:

> Violette's world and that of her companions had reduced to endless grey railway tracks and sidings, grey stations, grey platforms and the noise of grey guards and grey dogs. Even a few of the young women turned grey while screaming in pain or fear. Everything became grey – grey uniforms, grey bread, grey faces, grey world.

On 3 September 1944, Violette and six other women, including Lilian Rolfe, Denise Bloch and Eileen Nearne, were taken to Targau, another manufacturing slave labour camp like Siemens. Here they were forced to make ammunition but they made a stand, refusing to make bullets and shells that would be used to kill their brothers and fathers. Suffering bad whippings and faced with being shot, they gave in but did as much as they could to sabotage the work, slow down production as well as plan an escape. They were returned to Ravensbrück before they could act on their plans. Eventually, on the direct order of Heinrich Himmler, on 27 January 1945, Violette was taken out with Denise Bloch and Cécile Lefort to the yard beside the camp commandant's quarters and, after being forced to kneel, they were all shot in the back of the head. The Gestapo didn't want anyone providing evidence against them about their radio games and wanted to ensure SOE and SIS agents were disposed of. Of Violette, Odette Churchill simply said, 'She was the bravest of us all.'

After the war, in recognition of her bravery, Violette was posthumously awarded the George Cross – the first woman ever to receive it. The *London Gazette* of 17 December 1946 included a slightly inaccurate citation.

> Madame Szabó volunteered to undertake a particularly dangerous mission in France. She was parachuted into France in 1944, and undertook the task with enthusiasm. In her execution of the delicate researches entailed she showed great presence of mind and astuteness. She was twice arrested by the German security authorities, but each time managed to get away. Eventually, however, with other members of her group, she was surrounded by the Gestapo in a house in the south-west of France.
>
> Resistance appeared hopeless, but Mme Szabó, seizing a Sten gun and as much ammunition as she could carry, barricaded herself in part of the house and, exchanging shot for shot with the enemy, killed or wounded several of them. By constant movement she avoided being cornered and fought until she dropped exhausted. She was arrested and had to undergo solitary confinement. She was then continuously and atrociously tortured, but never by word or deed gave away any of her acquaintances or told the enemy anything of any value. She was ultimately executed. Mme Szabó gave a magnificent example of courage and steadfastness.

The French gave her and her husband the Croix de Guerre with clasps. Thanks to the efforts of Rosemary Rigby MBE, a museum was opened in Violette's memory by her daughter Tania, at Wormelow in Herefordshire in 2000. Annual reunions are held on the nearest weekend to Violette's birthday, 20 June, which attract many people who were involved directly and indirectly (http://www.violette-szabo-museum.co.uk).

Although Violette was the last woman agent mentioned by Clark as having been flown out of Tempsford, SOE records show that numerous other women were sent into occupied Europe after D-Day.

## Lilian Rolfe

Almost three weeks after Lilian Rolfe's thirtieth birthday, she was the next female agent flown into France by 161 Squadron. She was a passenger in one of two Lysanders from Tangmere on 5/6 April and landed one and a half kilometres east-north-east of Azay-sur-Cher, the same landing site that Julienne Aisner and Vera Leigh used. In fact, Julienne returned to England on the same plane. According to Verity, accompanying Lilian on the outward journey were Marie-Christine and André Studler, who Verity indicated were OSS agents. André was the head of the HISTORIAN and later the SQUATTER networks that needed lifting out to evade arrest. Whether Marie-Christine was his wife, girlfriend or worked in the Resistance is unknown.

Described by Escott as a dark-haired girl, with steady dark eyes and a mouth made for smiling, Lilian arrived in London at the outbreak of war with her twin sister, Helen, her British father and Russian mother. She and Helen had been born in Paris but were educated in Rio de Janeiro, Brazil. They lived in Woking outside London and Lilian joined the WAAF in May 1943, proudly wearing the Brazilian flash on her uniform. Being fluent in several languages, steady, mature and patriotic, she was accepted for training in the SOE in November.

An assistant second officer in the WAAF, Lilian went to work as a radio operator in George Wilkinson's HISTORIAN network in Montagris, near Orléans. Codenamed 'Nadine', she was also known as 'Claudie Rodier' and 'Recluse'. It was a difficult time as she was working in the towns of Montagris, Orléans and Nangis, formerly in the PROSPER network. Rebuilding it was Wilkinson's mission and Lilian had to arrange parachute drops to supply the growing number of men who were expecting an Allied invasion. The neighbouring networks of VENTRILOQUIST and HEADMASTER were also being rebuilt, as well as Pearl Witherington's WRESTLER network. Escott narrates how:

> When she arrived she carried a tiny transmitter and receiver strapped to her body. It was more fragile than the sturdier B2, one reason why she didn't parachute in … She had little cause to use, however, as she was separated from her organiser for several weeks, as he travelled around his circuit. She was able therefore to settle in the area, establish her cover story, met and get over the shock of her first Germans, get to know the routes she would have to use with her bike and make some useful contacts of her own, including the leaders of the local Maquis. Apart from a few messages she used her wireless very little until George, having got his circuit organised, came back to find her. Then she started work in earnest.

Although her mission was to report on German troop movements, organise arms and supply drops, she also took part in sabotage missions, including taking part in a gun battle in the small town of Olivet, just south of Orléans.

Shortly after the D-Day landings, Wilkinson, her organiser, was arrested but she kept on transmitting until she too was caught in Nangis on 31 July. Apparently, the house she was staying in was raided while the Germans were looking for someone else.

After being arrested she was taken to their headquarters in Orléans, where they shortly discovered they had caught an important member of the Resistance. This meant being transported to Avenue Foch in Paris for rough, intensive interrogation and brutal torture by the Gestapo. As she revealed little that helped them, she was transferred to Fresnes Prison but she did not stay long. Aware that the American forces were close at hand, on 8 August 1944 she and thirty-seven SOE men and women prisoners were taken by train to Germany. Lilian and the other women were sent to Ravensbrück. Three weeks later, she and two other women were sent to Torgau, another camp, where they planned their escape. The problem though, according to Escott, was that,

> although they should have been classed as prisoners of war, the Germans had ignored this fact and were treating them as civilian malcontents or political prisoners, and apart from not sending them to a prisoner of war camp – often a death sentence although they did not know it – they had never been brought to trial. In fact, none of the SOE girls was tried so their imprisonment was breaking all the rules of war drawn up in the Geneva Convention to which Germany had subscribed. But this was a small matter in comparison with the terrible crimes of which the Germans were later found guilty.

They were sent back to Ravensbrück before their plans could be materialised and, because they were relatively fit, were then sent to Königsberg to help clear land for the construction of a new airfield. The extreme conditions Lilian had to endure were described by Escott:

> It was now winter, freezing cold, with ice and snow. They were thinly clothed for the conditions, the food was bad and there was very little of it. They had to lift and carry heavy weights, to dig in deep frozen water for hours on end, to fill swamps with sand, to cut and lay slabs of turf, to hew and haul trees and tree stumps, to drag boulders and equipment, all in the open, without covering or shelter. There was no medical treatment and many died from pneumonia, dysentery, cholera and tuberculosis, if they did not break down from sheer exhaustion, malnutrition or cruel treatment by the guards, who thought nothing of beating women staggering with heavy loads or almost dying on their feet. Indeed when the German Air Force came to occupy the camp, so painstakingly created, even they were horrified by what they saw. Under these conditions, Lilian no longer spoke of escape. It was all she could do to survive. She was already sick with a spot on her lung and her breathing becoming hard and laboured. All her former cheerfulness failed her and she found it hard not to sink into the torpor which usually preceded a loss of will to live, and then death.

In January 1945 the three of them were transferred back to the main camp and put, not in the huts with the other women, but in the punishment block. From there she was put in an isolation cell close to the crematorium and, according to the testimony of the camp commander and guards after the war, had to be stretchered into the yard on or about 5 January. She had to watch the two other women sentenced to death being shot in the back of the neck before she too was executed. The bodies were then disposed of in the crematorium. Other sources state she was dragged out and executed on 27 January 1945.

Escott reported that Mary Lindell, who (like Yvonne Baseden) survived imprisonment at Ravensbrück, said after the war that she thought the three women had been told that they were to be sent to a POW camp near Lake Constance but that there is no evidence that any women were ever sent there. Mary felt that their deaths were a direct result of this; she added that the normal method of execution was hanging and she had been reliably informed that the women's clothing had been returned to the store unsoiled. In honour of her brave venture, Lilian was awarded an MBE, 'Mentioned in Dispatches' and awarded the Medaille de la Resistance and the Croix de Guerre.

## Muriel Byck

After four nail-biting attempts were cancelled because of poor weather conditions, eventually on 9 April 1944 petite, dark-haired Muriel Byck, a twenty-three-year-old French Jew, codenamed 'Violette', was flown out of Tempsford along with other agents to work as a wireless transmitter with Philippe de Vomécourt's VENTRILOQUIST network in the Orléans–Blois area.

Martin Sugarman, on the Jewish Virtual Library website, reports how Muriel was born in Ealing, London, but studied in Germany and went to university in France before the war. She returned to England and worked as an air-raid warden and a National Registration clerk in Torquay. She joined the WAAF in December 1942 and her fluent French drew her to the attention of the SOE, which she joined in July the following year. After an assessment at Winterfold and paramilitary training at Moeble, Inverness, and wireless training at Thame Park, Oxfordshire, she was, according to her instructors' records, given a high intelligence rating with a high grade for Morse and Mechanical Aptitude. Her observers described her as

> a quiet, bright, attractive girl, keen, enthusiastic and intelligent. Alert but not very practical and as yet lacks foresight and thoroughness. She is, however, self-possessed, independent and persistent, and warm in her feelings for others ... a girl of considerable promise who will require much training to help her overcome her lack of experience, her complete ignorance of what the work really involves and her general guilelessness. Her temperament would appear to be suitable for work as a courier, or possibly propaganda.
>
> (www.jewishvirtuallibrary.org/jsource/ww2/sugar2.html)

However, Vera Atkins, the woman in charge of all the 'F' Section women in SOE, thought Muriel very self-assured and committed to go into the hazardous work to defeat Nazism and all it stood for.

Escott commented that Muriel's 'pretty, chubby, tiny and almost childlike appearance masked the maturity and resilience of a 25-year-old woman'. De Vomécourt said: 'she looked so young, but I had seen enough of France to know that courage knew no barriers of age'. In fact, Muriel's youthful looks meant that she was given special training to make her look older by using a pencil under her eyes.

She got engaged to another French agent she met on the training course, who gave her a leather-covered powder compact. When Muriel arrived at RAF Tempsford for the flight, de Vomécourt said that she was not allowed to take the compact unless she agreed to make it look old. Nothing like it could be bought in France, so she agreed that it could be rubbed with ammonia.

Promoted to second officer before her trip, she parachuted into Issoudun where, because it was Easter, one of the reception committee pressed a small gold cross and chain into her hands – said by Escott to have been 'a kind of talisman against evil from which she was never to be parted'.

On her first day she was given a baptism of fire. Antoine Vincent, the owner of the garage in Salbris where she first stayed, took her out for a meal in a little restaurant on the outskirts of town with de Vomécourt. It was normally used exclusively by the Germans, and that day it was full of them. She was terrified and asked to leave but in his wartime memoirs, *An Army of Amateurs*, Philippe told her not to worry. 'We brought you here on purpose. You must get used to the sight of the Boches and realise there's nothing different about them. Once you're used to seeing them, you won't worry about them any more.'

When she was taken to her hosts' house, they were shown papers indicating that she was a secretary from Paris who had been given orders by the doctor to take a rest in the country. They specified that she had to ensure that her medicines were taken at specified times every day and night. This was to provide an excuse if they heard her alarm clock ringing at odd hours so she could make her scheduled wireless calls. The doctor also told them not to be surprised if she had the occasional visit from her 'uncle' who might pop down to see how she was.

Codenamed 'Michelle', she was also known as 'Michele Bernier' and 'Benefactress'. In *An Army of Amateurs*, de Vomécourt wrote that:

> Muriel was provided with three different photographs of herself for identity papers, each of them projecting an entirely separate person, by the adoption of a changed hairstyle. By drawing back her hair from her forehead, or by fluffing it out, untidily, she could assume different identities in an emergency. And she would have the identity papers, bearing the appropriate photograph of herself, to aid the transformation.

Her mission was to train local recruits in wireless transmission for the VENTRILOQUIST network. There were four sets in different places within a 16-kilometre radius of the garage. She ensured her operators never used the same set at the same time each day, and whenever reports arrived of Germans in the vicinity the set was moved to another spot. According to the Jewish Virtual Library website:

> Her circuit had four transmitters in different locations covering a wide area within a ten mile radius of Vincent's house, and – in accordance with her orders – were constantly moved about to avoid detection by the Germans, with transmissions being as brief as possible Her first transmission was on 7 May 1944 and she subsequently sent twenty-seven messages and received sixteen. She never used the same set consecutively or at the same hour on any day. She was thus continually cycling from one to the other, and although many a man's health and nerves degenerated under the stress, Muriel remained cheerful and buoyant despite her frail and youthful looks. Rushing from

location to location, she would encode, send, receive and decode messages, always on schedule, and on her own initiative often do this for other circuits as well, so messages would not ever be delayed. She also acted as a courier, alerting sabotage teams over a wide area.

Her base was in Vincent's junk yard, twenty-five yards from his garage which was used as a repair shop by the Germans. Her station consisted of a rickety hut with a rusted corrugated iron roof, with light filtering through cracks in the wall. She was surrounded by old tyres and car parts and the reek of oil and petrol. She had a box and table to work at. Whilst transmitting, a guard was posted at the yard gate to give her warning if need be.

One day in late April, (this date of de Vomécourt conflicts with the SOE file date given above) whilst transmitting to London, she noticed an eye looking through a hole in the shed wall. Her stomach lurched but she quickly switched to plain language to tell London she was being watched. Continuing to send, she picked up the set and approached the hole, in time to see a German soldier leaving the yard. Full of fear, and not understanding where her lookout was, she packed her equipment, threw dust over her box and table to disguise the fact that anyone had been in the hut, and slipped into Vincent's house and told him what had happened.

He decided at once to get her away in a car after consulting de Vomécourt, who came to collect her. When the Germans arrived – forty of them – they were already sceptical that their soldier had actually seen a pretty woman with a transmitter in a junk yard shed! They searched and found nothing and the soldier was given ten days detention for wasting his officer's time.

Securely relocated in a new safe house (with the help of the Resistance doctor Andrieux) Muriel returned to work; her story was that she was recovering from an illness and had come from Paris to recuperate. She had to take medicine during the night and her hosts should not be worried by her alarm going off at strange hours (this was, of course, to cover her wireless operations) or visits from her 'uncle', de Vomécourt.

(http://www.jewishvirtuallibrary.org/jsource//ww2/sugar2.html)

Following SOE analysis of her transmissions, in which she reported that the Germans were running trains into the military camp at Michenon and loading them with arms and ammunition, it was decided that the RAF would act on VENTRILOQUIST's plans and bomb the camp. She heard at 1400 hours on 7 May that there would be an attack the following evening. That was time enough for the Resistance to blow up the railway lines outside the camp to stop any trains from leaving and to inform those civilians living or working near the camp to evacuate. Things didn't go according to plan, however. The attack came at 2330 hours that night. Muriel heard the air-raid sirens and saw the incendiaries dropped by the pathfinder aircraft. Great explosions scorched the night sky. Tracer bullets streaked after the RAF bombers. Five plummeted in flames, smashing into the earth. The trains erupted like volcanic explosions of twisted and burning metal. Buildings rocked up to 20 kilometres away. Searchlights picked out the parachutes of pilots and crews who managed to bale out. Two separate search parties went out to find them, the Germans and the Maquis.

Muriel was badly shaken by the huge explosions. Philippe was so concerned by her exhaustion and listlessness that he had her moved into alternative accommodation with a blacksmith in Vernou, nearly 50 kilometres away. As there was a plane leaving shortly for Tempsford, he said he would arrange for any letters to be delivered to her parents. Shortly after he drove away, he had a premonition she had taken a turn for the worse. He returned to discover that she had fainted. The third doctor he rang turned up, diagnosed meningitis and had her hospitalised at Romorantin, Loire et Cher.

The nuns did all they could, but she died in Philippe's arms on 23 May. To prevent the disclosure of her real identity, he had her body put in a zinc coffin, gave a false name and arranged a quick funeral. Worried that the Germans might be able to arrest many of his network in one swoop, he stopped her friends from attending. In fact, he alone followed the hearse through the town to the cemetery, and during the priest's committal to the grave of the body, with its gold cross and chain, he heard one then another car arrive. With unusual sensitivity, the Gestapo waited until the service was over, by which time Philippe had taken cover behind the priest and altar boys and climbed over the wall where, by arrangement, his friends were waiting in a car.

His letter to her father was a moving tribute to Muriel, full of praise for her wonderful personality and beauty, her sense of duty and hard work, her laughter and gaiety, and it described her as a unique person who died as a soldier, giving her life for right and justice. She was 'Mentioned in Dispatches' and a memorial was built for her at Romorantin, visited by Resistance members. Her name is on the memorials at Valençay and the Lycée Français in Kensington.

## Odette Wilen

Odette Wilen joined the FANY early in the war and during her training course she met Pearl Witherington, who commented that Odette

> was very, very, very feminine. Of course there she didn't know what she was letting herself in for because one fine day we'd been blowing things up right, left and centre and she said, 'Pearl, I must ask you for some advice.' She said, 'What are we supposed to be doing?' I was so surprised and said, 'Don't you know?' 'Well,' she said, 'no, I thought I was coming into this because I was recruited as a bilingual secretary…' So I said, 'Well, you'd better go and talk to Major Watt about this because that's not what we're doing.
>
> (Witherington, P. 8689/2; 10447/3 IWM)

She went on to help train SOE agents until the need arose for her to be sent. Details of her activities in the field were revealed in communication on the Special Operations Executive user group on Yahoo.com which reported her being belatedly awarded her parachuting wings in 2007. Following the death of her husband, a Finnish volunteer RAF pilot instructor, in a flying accident, she volunteered to be sent into France. Given the urgency of the situation, she did not complete the requisite number of parachute jumps to qualify for her wings and was dropped near Issouden on 11 April 1944.

Codenamed 'Sophie', Odette was originally sent to act as a radio operator for Maurice Southgate's STATIONER network near Châteauroux. Having only been partly trained for that task, he sent her to work as a courier in the LABOURER network with a new codename, 'Waitress'.

While in the field, she developed a relationship with and got engaged to the network's leader but, following his arrest, she had to return to England. This involved a well-organised but nonetheless dangerous escape route which included a memorable bicycle ride down the Champs-Élysées in Paris, escorted by the thirteen-year-old son of a friend of her fiancé. Odette eventually crossed the Pyrenees into neutral Spain before being repatriated to England via Gibraltar. For the rest of the war, she acted as a conducting officer in 'F' Section.

It was during her escape that she met Santiago Strugo Garay, the head of the Spanish escape network. Despite having only known her for three days, he travelled to London when the war ended, found Odette and married her.

In Anne-Marie Walter's personal file in the National Archives, there is a note, dated 14 September 1944, expressing SOE's concern about Odette:

> We know most details of this lady's excursion into France. She struck me as suffering a little from a guilty conscience, but is in a very defiant mood. She states that she is anxious to make up for time wasted and not to be kept without useful employment for an indefinite period of time. I personally think it is unfortunate still that she should have arrived at a time when her fiancé had been arrested, and what is most regrettable is that she quite obviously placed her private affairs above any other consideration.
>
> (TNA HS 9/339/2)

Odette, Walters and Yvonne Fontaine were reported as having spent the night exchanging confidences in a London hotel, talking freely of the arrests of a great number of agents. The writer of the note expressed a wish that Miss Wilen and Miss Walters be requested to write their reports as soon as possible 'and be suitably disposed of'.

## Nancy Wake

At the end of April 1944, almost three weeks after Odette Wilen left Tempsford, Nancy Wake was flown out. Although born in New Zealand, the youngest of six children, she was brought up in Australia and ran away from home when she was sixteen and became first a journalist in Sydney and then a nurse in a mental hospital. Inheriting £200 from an aunt, she ran away to New York, then London, where she trained as a journalist. Becoming a correspondent for the *Chicago Tribune* in Paris, she reported on the rise of Adolf Hitler in Germany. Her obituary in the *Independent* told of a trip to Vienna in 1933 to interview Hitler which led her to become committed to bringing down the Nazis. Seeing Jews being tied to a kind of Catherine wheel and being whipped and pelted by Germans and Austrians, she commented afterwards that it was quite revolting: 'I thought … what had they done, poor bastards? Nothing. So I said, "God almighty, it's a bit much and I've got to do something about it."'

She upset her parents in 1939 by marrying Henri Fiocca, a wealthy French businessman, playboy and expert tango dancer in Marseille. Their taste for champagne and caviar in the morning and love in the afternoon came to an abrupt end when the

Germans invaded France in June 1940. She drove ambulances and helped a Resistance network on the Mediterranean coast, carrying messages and providing food and arms. Later, she helped British servicemen and Jews to escape.

She recalled how French women's *chic* was imitated by the Germans' wives and girlfriends, who joined the occupying forces when they took over the south of France. As French women didn't wear hats, the German women didn't, so the French ladies started wearing them again. This time they wore green feathers in them, which symbolised the green bean, *les haricots verts*, the nickname used for the Germans as they wore green uniform. Any women wearing a hat with a green feather was overtly insulting the enemy. When the newcomers started wearing expensive stockings, the French women stopped wearing them and used knitted stockings instead and still managed to look *chic*.

To avoid bringing attention to herself and her husband, Nancy worked under the cover name of Mademoiselle Lucienne Carlier, a doctor's secretary, while she acted as a courier for Ian Garrow and Pat O'Leary's escape line in the south-east of France. The SIS used to provide them with rolls of French francs carefully hidden in toothpaste tubes brought in from Switzerland. Loans from French businessmen were guaranteed by London and confirmed when a phrase of their choice was heard among the *messages personelles* after the 1900 hours news on the BBC's French Service.

In an interview after the war, Nancy asserted, 'I hate wars and violence but if they come then I don't see why we women should just wave our men a proud goodbye and then knit them balaclavas.' On one occasion, she was stopped by a roving police control and questioned as to why, as a secretary, she travelled so far in first-class compartments, wearing such good clothes. Blushing demurely, she said that she was a very *private* kind of secretary. The gendarme understood and let her go. Her obituary in *The Australian* detailed her experiences:

> It was perilous work despite her cover as the wife of a respectable businessman. She lived on her sharp wits.
>
> 'I'd see a German officer on the train or somewhere, sometimes dressed in civvies, but you could pick 'em. So, instead of raising suspicions I'd flirt with them, ask for a light and say my lighter was out of fuel,' she recalled.
>
> She told how she would get beautifully dressed and hang around making dates with Germans to get information.
>
> 'A little powder and a little drink on the way, and I'd pass their posts and wink and say, "Do you want to search me?" God, what a flirtatious little bastard I was.'

Working for the Resistance, she travelled all over southern France from Nice to Nîmes to Perpignan, with clothing, money and false documents. In Peter Fitzsimons's biography, she is quoted as saying:

> I played the part of a giddy Frenchwoman who didn't give a bugger what happened in the war. I was a good-time girl. I used to give Germans a date sometimes, sometimes three or four times if I was away on a long trip and give them a little bit of hope. I played the part – I should have been an actress.

Despite having her phone tapped and her mail opened by the Gestapo, Nancy managed to evade capture so well that they nicknamed her *la Souris Blanche*, the White Mouse. Every time they had her cornered, she managed to get away.

So determined were the Germans to stop her, they put out a 5-million-franc reward for her capture. According to Fitzsimons, she helped 1,037 downed Allied pilots and crew to escape over the Pyrenees into Spain, although this number is disputed by Keith Janes of escapelines.com.

After the network was betrayed, she feared for her life so had to follow the same escape routes as those she had helped. In Russell Braddon's *Nancy Wake: SOE's Greatest Heroine*, he details how, after she was betrayed, the escape organisation was compromised and her husband persuaded her to flee. She made six attempts and on one occasion she had to jump out of a moving train window and dodge bullets as she ran through a vineyard to evade capture, leaving her handbag with all her money and jewellery behind. She had to sleep in pigsties for five days, starved, got frozen and caught scabies.

When she was questioned at a checkpoint with 200 pounds of pork in a suitcase, she ended up being interrogated for four days, suspected of being involved in a Resistance attack on a cinema. She denied it and was locked in a stinking toilet overnight and only freed when Pat O'Leary marched in to see the Police Commissioner, pretended to be a close friend of Pierre Laval, the premier of the Vichy government, and demanded that his mistress be released.

Hidden under a pile of coal with two Americans and a New Zealander, she eventually succeeded in crossing the Pyrenees in espadrilles to reduce the possibility of the German guards' Alsatian guard dogs from hearing them. They made their way south through Spain to Gibraltar, where she spent the time waiting for a convoy to take her back to England doing two things: 'I went up to a hotel on the top of the Rock and got pissed every day, and I also read lots of newspapers catching up on what had happened in the war.'

Before Nancy's train pulled into London on 17 June 1943, Ian Garrow organised for the train to be stopped and a car whisked her off to St James's Hotel, where she was very warmly welcomed and suitably entertained by many of those pilots and aircrews she had rescued. But she was never to see her husband again. He was captured and tortured while she was out of the country, but he didn't reveal her whereabouts.

Her attempts to join de Gaulle's Free French Forces and be returned to France to fight the Germans were thwarted. Colonel Passy, the recruiting officer, refused her application. She thought he thought that she was a British spy. In fact, the following day she was approached by a representative of the SOE keen to know why she had been to see the Free French. She denied it, but when he proceeded to give her the time she went in and came out, what she was wearing and where she went to next, she realised they were the sort of organisation she wanted to work for. They quickly gave her a commission in the FANY as an ensign and sent her to the first training school at Winterfold, near Cranleigh in Surrey.

According to Juliette Pattinson, the author of *Behind Enemy Lines*, Nancy almost failed at the first hurdle. She was sacked from her course for drinking too much. Selwyn Jepson is reported as saying, 'We don't like our girls to drink.' Her report mentioned her being charged with being drunk and disorderly in the village outside the training camp. Buckmaster must have recognised her potential as he overruled Jepson, saying, 'It sometimes happens, I think, that this woman's high spirits, are sometimes mistaken for drunkenness … she was a real Australian bombshell. Tremendous vitality, flashing eyes. Everything she did, she did well. With all her gay laughter, she had a serious and sensitive streak.' Jepson's comment underneath was the reverse.

More light on the circumstances was shed in Fitzsimon's biography. Nancy had been in the room when there had been a great argument between a Frenchwoman on the course and Denis Rake, an openly homosexual weapons training instructor who later became an agent himself. Nancy ignored it but, after Rake had stormed out and slammed the door, the Frenchwoman asked her to witness what he had said to her, wanting to get him sacked. When she refused, the Frenchwoman,

> sensing that Nancy might have been slightly tipsy after the lunch she had just returned from, accused her of being drunk, and quickly reported this 'fact' to one of SOE's more punctiliously proper officers, Selwyn Jepson, together with the fact that Ensign Wake was refusing to acknowledge what she had heard Rake saying to her. Jepson called for Nancy and upbraided her. She promptly told him, in highly specific terms, where he could stick his upbraiding. He, white-faced with fury, ordered her to leave the premises and return to her flat in London.

She is reported to have told Jepson that he could have her FANY uniform back if he came to pick it up himself. Garrow pleaded her case, arguing that she was volatile, passionate and fearless – exactly what was required of an agent in the field. Buckmaster agreed and she was invited to rejoin the course. He must also have recognised how pro-British she was. In fact, Rake had previously been caught with his radio, imprisoned and had a number of bones in his foot broken during interrogation. After managing to escape, he crossed the Pyrenees and returned to London, where Buckmaster gave him a job as Nancy's conducting officer. They were to develop a remarkable operational relationship. On the train to her next course in Scotland, Nancy explained that

> when I looked out of the carriage window … I was looking into the backyards and tiny gardens of all these houses that backed onto the railway line, and what do you think? They were all growing vegetables. All of them had these great vegetable patches going wherever there was a spare patch of dirt. They were magnificent! England, and the people of England, were growing everything themselves, never mind what the war had to say about it. And they could feed everybody, I've never forgotten it. I don't give a bugger what anyone says – we owe a lot to Britain. I loved Great Britain – and I will die loving it…

She was thirty-one when she was sent for paramilitary training in Achnacharry, Scotland, and admitted evading physical exercise by saying she had a period or had a cold. She cheated on cross-country courses and took shortcuts whenever she could.

> We also had a lot of fun, and a lot of laughter. As a relief from the seriousness of everything else, there was a lot of skylarking and pranks, and that sort of thing, and being a bit of a skylarker myself I absolutely loved it.

In her book *The Autobiography of the Woman the Gestapo called the White Mouse*, she recalled an incident at Ringway.

> All our meals were served in a huge dining hall. The commanding officer and his staff sat at a long table running the full width of the room, with their backs to the wall and facing the students. The students were seated at both sides of several long tables running lengthwise, from the top table to the other end of the room. Thus the staff were in a position to observe everything that occurred in the dining hall.
>
> One morning at the breakfast table an American sergeant sitting opposite me passed me a small packet, saying that it was a present. Although Raymond Batchelor sitting on my right whispered in French not to accept it, I did so, thinking it was chewing gum or chocolate. I knew what a French letter meant in English, just as I knew the French name for it, but I did not know what a condom was until I opened the packet and saw three of them lying there together with the instructions.
>
> I don't know what reaction the American expected, especially at a breakfast table. There was silence all round me. Then I proceeded to read out the instructions, much to the amusement of everyone at our table except the American, who, red in the face, left the table. I put them in the pocket of my battle dress and continued eating my breakfast. As we left the dining hall the CO called me to one side, apologised for the behaviour of the American and offered to disembarrass me of the unmentionables. He was surprised when I declined his offer, adding that they might come in handy later on. We never saw the American again. He vanished. I feel sure he was reprimanded.

Having survived the parachute training at Ringway, she went to Beaulieu, where she found occasions to use her present later on, surreptitiously attaching them to various instructors' clothing, much to the amusement of her fellow trainees. One day, hearing that the top brass were about to make an inspection, she used the skills she had been taught to snatch the keys of the filing cabinet where the agents' assessment files were kept, press it into a lump of plasticine she had brought specially for the task, put the key back, then went to the workshop the following day and poured some molten brass into the mould. That evening, while her friend Raymond was on guard, she slipped into the office and sneaked both their files. Hers was very good. She recalled it saying, 'Her morale and sense of humour encouraged everyone.' This was clearly demonstrated in her choice of code poem:

> She stood right there,
> In the moonlight fair,
> And the moon shone,
> Through her nightie,
> It lit right on,
> The nipple of her tit,
> Oh Jesus Christ Almighty!

Much to the amusement of the others, one day she and Violette Szabó managed to pin down one of the instructors, pull his pants off and tie them to a flagpole. When the camp commander didn't invite them to a party, they broke into his room, removed all the furniture and then barricaded themselves into their own room for the night.

Vera Atkins remembered her as 'a real Australian bombshell. Tremendous vitality, flashing eyes. Everything she did, she did well.' Her training reports record that she was 'a very good and fast shot' and had a good eye for fieldcraft. On several occasions, she 'put the men to shame by her cheerful spirit and strength of character'.

Her mission was to act as a liaison officer for STATIONER, the codename for the Maquis group in the Auvergne, the mountainous region of central France. As there was no moon visible on 28 April 1944, her flight back from RAF Tempsford into occupied France had to be postponed. This gave her the chance to visit Cambridge and see the sights.

The next night was less cloudy and Nancy, codenamed 'Helene' and known as 'Madame Andrée', was seen off personally by Colonel Buckmaster, who gave her a silver compact makeup case. In the late evening of 29/30 April, she was handed up into the belly of a black Liberator B-24. According to Braddon, her codename for the journey was 'Witch'. 'The dispatcher, a lean, good-natured Texan, sidled up to her and asked, "Are you really a witch?" "I am. And don't get your letters mixed." "Gee," he muttered, "a woman! We ain't never dropped a woman before."'

She was parachuted into the outskirts of Montluçon with Major John Farmer, an SOE agent codenamed 'Hubert'. Suffering from a double hangover and half-frozen, she had her parachute caught in a tree, and Henri Tardivat, the French agent who helped her down, told her that he wished all trees could bear such beautiful fruit. As a typically straight-talking Australian, she was unimpressed by his Gallic charm and told him, revolver in hand, not to give her 'that French s**t'. Fitzsimons tells us that:

> She was dressed, oddly enough, as a very lumpy version of her normal self. For the jump she had on her favourite camel-hair coat atop regulation army overalls, but beneath this army issue she wore silk stockings and stylish shoes beneath heavily bandaged ankles to protect her bones and tendons against the impact of landing. In the pockets of these clothes were two revolvers. On her head, a tin hat. In her small backpack, she had several changes of clothes, and among other things, a red satin cushion that she simply adored and two hand-embroidered nightdresses she'd insisted on bringing. On her arm, topping the whole thing off, her handbag stuffed full of over one million French francs with which she hoped to help finance the Maquis, plus her favourite red Chanel lipstick and tightly packed articles of feminine hygiene, while securely memorised in her head she had a list of targets for demolition – railway junctions, bridges, underground cables and factories that had to be attacked and destroyed the moment D-Day arrived. In the same spot, securely stored away, she also had the addresses of various safe houses in the area, together with the names of their residents and the passwords by which she would be recognised. Finally, secreted in the second button of the cuff on her left sleeve was a cyanide pill which guaranteed an all-but-instant death should she ever find herself in a situation where that was clearly preferable to what lay before her.

Captain Dennis Rake was dropped separately. He had convinced Buckmaster that he was fit enough to return as Nancy's radio operator. As well as making arrangements to provide the Resistance with funds, their mission was to help the French establish ammunition and arms caches and to arrange wireless communication to England in preparation for the D-Day landings. She lived in the forested hills, criss-crossed with tracks, with about 7,000 male *résistants* and wore army boots, khaki trousers, shirt, tie and beret.

Howarth mentioned that shortly after her arrival, Nancy overheard one of the Maquis suggest to another that he should seduce her, murder her and then take her money. This influenced her judgement as to which group she would arrange arms for. This involved sending messages to London for weapons, ammunition, food, clothes, money and Elizabeth Arden face cream.

On the first morning, when she went out to urinate, she noticed that all the bushes around her were shaking. Although she understood, she insisted that, once they had seen her it was to be the last time. When ten men in her camp refused to do the water-carrying duties, she persuaded them by emptying a bucket of water over each. During the day she would join them in physical training, go on reconnaissance with them and provide them with weapons training. In the evening, she would sit around the camp fire swigging whisky and having drinking competitions, which she claimed she always won. She played cards, swore blindly and joined in with raucous singing. When she went to bed, she reasserted her femininity by putting on a silk nightdress and applying her face cream.

During her time in France, she developed two great passions: a taste for 'Baba a Rhum', (sponge ring doughnuts steeped in rum, and served smothered in whipped cream with a glacé cherry on top), and Pastis (a French anise-flavored liqueur and apéritif). Anecdotally, it is said that, after a Pastis session with her Maquis colleagues, she became maudlin and 'fell' for a 'lonely' horse in a nearby field and transported it to the ramshackle bathroom made of corrugated iron that the Maquis had built for her. During the night there was a torrential thunderstorm, and the heavy rain on the iron roof spooked the horse, which kicked the place to pieces and bolted into the night.

Her Maquis colleagues, when asked for a code phrase to report safe delivery of their supplies, came up with 'Madam Andrée has a horse in the bathroom!' 'Madam Andrée' was the nickname the Maquis gave her. According to her obituary in the *Guardian* (8 August 2011):

> Circumstances gave her considerable freedom of action. The circuit's orders were to help organise and arm the local maquis, and soon Wake was fighting alongside them in pitched battles with the Germans. 'I liked that kind of thing,' she said, although she had to prove herself first as an honorary man, a feat easily accomplished by regularly drinking her French comrades under the table. 'I had never seen anyone drink like that,' confessed Farmer, 'and I don't think the maquis had either. We just couldn't work out where it all went.'

On the night of 15/16 September 1943, a bombing raid of 389 RAF planes halted production of the Dunlop rubber factory in Montluçon. The following year, when it was back in production, it only took two pounds of plastic explosive planted by Nancy's team to bring it to its knees. She played a prominent role in blowing up the bridge over the

Allier River. She and four men, with explosives strapped to their bodies, climbed down the struts of the bridge to lay the charges. Fitzsimons reported her ambushing German convoys using home-made bombs, which would result in the deaths of twenty to thirty soldiers. She shot dead four German officers at point-blank range, fought her way out of roadblocks and went into battle with German troops on numerous occasions when the camps were attacked. She led a raid on the Gestapo headquarters in Montluçon, throwing a grenade into the room before retreating. 'Several dozen Germans did not lunch that day, nor any other days for that matter.' When she found out that a group of her men were torturing and sexually abusing three women who had been collaborating with the Germans, she interviewed the women, released two and ordered the third shot, even offering to execute the woman herself since the Maquisards' sense of honour permitted her rape but not her killing. 'It didn't put me off my breakfast,' she said. 'After all, she had an easy death. She didn't suffer.'

On another occasion, Fitzsimons tells us, a disaffected and drunken communist Maquisard was threatening to shoot Madame Andrée for not providing him with weapons. She hadn't because of his slovenly, disorganised organisation. When he came out of the bar to throw the grenade at her car, he took the pin out but didn't throw it in time. 'All I knew was sitting in the car and bits of flesh were going all over the place, landing on the bonnet and the windscreen.'

In an interview with Pattinson, Nancy explained why she had become so aggressive and desensitised to the violence of war. It was witnessing anti-Semitic actions in Vienna, observing a seven-month-pregnant Frenchwoman being bayoneted in the stomach and hearing about a male colleague who had been beheaded. Asked about the source of her courage, she replied, 'Freedom is the only thing worth living for. While I was doing that work, I used to think it didn't matter if I died, because without freedom there was no point in living.'

Fitzsimons reports her saying that she proactively sought to kill as many Germans as she could as she 'longed to break their fucking necks'. After being cut in the arm by a sentry's bayonet during an attack on an armaments factory in Mont Mouchet, she killed the man with a karate-like chop to the back of the neck to keep him from alerting the guards. 'They'd taught this judo-chop stuff with the flat of the hand at SOE, and I practised away at it. But this was the only time I used it – whack – and it killed him all right. I was really surprised.' Fighting, she believed, was part of war. The idea of women having a homely, peace-loving, compassionate, caring nature was not found in Nancy during her war years. In her interview with Juliette Pattinson, she commented on her position among so many men:

> If I had accommodated one man, word would have been spread around. They would have been coming over from the next mountain! [laughs!] I would have had a very sore arse! [raucous laughter] The pine needles! And when would I have done the work that I had done and would those men have had respect for me? They wouldn't have. They wouldn't have.

There was one occasion when Nancy had to adopt the disguise of a middle-aged peasant to avoid detection. According to her autobiography,

I borrowed a long white piqué dress which must have been fashionable before World War I ... I was ... looking like a real country bumpkin, wet hair pulled back tight, no make-up, an old fashioned dress, and wearing a pair of the farmer's old boots ... Our cart and the produce were inspected several times by the Germans as we entered Aurillac; they did not give me a second look, even their first glance was rather disdainful. I did not blame them. I did not look very fetching.

In Russell Brandon's biography of Nancy, he said that the dress dated from 1890 and had been borrowed from an elderly lady. 'The Germans questioned him [the farmer] and searched the vegetables, but they showed no interest at all in his revolting-looking daughter.'

Having lost her radio and codes during a skirmish with German troops, she was unable to make contact with her controllers in London. Without a radio she could not receive, order or arrange air drops of weapons, ammunition and food. Accordingly, she volunteered to cycle more than 400 kilometres over rough terrain with no identity papers to deliver a vital message. It took her three days. So as not to look unkempt she took her dress off at night when she slept in deserted barns. One time, desperate to go to the toilet, she knew that she would never be able to get back onto the bike if she got off. So, she hitched her dress up, moved her underwear to one side and urinated onto the ground. She commented in her autobiography that she was fortunate that she didn't have to do the other. 'I was just a normal young woman ... I cycled to the local markets and filled my string bag with all the fruit and vegetables I could buy without food coupons hoping that I would pass for a housewife out shopping.' When she was stopped, she said she only had to 'look over to the officer, flutter my eyelashes and say "Do you want to search moi?" And they would laugh flirtatiously, "No, Mademoiselle, you carry on."' On her return, she was asked how she was. She cried. 'I couldn't stand up, I couldn't sit down. I couldn't do anything. I just cried.'

After the Normandy landings, her circuit was getting up to four drops a week with fifteen containers of supplies, including army trousers and black boots and 15 million francs (£85,000) a month to pay the wages and pensions of her 7,000-strong force. Rake commented that 'it was no exaggeration to say that Nancy Wake armed and supplied the vast majority of them'. They were attacked by 12,000 SS troops in June with aerial bombing, artillery, mortars and machine guns. Working with two American officers when the Germans launched an attack, she took command of a section whose leader had been killed and with exceptional coolness directed the covering fire while the group withdrew with no further loss of life.

Although Nancy managed to escape, a hundred of her colleagues were killed and 1,400 German troops lay dead on the plateau above Chaudes-Aiguwes. Speaking about a film she made after the war, she denied feeling any anxiety.

I never had any time to worry and I must admit some people don't believe me. I never was afraid and sometimes I think that people probably think I'm mad or that I'm telling lies. But I can honestly say I was never afraid. I was too busy to be afraid.

On 25 August 1944, the day Paris was finally liberated, she led her celebrating troops into Vichy. Her exuberance was only halted when she was told that Henri, her husband, was dead. He had been arrested and interrogated to reveal her whereabouts. When he refused to do so, he was tortured and finally shot. She blamed herself. If it had not been for her, he would have survived the war. Farmer ordered her to work with an SOE network whose headquarters had moved to Paris. Probably owing to the stress of the preceding summer, she fell ill and did not report back after sick leave. She subsequently wrote to SOE headquarters in London, requesting to be 'sworn out' of the organisation.

In her interview with Pattinson, she claimed that Tardivat, the French Resistance leader, said that:

> 'She is the most feminine woman I have ever met in my life, but in battle she's worth ten men!' So I changed. I was feminine but fighting. All I wanted to do was kill Germans. I didn't give a bugger about them, to kill Germans. Didn't care about it. I hated, I loathed the Germans. I loathed them. As far as I was concerned, the only good one was a dead one and I don't care what anyone thinks of me. A dead German!

After the war, her bravery and leadership were recognised and she was awarded the George Medal, Croix de Guerre with two palms and Silver Star, Chevalier de la Legion d'Honneur, French Resistance Medal and the United States Freedom Medal. It was said that she used to threaten that if the Australian government ever got round to giving her a medal, she would tell them 'to stick it where the sun don't shine'. In 2001 they eventually awarded her the Companion of the Order. In fact, Nancy was the most highly decorated servicewoman in the Second World War.

Wake continued working for British intelligence in Europe after the war until 1957, when she moved back to Australia and married British RAF fighter pilot John Forward. When an Australian television drama was made about her wartime experiences, she commented, 'For goodness sake, did the Allies parachute me into France to fry eggs and bacon for the men? There wasn't an egg to be had for love nor money, and even if there had been why would I be frying it when I had men to do that sort of thing?'

She moved back to Britain in 2001, four years after Forward's death, and is said to have inspired Australian actor Cate Blanchett's role in the film *Charlotte Gray*. She never had children and died on 7 August 2011. According to her wishes, her ashes were scattered in Montluçon, where she fought a heroic battle in 1944 at the Gestapo headquarters.

In September 2010, the former Olympic gymnast Suzanne Dando led a group of young women on a charity trek, *Le Chemin de la Liberté*, across the Pyrenees on behalf of the Royal British Legion. They followed in the footsteps of Nancy Wake and thousands of civilians and servicemen who escaped from France during the war.

## Phyllis 'Pippa' Latour

On 1 May 1944, Carpetbagger Crance's mission parachuted twenty-two-year-old South African Phyllis Latour, another second officer in the WAAF, into Mayenne, near Hardanges. Using three codenames, 'Geneviève', 'Plus Fours' and 'Lampooner', she worked as a radio operator in the revived Scientist network in south Normandy under the command of Lise de Baissac.

In Judith Martin's interview with her for New Zealand's *Army News*, she described how she was born on a Belgian ship tied up in Durban, South Africa, in March 1921 to a French doctor and a British mother. Her father was killed in fighting in the Congo when she was three months old. Her mother remarried when she was three and Phyllis went to live with her stepfather and his sons in the Congo.

> 'My stepfather was well off, and a racing driver. The men would do circuits and they would often let their wives race against each other. When my mother drove the choke stuck and she couldn't control the car. She hit a barrier, the car burst into flames, and she died.'
>
> Her father's cousin became her guardian, and she went to live with him, his wife and his sons in the Congo. 'They were really the only parents I knew. When I was seven my "new" mother went riding as she always did. The horse came back without her, and a lot of time elapsed before they found her as they did not know where she had been riding. Apparently the horse had stepped on a puff adder. She was thrown, and then bitten in the face by the adder. When they found her she was dead.'
>
> (http://www.army.mil.nz/at-a-glance/news/army-news/400/pw.htm)

Known by her family and friends as Pippa, she grew up with her 'brothers', who taught her how to shoot. When she arrived in Britain is uncertain but, fluent in French, she joined the WAAF in November 1941 as a flight mechanic. She had visions of working on an airfield and interviewing French air crews returning from sorties. Two years later, her fluency in French brought her to the attention of the SOE. After a successful interview, she was commissioned as an Honorary Section Officer and trained as a radio operator.

> 'They took a group of about 20 of us away for training. It was unusual training – not what I expected, and very hard. It wasn't until after my first round of training that they told me they wanted me to become a member of the SOE. They said I could have three days to think about it. I told them I didn't need three days to make a decision; I'd take the job now.'
>
> The training members of the SOE were given was tough, and women were given no quarter, says Pippa. The men who had been sent in before me were caught and executed. I was told I was chosen for that area (of France) because I would arouse less suspicion.
>
> As well as extensive physical fitness training, the operatives were given other training to suit their work. 'We climbed ropes, and learned to climb trees and up the side of buildings. Our instructor was a cat burglar who had been taken out of prison to train us. We learned how to get in a high window, and down drain pipes, how to climb over roofs without being caught.'
>
> '… I was scared. I didn't like jumping, no matter what part of the aircraft it was from.'

Understandably, she did not mention that she had to be helped to be disentangled from the only apple tree in the drop zone area. She claimed in her interview to have been motivated by revenge. Her godmother's father had been killed by the Germans and her godmother committed suicide after being imprisoned by the enemy.

Her arrival in France came at a time of great upheaval in the de Baissacs' networks following hundreds of arrests in and around Paris. In Ross Dix-Peek's article, 'A South African Girl in the Special Operations Executive', he commented that her codename was intriguing,

> as 'Genevieve' was the name of the patron saint of Paris, a shepherd's daughter who lived in the 5th century, and who encouraged the citizens when threatened by Attila and the Huns, and also brought them aid when Childeric attacked the city. And, 1500 years later, yet another 'Genevieve', this time in the form of a young lass from South Africa, was again helping France to resist the invader. Latour operated bravely and stoically, sending a plethora of coded messages back to London, all the while evading the enemy.
>
> (http://peek-01.livejournal.com/27044.html)

The rebuilding of a more secure network took time and Pippa had to keep tight security, transmitting at different times from different houses using the three sets that had been dropped with her. To assist her getting about, she had six bicycles hidden around the countryside and dressed like a fourteen-year-old schoolgirl living with her extended family to avoid the bombing.

> With just one blue cotton dress to her name she pedalled across the countryside selling soap to mostly German soldiers, crossing fields on foot to where she had hidden another bicycle.
>
> The Gestapo and SS were everywhere. And to add to the confusion and danger a double agent was working in the area. The SOE operative was friendly and talkative whenever she met German soldiers – 'I'd talk so much about anything and everything, trying to be "helpful" and they'd get sick of me' – and was constantly moving through the countryside where she was transmitting the information urgently needed by the Allied Command.
>
> It was crucial the information she transmitted was accurate – the lives of thousands of Allied soldiers depended on it.
>
> 'I always carried knitting needles because my codes were on a piece of silk – I had about 2000 I could use. When I used a code I would just pinprick it to indicate it had gone. I wrapped the piece of silk around a knitting needle and put it in a flat shoe lace which I used to tie my hair up.'
>
> Once she was loaded into a truck along with other locals and taken to the police station for questioning. 'I can remember being taken to the station and a female soldier made us take our clothes off to see if we were hiding anything. She was looking suspiciously at my hair so I just pulled my lace off and shook my head. That seemed to satisfy her. I tied my hair back up with the lace – it was a very nerve wracking moment.'
>
> Pippa had no real base, sleeping rough in the countryside and in the forest. She had a courier, and a local married couple who she could contact should things go horribly wrong.
>
> She was constantly hungry. 'One family I stayed with told me we were eating squirrel. I found out later it was rat. I was half starved so I didn't care.'

While she had a Sten gun and a 7mm pistol with a silencer, she couldn't carry a weapon routinely as it would give her ruse away should she be stopped. She used the training she had been given but lived largely by her wits.

'Germany was far more advanced with their DF [direction finding or radio detecting apparatus] than the Allies. They were about half an hour behind me each time I transmitted. Each message might take me about half an hour so I didn't have much time. It was an awful problem for me as I had to ask for one of the three DF near me to be taken out. They threw a grenade at it. A German woman and two small children died. Then I heard I was responsible for their deaths. It was a horrible feeling. I later attended the funeral of a grandmother, her daughter and her two grandchildren, knowing I had indirectly caused their deaths.

I can imagine the bomber pilots patting each other on the back and offering congratulations after a strike. But they never saw the carnage that was left. I always saw it, and I don't think I will ever forget it.

(http://www.army.mil.nz/at-a-glance/news/army-news/400/pw.htm)

Just before the D-Day landings, she and the de Baissacs were working in the same half-derelict farmhouse. On the first floor they sat on wooden benches, slept on piles of straw and foraged the local countryside for food and water. They spent hours coding and decoding the messages she sent to and got back from London and then passed the instructions to various members of the network. Escott says she sent 135 messages while in France. She also arranged the arrival and accommodation of the VERGER Jedburgh team, who undertook useful sabotage missions until they were caught and shot. However, she admitted after the war, 'I hated what I was doing. At first I was proud of myself because I was doing something for the war effort. But when you see what the bombers do…'

Following the invasion, almost every foot of soil in her area was being fought over. Another Jedburgh team was welcomed and put into action while the men harried the arriving German reinforcements in order to allow the Allies to move further east towards Paris. According to Escott:

During this period Pippa had many narrow escapes, flitting to and fro over Orne from one hidden radio set to another, or following after Lise who frequently carried her wirelesses ahead of Pippa. One day during the German retreat, she was on her way to a distant farmhouse from where her next transmission was expected to go out. As the area was filled with Germans, Claude, having no one else to spare and knowing that it was not safe to let her go alone, sent his sister Lise to accompany her. The Allied victories which Pippa constantly heard on the BBC had sometimes made her less careful of her safety and less conscious of the danger surrounding her. This worried Claude, as his pianists were too valuable to lose, and Pippa was both too young and bold for her own safety, only measuring the demoralisation of the mass of soldiery by those units she saw in flight, rather than the individual soldier, who might be driven to revenge if he suspected her mission. They were both on their bicycles and Lise was carrying some spare parts for the set, hidden in the belt around the waist of her dress, believing that what was in full view was less likely to be searched.

As they came to a bend in the country road they had taken, believing it clear of Germans, they saw a soldier at the side examining all those passing by. There was no way of avoiding him. So they rode casually up to him and getting down from their bicycles produced their papers for his inspection. But more followed. He wanted to search them for arms or sabotage materials. The resistance had been quite active over the past week in this area, and the Germans knew that they were being helped by many in the locality who, with the Germans in retreat, were becoming more open in their hostility. A thorough search might mean removing clothes and examining different parts of the body and was usually carried out at the police headquarters, but a wayside search usually meant passing the hands over the body, clothes and all, to detect any unusual lumps or bumps on the person. Pippa was all right, but would the German find the parts in Lise's belt? Quietly Pippa submitted to the search. Then it was Lise's turn. What would they do if he discovered the spares? A minute lasted like an hour, and then Pippa felt like laughing, the German did not bother with the belt, not even noticing that it was rather an odd shape. He merely grunted, and stood back motioning them to go.

The search was satisfactory. They mounted their bikes, overwhelmed with relief, when suddenly there was a clatter on the road at their feet. One of the spare parts had fallen out of Lise's belt. Surely this was the end? To Pippa's astonishment the German hardly seemed to notice, being already busy with another couple riding behind them. Quickly Lise bent down to retrieve the part and then they were off cycling like the wind, in case the German had second thoughts. But he didn't and they got away without further mishap. Nevertheless they had both had a great fright.

When the American forces drove into the village where she was staying in August, she lined up with the other residents, waving, shouting and laughing. There was clapping and cheering, attempts to catch hold of the soldiers as they passed in their cavalcade, and the throwing of flowers and blowing of kisses to the men. As Escott put it, 'No one particularly noticed the girl from SOE, in her faded summer dress, and yet she as much as any of them had paved the way for their victory. She had sent over 135 messages to London and carried out her mission safely and successfully.' Shortly after she returned to England, in appreciation of the contribution she made in helping the French shed the yoke of tyranny, she was awarded the Croix de Guerre and an MBE. A South African newspaper commented after the war that:

It was lonely work in a land of strangers, and anxiety was an ever-present emotion – anxiety as to what was happening to family and friends, with whom she could not communicate; anxiety about making contact with certain persons at specific times, and the endless anxiety as to how long the deception could be kept up. All this on the shoulders of a girl but twenty-three years-of-age, but triumph she did.

(http://peek-01.livejournal.com/27044.html)

## Marcelle Somers

On 3 May 1944, the moon period before D-Day, Flying Officer Harold Ibbott took eight passengers in his Hudson to a field 3 kilometres north-north-west of Manziat, north-north-east of Mâcon. Marcelle Somers, codename 'Albanais', was accompanied by seven other passengers, including Commandant Maurice Barthélémy, codenamed 'Barrat', Colonel Paul Hanneton, codenamed 'Ligne', and Jacques Davout d'Auerstaerdt, codenamed 'Ovale'. Exactly what Marcelle's role was has not come to light, but in Gibb McCall's *Flight Most Secret* he says that she worked with the CONE network and arranged her daughter's parachute reception two months later. After the war, she was awarded the MBE and the Croix de Guerre.

Eight other passengers were returned in the Hudson, including Mme Fleury and her baby daughter, who celebrated her first birthday in the Royal Patriotic School in Wandsworth. Mme Fleury had only recently been released by the Gestapo after four months' imprisonment for questioning over her husband's clandestine radio operations. A stool pigeon, someone planted to win her confidence in order to make her talk, had been in her cell with her but she didn't provide any information. Her husband told Verity:

> This is why the British and the French decided to bring her and the baby out of France. This is how one was able to see a strange sight on their arrival in England: a tall pilot in operational uniform getting out of the aeroplane and, confronted with a tiny baby, asking her: 'are you a terrorist?' But the reply would have been too long to give him.

## Marguerite Knight

Twenty-four-year-old Lieutenant Marguerite 'Peggy' Knight was brought up in Paris, the daughter of a Polish mother and British father. She was fluent in French when she moved to London and, when war broke out in 1939, she moved from working as a shorthand typist for Asea Electric in Walthamstow to a position in the WAAF. After being invalided out in May the following year, she found a typing job in an engineering firm. Escott narrates how

> one day she was present at a party given in the lounge of a London hotel. While the social chatter went on around, her attention was caught by a man, whose book seemed to have slipped from under his arm without his noticing it. When she retrieved it he had moved away, giving her time to glance at the cover, the title of which appeared to be in French. Probably its owner could also speak it. Unobtrusively she found her quarry and almost apologetically handed his book back, adding a few courteous and appropriate words in French. The man raised his eyebrows and complimented her on her good accent. Then switching the conversation to French he soon found out how fluent she was. Before the party broke up she found herself the possessor of a name and telephone number, which she was to ring up if she wanted to change her job. This was her entry into SOE and in April 1944 she joined the FANY.

After successful interviews, she started the SOE's 'Students' Assessment Course' at Wanborough on 11 April 1944. Described as well educated, well above average intelligence, thoughtful, practical and quick, she was considered by her instructors as an ideal candidate to be a courier. But with time pressing, her call to arms came despite one instructor feeling that she needed more training: 'I could accept no responsibility for passing her out as fit for the field.'

There must have been a degree of urgency with D-Day approaching as she only did one parachute drop at Ringway. After further radio training at Thame Park and briefing for her mission, she was parachuted by USAAF Carpetbagger mission FENSTER from Harrington on 5/6 May 1944. In an interview with Cameron Ramos, she told how she and Henri Bouchard, the radio operator, codenamed 'Noel', landed at Marcenay on the Cote d'Or. She jumped from 200 feet, when the plane was doing 150 mph, onto a drop zone lit up with torches in the shape of a letter 'T'. Her report said that she showed no sign of nervousness in the aircraft.

They were met by a 'very bad' reception committee under the command of Casse-Cou, which forced them to hang around the field for more than an hour as they were asked questions and had their cigarettes, chewing gum and even their parachutes taken from them before the threat of discovery forced them to the nearest village. Ramos told his readers in the *Harrow Times* how

> her time there was marked by constant feuding. Three of her colleagues were shot as traitors, another survived a bungled assassination attempt by two comrades and her circuit organiser was betrayed.
>
> In this atmosphere Peggy had to use all her instincts to survive and managed to remain undiscovered for six months while sending vital information to the Allies.
>
> Colonel Maurice Buckmaster said of her in June 1945: 'A young girl of an altogether exceptional courage and good sense and very marked intelligence.
>
> 'She has rendered services of a remarkable nature without regard to the risks she ran.
>
> 'Courageous in front of the enemy, she has shown a completely unexpected military sense and has been an inspiration to her comrades.'

Her mission was to work as a courier in Henri Frager's DONKEYMAN network in Yonne and the Cote d'Azur. According to Foot (1999), she had only had a fortnight's training. 'She was naïve, modest, efficient, and self-effacing; her French was good; everyone liked her and no one noticed her. She was quite out of her depth in the personal and political intrigues that riddled DONKEYMAN.'

Little else has emerged of her exploits, except that she was codenamed 'Nicole' and her cover name was 'Marguerite Chauvan'. Her *réseau* was involved in attacking railways, airfields and oil storage depots. Escott tells of Peggy narrowly avoiding capture and her group having to disperse. When the Americans arrived, she had to cross German lines to keep in contact with her group and the Allies. Her courier work by bicycle was gruelling but, in time, she was another of the female agents brought safely back to England in September 1944. She resigned her FANY commission when she got married in November 1944 and was subsequently awarded the MBE, the Croix de Guerre and the Médaille de la Résistance.

Ramos related how Peggy's story was brought to the public attention in 1947 by a reporter from the *Sunday Express* who wrote an article entitled 'Mrs Smith: Train-wrecker, spy and Nazi-killer'.

> You would not expect that the prim little woman who comes out of the newly built house, 61 Eastfield Road, Waltham Cross, Essex (sic), wheeling her 16-month-old and

four-month-old in a second-hand pram … with shopping basket on the handrail, is our trusted and well-beloved Marguerite Diana Frances Smith who once blazed away with a Sten gun at Germans hunting her down as a secret agent in France.

(http://www.harrowtimes.co.uk/news/579480.from_the_ typewriter_to_blazing_sten_gun/)

The caption underneath the photograph showing her playing with her two children in front of the fire read: 'I like a good fight, whether it's with a gun in your hand or whether it's just against circumstances, but I honestly think my present job as a housewife is more exacting.'

## Madeleine Lavigne

According to Hugh Verity, Madeleine Lavigne was recruited in France by Robert Boiteaux , an SOE agent dropped in Ance in the south-west Pyrenees in June 1942. As he needed her trained in England, he arranged for her to be picked up. She returned in a Hudson flown by Squadron Leader Ratcliff on 4/5 February 1944 from a field a kilometre south-east of Soucelles, north-east of Angers. The other eight passengers included Robert Benoist, Philippe Liewer, Bob Maloubier, H. Borosh, Col. Limousin, 'Le Berbu', the innkeeper at Tiercé, her husband and Mme Gouin, the wife of a French politician. In Ratcliff's memoirs, he told how he had been ordered to bring Déricourt back, but he refused. Whether they landed at Tempsford is unknown.

After her training, Madeleine was taken to Tempsford on 24 May 1944 and Geoff Rothwell of 138 Squadron reported dropping her at Soane-et-Loire, near Reims in the Ardennes. She was described by Wilf Burnett, 138 Flight Commander, as a VIP agent. Geoff was impressed by her height, good looks, and perfume. When he asked Bob Willmott, one of his crew, if he had noticed her heavy make up, the response was: 'All these women Froggies make the 'ole bloody aircraft smell like a bleedin' whore's boudoir!'

Major Charles Tice, the Liaison Officer, had told Geoff that she was going back 'into the field' for the second time. She had been captured on her first trip working for the SILVERSMITH network and the Gestapo stubbed out lit cigarettes on her face to try to get information out of her. The make-up was to hide the scars. After a daring escape from her jailers, she was picked up, returned safely to Britain and prepared for her second trip.

A volunteer FANY, Madeleine worked as a courier with the SPRUCE network with the codename 'Isabelle'. When the Germans successfully penetrated her network, she went on the run, staying in one of Henri Déricourt's safe houses not far from the DZ. She died of an embolism in Paris on 24 February 1945. She was awarded the King's Medal for Brave Conduct and the King's Commendation for Brave Conduct.

## Sonya Butt

Four days after Madeleine Lavigne arrived in France, Sonya Butt was flown out on Carpetbagger CHOPER mission and parachuted into La Cropte, a small community west of Le Mans. It was a fortnight after her twentieth birthday. Codenamed 'Blanche' and with the cover name 'Suzanne Bonvie', she had important courier work to do. According to the now defunct 64 Baker Street website, she was born in Kent but her father, an RAF Group Captain, separated from her mother and she attended a private school in the south of France.

Following the German invasion of France, fifteen-year-old Sonya returned to Britain. At seventeen, she joined the WAAF and carried out tedious administration duties. In time, she got to hear of people joining de Gaulle's Free French Forces and felt that she could do more interesting work by exploiting her fluent French. She requested a job as a translator, but, once Colonel Passy discovered her English background, she was refused. Shortly afterwards, she was taken on and trained by the SOE.

During her training, she got to know Nancy Wake and Violette Szabó and they had many good times together before their missions. Not having a mathematical or logical brain or being good at map reading, she did not think she was suitable material for coding or signals work. The part of the course she enjoyed most was weapons training. Students had to learn everything there was to know about every type and make of weapon that they might encounter, whether they were British, American, German or other foreign makes. They also had to be able to take them apart and reassemble them in the dark and use them accurately. However, her speciality was working with explosives.

Her instructor introduced her to Guy Artois, a Canadian soldier who was also training as an agent. Romance blossomed. Even though she had only known him three months, they got married in London before the SOE had decided upon their missions. Buckmaster was said to not have being very amused by the wedding, because he would not be able to send both into the field as a married couple. Following Guy's departure to France, Buckmaster realised how upset Sonya was and could not refuse her request to be sent on a separate mission.

Sonya was parachuted into the Le Mans area on 28 May 1944 with two other agents to help Sydney Hudson's HEADMASTER circuit. Her cover story was that she was an employee of a fashion house in Paris, but, suffering from bronchitis, she had been sent to the country to recuperate in a chateau. She landed in a ditch, but the container carrying her clothes and other belongings landed on a nearby road and was almost immediately picked up by a German patrol. It was said that she was more annoyed that she had lost her designer clothes than that the Germans now knew that there was a new female operative in the area.

Over the next few months she was constantly on the move, only staying in someone's home or hideout for a maximum of two nights. By day she and her colleagues were recruiting new *résistants* and training them in weapons and explosives techniques. By night she helped pick up 138 Squadron's drops of weapons and explosives. Her team then used them to attack railway lines, roads and bridges.

Just before D-Day, she and Hudson successfully blew up Le Mans telegraph office, forcing the Germans to transmit wireless messages which were intercepted by Allied code breakers.

In Hudson's memoirs, *Undercover Operator*, he recalled that on the morning of D-Day, they were staying at No. 8 rue Mangeard in Le Mans. Presumably to protect Sonya's identity, he changed her name.

Madeleine was sleeping upstairs and I was installed on the sofa on the ground floor. We were awakened by the sound of bombs falling nearby. Allied bombers were targeting the railway station; in fact it had already been destroyed. Thinking that Madeleine might be frightened I dashed upstairs to her room. I need not have bothered; she was completely unperturbed. The bombardment did not last long and soon all appeared normal on the streets of the town.

The area where she was working was full of Germans, but, rather than hide from them, she was said to have blatantly and brazenly mixed with them. An attractive blonde, she knew she would be noticed, but Sonya was confident with her cover and false papers. On one occasion, she was cycling to a house to tell a group of *résistants* about their next meeting when a sixth sense told her to stop and wait. Just then, a group of German soldiers swooped on the house and arrested the people she was going to meet. On another occasion, she was in a café sitting close to several German soldiers when she accidentally dropped her handbag containing her .32-calibre handgun, When one of the officers reached down to pick it up for her, she managed to beat him to it. The weight of it would very probably have given her away.

After the D-Day landing the fighting by the *résistants* was far more open and Sonya was involved in major attacks involving groups of between twenty and thirty fighters. Trains were stopped and German soldiers captured. Once the Americans troops arrived, she was told she could return to London via Paris. When she and the head of her circuit refused, they were given the task of identifying German troop positions and strengths by travelling back and forth over the front line.

On one incursion, her group were conscious that a German patrol was close by. To avoid being caught with their Sten guns, they buried them in the woods. Although they were caught and interrogated, the Germans didn't know what to do with them and so they let them go.

On another occasion she and Hudson walked into a German-held town, only to find it empty and deathly silent. All the men had been rounded up and were under armed guard in the market square, while the women had gone into hiding. It turned out that the Germans were hoping to bargain for their own safety by using the men as hostages. Although Hudson was arrested, Sonya was allowed to leave and went in search of safety. Eventually, the Germans surrendered and their prisoners were released.

Sonya returned to the American lines and continued working for them until she went to Paris. After several weeks of celebrations, she was joined by her husband. After completing his own SOE work, he had been searching for her in other parts of France. She became pregnant with the first of their six children, and, after a period in England, they went to live in Canada.

Sonya was awarded the MBE and 'Mentioned in Dispatches'. More details of her wartime experiences can be found in Escott's *Mission Improbable*.

## Germaine Heim

Germaine Heim (Heem), codenamed 'Danubien', was another member of the Corps Auxiliaire Féminin in the RF section who was parachuted in to work with the Scope and Périmétre networks on 5/6 July 1944. Little has come to light of her work, except that she managed to survive being caught until Liberation.

## Ginette Jullian

Far less detail has emerged about the other women sent to France in 1944. Lieutenant Ginette Jullian, codenamed 'Adèle', was dropped at St Viatre the day after D-Day with Gerard Dedieu. Maybe she was the Ginette referred to as helping on the Marie-Claire line. She worked as a radio operator in the PERMIT network until she was picked up and returned to Britain.

## Krystyna Skarbek (Christine Granville)

Twenty-two-year-old Krystyna Skarbek, the slim, olive-skinned, raven-haired daughter of a Polish count, was the next agent to be flown into France. Although there is no documentation showing that she was taken out from Tempsford, it was thought to have been an SOE-inspired mission from Massingham, their forward base in Algiers.

Born in Poland to a Jewish mother, she was brought up a Catholic by her father and described by Hugh Davies, an SOE enthusiast, as 'the sort of woman our mothers warned us about'. Working first in an agency for Fiat cars and then as a journalist in Paris, she spent her holidays skiing in the Polish resort of Zakapone, making extra money by smuggling. There she got to know some of the mountain people who would be of help later in the war.

She married in 1938 and was in Addis Ababa with her Ukrainian husband, Jerzy Giycki, when the Germans invaded Poland on 1 September the following year. The gold ring she wore on her middle finger had a band of steel in the middle which she claimed was in memory of the heroic times in the fifteenth century when her ancestors drove the Teutonic knights out of Poland. She was reported as saying that when Jan Skarbeck was told by the Emperor, Henry II, that resistance was futile and he had coffers full of gold to pay his soldiers, he took his gold ring off and threw it in with the coins, saying 'Let gold return to gold; we Poles prefer steel.'

Her mother, the daughter of a Jewish banker, was deported from Warsaw. Krystyna and Jerzy managed to get to London, where she successfully applied for British naturalisation. Her husband was determined to make his way to Finland to fight against the Red Army, but Krystyna had other plans. Wanting to help the Polish resistance, she contacted the SIS. She joined the WAAF and underwent training and a flight was arranged for her to get to Budapest.

George Taylor, one of SOE's early officers, had a rapport with Krystyna and arranged her cover story as a journalist with a mission she largely created herself.

> Once established in Hungary, her intention was to make her way into Poland with propaganda material which, she hoped, would convince her compatriots that, contrary to nearly all the evidence, Britain had not abandoned Poland and would continue to prosecute the war vigorously.
> (Howarth, *Undercover: The Men and Women of the Special Operations Executive*)

In Madeleine Masson's biography, *A Search for Christine Granville*, she details how in Budapest, Krystyna, codenamed 'Granville', met up with Andrezej Kowerski, an old friend and hero in the Polish army, and engaged in espionage, sabotage and a *ménage à trois* with another Polish agent. Vera Atkins said of her that 'she was no plaster saint. She was a vital, healthy, beautiful animal with a great appetite for love and laughter.'

Having rescued members of the Polish army from internment camps, she used her skiing skills to escort them over the snow-covered mountains into Yugoslavia. Despite being arrested twice in Hungary and once on the Czechoslovakian border, she managed to escape, convincing her guard that she had tuberculosis. She was able to provide the Allies with a microfilm showing German forces preparing to invade the Soviet Union in June 1941. Sir Owen O'Malley, the British ambassador in Budapest, who knew her well and issued her with a British passport, said, 'She is the bravest person I ever knew, the only woman who had a positive nostalgia for danger. She could do anything with dynamite except eat it.'

She and Andrezej escaped over the Yugoslavian border in the boot of a car and made their way through Istanbul, Syria, and Palestine to Cairo, where she was recruited into SOE using the name Christine Granville. In a lecture at Bletchley Park in January 2010, Dr Mark Baldwin, an SOE historian, added that, on her way through Syria, she made a detailed study of all the bridges – invaluable information for the SOE, who were instructed to protect the Syrian oilfields in case of a Nazi attempt to capture them.

Said to have been the most highly trained of all the SOE's female agents, her instructor said of her that she was as brave as a lion and as SOE-minded as any of the Poles. Following a commission as a flight officer in the WAAF, she was the first agent to be flown out of Algiers. Despite a terrible gale, the pilot managed to drop her on the Vercors plateau on the night of 7/8 July. She landed badly, several miles off target. The butt of her revolver was smashed, but she hobbled on with a badly bruised hip. When she reached the reception committee that was waiting for her, the more conventional among them were said to have been shocked by her language.

Codenamed 'Pauline' and also known as 'Jacqueline Armand', she replaced Cécile Lefort as Francis Cammaerts' courier in the JOCKEY network. They managed to leave the wooded Vercors plateau before the German attack on 17 July. Travelling by car, they took the back roads and trails to Seynes-les-Alpes in the Basses Alpes. Her mission then changed.

She was to contact Italian partisans on the border and win their active co-operation with the Allies. This mission successfully completed, not without danger, she was next sent off to win over the Russians serving with the Oriental Legion of the German 19th Army. Her gift for languages and her ability to inspire affection made her welcome and again she succeeded in her object. Once on the journey, while hiding from a German patrol, she was scented by one of the Alsatian tracker dogs which, coming under her strange charm, lay down beside her, instantly changing its loyalties, and never afterwards leaving her side.

Being thoroughly feminine, she was certainly conscious of her appearance, though she frequently dressed in a manner which attracted little or no attention. This I believe, derived from a certain chameleon quality which helped her to be so supremely successful as a secret agent …

In reality she was a peculiarly gentle being who disliked noise in general and firearms in particular. When she was being taught how to use a pistol she shut her eyes every time she fired and announced that she could never bring herself to shoot anyone. Nor did she. In emergencies she employed other weapons, including her formidable power of persuasion. This derived partly from feminine charm, partly from a controlled indignation which, it was easy to believe, might suddenly erupt into fury, and partly from an ability to persuade any man on whom she was working that he was unusual in being perceptive enough, not only to understand the arguments she was advancing, but to agree with them.

(Howarth, *Undercover*)

On one occasion, when faced with a German patrol, she calmly took out of her bag the SOE escape map, which was printed on silk, and used it as a headscarf. Part of her mission was to encourage a group of Polish nationals who had been forcibly enrolled in the German army to desert.

She managed to contact some who ran a clandestine organisation centred at Mont-Dauphin. A more difficult assignment was to make her way to a fort in the Col de Larche on the Italian border south of Meyronnes, where 150 Poles were manning the garrison. A French patriot took her by motorcycle to the house of a guide, who led her up the 1,994 feet of precipitous mountain, mainly through woods of larches. She achieved a meeting with her contacts and many Poles defected as a result, with their arms. Before doing so, fifty of them removed the breech blocks from the heavy guns and brought with them mortars and machine guns to join the maquis.

(Pawley, *In Obedience to Instructions*)

According to Pawley, when Cammaerts and two other leaders of the Jockey network were arrested at a roadblock on 13 August, they were taken to a prison in Digne. The driver, Claude Renoir, the son of the famous painter, was allowed to get away and he told Christine. She then bicycled the 25 miles to Digne and, pretending to be Cammaert's wife, succeeded in entering the prison.

In Foot's *SOE in France* he said how, three hours before the men were due to be shot, Christine used a combination of steady nerve, disguise, feminine cunning and sheer brass to secure their release. She told Albert Shenck, the liaison officer between the French prefecture and the Germans, that she was Cammaerts' wife, the niece of General Montgomery and a British agent, and that she would arrange to have him killed by the Maquis within days once the American forces arrived. She offered to bribe Max Waem, the Belgian Gestapo officer who acted as an interpreter for the German secret police, with 2 million francs. Her plan worked. The money was dropped by parachute on 17 August after her urgent request to Massingham, the Allied headquarters in Algiers.

The *message personelle* on the BBC included the words: '*Roger est libre; félicitations á Pauline*.' She then accompanied the two men over the Pyrenees into Spain and then back to England, from where, after a brief respite, the SOE sent her to Cairo for her next mission. The plan had been to infiltrate her into Poland, but the speed of the Russian advance towards Germany thwarted the mission.

Following the German surrender and demobilisation, Christine returned to England, where she was awarded the George Cross and the OBE. The War Office had initially been reluctant to recommend the awards as she was from Poland, but many recognised that her bravery deserved recognition. De Gaulle awarded her the Croix de Guerre.

She found work as a telephonist in India House in London, then as a salesgirl in Harrods department store before getting a job as a stewardess on the SS *Rauhine*, a liner plying between Southampton and Australia. Dr Baldwin reported how the captain suggested one evening that everyone should wear their war medals. There was amazement when Krystyna wore her three. It was on this ship that she met George Muldowney, an Irish steward, who became obsessed with her. Although his romantic propositions were rejected, he found her lodgings in London and, in June 1952, he stabbed her in the heart outside the Shelbourne Hotel in Kensington when she still rejected his advances. Muldowney was hanged for her murder on 30 September 1952. The Wordiq website states that:

> Since her death, it has been speculated by some that because author Ian Fleming used the beautiful Krystyna as the basis for the double agent, 'Vesper Lynd' in his first James Bond, that Krystyna herself may have actually been a double agent. However, no such claim has ever been suggested by any legitimate authority and SOE's Vera Atkins, who had access to all files and knew her well, stated that Krystyna Skarbek was 'utterly loyal and dedicated to the Allies, and nothing would have made her betray her trust'.
> (http://www.wordiq.com/definition/Christine_Granville)

More details of Krystyna's daring escapades can be read in Escott's *Mission Improbable* and a film about her exploits, entitled *Christine: War My Love*, is in the making.

## Josiane Somers
On the same night that Krystyna was dropped, 6 July 1944, Bill Strathern dropped nineteen-year-old Josiane Somers in France. The location was not documented. Also known by her married name, Josiane Gros, she was another member of the Corps Auxiliaire Féminin, sent in to join her mother as a radio operator for CONE, one of the RF *réseaux*. Apart from her codename 'Venizien', little is known of her mission, except that she had joined de Gaulle's department in London in 1942. Both mother and daughter survived the war when the Americans overran their area.

## Eugénie Gruner
On the night of 10/11 August 1944, Wing Commander Boxer flew a Hudson mission to a field near Garlin, 30 kilometres north of Pau in the Pyrenees. Eugénie Gruner disembarked with five other passengers, part of the Proust team. She was another of de Gaulle's RF section women, sent in to work with the RECTANGLE network. Apart from her codename 'Bulgarian', little is known of her and her mission, except she was in place when the Allies arrived.

## Cécile de Marcilly
Pierre Tillet's research shows that Cécile de Marcilly (née Pichard) also went out on 11 August 1944. Her brother, Michel Pichard, was the head of General de Gaulle's Air

Liaison, who co-ordinated the flights from Tempsford and Harrington into occupied France. A number of photographs of her being kitted out prior to her flight have survived.

Thomas Ensminger, historian of the Carpetbaggers, told me that Cécile was a member of the Corps Auxiliaire Féminin. Also known as 'Jacqueline', she was flown out with Wood's Carpetbagger crew and accompanied by Maurice Rosenbach, codenamed 'Sevilan', as part of an Inter-Allied Mission team known as Anis on operation Bob 242. They landed near Rivière les Fosses, Haute Marne, but very little has come to light of her mission, except that it was in Altesse region. Verity mentioned being contacted by Michel Pichard, who had told him:

> Yeo-Thomas was to be picked up with Claude Bouchinet-Serreulles ('Sophie') and myself. I got to Arras around the 11th with my secretary Bel-A (actually my sister Cécile, whom we call Jacqueline, now Jacqueline de Marcilly as she kept that Christian name) in case there would be room for her; she had worked with me since January and was 'blown'.
>
> On November 12th or 13th I rushed back to Paris after hearing that eight BOA (Bureau d'Opérations Aériennes) agents had been arrested at Café Dupont, Versailles … the situation was quite alarming and I decided to stay.
>
> Serreulles, disregarding London's instructions, did not show up; so, this left two 'seats' available, and Yeo-Thomas flew back with Mademoiselle Virolle (his agent de liaison) and Mademoiselle Pichard.

## Marguerite Gianello and Aimee Corge

The next Corps Auxiliaire Féminin agent, Marguerite Gianello, was parachuted into France on 1/2 September 1944. Apart from her codename, 'Lancel', no further details of her Péritoine mission have come to light. Similarly, little is known of Aimee Corge,

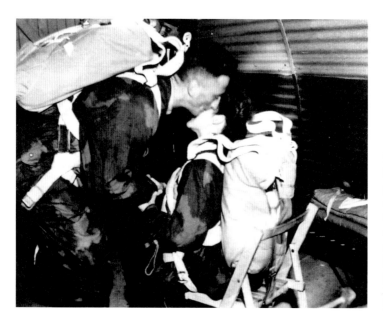

Cécile de Marcilly's final kiss before getting on the plane on 11 August 1944. A member of the Corps Auxiliaire Féminin, she was parachuted back into France as part of Sussex Team Anis. (Courtesy of Pierre Tillet)

Corps Auxiliaire Féminin, codenamed 'Helene', who was flown out on 11 September. All these women survived when the Allies overran their positions.

## Marie-Madeleine Fourcade

The next woman flown out was Marie-Madeleine Fourcade. Her autobiography, *Noah's Ark*, details how she was born Marie-Madeleine Bridou, the daughter of the executive of a steamship company, in Marseille in 1909. She married Monsieur Fourcade in 1929 but they separated, leaving her with two children.

Until war broke out she worked for a publishing company in Paris, and when Pétain signed the armistice in June 1940, she joined the Resistance. Working with Georges Loustaunau-Lacau in the ALLIANCE network, she took advantage of her contacts in business, politics and the military to provide the Allies valuable and continuous information about German troop movements, their supplies, submarines and ships. It was sent to England along with their political plans, scale drawings of U-boat bases, the launch sites of 'secret weapons' and anything potentially useful to the Allies. When her organiser was arrested in May 1941, she took command. The British military authorities were so impressed with the quality of this information that they sent her a radio operator in August. Unfortunately, he was a double agent who betrayed many members of her network to the Gestapo. She was arrested but managed to escape and got into Spain inside a post bag in the back of a diplomatic car.

Fearing German reprisals, she was infiltrated back into France where, once she had her children taken into neutral Switzerland, she restarted her resistance work, helping to get downed Allied airmen back to Britain.

In Keith Jeffrey's history of MI6, there was an account of how, in 1942,

reliable information was received that an agent known as Bla, a former French farm manager, had been captured by the Germans and was now working for them. He was caught in France by agents of Alliance, a network of French spies reporting to SIS. Bla was taken to an Alliance safe house where he was interrogated by the French agent Marie-Madeleine Fourcade (among others) and confessed to 'having given to the Boches all details known to him about us'. They first tried to kill him 'without him knowing it', by putting lethal drugs in his food, but this failed and merely alerted the unfortunate man to 'the attempt we were making'. When he was killed (he was shot) he faced his fate with what Fourcade reported as 'extraordinary moral courage' and 'astounded us by his calm attitude in facing punishment'.

'The way he died,' she wrote, 'did something to mitigate his past record.' Although in her memoirs Fourcade relates that an 'execution order' was received from London, nothing so explicit survives in the relevant files, and her contemporaneous report asserted that over the weekend when Bla was in Alliance hands no contact was established with London.

A subsequent minute, nevertheless, by the Free French Section in Broadway (SIS headquarters) recorded that because the leading Alliance figures were 'known personally to [blanked out], the danger was such that eventually we instructed them to do away with him should the opportunity occur'.

When his widow made inquiries about him towards the end of 1944 she was simply told that the authorities had had no information of his whereabouts 'since 1942'. As one SIS officer minuted, 'if any sleeping dogs should be let lie I think this is one'.

Following more arrests, MI6 thought it was too dangerous for Marie-Madeleine to stay in France, so they arranged for her to be brought to Britain. The Germans called her network 'Noah's Ark' as all her agents' cover names were animals. Hers was 'Hedgehog'. On 5 July 1943, Johnnie Affleck was said to have flown his Hudson to pick her up, along with her latest batch of airmen. Whether he did or not is uncertain as Hugh Verity says she was returned in a Lysander from a newly cut cornfield at Bouillancy, near Meaux on 17/18 July by Flight Lieutenant Peter Vaughan Fowler, who was able to add a *fleur-de-lis* on his cockpit for another successful mission. Once she was safe in England, the BCRA provided Marie-Madeleine with accommodation in Chelsea, from where she continued supervising her network and arranging pick-ups.

Aware of the Allied plans to invade Europe, she browbeat her minders into allowing her to return to France. Yvonne Fontaine and Pierre Mulsant arranged her landing the day after D-Day. In her memoirs, *Noah's Ark*, she said that she was given two hours' notice of her departure and had to pack into the false bottom of a large, soft holdall the crystals for her wireless set, replacement codes, money and a set of dentures that transformed her into a French housewife. Her clothes were in a light fibre suitcase and in her handbag she carried a forged identity card and her 'L' pills.

> I gazed at Alliance House for the last time, at the large-flowered cretonnes, the camp-bed with its tearful night-time memories and the telephone that had so often been the bearer of appalling news.

She, Pierre Giraud and Raymond Pezet, her 'husband' for the return visit, were driven out of London in a long, black car. From her description, it is not clear whether she went to The Hasells or Gaynes Hall. Her account of her visit is worth including for the light it sheds on the agents' preparations for the trip.

> We drew up at dusk before the steps of a country house and were immediately taken to a huge dining room that had been converted into a mess, where waiters in white jackets above their service trousers were bustling about.
>
> 'So it's to be tonight?' Teutatès asked Ham, who had come back from the phone box.
>
> 'No, it's postponed until tomorrow.' My heart sank. After dinner I invited Ham to drink a last whisky with me.
>
> 'You're frightened about going back, Poz?' he asked.
>
> 'Yes, I'm frightened; I'm really in a blue flunk. I'm going to be arrested and yet I've got the feeling I shall get away with it.'
>
> We talked until dawn, going over all the ups and downs we had experienced together… His kindness and his tact were a great comfort.
>
> I woke up very late, certainly not before the afternoon. The huge place felt like a haunted house. One sensed the presence of a lot of people lurking behind the partitions, but … no one ever met anyone else. Kenneth Cohen appeared.
>
> 'It won't be long now, dear Poz,' he said, greatly moved. 'Mary asked me to give you her best love and we'd like you to have this little memento. It's an heirloom.' He handed me a charming ring with a heart-shaped stone. 'Take it with you. It'll bring you luck,'

he said when I protested. 'That's why we're giving it to you. And here's a luminous watch from British Intelligence. It's Swiss and it keeps perfect time…'

The airfield presented an extraordinary sight with aircraft lined up wing to wing as far as the eye could see, and in the middle a crowd of agile and athletic-looking RAF men moving about. 'You're not going to tell me that all these are off on secret missions?'

Kenneth Cohen laughed. 'No. They're bombers and will be taking off in waves from dusk to dawn. You're going in just behind them, so that the enemy radar won't be able to pick you out. They'll think you're one of the raiders.'

On arriving at the mess I saw my travelling companions sitting apart with Ham and, in another corner, half a dozen men of all ages and ranks. 'Those are the other passengers,' Kenneth said, going over to greet them, 'but I'm not making any introductions. Take no notice.'

'But we shall meet on the plane. Do you really imagine we will cold shoulder one another in these circumstances?'

The sun began to go down and waves of aircraft headed eastwards, disappearing into the oncoming darkness. An officer asked us to follow him. Another, with a poet's face, came over to us with a pile of little cages, each containing a white pigeon. I received one like the rest.

'You'll slip a message into the ring on its leg as soon as you land,' Kenneth told me.

'This seems very strange on the day of the V.I.'

'No, we do it for people who haven't any transmitters. That's not the case with you, but as you're with a lot of other people you're getting one of your own, so that nobody's jealous.'

We were driven to the tarmac, where I could see the burly outline of a Hudson, its paintwork chipped by machine-gun fire. I fell for it at once. I had the honour of being the first up the ladder into the fuselage, where I bumped into all kinds of containers piled up by the entrance, and went sprawling.

Our party came in one by one and crouched down in any available corner, the sergeant making sure that the weight was equally distributed; then our luggage and the pigeon cases were passed to us and the door shut with a loud bang. I stood up to try to catch through the window a last glimpse of Kenneth Cohen's tall figure in naval uniform and Ham's familiar cap. I felt a terrible urge to cry.

When they arrived, there was no sign of a reception committee. The pilot had to abort the mission and return to Tempsford. Marie-Madeleine got back when the other planes were returning from Germany in the early hours of the morning. With the Liberation of France imminent, many more missions were diverted eastwards. Marie-Madeleine awoke the next afternoon and relieved the tension by playing a piano, but she admitted that her fingers had lost all their agility and she couldn't remember her favourite piece.

She said that, after a day's wait, she was eventually landed in a field at Maisons-Rouges, near Nangis in the forest of Fontainebleu. Verity claims she was taken out with seven other passengers on 5/6 July in a Hudson piloted by Flight Lieutenant Affleck. In just under three hours they landed two and a half kilometres north of Égligny, south-west of Provins. Eight others replaced them for the return journey.

Her first words of welcome were 'Hello, Marie-Madeleine'. After a hearty meal in a nearby farmhouse, she and Pezet hitched a lift in a peasant's cart with squeaky axles to the station and managed after three days to get to Marseille. Within a fortnight she had arranged a drop of six tons of supplies and 4 million francs. A few days later she was caught and imprisoned by the Gestapo in Miollis barracks. Aware of what would be in store for her, she managed to escape by removing her clothes so that she could squeeze through the bars of a window in her cell room, her slender body lubricated by the sweat of fear. Picking up her batik cotton dress that she had dropped outside, she managed to find safety with the American troops who had just landed on the Mediterranean coast in August. She later found out that 438 out of an estimated 3,000 members of her network had been executed.

## Jeannette Guyot and Evelyne Clopet

Prior to the Allied invasion, a joint operation was planned by the SIS, OSS and the BCRA. Small groups, normally two-man teams called SUSSEX teams, undertook the same training as SOE agents and were parachuted into northern France on a mission to collect and send back information on the German order of battle and their troop movements by identifying the different units and counting the amount, type and direction of their rail and road traffic. The information was then passed back to Allied Command via S-phone to the radio operators on board overflying Mitchell bombers of 226 Squadron. These planes returned to their base at RAF Hartingbridge, now Blackbushe Airport, where the information was passed on to High Command. The SUSSEX teams were a prelude to the Carpetbaggers, RED STOCKING missions over Germany.

According to the Le Plan-Sussex-1944 website, two French women, Lieutenant Jeannette Guyot and Sub-lieutenant Evelyne Clopet, were part of two teams. Evelyne is documented as having flown from Harrington, but Jeannette may have been sent out of Tempsford. They were trained at Prae Wood, near St Albans, under the command of British Major Guy Wingate and American Colonel Malcolm Henderson. Prior to their deployment, these teams were provided with 'safe houses' at Grendon Hall, Northamptonshire, and possibly Hasells Hall.

Jeannette undertook one of the first two 'pathfinder' missions. She and Georges Lassale, the radio operator, were dropped early in 1944 with orders to locate parachute and landing sites, to establish contacts with the Resistance and to help them build up caches of arms and equipment. After arriving in Paris, she decided to visit her cousin, Mme. Kiehl, who ran the 'Café de l'Electricite' in Montmartre. There she got to know others in the Resistance and, with the second team, they found and organised twenty-two landing operations, some of which were used twice, as well as finding almost a hundred safe houses to accommodate fifty-three subsequent SUSSEX teams. She survived the war and was one of only two female recipients of the US Army's Distinguished Service Cross. The other was Virginia Hall.

The second woman, twenty-two-year-old Evelyne Clopet, was flown out at 2237 hours on 3 July but, according to Merrill, the Carpetbagger pilot, 'Everything out OK. One didn't get to the Joe-hole in time. Made another pass, – lites were out.' The pilot returned to base at 0415 hours. She was returned on the 8th by Ben Mead and his crew, who noted, 'Dropped on center light – Body went out on middle light + packages strung along.' Team Colére were parachuted into Chateau l'Hermitage in the Sarthe to join two other teams. Using the alias 'Chamonet', Evelyne went on to provide valuable information on German troop movements.

On 9 August, as her and two other teams were driving in a truck towards Vendome, they were stopped just before Lavardin by a group of retreating German troops who wanted to commandeer their vehicle to help them escape to the north. When asked to show their papers, they handed over their fake documents. The Germans were suspicious that the truck had been stolen, so Evelyne and her team were forced to get out and open their luggage. Their weapons and radio were found and apparently Evelyne urged the others not to fight. They were ordered into the back of the truck and the Germans then drove them to the feldgendarmes in Vendome. One person managed to jump out and escape but the other five were interrogated and tortured until 0130 hours. When the Gestapo and the SS got tired, they drove them out on the road to Paris, stopped at a quarry near the little village of St Ouen in Loir-et-Cher and shot them (http://www.plan-sussex-1944.net).

## Francoise Dissart

McCall (1980) noted that in late July 1944, Wing Commander Boxer and Flight Lieutenant Helfer flew their Hudson to the disused Le Blanc airfield between Châteauroux and Poitiers. The reception committee had repaired it a few days after the retreating Germans had criss-crossed it with a plough. Tempsford's Station Commander had been invited by the local mayor to a splendid luncheon that was laid on in honour of Francoise Dissart, a rather special woman who they had to take back.

She was described as a white-haired woman in her sixties who had worked on the PAT escape line for much of the war. Her safe house was not far from the Gestapo HQ in Toulouse. Many of the young evaders who were helped to return to England thought she looked like a witch, always dressed in black, chain-smoking with a black cigarette holder and stroking Milouf, her cat. As the network was collapsing around her, she managed to avoid arrest, secure in her cover as a crotchety old woman who wanted nothing to do with the war. She told Boxer that she was going back to Tempsford with him on the instructions of MI9 to receive a decoration from the King at Buckingham Palace.

## Elaine Madden

Online searches for information on female agents sent into occupied Belgium unearths data for just two: Elaine Madden and Olga Jackson. The cometeline website, which focuses on the escape route from Belgium through France to Switzerland or Spain, mentioned that Elaine, codenamed 'Alice', was the only female Belgian agent sent in. Operation MANDAMUS on 3/4 August 1944 involved dropping her, André Wendelen and Jacques van der Spiegle near Beauraing, a small town south-west of Liège. She was to act as their courier. It appears that André was a clever young Brussels lawyer who had joined SOE in 1940, went down the Comète line himself and this was his third drop into Belgium. Jacques was the radio operator. In Michael Foot's *SOE in the Low Countries*, he said that their mission was to locate Prince Charles, King Leopold's brother, and bring him back to England.

However, Elaine's personal file in the National Archives tells a very different story. Lieven Saerens of the CEGES/SOMA website told me that, according to her extensive dossier on the Belgian State Security, Elaine was born in Poperingen on 7 May 1923 to an English father, Harold Madden, and a Belgian mother, Caroline Duponselle. After attending the British Memorial School in Ypres, and following the invasion of Belgium on 10 May 1940, she dressed up as a soldier and was evacuated to England at Dunkirk. Arriving on 1 June 1940, she continued her studies at St Ellen's College, London, taking up a profession as a 'comptable steno-dactylo'. By March 1944, she was working for the Belgian State Security and had been recruited by the SOE.

Her personal file in the National Archives sheds no light on her background. It is a report on her mission, codenamed IMOGEN. There was no mention of Elaine Madden, either. The name on the earliest forms, dated 8 May 1944, almost three months before she was dropped, was E. Meuus. This was probably Elaine Meuus, a codename used while she underwent SOE training. The name on the identity card she was to use in Belgium was Hélène Marie Maes, supposedly issued by the Belgian office in Nice. There were salary receipts and a residence permit for an apartment in Paris owned by a Mme. Dervaux. Her papers told her that, before she left, she would be given a 'Gestapo-style' interrogation to discover whether her cover story had any weaknesses. Part of it was provided, which she had to learn off by heart:

> At about noon on the 17th May 1940 after the first air-raid on Paperinghe [*sic*] I walked down the Rue de l'Hopital with my aunt named Simone. There was considerable damage everywhere and the services responsible had not yet had time to clear away bodies that were scattered about in the streets. We hadn't walked 100 yards when we saw the head of a man lying in the gutter. Although gruesome it was a fascinating sight and one that neither of us will ever forget. We stopped for quite a few minutes and stared not being able to believe our eyes and then walked away feeling slightly sick and dazed. From there we went on up the Rue de l'Hopital and turned right down the road to the house another Aunt named Antoinette occupied. We stayed there until about 6 p.m. and made our way back home. The streets had been cleared by this time and there were no further incidents.
>
> (TNA HS 6/112)

She was told she would be provided with appropriate clothing and toiletries for the three months she would be in Belgium and given whatever 'equipment' she thought suitable for her parachute jump and landing. Agents were normally offered a knife, revolver and a variety of pills, one being the 'L' pill. Details were provided for her return trip to England once her mission had been completed, and there were pages of coding that she had to master with the help of Captain Whittaker.

Annexe 'K' in her personal file provided fascinating details of the coding system being used in the run-up to D-Day. On 31 May 1944, while she was at S.T.S. 35 (SOE code for one of their Special Training Schools in the grounds of Beaulieu, near Bournemouth), she met with a Captain Whittaker. He went through the codes she had to use when communicating with HQ from the field.

The cipher being used was Playfair Rimmer with the keyword BAYSWATER. See if you're as bright as she was. The special arrangements included suppressing the letter 'Z',

K = CH, X = EX, Y = IN and Z = EZ. Numbers one to ten were their equivalent letters in the alphabet. The 'dud' letter used for null was X. The security check in case she was compromised was to have twenty-one words in the first sentence. The code was to start at the first word in the third sentence. The interval between pregnant words had to be every fifth, and the code was to end at the last exclamation mark. Courtesy forms at the beginning and end were to be ignored, apostrophes and hyphens were both 1 and the specimen cage of a square was:

BAYSW

TERCD

FGHIJ

KLMNO

PQUVX

Having mastered that, in a document dated 27 July 1944, a week before her flight, she was provided with her codes. See whether you can get your head round them. She was informed that the prefix for all her incoming messages was 578 and, for her outgoing ones, 195. The T.15 check was that 1 and 2 were to be added on the 3rd and 4th and that 'E' would be used for dead letters. Annexe 'J' included her MENTAL ONE-TIME PAD PLUS MENTAL INDICATOR, with the remark that the substitution square letter was 'Y'.

| A | SEQUESTERED | N | SAVETHE |
|---|---|---|---|
| B | FROM | O | SACRED |
| C | THIS | P | MONUMENTS |
| D | NOISY | Q | OVER |
| E | WORLD | R | WHICH |
| F | COULDI | S | THE |
| G | WEAR | T | WINGS |
| H | OUT | U | OF |
| I | THIS | V | CENTURIES |
| J | TRANSITORY | W | HAVE |
| K | BEINGIN | X | SILENTLY |
| L | PEACEFUL | Y | PASSED |
| M | CONTEMPLATION | Z | BY |

| A | CONTINUOUS | N | OTHER |
|---|---|---|---|
| B | POUNDING | O | ALLIED |
| C | OFENEMY | P | AIRCRAFT |
| D | TARGETS | Q | HAS |
| E | BY | R | SOFAR |
| F | LIBERATORS | S | PROVED |
| G | FORTRESSES | T | VERY |
| H | MOSQUITOES | U | SUCCESSFUL |
| I | MARAUDERS | V | MANY |

| J | THUNDERBOLTS | W | FACTORIES |
|---|---|---|---|
| K | MUSTANGS | X | HAVE |
| L | LIGHTNINGS | Y | BEEN |
| M | AND | Z | DESTROYED |

POEM FOR MENTAL INDICATOR

| A | RESISTANCE | N | SETBY |
|---|---|---|---|
| B | CONTINUES | O | THEIR |
| C | MEN | P | BRILLIANT |
| D | WORK | Q | AND |
| E | INDEPENDENTLY | R | COURAGEOUS |
| F | ORWITH | S | LEADERS |
| G | ORGANIZATIONS | T | PROPITIOUS |
| H | FOLLOWING | U | HEAVEN |
| I | THE | V | MUST |
| J | GREAT | W | SURELY |
| K | AND | X | SAVE |
| L | INSPIRING | Y | THESE |
| M | EXAMPLES | Z | HEROES |

The code word she had to use with the above poem was WORLD. Her true check in every message was the fifth letter indicator chosen by the Mental Indicator System. Just in case she was transmitting under duress, she was given a bluff check which was: '7th letter of message increased by alphabetical equivalent of number of message gives 1st letter of 7th word.' The Mental Indicators were prefixed with the keyword WORLD.

| | | | | |
|---|---|---|---|---|
| NTRGP | IKFEO | ENTRE | HGRUE | FERCL |
| FOTSA | PHLMN | CDAPB | TASGI | TLSHD |
| SZUYC | FEWIR | TMIGN | DINPO | AFTVE |
| SOJIR | IENAG | HOTER | EABLS | XTSOU |
| LDFEN | SRTLO | PEOIN | IEODP | WOLMU |
| HILWN | ATONS | RENAS | POEQN | VIESU |
| IEHNR | FYIAE | UTRDS | UIEVT | BSTVA |

Do you understand that? Good. The SOE advisers showed advanced planning and foresight. She was given an address in Basle for any 'innocent' letters she might want to write. In them she had refer to herself as Marie Antoinette, use one if 'the address was her safe house', two if 'the first has been cancelled, here is my new one', three for 'I am in my safe house, come and find me' and four for 'I am going to Nancy'. The signature she was to use was 'Barnabe'.

Letters concerning her return to England had to be sent to either an address in Seville or one in Lisbon. These had to be learned off by heart. Her password in Nancy was '*Je cherche le bougniat*', and the reply would be '*Vous voulez dire le marchaud de charbon*'. Once in Spain her name would be Miss Mary Townsend and, if she got out via Switzerland, she had to ask for Mr Bateman at the British embassy.

To be sure she understood the danger of her mission, she was informed that she would be paid as a third-class agent and, in the case of her death, her salary would continue being paid into her account for the next six months.

She was provided with 5,000 Belgian francs to carry on her person, but hidden in a box of talcum powder were a further 50,000 Belgian francs for her mission and 10,000 French francs for her return. The One-Time-Pad was hidden in her wallet, along with microfilms of questionnaires she had to encourage Belgian sympathisers to fill in. Six identity photographs were hidden in a secret pocket. Her valise and the wireless set to be used by 'Donalbain' (Jacques Van de Siegle), the radio operator who would accompany her, were to be dropped with them when they parachuted in.

The date of her flight, presumably from Tempsford, was not specified in her file but she was told it would be one night during the moon period between 30 July and 12 August 1944. Records suggest it was on the night of 3/4 August. Documents in her file, dated 22 November 1944, six weeks after the Allies invaded Belgium, showed that she made a perfect landing at 0130 hours 7.5 km SSE of d'Houyet and 3.5 km NE of Pondrome and rendezvoused as instructed at 'Ferme du Fisique' without any mishap. It was situated on the crossroads of two farm tracks on the edge of Chy Wood. The password she had to use was: '*Je viens chercher le kilo de Café emballé dans la serviette et apporter de quoi faire use nouvelle bride pour l'etalon.*' She was told that 'Tybalt' (one of André's codenames) had already left the coffee with the farmer, and warned that she didn't have to take the train to Martouz-in-Neuville: '*Le chef de gare est Rexiste et dangereux.*'

'Donalbain' was to be known in Belgium as 'Foxtrot'. Elaine's codename in Belgium was to be 'Alice' and her 'Chef de Mission' was codenamed 'Brabantio' (André), but known in Belgium as 'Odette'. The password she had to use with him was '*Je viens chercher Mlle. Olive Chartres*' and the response had to be '*Vous voulez dire la cousine de Georges*'. In case additional proof of her identity was needed, she was told that a personal message, '*Nous irons cueillir les murons*', would be broadcast at 1915 hours on Radio Belgium for the first three days after her arrival and repeated on the twelfth.

'Odette' was to put her in contact with 'Huguette', another SOE agent who had been parachuted into Belgium in May 1944 to co-ordinate sabotage of the railway network. Philippe Connart told me that 'Huguette' was twenty-nine-year-old Baron Jules Rolin, an artillery reserve officer also known as 'Messala' and 'Ridder'.

Following the D-Day landings in Normandy in June, the next targets for the Allies were the capture of Paris and the liberation of Belgium. This gave Elaine's mission a particular importance but also imposed strict limits on it. What she was warned about was the need for strict discipline. Her briefing notes told her:

1. You are going to find yourself amongst people who have resisted magnificently an unprecedented oppression. This will make you ask yourself some questions, to suggest potential contacts, to offer you some actions that haven't been foreseen in your mission. It is an exceptionally dangerous situation, one in which you must not put yourself at any risk. The essential condition amongst all these operations is security and everyone must accomplish their tasks to the best of their ability.

2. You have to avoid engaging the Belgian government or the British authorities in the field of politics. Every initiative in this mission has the possibility of creating a dangerous confusion in the actions and plans of the War Cabinet.
3. The duty of ambassadors like you is to be especially focussed on quiet reserve and to use the utmost discretion as an observer, concerned with your own mission and its planning. Knowledge of both the British and Belgian points of view needs to be at its heart.

Her plan of action, included in Annexe I of her personal file, was to follow SHAEF's (Supreme Headquarters Allied Expeditionary Force) aims and objectives. The first was to slow down the arrival of enemy troops before they could engage the invasion forces, in particular their artillery units, tanks and armoured cars. The second was to slow down the placement of reinforcements in areas near the Allies' bridgeheads. The third was to hinder German aerial attacks on Allied troops. The fourth was to hinder river transport, and the last was to transmit back to London all information about military matters, no matter how great or small.

She was instructed to inform Huguette, SOE's main organiser, who would execute SHAEF's orders. As his courier, she would be the go-between between him, SHAEF and the different Resistance groups. To pass on messages, she had to use Huguette's existing contacts. Any personal contact she might have with the chiefs of the Resistance groups had to be kept to an absolute minimum. Her security was not to be put in danger. The individuality of the Resistance groups had to be respected and, where possible, they were to be given autonomy in carrying out appropriate action.

The principal groups Elaine was told she would be working with were the Front de l'Indépendance, Group G, Group Nola and the Mouvement National Belge. In the section headed GENERAL NOTES, she was told that the group targeting the railways had to immobilise rail transport. Another had to cut all telephone communications by bringing down pylons, cutting telephone cables and attacking Brussels' central telephone exchange.

She had to insist that none of the groups had overall control of discipline. Their orders had to come through SHAEF, which included targets for sabotage.

The Allied Command wishes concentrated coordinated attacks to be made on the following types of target when special Action Signals are given:
Railways: Action against the railways will consist of:
a) The elimination of key enemy personnel brought from Germany to control military transport by rail.
b) The destruction of railway lines by the use of explosives or, if sufficient time and personnel are available, by the removal of lengths of rail.
c) The destruction of breakdown trains.
d) The interruption and disorganisation of railway telephone and signals systems by the cutting of lines, destruction of cabins, etc.
e) Destruction of railway turntables.
f) Light destruction of the railway watering system, e.g. by cutting of mains.
   General Note: Complicated or heavy installations which would require more than a week to repair should not be destroyed, but should be sabotaged by having their

essential parts removed. These parts should be kept carefully and placed at the disposal of the Allied Forces on their arrival. It should be born in mind that as a general rule the continuity of railway dislocation must depend on the repetition of the derailments and light sabotage, rather than on massive destruction.

1. Enemy Road Movements. It is certain that the enemy will use the roads for the massive transport of troops and equipment when invasion takes place. Every effort should be made to sabotage such movements, e.g. by improvised road blocks; displacement of traffic signs; setting of booby traps; placing of small mines. Such action should be entirely clandestine, and no risk should be taken of being involved in pitched battles with enemy effectives.

2. Telecommunications. The cutting of telephone and telegraph lines and cables (preferably undetectably) and the removal and safe-keeping of essential parts of such installations. Installations of this kind, even in cases whether have been requisitioned by the enemy, are not to be destroyed but only lightly sabotaged.

3. Waterways. Dislocation of communications by inland waterways, e.g. by the destruction of lock gates; and by the sabotage of enemy munitions shipments.

4. Air Targets. Sabotage of enemy aircraft; airfield installations; light repair plant and aviation fuel dumps, particularly in the area between Courtrai/Ghent and the coast. Enemy flying personnel should be sniped where occasion presents itself, without the risk of becoming engaged in a stand-up fight with the enemy.

Note: The procedure regarding action signals is known to NELLY and HUGUETTE.

Action signals were the coded instructions to the Resistance to commence their planned activities. They were to be broadcast by the BBC in their *messages personelles* after the 1900 hours Belgian news. All the information she collected had to be forwarded to London, taking into account of the fact that the expression 'large bodies of troops' meant units of approximately 500 men or more and included concentrations which couldn't easily be seen from the air, e.g. bivouacs in woods. Exact grid references would be essential. Field post numbers or the divisional signs on vehicles had to be provided. Wireless aerials and despatch rider activity often indicated the presence of a headquarters, which could then be identified by its pennants or painted signs. Any information about petrol and ammunition dumps would be particularly important, as would any information about rockets, flying bombs and other secret weapons. It was urged that her reports had always to include:

a) The date and time of observation, as opposed to the time at which the source may have originated the telegram. It must be clear whether zone time (G.M.T.) or local time is being used.

b) A description of the place in sufficient detail to enable it to be pinpointed, in the case of static targets, with a six-figure map reference if possible.

In addition, reports should show whether the originator is himself the source; if the report has been received from a third party, the latter's identity or reliability should be stated.

These instructions do not affect the original proviso that there is no onus on any agent to send information and that he must never allow the despatch of information to jeopardise his other activities or his security. Nor should vague deductions be made, though reliable indications of future moves and negative information are of value.

The questionnaire she was provided microfilm copies of was particularly interesting, revealing not only the extent of the Allies' existing knowledge of Germany's latest weaponry but also their very serious concerns about its use.

1. Information is required as to the methods at present in use for transporting component parts of the flying bombs, its launching trolley, and the materials used for fuelling the bomb and providing rocket propulsion, to the depots where it is stored prior to use.
2. The bomb may be transported in one piece (without planes), in which case the length would be 22 ft. and the diameter about 3 ft. alternatively the war-head may be transported separately; it is a truncated cone of length 47 ins., minimum diameter 28 ins., and maximum diameter 33 ins. The forward end is rounded and the base hollow.
   It is required to know if the above parts can be identified as travelling by road or rail, if there are completely crated or merely protected by a skeleton crate, how they are guarded, and if there is any possibility of access during a halt or during marshalling.
3. The launching trolley with the rocket propulsion unit may be transported separately by road or rail.
   We want complete details of the trolley, and if possible, a sketch or photograph.
4. At some time prior to launching, the bomb is fuelled with petrol and the rocket propulsion unit on the trolley is filled with hydrogen peroxide.
   Where is this done? Probably one filling station serves a number of launching sites.
5. An important constituent of the rocket propulsion fuel is almost certainly hydrogen peroxide. This is stored in 2500 gallon aluminium tanks, which may be above or below ground. The storage tanks are supplied by road or rail. Rail transport may be either (i) by large aluminium tank wagons (length of wagon 60 ft.; tank diameter 8 ft. 6 ins.; tank length 30 ft.) or (ii) by a number (12/14) of small aluminium tanks 4 ft. in diameter and 4 ½ to 5 ft. high, arranged in close contact in a double row.
   Is there any evidence of road transport? This may be in carboys of 13 gallons capacity.
   In the case of rail transport, we wish to know if there is a wooden floor or other woodwork in the tank wagon construction.
   Is there any opportunity of access to the wagons at sidings or marshalling yards?
   Is there any opportunity of attacking the wagons by rifle or mortar fire from a distance of say 100 yards?
6. If any depots, assembly or filling points are located, we want to know what kind of road transport is allowed to enter them.
   Are any foreign workers allowed to enter?
   Are lorries subjected to careful inspection at the entrance?

Is it possible to approach to say within 100 yards of the boundary fence after dark?
Are there any trees or other means of concealment in the vicinity?

How successful operation IMOGEN was is uncertain. We have to presume she managed
to pass on SHAEF's directives to the right contacts, who acted on them appropriately.
The only indication was a couple of paragraphs in her file:

> There was no time to work on my personal mission owing to the fact that I was
> 'Courrier' for Odette. The majority of the time I didn't know which mission I was
> working for, but information could be obtained from Odette's report. I travelled
> considerably in the Ardennes, carrying messages, transmitting sets and bringing the
> revolvers back to Brussels. I was put in contact with Huguette and did some 'courier'
> for him. Apart from that, I was in charge of the "service de protection" for Foxtrot
> and recruited three people to help us. Two were permanent staff and third part-time.
> I was part of the 'service de protection' on every occasion and usually transported the
> soul myself to the house elected. The finding of safe houses was also left to me. I never
> had any trouble of any kind, except once when I was followed for several hours by
> a suspicious looking character. I managed to shake him off by taking various trams
> and wandering around the town. This happened after I had been to rendezvous with
> C. Lapoivre (operational name unknown).
>
> Help and assistance were given by Mlle Denise Leplat, 19 rue de Anges, Liège and
> Jean Smets (address unknown) who worked full-time as 'service de protection'. Also
> Anton Smets who worked part-time. The two sisters Lucy and Jeanne Rouffignon, rue
> Chants d'Oiseaux, Bruxelles, also helped considerably by letting us transmit from their
> house and in helping me find other houses to transmit from.

Foot's mention of Elaine being involved in the rescue of Prince Charles was hinted at in an
interview she gave after the war in *Histoires*, a documentary on Canvas, one of Belgium's two
public TV channels. According to Foot, the prince was on the run from the Gestapo and
plagued with sciatica. Unable to travel easily, he had had been in hiding in Sart-Lez-Spa.

> My chef de mission said that I was to come to Ciney (south-east of Namur) and look
> after this important gentleman. I met him [there], I thought he was very charming. We
> used to talk, play ping pong together, we used to go walking in the woods. And once
> we were away from other people, he would speak to me in English. His English was
> fluent and we had a lot of fun … He used to question me about London, and London
> during the wartime, and what was happening … I thought he was somebody in the
> resistance who was very important. So, I was his liaison between London and here, I
> used to code and decode messages. And we were trying to find a small landing ground
> so the Lysander could come and fetch him. Because the idea was that we wanted to get
> him to England … When eventually we did find a landing ground (Sovet) … it was
> already so late in the war. The Allies were arriving so quickly after Normandy, that he
> decided he didn't want to leave because it was too late. That he wouldn't have time to
> get out of the plane in London, before getting into another plane back to Belgium. So
> the mission was dropped.

Additional information was provided by Philippe Connart, who said that Elaine hid in the castle of Walter de Sélys-Longchamp in Halloy, near Ciney. He was an important figure in Group G. Also staying with them was a 'Monsieur Jules Bernard', an English-speaking gentleman who had been educated at Eton and Dartmouth. He was in hiding from the Germans and was being helped by Baron Robert Goffinet, who once gave a golden guinea to James Cromar, and a few other Comète evaders. Mr Bernard should have been picked up by Lysander from a small private airfield, but the mission was aborted.

When the Prince Regent gave Elaine an award after the war, she only then realised that he was the prince of Flanders.

## Jos Gemmeke

Twenty-two-year-old Jos Gemmeke, codenamed 'Sphinx' and also known as 'Els von Dalen', had been active in the Dutch resistance as a courier printing and distributing the underground newspaper *Je Maintiendrai*. She did it so well she looked after several other journals' distribution as well. Later on, she worked as a communications officer, carrying wireless equipment and other goods dropped by 138 Squadron.

In October 1944, despite being shot at by British planes as she cycled south out of occupied Holland, Jos managed to charm a *Feldwebel* into allowing her to cross the River Waal into Belgium. There, she delivered important papers and microfilm hidden in her powder compact and shoulder pads to the headquarters of Prince Bernard in The Hague. They were destined for the Dutch Secret Service in London. The prince arranged for a plane, a green Dakota, to fly Jos to England where, once she had been debriefed, she started specialist training for the SOE. In Foot's book, he quoted her officers describing her as 'a very level and cool-headed young woman, completely unemotional, very reserved and very determined'. She passed her parachute training at Ringway, was considered outstanding while at Beaulieu, and was awarded a commission in the FANY.

After being flown out of Tempsford, she was dropped at Nieuwkoop on 10 March 1945. Although she was injured parachuting from a low altitude, she managed to complete her mission. She kept as souvenirs her pistol, a bottle of strong drink that she drank to mitigate the impact of her jump, and the belt that held the 100,000 guilders she had brought for the resistance movement. Her mission was to follow the Allied advance into Germany under the guise of a secretary to a businessman and work with Dutch labourers in German factories at sabotage and slow downs. As relations between the two countries had broken down by then, her mission was aborted, but not before she sent back awful accounts of foreign workers' treatment. She survived the war to be appointed the chairwoman of the *Vereniging Ridders in de Militaire Willemsorde* (Society for Knights in the Military Order of William).

## Olga Jackson

Searching for information on Olga Jackson, I found an intriguing snippet on the Adam Matthew Publications website's section on SOE's operations in Western Europe:

> EMELIA. Belgium, August 1944, Mrs Olga Jackson, field name Babette, independent propaganda mission for undermining of morale in Brussels, Ghent, Liege, Antwerp, Charleroi; organisation of prostitution circuit aimed at German officers.

(http://www.adam-matthew-publications.co.uk)

Olga's personal file in the National Archives contains a fascinating story, worth detailing as it shows what other kinds of political intrigues were thought up by the SOE. On the night of 4 August, the same day Elaine was dropped, she too was parachuted into Belgium. Whether they knew each other in Belgium, had trained together at Wanborough and Arisaig, got their parachute wings at Ringway and attended the Beaulieu 'finishing school' remains unknown. She was born on 6 January 1909, was called Olga Thioux and was a British citizen. Her personal file mentions nothing of her early life.

For whatever reason, she jumped before her luggage and two companions. Their intended drop zone was supposed to be 13.5 km north of Hals, near Ledeberg. Instead, she landed about 3 kilometres from Pamel, a small village between Ninove and Brussels, and couldn't make contact with the others, two agents, 'Eugénie' and 'Yvonne'. Whether they really were women and whether those were their real names is unknown. The only other reference to them in Olga's file was their mission names, MENAS and CIMBER. Eugénie's MENAS mission was to contact Samoyède II, Freddy Veldekens's propaganda mission for pre- and post-liberation work and jamming German wireless installations with the aim of helping the Allies after D-Day in the use of the press, cinema and radio. She, if Eugénie was female, also had to contact STENTOR. Who or what STENTOR was has yet to come to light. Yvonne's CIMBER mission, if she was female, involved the transmission of microfiche messages.

After hiding her parachute in some bushes, Olga made her way to the capital. With the help of someone she met on the road who was convinced she was a black marketeer, she avoided the checkpoint and arrived at 0700 at her safe house, the home of Madame and Monsieur René de Pot, the Police Brigadier. When she showed him her identity papers he was suspicious, but a personal message following the BBC news convinced him of her credentials. With the help of one of his friends he got her better identity cards, but as this friend was arrested the following day, she had to be quickly provided with others, just in case he talked. Arrangements were made for her to meet M. Schakewitz, the Joint Police Commissioner and Chief Inspector of Police, who listened with interest to her plans. Although he didn't show much enthusiasm for her enterprise, he promised to help. There was no mention of her being reunited with her luggage or companions.

She then went to Liège and met Frans Banneux. Whether he was another police official, government or Resistance member isn't clear, but she made arrangements with him for her safe house in case the Germans found out what she was up to. What else she did while in Liège is not recorded. When she returned to Brussels three days later, she had another meeting with the Chief Inspector and insisted she be introduced to Monsieur Delecourt, the King's Public Prosecutor. While she was waiting, he introduced her to Monsieur de Lobel, the Chief Bailiff, who agreed to help her. He allocated a room in M. Jungelaus' Brussels office and allocated two women to assist her in collecting information on the private and public lives of important German figures stationed in Belgium. Over time they compiled a list which included: 'General von Falkenhausen Alexander, Dr. Reeder President Eggert, von Harbou Obest. Von Schon, von Graushaar General, Dr Bayer, Bennewitz Hauptbannfuhrer, von Hammerstein Freiherr Lieutenant-General, Dr. Schulze Adolf, Landesgruppenleiter, Dr. Gentzke, von Clear General, Dr. Busch, Gayler, Angelmann Lieutenant-Colonel, Bruns Major General, von Werder, Dr. Mallia, Schmidt, Dr. Griesbauer, Feldberg, Schindlmayer and Moskopf.'

The 'independent propaganda' she was involved with was 'to complement the campaign already being waged by the Mandrill organisation'. This was a Political Intelligence Department mission sent into Belgium in 1943 to liaise with the existing CORDIER mission to demoralise support for the Germans and co-ordinate the reception of propaganda in Lille, Liège and Ghent. Olga's work, it was stressed, was 'in no way connected with espionage and it must be clearly understood that your task is not the collection of military information. By doing so you would be liable not only to jeopardise your own security but also the success of the mission itself.'

The mission included finding every opportunity to tell people of the imminent arrival of the Allies, of their impending liberation and release from the yoke of German oppression. The members of the Belgian resistance had to be told to wait until they were given instructions by the Allies' High Command. Olga had to recruit and instruct responsible people to help with her work of disseminating rumours and lies about the enemy and about an imminent Allied landing. This included setting up a radio listening centre, typing false stories to be leaked to the media and narrating them to people she met. Her list of people to meet included those dealing with news broadcasts, editors, radio announcers, technicians and Morse operators. She had instructions as to what action the civilian population had to take following the Allies' arrival, in particular technicians in the gas, electricity, water, rubbish, railway, tramway and telecommunication industries as well as factory workers, road workers, dockers, mechanics and miners.

She had to disseminate supposedly police-generated information about the Allies' plans, their estimated troop numbers, predictions of their movements, military equipment, weapons, food stocks, etc. Where possible she, and those supporting her, had to cause delays and obstruct collaboration with the Germans, undermining their and their collaborators' positions by spreading malicious rumours about conflicts between them, denunciations and recriminations and what those on the side of the Allies might do to them. Detailed notes had to be made of the preparations the Germans were making for the invasion, what demolition work they were undertaking and their troop movements so as to supply it to the Allies when they arrived. Attempts had to be made to warn the Allies as to the Germans' eventual retreat and to try to ensure that Allied supplies were spread over a wide area.

Another task was to undermine the morale of the German troops, to depress them and make them nervous by spreading stories that parts of Germany were being overrun by Allied troops, that German villages were being bombed and how other German soldiers stationed in Belgium were becoming irritated and exasperated by what they saw as indiscipline.

According to Olga's instructions, she had to find an organiser in Brussels, Liége, Anvers, Ghent, Namur and Charleroi and provide them with a list of generally high-ranking German military or administrative officials to 'attack'.

It will be necessary to establish the identity of the Belgian and other non-German mistresses kept by German officers and officials and then to determine how many of them can be utilised either because they are good patriots or for other reasons. Those selected should, through suitable outlets, be approached. Tactics at this point will depend entirely upon the type of individual concerned but in order to obtain their co-operation it will not be necessary to use financial or other material inducements. The women thus to be approached will fall roughly into two categories:

(i)  those who have a genuine personal affection for their German masters,

(ii) those who from force of circumstances or otherwise find it easier thus to earn their living and whose personal feelings are not to any extent involved.

As regards (i) these may be the most difficult to enlist but having once convinced them good results should be obtained. It may not be necessary to take this category into your confidence provided they are convinced that defeat for Germany means added danger for their protector unless he covers himself. The line to be taken is that they will clearly wish to do the best for their 'friends'. Whether or not an appeal should be made to their patriotism must be left to the consideration of the person contacting them. The 'amie' must first be thoroughly convinced that Germany has lost the war and her thoughts must be directed to what is to become of her 'friend'. This thought she must discreetly sow in the mind of the officer or official himself, thus inducing him to defer a decision for a few weeks or months? And if he is not killed on one of the fronts what will he find when he gets home, after most of the others? Or will he, realising how things are going, take steps to see that he at least gets back to Germany alive. What is happening to his family with all the foreign workers at home? Who is to protect them if there is an armed uprising in Germany. How is he viewed by his men and the Belgians? Will the latter give him a good character or is he a 'war criminal'? Other German officers are already taking steps for their own protection and the higher the rank the more active has been the urge to anticipate the future.

The subject must be introduced discreetly and not exaggerated and progress judged in the light of the 'protector's' reactions. If it is clear that he has already been thinking along such lines himself, progress can be more rapid. If however, it is patent that the subject cannot be seduced from his duty by such means then he should be induced to exaggerate any weaknesses he may possess, drinking, general self-indulgence, laziness, gambling.

With younger officers, particularly they are of an adventurous type, it will be necessary to adopt different tactics.

They should be shown that their authority is nearly over and the 'good times' that went with it. They should be encouraged in any vices they may have and led to excesses in self-indulgence. They should similarly be encouraged to neglect their duties and finally if so inclined to desert altogether to some occupation in which there is a future.

It may be desirable to offer financial assistance to this class of woman, though it should not be on a lavish scale.

(TNA HS 6/84)

Ideally, Olga had to recruit loyal and dependable proprietors or tenants of brothels who would pass on instructions to the women employed there. No attempt was to be made to contact German-run brothels, though non-German women employed there could be approached. They didn't have to give their clients any grounds for reprisals but had to ask seemingly innocent questions. Among the tactics suggested was to regretfully emphasise the level of Germany's moral and political decline, the decadence and ruin that menaced it, and the dark future that it faced if the war continued. They had to underline the regret that Germany was committing treason by allying the white race with the yellow peril. During British and American bombing raids, they had to show intense fear and express awe at what potential they had. They were encouraged to spread stories about the enormous damage being done by the bombing in Germany, ask whether a miracle was possible that would stop the progressive destruction of the entire country and enquire how many years they would have to endure. They had to sympathetically ask about the men's wives and families, whether they were evacuees or requisitioned for compulsory labour. They had to show fear about epidemics, venereal disease and other ailments which were ravaging the country, frequently ask for explanations and whether it was true that a typhoid epidemic had broken out in a distant region. It was suggested they spread the slogan 'Schluss' (The End) around, ask what the significance of the griffon was on all the walls and in the toilets and spread the story of a new flu epidemic coming from the East. They had to remind the Germans of the Spanish flu epidemic after the Great War, which killed about 18 million people and express doubt whether there was sufficient medicine, clothes and food. They were to reinforce the natural feeling of envy about the number of government members and high officials who had left the country and were living in comfort and safety after having enriched themselves. They had to emphasise the laziness caused by five years of war, ten years of mobilisation, the long hours of work and the difficult living conditions. They had to accentuate the bad feeling there was about fewer imports and the voluntary reductions people were expected to accept. They had to deplore the inevitable hypocrisy caused by such grievances, especially when many of those who were suffering could see important Germans living a good life.

> To incite or assist a German officer to desert requires very careful planning and the seed must be planted very carefully and nourished without apparent intention. However, when an officer has demonstrated his considered intention to desert help should be given him. He will require two essentials, first civilian clothes and second a temporary hide out. Suitable addresses should be given to him and in both cases he should be required to pay for them.

One has to presume that Olga was involved in such arrangements as well as arranging the writing and sending of anonymous letters to officers' wives. These, she was recommended, had to be written on the type of paper that could then be obtained at any stationer's, to have no address and be posted from one of the central post offices. Her advice was that they

> should not normally be written in a threatening vein but rather in the guise of a well-wisher or friend warning her of the misfortune which will befall her or the treatment planned for Germans and their wives. Reference should also be made to the risks run by her husband, of the necessity of his securing employment after the German army had been defeated.

There was also advice on how she could use vice to target those already known to have 'vicious habits, those susceptible to acquire them or those suffering from diseases rendering them particularly susceptible to demoralisation'. The aim was to lower their efficiency and encourage them to neglect their duties. The information in the section on drugs mentioned that drug traffickers who had been arrested in Brussels had been selling opium with a street value of 60,000 francs a kilo. To put this in perspective, Olga was provided with 15,000 francs a month for spending, 10,000 for accommodation, 15,000 for clothes and 3,500 for postage. The opium had been grown in countries which had developed by increasing their production of oil from poppies. It would only be possible for Olga or her contacts to find out who the drug users were through loyal officers, and they would only be able to get hold of drugs via theft from military pharmacies or drug dealers. It was extremely difficult to get hold of products such as cocaine, heroin and morphine because they had almost disappeared from the marketplace. Offering such 'merchandise' to serious Germans had to be avoided because they would almost certainly inform their superiors, who would make enquiries as to where they had come from. Importantly, they hadn't to let them fall into the hands of the Belgians. The only places where drugs should be on sale were night clubs or other places specialising in such trade. Some individuals, such as pimps, could be supplied with drugs, as long as they would be able to resell them and make a reasonable profit. However, if drugs were offered to the wrong people, they would immediately believe it was 'a truly shocking and dangerous business'.

Doctors, Private V.D. Specialists and Clinics
The co-operation of those of the above known to be patronised by German officers and officials, should be sought. The patient who suffers or believes himself to suffer from V.D. is particularly liable to be demoralised and the object here is to induce doctors to play up to this weakness to the ultimate demoralisation of the subject. Some difficulty may be anticipated as the more serious members of the medical profession are unlikely on moral grounds to co-operate but on the other hand this field covers a number of quacks and near-quacks to whom the same considerations would not supply.

Officers, Olga was told, had great pleasure in drinking alcohol and often broke the rules and paid a lot of money to get hold of it. Drinking spirits that had been fortified was on the increase, but there were cases of adulterated and dangerous spirits. To further the Allies' aims, Olga was encouraged to get hold of spirits of doubtful origin. If they could be supplied only to the Germans it would be perfect, but it was acknowledged that unfortunately that wouldn't be the case.

As regards jealousy, Olga and her contacts were to target those Germans with wives or girlfriends, telling them that the massive increase in foreign workers in Germany was creating a special situation. Olga would be provided with pamphlets and leaflets and given suggested graffiti, conversations and rumours to get the attention of German soldiers. There weren't very many men left in Germany and those who remained were too old, too young, wounded, or infirm and had their own wives. It had been a long time for their wives, sisters and daughters to have been left alone, especially now that there were formidable numbers of foreign men working in Germany, men who had been sent because they were fit and healthy, the very great majority of whom '*sont originaires de races aux facultés beaucoup plus amoureuses que celle des Allemands (Italians, Français, Belges, etc.)*'. The nervousness caused by Allied bombing and the privations experienced must '*relâcher les consciences*'.

### CINEMAS, THEATRES, ETC.

It is anticipated that however willing the managers and proprietors of such establishments may be to co-operate the limit within which they will be able to will be very narrow.

Cinema managers will have very little scope in their choice of films, but where they are able to do so they should present those stressing the pleasures of peace and the horror of bombing (civilian populations, enemy); films implying the ultimate liberation of the occupied countries and the return to normal occupation of the inhabitants.

As regard theatres the situation is more difficult. Where possible plays, operas, etc, in which liberation or democratic themes appear should be presented. Tunes, songs, etc, which are identified with similar sentiments should be chosen.

Last war songs, Tipperary, Pack up your Troubles, Over There (?) Décor should be so displayed as fortuitously to represent the Allied and national colours – without risk of reprisals – reminding the enemy of approaching defeat.

There were instruction on different types of rumours to be spread among the Germans, and the list of those who might help included traffickers and fraudsters, railway employees, waiters in cafés, hairdressers, priests, doctors, members of the Resistance, sales representatives, gossips, people in queues and a group described as *les filles de vie*.

The fact is that this kind of woman is frequently in contact with Germans. That they often speak of what's going on in the war is doubtful as it wouldn't be commercial. Moreover, night clubs etc, are frequently under German police surveillance. It's inevitable that with women, and particularly with these kinds of women – many soldiers let themselves go and confide in them. They think of them a bit like comforters. Although many of these women are very patriotic, it is only with great difficulty possible to envisage them being of use. And yet, if a rumour is convincingly presented it will be passed from one Belgian or another who visits these places before the beginning of the evening. In offering a glass (not two, or there'll be financial interest and risks of exaggerated dependency), he will be able to appear the 'Man in the know' and secretly to take these women into his confidence.

There was plenty of money to finance the EMELIA mission. Before leaving England, Olga had been supplied with 248,500 Belgian francs in 100 franc notes, presumably in a money belt. Two 1,000 French franc notes, 100 Spanish peseta notes and 4,075 US dollars in mixed notes were hidden in a box of talc to be used on her way back to England three months later. A letter, photograph and two coins were hidden in her nail brush. There were also details of passwords and replies for her rendezvous, including those needed in Spain and Portugal.

Her file refers to her throughout as 'Jenicot', but she had several other cover names. As she had no radio operator, she had to sign letters to SOE post boxes in Barcelona and Lisbon as 'Zoe'. When she escaped through Spain, she was to be known as 'Irene Thompson'.

In Foot's *SOE in the Low Countries*, he referred to 'Mrs Jackson' but made no mention of prostitution. According to his research, she was born Belgian, had married an English husband and had lived in England since 1935.

She had a strong, self-confident, humorous personality, and was a junior FANY officer. She joined SOE in March 1944, and was dropped into Belgium on 4/5 August, with an odd mission: though she spoke not a word of German, her task was to introduce herself to as many senior German staff officers as she could, and proceed to rot their morale by explaining to them that Germany had already lost the war. In the few weeks that turned out to be available to her, she set about her task with such considerable aplomb that she was mentioned in dispatches for courage and enterprise; concrete results were necessarily slight.

## *Frédérique Dupuich*

My research has revealed that another women agent was Lysandered into Belgium the day after Olga Jackson. Her name was Frédérique Dupuich. There has been no mention of her in any SOE literature. Details of Frédérique's early life have yet to come to light. Born in 1900, she was an English girl, known to some as Miss Richards. During the 1930s, she worked as a company secretary in Brussels but, four months after the German invasion, decided to join the Belgian underground movement. What work she did for them is unknown, but in July the following year, when one of her friends in the Resistance was betrayed to the Germans, she decided to get out. Being interned for the duration of the war was not what she wanted. The Comète escape line had been in operation for some time so, along with ten other Belgians, she was accompanied by Andrée de Jongh, known as 'Dédée'.

Once they reached the small town of La Corbie near Amiens, on the banks of the River Somme, which formed a line known as Zone Interdite or Prohibited Zone, they had to find a way of crossing the Somme, without being detected, as it was regularly patrolled by the enemy. Most of the men and Miss Richards couldn't swim and therefore, the inner tube of a large tyre was used with Andrée having to make several return trips pushing them across before they could rest and sleep in the farmhouse of a woman named Nenette in the village of Hamelet on the opposite side of the Somme. 'Next time,' Andrée thought, 'we will need the use of a boat.' The following morning the party made their way to Paris and then by the overnight train to Biarritz and the home of Madame Elvire DeGreef. A Basque guide was then employed to guide them over the Pyrenees, and to the Spanish side of the border, where they were left to make their own way to San Sebastian. The journey had been a success, or so it was thought until Andrée and Arnold returned to Anglet and learnt that their party had been arrested in Spain and taken back to the border and handed over to the Germans. 'Next time,' Andrée said, 'evaders must be taken direct to the British Consulate in Bilbao.'

(http://cometeline.blogspot.com)

According to Frédérique's obituary in the *Dorset Evening Echo*, the soldiers who were taking her to the authorities for questioning stopped at a café where Frederique was able to slip a note, addressed to the Belgian consul, to the café proprietor. She thought it was his intervention that allowed her out of Miranda Prison after ten days in captivity. From there she made her way to Tangier, where her sister lived, and then managed to get across to Gibraltar.

She reached England in October 1941 and quickly gained employment as the section head of the London-based Political Warfare and Propaganda Department of the Belgium Sürète de l'Etat. There she must have met Airey Neave, the SIS intelligence officer who, in his *Little Cyclone*, described her as 'the plump lady with the panama hat'. Prior to her mission, she undertook training and her commandant's report stated that 'Miss Dewaay', her codename at 'finishing school', was

> well and widely educated, is intelligent and has plenty of practical ability. She is observant and learns quickly and possesses plenty of presence of mind and has imagination.
>
> She is keen and worked hard, displaying good initiative. Her character is strong. She is determined, steady and reliable, but at the same time modest and unassuming.
>
> Her personality is pleasant, she is a good mixer with considerable charm of manner, tact and sociability. She should inspire confidence and is generally liked.
>
> She has good powers of leadership and should do well in any position of trust and responsibility.
>
> (TNA HS 9/460/3)

In 1944, she volunteered for an important mission in occupied France. Exactly what it entailed has yet to come to light. On 6 August she was said to have been flown in a light plane, thought to have been a Lysander, to France. The records of 138 and 161 Squadrons do not mention specifically the dropping of a female agent. As her name didn't appear in any of the SOE literature, it is possible she was an SIS agent. She spent weeks working in a region where the Germans were harassing the French Maquis. Her work was considered very valuable as, according to her obituary,

> After crossing the lines to find the American 9th Army in Brittany, she returned to England and later enrolled in the First Aid Nursing Yeomanry. She served with them in South East Asia, India, Malaya, Sumatra and Hongkong.
>
> Miss Dupuich's exploits earned her the King's Medal for Courage, which was presented to her at the War Office by General Montgomery, the Croix de Guerre avec Palme, the Chevalier de l'ordre de Leopold II for exceptional service rendered to her country, the Croix des Evades, the Resistance Medal, the General Service Medal with clasp and the France and Germany campaign medals.

She had been a much-appreciated intelligence officer at PWE (Political Warfare Executive). By January 1944, she had been trained and fully briefed for a mission but, for whatever reason, it was aborted. When she finally went in, she was the head of an important liaison mission, was captured and imprisoned by both the French Resistance and the French authorities, but managed to survive their interrogations. Even at forty-four, she never ceased from trying to reach Paris, eventually crossing the front line at night on her own.

## Missions of a Sensitive Nature

Given the sensitive nature of the abovementioned operations of Olga Jackson, understandably very little has emerged in SOE literature. There's evidence that both the OSS and the SIS employed women to seduce their way to obtaining information vital to the Allies' cause. Wilfred Deac tells the story of Amy Pack (née Thorpe), codenamed 'Cynthia', who worked for the SIS (http://www.historynet.com/amy-elizabeth-thorpe-wwiis-mata-hari.htm). Having charmed naval codes from the Italians, Betty was sent to Washington, where she had an affair with Brousse, a married official at the French embassy. With his connivance, she managed to unlock the safe holding two French code books, and arrange for them to be photographed and returned without the military attaché knowing. The precious ciphers were sent to London within 48 hours of the theft and were used before and during the Allies' invasion of North Africa.

It is acknowledged that lots of valuable information was obtained from German-frequented brothels. Claudia Pulver, the Viennese dressmaker who created suitable attires for female agents, admitted that:

> We also had quite a lot of prostitutes from the brothels of Paris coming in. We made appropriate underwear, very provocative, whatever they needed. They were very important to whoever was in control of them because their clients were a lot of German officers and they got quite a lot of information out of them. They were the ones that came backwards and forwards more often than others, because I think possibly they had to bring their information back personally. We had one who came backwards and forwards ten or twelve times and survived, only to die of a botched abortion after the war, which was quite sad.
>
> (Quoted in Miller, *Behind the Lines*)

As these women were not official SOE agents, it's possible that Hugh Verity and Freddie Clark did not find them in 161 and 138 Squadrons' records. Might they have been sent in by SIS? Such activities are neither confirmed nor denied.

Verity mentions a *fille de joie* in his autobiography but does not indicate whether she was infiltrated or exfiltrated. Numerous surnames with initial letters appear in the appendices of their books, and any number of the names could have belonged to women.

Hugh Davies, an SOE enthusiast, has lectured on the subject of Fifi, the nickname of Noreen Riols, a young lady employed by the SOE to seduce men while they were at Beaulieu. She had joined the Wrens aged seventeen rather than work in a munitions factory, saying that she would look really smart in their lovely hats. Being fluent in French, having studied at the Lycée in London, she was transferred to the SOE in 1941 and sent to Beaulieu to work as a secretary and driver. In an article in the *Daily Mail* about 'Churchill's Secret Spy School', the eldery Noreen reflected that 'Security was very, very tight. It was like being in a very enclosed family … I knew I had to keep my mouth shut and not ask questions. My mother thought I was working for the Ministry of Agriculture and Fisheries.' Later, she was required to use her seduction techniques to test how easily it was to get information out of the agents. One strategy was for the target to be invited out for a meal in a hotel in Bournemouth by a businessman who brought his secretary along. During the meal the guest was plied with drink until the host excused himself to make a phone call, came back, apologised profusely and said he had to leave. He told his guest to stay and enjoy the rest of the meal, puts his room key on the table and money to pay for the bill and insists they enjoy the rest of the evening together.

'Then it was up to me,' says Noreen. 'The hotel had a balcony overlooking the sea, and if I could get the man out there on a moonlit night that always helped.' In most cases, she insists, the agents didn't talk. 'But if they were very young and far from their country and their families, they might,' she says. If they did, Noreen had to report it.

In David Stafford's *Secret Agent*, he said all the secretaries seemed to know about 'Fifi', the ultimate Agent Provocatrice, gorgeous, enticing and who 'went all the way' (at least for the male trainees). What temptations, if any, were provided for female agents remains a mystery.

Pattinson commented that FANYs were encouraged by the SOE to test the male agents at Wanborough, particularly after they had been plied with drink. There was no distinction in gender in the surveillance of students' alcohol consumption; but only inebriated male students were encouraged to reveal personal details about themselves.

The use of young women to extract information suggests that the male students were assumed to be heterosexual. It appears that women were not subjected to this test. This is perhaps because it was thought that unlike men who were considered liable to succumb to women's advances, female agents were less likely to be duped by agents provocateurs into revealing information. The testing of men only illustrates assumptions about the workings of gender and heterosexuality.

Pru Willoughby, one of the conducting officers, told Pattinson about Christine, one of these *agents provocatrices*:

I was in charge of a very nice girl who was a prostitute. We told this girl, Christine, to go to the pub and try to break this chap down and try to get him into bed. After the week was up, he came back to Baker Street and there was a committee of people to interview him about what had happened during this week and he found to his horror that there was this girl amongst the people. Christine could also detect whether they talked in their sleep and note in which language. Some students, however, outwitted the SOE's ploy to ensnare them. Bob Maloubier recollected his 'blind date' with an attractive woman whom he immediately realized was a plant. When they retired to his bedroom, he confronted her: 'We talked the matter over in my room. Anyway, she said, "Now what are we going to do?" "I'm going to kill you". [Imitates gun and laughs] I said, "You're dead." We talked the matter over. I said, "Ok. You can tell the people that employ you that you came up to my room to extort information out of me and I killed you!"'

In Philippe de Vomécourt's *An Army of Amateurs*, his account of his role in the French Resistance, he described being told by a Parisian oculist that heroin had the opposite effect of carrots in that it seriously affected night vision. He arranged for a kilo of the stuff to be sent from London in the diplomatic bag of a neutral military attaché. He then supplied it to the prostitutes in the brothels in Tours which were frequented by German night fighters. It worked, but after a month or so their doctors realised the cause and interrogated the pilots about their habits, their movements, what they ate and drank and how much they smoked. This led to police raids on the brothels. While some of the women may have been successfully lifted out and flown back to Tempsford, two were arrested and shot. Philippe continued his resistance work elsewhere.

There was another woman said to have been parachuted into France, but of whom little has come to light apart from a paragraph in Jerrard Tickell's *Moon Squadron*. If his story is true, it's quite possible he deliberately changed her name to help her remain anonymous.

Her Worship, the Mayoress of a town in the Bordeaux area … was the daughter of an English father and a French mother. Under the code name of Chloë, she was parachuted into France to work as a radio operator with Achille, leader of the local resistance. To explain away her constant association with him, it was agreed that Chloë should pose as Achille's wife. So popular did the couple become, that, with the cordial approval of the Gestapo, Achille was elected Mayor. Here the years that Chloë had spent at an English public school stood her in good stead. To her duties as Mayoress, she brought all the dignity that she had acquired as a prefect at Roedean, playing the part of a civic hostess as to the manner born. She dispensed cake and conversation to the entire satisfaction of the townspeople – and of the Germans. It was sad when she had to go away for a fortnight into some unspecified place in the sunshine because of a persistent cough. She returned, looking sun-burned and much better. She resumed her duties and a small party was given to celebrate her homecoming. An affecting speech was made by the chief of the Gestapo who was quite unaware that, during her absence, Her Worship the Mayoress had attended speech-day at Roedean, caught a one and a half pound trout in the Test and replenished her make-up box in Dover Street, London, W.1.

Another woman that Tickell refers to, not in the SOE records, is Philippe Livry-Level's second daughter, who was described as a British agent. Philippe was a pilot at Tempsford himself, flying on 161 sorties. His wife and daughter were both imprisoned by the Germans and condemned to death. She managed 'by wit of her inherited wit and ingenuity, to escape whatever passport to eternity the Germans had decided for her. She lived to match her father's Croix de Guerre with her own.'

## Josephine Hamilton

Jelle Hoolveld gave me the names of the two other female agents sent into Holland, Josephine Hamilton and Jos Gemmeke. They were in SOE's 'N' Section, Bureau Bijzondere Opdrachten, which translates as Bureau of Special Duties. On 10 August 1944, a month before the Battle of Arnhem, Flight Lieutenant Terence Helfer of

161 Squadron took off from Tempsford at 0018 hours in his Hudson. Despite poor visibility, at 0204 hours he dropped Antonia and her brother Frank Hamilton with a container of weapons and two pigeons near Abbekerk, a rural community about two miles (5 km) north of Hoorn and 20 kilometres north-east of Alkmaar. Given the previous disasters, they were dropped blind, without a reception committee.

Their personal files in the National Archives provided fascinating details of their missions. While in training in Britain, Antonia was known as Josephine. In line with the names of games 'N' Section was then using for its agents sent into Holland, hers was TIDDLEYWINKS and Frank's was ROWING. In the field, her codename was HEMERIK (TNA HS 6/767; see also the author's *Return to Holland*, 2009).

When they arrived at the barn at Gibraltar Farm, they were issued with the equipment listed on the Air Transport form. Antonia's was stamped MOST SECRET and dated 26 July 1944. It gave her height as 1.72 metres and her weight as 125 pounds – information valuable for the issuing officer, who would be able to locate all these items on the three-foot-wide concrete shelves that ran around the inside of the building. She was given a Colt .32 revolver with fifty rounds of ammunition, a locking knife, a pocket compass, field dressings, a torch with one spare battery and bulb, a pack of Lyons emergency rations and a flask of cognac. Over her ordinary clothes she had a striptease parachutist's suit; harness; parachute; an old-type helmet; spine, knee and heel pads; ankle bandages; overboots; and a spade for burying the parachute after she landed. The 'L' pill was not issued but she took four 'B' tablets, Benzedrine, to help keep her awake.

The cover story she was given had to be as close to the truth as possible. Should she be captured and interrogated, she needed to know the story off by heart. The name on her identity card was 'Antonia Wouters', born on 22 May 1910 at Breda. She grew up at Ginnekenweg 8 and was known to everyone as 'Ton'. Her parents, Anton and Hendrika, were both Dutch and their dates of birth were provided. Her father was a wood broker and her mother a housewife. It detailed which schools she went to and that she helped around the house when she left. From October 1930 until summer 1932 she worked as a housekeeper for Mrs van Oerle of Oegstgeesterweg 8 in Lieden, but when her parents decided, for business reasons, to emigrate to America, she went with them. They lived at 444 Central Park West in New York. Mr Wouters engaged in the wood trade with various American businessmen.

Aged only twenty-two when she was in America, 'Ton' did very little work, just lived off her father's earnings. In 1934 she got engaged to Derek van der Linden, but he broke it off in summer 1938. Heartbroken and rather tired of the Americans, she decided to return to Holland. Although her parents were not keen on this, she was an adult and was determined to leave. The SOE had done their homework. They had gone to the trouble of contacting various shipping agencies to get the correct details for the cost of her return tickets from Rotterdam to New York. She sailed on the SS *Volendam* of the Amerika Line in a cabin which cost £69 in 1932 and £65 10s 0d in 1938. The prices for Tourist-class return tickets for the same years were £43 5s 0d and £50 15s 0d, and third-class £33 5s 0d and £38 10s 0d. They even provided all the dates she needed to convince anyone making enquiries about her travel arrangements.

'Ton' went to work at a friend of her father's in Amsterdam, Dr H. J. Damen of Prinsengracht 1019. In return for looking after the house she was paid a little, but her father had given her sufficient funds to be quite comfortably off. She stayed there during the war until she was called up by the Arbeidsdienst (Employment Bureau) and ordered to work as a kitchen inspector in the Oorlogstijd Afdeeling Massa Voedeing (Wartime Mass Feeding Programme) in Amsterdam. How and when she got to England was not documented.

The relevant documents, a Legitimatiebewijs Voedselvoorziening in Oorlogstijd and a Dutch Identity Card, were provided. She had previously been interviewed by an officer regarding the use of neutral post boxes and passwords. Camouflaged in her handbag were a one-time pad, documents for the journey from Holland to France in case of emergency and a W.O.K. (Worked Out Key) Code.

The Adam Matthew Publications website provides details, her operation, codenamed TIDDLEYWINKS. She had to re-establish propaganda links and send messages to the underground press on behalf of Queen Wilhelmena, but the mission had to be aborted as she broke both her shin and splint bones on landing in a canal. Despite the pain, she managed to hide for a couple of nights until she was discovered by the Dutch resistance, who took her to Haarlem via Alkmaar, where she was put in hospital under a fake name. The flask of cognac would have come in handy to dull the pain until she got to see a doctor. She stayed with another Dutch SOE agent, Tom Biallosterski, 'Draughts 2', until Frank found her a safe, isolated farmhouse where she survived the rest of the war.

## Sibyl Anne Sturrock

The last recorded WAAF I have come across who was parachuted into occupied Europe was sent by the SIS, which may or may not have records of this. As the woman was in the WAAF, Escott included her details in the postscript to *Mission Improbable*, and her story is worth mentioning here. Whether she was flown out of Tempsford, Tangmere or Harrington was not mentioned, but it is possible she flew from one of these locations as long flights to Algiers did originate from these airfields.

Sibyl Anne Sturrock was born in Berlin in 1921, and as her father worked in the Foreign Office she spent time studying in schools in Hungary, Yugoslavia and Austria. Known as 'Chibi' to her friends, she was fluent in several languages.

Early in the war she moved to England and joined the WAAF in July 1940 and became a sergeant radio operator employed on direction finding. She was described by Escott as

a convinced anti-fascist. She quickly found the rules and petty discipline of her life restrictive, being of an independent, outspoken nature, and felt her abilities wasted until SIS, recognising her peculiar talents, had her seconded to its service. At its insistence she was sent for officer training before working at the Yugoslav desk in London and then Bari [in Italy].

Escott provided background of the politics of Yugoslavia, which were as complicated as those in France. In September 1944, Sibyl was parachuted in

to work on operations, intelligence gathering and building up good relations with the Yugoslavs, under the leadership of her organiser Major John Ennals and their radio operator Eli Zohar. They were attached to the 10th Corps of the partisan General Tito in the partly liberated territory of Moslavina, about 45 km south-east of the Croatian capital of Zagreb, and surrounded by enemy-held lines of communications.

In the winter snow, at the end of the year, she travelled with the partisans on foot and on horseback as they retreated painfully, step by step into Slavonia. 'Life was very serious and danger a constant companion.' Her willingness to share their hardships and champion their cause made her very popular and helped to establish confidence between the Allied and partisan authorities.

By about March 1945, they had gone back as far as they would go and the Yugoslav army prepared to take the offensive, eventually advancing into Podravina and joining the advancing Red Army of Russia, Sibyl still accompanying them. In May 1945 Zagreb was finally liberated and she took part in the great victory march through the city. Now her part in the war was over and shortly afterwards she left.

In recognition of her work, she was awarded the OBE in 1946.

## Carpetbaggers' Women

Bowman (1988) mentioned two other women who were flown by Carpetbagger pilots from Harrington. Douglas D. Walker, a pilot who arrived in January 1945, recalled in his memoirs being part of Sergeant Swartz's crew.

> I was in the waist of the Liberator preparing for the mission while I awaited the arrival of the Joe. The generator was running, so I had a dim light to work by. I looked up as the Joe stepped into the aircraft. I nodded to him, not paying too much attention, as I was busy arranging the static lines.
>
> An OSS Colonel stepped in behind and walked over to me. 'Sergeant', he said, 'Take good care of your Joe tonight – she is a special cargo.' I turned to look and she had removed her helmet, unveiling a casket of blonde hair down to her shoulders, I smiled at her in welcome and told the colonel, 'Don't worry, we'll deliver her in good condition.'
>
> He then told me that she understood only French and German and that her mother and father in France had been killed by the Nazis – the reason she had volunteered to be dropped into Germany, Seems we were dropping her into the Bavarian Alps region to determine if Hitler was really setting up a 'last ditch' stronghold in the so-called mountain redoubt, to hold out against the Allied armies.
>
> After we took off, I made her as comfortable as I could – as comfortable as could be managed in a drafty, unheated bomber on a cold night in January.
>
> With my fractured French and her equally disjointed English, it was difficult, but we managed to communicate so that I could at least keep her mind occupied until the time came for her to jump into Germany.
>
> I'll never forget the sight of that pretty, brave girl, as she sat in the Joe Hole awaiting my signal to jump into the night! Here we were, flying in pitch darkness over enemy territory at 2,000 ft and she had the courage to parachute into enemy skies, not knowing what fate awaited her below! I wished her 'Bon Chance' as she jumped and she answered with a smile – 'Merci Mon Ami'.

The tail-gunner, Ralph Schiller, reported that her parachute had opened and 'we flew back to England and safety – leaving a very brave woman behind in a very unsafe place! We never learned what happened to her, but we all agreed that she was one of the bravest people we had ever met!'

Lieutenant John L. Moore, a navigator in the carpetbagger outfit, also fondly recalls one female Joe. 'I briefed the crew, captained by Lieutenant West, which dropped her over south-central France. She was a little thing, 5 ft 2 or 3 in and about 105 lb. How many stone would that be? Beautiful in spite of her Second Lieutenant uniform. Some of the Joes wore British or American uniform so if caught in their 'chutes they would have a part of a cover story. I doubt if the uniforms helped them live long if caught. Hope she lived through the mess.'

During World War Two thousands of agents were parachuted into occupied Europe, and many were female. SOE for instance dispatched 10,000 men and 3,200 women agents and operatives into Europe during the war.

Pattinson commented that these figures are often cited when speaking about the total numbers of men and women who served in SOE. The 3,200 refers to the FANYs mainly, who were employed as radio operators, coders, secretaries, etc., in Britain, Italy, North Africa and the Far East, and to a lesser extent to civilians (who worked in Baker Street and as seamstresses in The Thatched Barn, for example) rather than operational agents. So the sentence is highly misleading.

Sometimes there was some comic relief, even for the Carpetbaggers. One crew returned from a mission and told the story about a female French agent they were carrying.

She was slow getting to the Joe-hole because of the heavy gear she was wearing and was not allowed to jump, as the reception light went out before she was ready. She sulked on the way back until nature put her under pressure. She was directed to the 'relief tube' in the airplane's rear section. The dispatcher gallantly turned his back while the girl struggled with her zipped up man's flying suit, in an effort to use the tube that was, unfortunately, designed for the male's anatomy. Finally, the girl burst into laughter, and when the dispatcher turned around, she demonstrated to him in rapid-fire French and gestures that her personal 'operation' had not been completely successful. She was considerably dampened below the waist (but not in spirits) …

Another time a radio operator reported that as the aircraft crossed over a target without making the planned drop, he heard a woman's voice on the ground S-phone yelling in a cockney accent. 'For Christ's sake, come back 'ere: Turn around and come back!'

(Fish, *They Flew By Night*)

David Oliver quotes Roy Buckingham, who was posted to 138 Squadron in June 1944.

On one occasion we had to bring our 'Joe', a young lady, back with us to the forward base at Kinloss in Scotland after the 'Joe' hatch had frozen solid over a DZ in Denmark.

It was my duty with Bill Clarkson, the dispatcher, to make sure that no one talked to the agent while we were away from the base. We had to stick close to her even in bed – we were all fully clothed – and when she went to the toilet, the door remained unlocked. We were standing outside the women's toilet when a senior WAAF officer wanted to go in. We barred her way and she demanded to speak to our commanding officer. We gave her the number and when she got through, her face went bright red when he told her in no uncertain terms that she should leave us to do our duty.

(Oliver, *Airborne Espionage*)

Who she was, what her mission was, and whether she went on a subsequent trip remains a mystery.

## The Women's Motivation

Of the fifty female SOE agents sent into France, fifteen were caught by the Germans. Only three survived. The French captured three others, two of whom escaped. One died of meningitis in the field. Although I have found evidence of over sixty women sent into occupied Europe, the exact number remains unknown.

The motivation for many of these women to undergo specialist training and be sent into enemy-occupied territory knowing about the possibility of arrest, torture and potential execution, was not the love that Sebastian Faulks' heroine, Charlotte Gray, had for her missing RAF pilot downed somewhere in France. According to Vera Atkins, it was their loathing of Nazi ideology, a love of freedom and a desire to make an individual contribution to the liberation of France, Belgium and Holland. They were messengers of hope to the Resistance. In an interview recording at the Imperial War Museum, Atkins said:

I've always found personally that being a woman has great advantages if you know how to play the thing right and I believe that all the girls, the women who went out, had the same feeling. They were not as suspect as men, they had very subtle minds when it came to talking their way out of situations, they had many more cover stories to deliver than most men and the performed extremely well. Also they're very conscientious – I'm not saying men are not. They were wonderful radio operators and very cool and courageous.

(Atkins, V. 9551/3; 12302/1; 23237/3; 31590/3; 31592/3; 31586/3 IWM)

Elizabeth Nicholas's research led her to be quite critical of the SOE. According to Vera, the women sent to France by 'F' Section were mostly in their early twenties, telephonists, shop assistants and clerks. Most had lived in simple, modest accommodation. Some spoke imperfect French and, after only a few weeks of training, 'were sent to pit themselves against German counter-espionage services manned by men of the utmost shrewdness, highly-trained, with many years of experience in that field'. The men in London who controlled them, she described as 'amateurs'.

There were some involved on the British side and many on the French who suggested that the British government sacrificed the lives of many of its British and French agents and subagents as part of a grand deception scheme. Its details are outlined in Kramer's *Flames in the Field*. There are many in Holland and Belgium of the same opinion. They argue that, as part of Churchill's agreement with Stalin, a plan was created to distract

Hitler from the Eastern Front by pretending an Allied invasion in the Pas de Calais was planned for the summer or autumn of 1943. The intensified provision of agents, arms, ammunition and supplies to the Resistance and their increased sabotage activity in the north of France was part of the scheme.

One female agent interviewed by Pattinson detailed some of her experiences in Normandy and asked to remain anonymous. Not long after D-Day and with the American army advancing towards Paris, she and her organiser drove back and forth across the lines. Her mission was to provide the Americans with intelligence about the German military disposition. At one point, the car was ambushed and fired on. She admitted that she survived by trying to be nice with the enemy.

> You just react to the moment and think. I'll get by alright with a nice smile. I just sort of smiled and waved to them. All the time. Women could get by with a smile and do things that men couldn't and no matter what you had hidden in your handbag or your bicycle bag, if you had a nice smile, you know, just give them a little wink. It just happened constantly, all the time. So I got away with it. It becomes sort of second nature … You did that [flirted] automatically. Absolutely. That was just par for the course. Just sort of went into the role automatically, just quite naturally.

On one occasion, the car she was travelling in was stopped and she was forced out. Her papers were hidden in her girdle.

> I heard this marching behind me and I turned around and there were these two guys so I just smiled at them and went on my way and they followed me in and they raped me. One held me down. My first instinct was to put up a fight and then I thought no, I can't. I've got these papers. If I put up a fight, they're going to overpower me and then they'll probably strip me and we'd be in a worse mess than we are already in. I've just got to let them do it and get on with it … Anyway, it was quite an experience! But they didn't get my papers! [laughs]

Three survivors interviewed by Pattinson described being badly beaten. Testimonies of locally recruited French Resistance workers note that some women had electric currents run through their nipples, electrodes inserted into their vaginas, their nails extracted, their breasts severed and some were raped by guards, sometimes in front of their male colleagues.

The horror of being robbed of one's dignity after having been stripped, shaved and been given shapeless prison clothing and a number was mentioned by many survivors. Lillian Kremer, who researched the Jewish survivors of the Holocaust, said that women were

> shamed and terrified by SS men who made lewd remarks and obscene suggestions and poked, pinched and mauled them in the course of delousing procedures and searches for hidden valuables in oral, rectal and vaginal cavities.

Prisoners were forbidden to exchange their camp clothing, to dress well, to wear make-up, to style their hair – they were, in a word, defeminised. Many had to cope with diarrhoea, cystitis, malnutrition, excessive exercise and lack of sanitary products. These problems, in addition to maltreatment, often led to the cessation of menstruation. Tania Szabó reported that 'those for whom periods continued, through intentional lack of hygienic material to prevent the menses flowing down the legs of the women … they suffered great distress and humiliation'. Some were worried that bromide had been put into their soup to stop them from having children.

One poignant account was given by Geneviève de Gaulle, a captured member of the French Resistance, who was celebrating her birthday. She had been given a birthday cake made from compressed breadcrumbs which had been kneaded together with several spoonfuls of a molasses-like substance they called 'jam' or 'jelly'. Twenty-four twigs were used as candles and leaves picked from the banks of the nearby swamp decorated the edges (http://www.seanet.com/~raines/conflicts.htm).

What I found interesting in the accounts of all these women is that there were very few records of them taking advantage of their 'L' pills, the cyanide capsules they were to use *in extremis*. It could well have been that they were convinced that, if they kept to their cover story, they would be able to bluff their way through, even survive the torture. In Marcus Binney's *The Women who Lived for Danger*, he beautifully summed up the role of the SOE women:

> In an organisation that recruited numerous outstandingly brave and resourceful men, who repeatedly carried out the most hazardous missions in enemy-occupied Europe, constantly facing the threat of betrayal, arrest and torture by the Gestapo, these women were to show corresponding valour, determination and powers of endurance, serving alone or in small groups. Without hesitation, they risked their lives on an often daily basis. For this they had no previous military or professional training, as many of the men had. They had to be alert, quick-witted, calm and unruffled while constantly acting a part. Women had never had such a role to play before, yet again and again they surprised their comrades with their astonishing mastery of clandestine life.

The Tempsford crews were probably completely ignorant of the women's missions. They were not supposed to know. They undoubtedly heard on the grapevine, or sometimes first-hand, what happened to their colleagues if they crash-landed and survived. If they were very lucky, they themselves might be rescued by the Resistance and sent down the escape line back to Britain. However, there was always the chance of being captured and imprisoned. As prisoners of war, they knew they would be reasonably well treated until the end of the war. However, they probably guessed what happened to captured agents, especially women. Of course, the details of what happened to the women referred to above only came to light well after the war ended.

Yet another woman said to have been sent into France has recently come to light. Friends of the deceased Madge Frith Wilkinson (née Crabtree) believe she was an SOE agent in France and have been trying to find out information about her. Born on 4 February 1921 in Rochdale, she was fluent in French and Spanish and was thought to have been recruited into SOE when she was about twenty. She would have been married at this time but may have used her maiden name of Crabtree or her mother's maiden name of Frith. They did not know her codename. From the few details she gave them, they believe that she was sent out in a submarine to Gibraltar and then made her way up through Spain, across the Pyrenees and into France. The work she did there was largely a mystery to them, but they believe that she was involved in sabotage and returning intelligence to HQ in London. As there are no records of her in the SOE files, it is possible she was employed by the SIS.

Pattinson's investigations revealed that two female agents were arrested at checkpoints while travelling in cars loaded with weapons. One was arrested when she visited her network's radio operator following a transmission which allowed the Abwehr to locate the operator's position. Five agents were arrested at safe houses under German surveillance. Two were arrested following delation, denunciation by acquaintances hoping for at least a 10,000-franc reward. Another was trapped by a German agent impersonating a new recruit to her network.

Two female radio operators were captured by their sets having been located by *gonios*, the detection vans. One was denounced by a jealous wife who believed the agent was having an affair with her husband. Another was captured following a young member of her network revealing under torture the address of a safe house they didn't think she would be using. One was caught in a Gestapo raid on a landing field when she was trying to capture someone else, and another was captured immediately on landing by a German reception committee. All told, seventeen were arrested and incarcerated in French prisons. Blanche Charlet managed to escape from Castres along with fifty-three other inmates on 16 September 1943, and Mary Herbert was released after two months because of lack of evidence.

Many of them were said to have feigned ignorance and confessed to being gullible when interrogated. An SOE report in the National Archives notes that:

> A woman agent 'admitted' to having been engaged in subversive activity, but said she had gone into it with her eyes closed and, at first, had no idea of what she was doing. Later, when she did realise she was afraid to give it up. In this way, she was able to represent herself as having been locally recruited, when, in fact, she was a parachuted agent.
>
> (TNA HS 7/66)

In Pattinson's 2006 article, "'Playing the daft lassie with them': Gender, Captivity and the Special Operations Executive', she noted that many played on stereotypically feminine traits, such as foolishness, innocence, lack of common sense, anxiousness and timidity.

Along with the 104 arrested male agents, fifteen women agents were deported from France to concentration camps. Seven were executed shortly after arrival; the others suffered months of incarceration, some in solitary confinement. Three were injected with phenol at Natzweiler concentration camp. Four were shot at Dachau. Three were shot at Ravensbrück, one died in the gas chamber there and another died of starvation and typhus at Belsen while awaiting repatriation. Only three women and twenty-three men managed to return from the camps.

## *Baroness Crawley's Debate in the House of Lords*

On 6 June 2011, Baroness Crawley started a debate in the British House of Lords in an attempt to persuade the government to commemorate the SOE women sent into France.

> The women concerned were recruited to serve in occupied France. They acted variously as couriers, wireless operators and saboteurs. They found places for planes to land, bringing more agents and supplies. They established safe houses and worked with resistance movements to disrupt the occupation and clear the path for the allied advance.
>
> Those women did these things, given wartime pressures, after a very brief period of training. Apparently, they had each been told when recruited that there was only a 50 per cent chance of personal survival – yet, to their eternal credit, off they went. Some had been born in France, some in Britain, a couple in Ireland and some still further afield. Some were Jewish, some convent-educated, one Muslim. Some were already mothers, some just out of their teens; some shop assistants, some journalists, some wives; some were rather poor. In France, they often had to travel hundreds of miles by bike and train, protected only by forged papers, and as they went about their frequently exhausting work they were under constant danger of arrest by the Gestapo. Some were even exposed to betrayal by double agents and turncoats.
>
> The story of what happened to some of those women is often unreadable and, in 21st-century Britain, is perhaps too easily under-remembered. A number were captured in France, horribly brutalised and sent to camps in Germany. There, the torment was often sustained over weeks and months on starvation diets, the women crammed in unsanitary and overcrowded huts with disease rampant. Four of them were killed in Natzweiler by being injected – scarcely credible as it is – with disinfectant. A number, once worked and beaten to a standstill, were shot and hanged at Dachau and Ravensbrück.
>
> (http://www.memorialgrove.org.uk/SOE%20Women.pdf)

Many speeches followed, honouring the women involved, not just those sent into France. This book will help keep alive their memories.

# 6
# Life at RAF Tempsford

## The Americans at Tempsford

When the Americans joined the war, a squadron was allocated to assist the SOE with its secret work supplying the resistance groups in occupied Europe. Their pilots and crews spent a month at what they affectionately called the 'Tempsford Academy', learning the skills of night flying before being transferred to their base at Harrington. All their personnel were issued with a little book to help them better understand British culture and, in particular, the women they might come into contact with while stationed in England. In it was a section on BRITISH WOMEN AT WAR:

> A British woman officer or non-commissioned officer can – and often does – give orders to a man private. The man obeys it smartly and knows it is no shame. For British women have proven themselves in this way. They have stuck to their posts near burning ammunition dumps, delivered messages afoot after their motorbikes have been blasted from under them. They have pulled aviators from burning planes. They have died at the gun posts and as they fell another girl has stepped directly into the position and 'carried on.' There is not a single record in this war of any British woman in uniformed service quitting her post or failing in her duty under fire.
>
> Now you understand why British soldiers respect the women in uniform. They have won the right to the utmost respect. When you see a woman in khaki or air-force blue with a lot of ribbon on her tunic – remember she didn't get it for knitting more socks than anyone else in Ipswich.

## After the War

After the war, when information was eventually released showing the role of SOE women, they were eulogised by the British media. Two of them appeared on Eamonn Andrew's TV show *This is Your Life*. A TV series, *Wish Me Luck*, shown on London Weekend Television between 1989 and 1990, was based on two imaginary women sent to France. Sebastian Faulk's based his novel *Charlotte Gray* on one of the women. Various documentaries have been made about the SOE which mentioned the women, and in 2008 the film *Female Agents* was released, focusing on the lives of four agents sent into wartime France on a rescue mission which ended up being an assassination job.

A number of publications emerged after the war which covered the work of the SOE, many of which have been referred to earlier. Pattinson noted that the pattern of biography publication illustrated the public's preoccupation with the experiences of female agents, largely because it was the first time women were engaged in combat situations instead of in domestic situations with men fighting to protect them. Of the thirty-nine women sent by SOE's 'F' Section into France, six have been subjects of published biographies, three of whom have been written about by more than one author. Five books contain chapter biographies of several female agents, whereas only two biographies have been written on the 441 men sent to France and two books include chapter biographies. On the other hand, far more men have had their autobiographies published. Only three of the female agents have published their memoirs. In *Behind Enemy Lines*, Pattinson has written:

> That most written SOE testimonies are male authored reflects a more widespread pattern in published autobiographies; whereas men represent themselves, women are more likely to be represented by others. One agent who failed to find a publisher for her autobiography, was told that the manuscript lacked drama and was advised to 'pad it out' by injecting more excitement into the descriptions of resistance in France and life in Germany as a prisoner. Those who were successful in locating a publisher generally adhered to the conventions of the spy and thriller genre; these were gripping tales of derring-do and close shaves. Hence the agents themselves were involved in shaping the public image of the clandestine operative.

Pattinson made very perceptive comments, suggesting that the interest was because the women transgressed the conventional codes of behaviour and notions of women's 'appropriate' role in war. They didn't stay at home and look after the children, waiting patiently for their husband's return. They went out and did something about it themselves.

> This interest in war women is heightened when it becomes common knowledge that young women, trained in unarmed combat and silent killing techniques, were infiltrated behind enemy lines to wage war against the might of the Nazi war machine … In a total war, anything goes and it is this which is of infinite interest to the public.
>
> [They] were highly motivated, often driven by the desire for revenge and hatred of the Germans, were alert to the dangers they faced, were determined to proceed with their missions, despite the obstacles that were put in their way and accomplished their work with varying degrees of success.

## Romances on the Job
Pattinson's researches into SOE personal files revealed that a number of the women had relationships with fellow agents on their training courses. Sonya Butt and Guy d'Artois, Eliane Plewman and Eric Cauchi, and Muriel Byck and an unnamed male agent identified as 'No. 15' became lovers. In the field, Mary Herbert became pregnant during a relationship with Claude de Baissac. Odette Sansom had an extramarital affair with Peter Churchill, Sonya Butt with Sydney Hudson, and Andrée Borrel with Gilbert Norman. Pattinson suggested that many others developed attachments which were not disclosed.

## Romances at RAF Tempsford

When the US personnel arrived at Tempsford, they provided quite a stimulus for the local women and girls on and around the base. Having more money than most of the other armed forces, the Americans were keen to have a good time. In fact, having a good time was very high on most people's priority list. The high anxiety, stress and trauma of the war put enormous pressure on the Tempsford personnel. Strong friendships between pilots and aircrew have lasted until this day. Getting a boyfriend or girlfriend was just as important then as today. Although very few accounts have come to light, Freddie Clark mentioned that Leading Aircraft Woman Iris Lawdy, who worked in the officers' mess, fell in love and got engaged to Fl/Sgt A. H. Beggood. Imagine her distress when told one morning that he had been lost on a mission.

Another story told by Terry Crowdy in his *SOE Agent* was of the SOE sending one of their staff to speak to an agent's girlfriend with a proposal of marriage. He had not had time to pop the question before he left and had realised how important she was to him. Her acceptance was signalled back with a demand for a suitable engagement ring.

A number of WAAF had their autobiographies published by Woodfield Publishing. On their website, it states that:

> These indomitable young ladies worked in a wide variety of trades and made an invaluable contribution to the war effort. They also, of course, worked in close proximity to the young men of the RAF and, inevitably, many romantic liaisons flourished … But the terrible attrition rate of the air war meant that thousands of young women lost their sweethearts and thus their memories of this era are bitter-sweet – nostalgic for the wonderful camaraderie they shared with their WAAF and RAF colleagues but also tinged with sadness. Their stories make for fascinating reading.

Some evidence of romantic liaisons has come to light. Clearly there would have been numerous romances with local women and girls as there was plenty of socialising. Some WAAFs must have attracted the attention of the Americans because, in the Harrington Aviation Museum at Harrington, there is a photograph of three Tempsford WAAFs outside one of the huts with a romantic poem written on the back.

> If we could take the tiny freckles on your nose,
> Each one to be as a million years and more,
> Then multiply, as far as multiplying goes,
> Add the stars; then total up the score,
> We would have for all the world to see,
> And envy too,
> Half the years my dear, that I shall be,
> In love with you,
> At Tempsford WAAFERY.
> (Courtesy of Harrington Aviation Museum)

During the war, the government's need for gold resulted in them issuing a directive to jewellers restricting the size of wedding rings to the equivalent value of one guinea (£1.10).

Undated photograph of three WAAFs at RAF Tempsford. (Harrington Aviation Museum)

Lucy Bittles, a daughter of one of the Tempsford WAAFs, provided details of her mother's wedding for the BBC's People's War website. Anne Bittles from Newry, Northern Ireland, was a Nursing Orderly at RAF Tempsford. She had enlisted on 21 October 1941 and was a corporal when she had a 'Forces Wedding' on Tuesday 14 March 1944 in St Mary's church, Everton. Her husband, Robert Hanna, was a gunner in the Royal Horse Artillery who had recently returned from British North Africa, after six years' service, during which he served with the Eighth Army. The vicar was Revd F. C. Hamlyn and RAF Padre Bruce officiated, assisted by Cpl Turner. L/A/C Turner presided at the organ for the hymn 'O Perfect Love'. The bride was given away by her friend Cpl Green, RAF, and the groom's sister, Cpl Ann Hanna, WAAF, was the bridesmaid. Cpl Leslie Clark, RAF, was best man. The couple were both in uniform and had a guard of honour of WAAFs. After the service, they had a reception at Manor Farm, Everton, the home of Mrs Gurney, who was a friend of the bride.

This account prompted me to investigate the parish registers of St Mary's church, Everton, and St Peter's church, Tempsford. Apart from Lucy Bittles's wedding, there were eleven recorded 'forces-related' church weddings in both parishes between 1941 and 1945. The certificates did not specify whether the bride or groom was stationed at RAF Tempsford. In the section on their rank or profession, it most often said: 'His Majesty's Forces'. Two were marked AAF, which may refer to the Australian Air Force. On 28 July twenty-four-year-old Frederick Higgins, a corporal in the RAF, married seventeen-year-old Dulcie Thurley of Church Street, Tempsford, at St Peter's. On 8 August 1942, twenty-one-year-old Eric Dilley, HMF, married twenty-two-year-old Evelyn Ingram, a domestic servant, from Tempsford. On 24 April 1943, there was a double wedding. Twenty-four-year-old Donald Urquart, HMF, married nineteen-year-old Joyce Wilkins, HMF, while thirty-one-year-old William Walton, HMF, married twenty-two-year-old Ethel Crawley of the Women's Land Army.

On 21 January 1942, twenty-three-year-old Robert Young, AAF, married twenty-one-year-old Norah Malone at St Mary's. On 30 October, twenty-six-year-old Horace Gurney, HMF, of 8 Sandy Road, Everton, married twenty-two-year-old Annie Vine, WAAF. On 7 February 1942, twenty-one-year-old Raymond Norman, AAF, married nineteen-year-old Elsie Wisson of Woodbury Lodge, Everton. The Hanna and Betts wedding was on 14 March. On 28 October, Alec Culverwell, HMF, married Edith Davenport, HMF. On 12 December, Leslie Dibdin, HMF, married Gwyneth Lawson of Everton. On 19 April 1945, twenty-two-year-old Ernest Hollett, a petty officer in the Royal Navy, married twenty-two-year-old Carolina Froud, Leading Aircraft Woman in the WAAF. On 28 April the last wartime 'forces' wedding was recorded between Dennis Sear, HMF, and Maud Hull of Everton. Examination of the marriage registries for churches of other denominations and the civil marriages will probably reveal more; so might an examination of the baptismal records to see if there were any forces-related babies.

Pat Darlow told the story of her grandmother Jenny Willmott, whose husband George was the tenant farmer of Gibraltar Farm in the 1930s. She and their seven children were rehoused at Woodbury Farm when their house was requisitioned. Their son Hugh married Mabel, a barmaid at the Anchor Hotel in Tempsford. As she already had a baby from a relationship with an RAF officer stationed at RAF Tempsford, they had to move out of the area to avoid the gossip. It was suggested that Mabel never revealed the father's identity because the man was already married.

Pattinson's research into the lives of the female SOE agents sent to France showed that they eagerly embraced marriage and motherhood on their return. 'Of the twenty-six who returned, just four remained single; three returned to their husbands, three had been widowed (two of whom later remarried) and the others married within five years of the war ending.' In an interview in 1950, Vera Atkins said that the majority were happy wives and mothers and the others settled into different everyday jobs (Atkins, V. 9551/3; 12302/1; 23237/3; 31590/3; 31592/3; 31586/3 IWM).

At one of the reunions on the airfield, I overheard a woman telling her Canadian son that he had been conceived behind Gibraltar Barn on the night of VE Day.

The celebrations in Everton and down on the airfield on VE Day were immortalised by D. Summerhayes in her poem.

### V.E. Day

> I was a W.A.A.F. who loved to jive,
> Way back at TEMPSFORD in '45,
> When news came through on that GREAT DAY,
> OH! How we cheered – A PUBLIC HOLIDAY.
> We jumped on our bikes to CELEBRATE,
> At our local Pub, a mile from the Gate,
> The singing and dancing – the kissing and fun –
> (My chain coming off on the homeward run).
> A kip for an hour, and a freshen up,
> Then a good drink of CHAR from a NAAFI cup,
> Then back on our bikes, for a ride DOWN the Hill,
> To the main RAF Camp for a Beer Drinking swill.
> We backed our winners and shouted 'ENCORE'
> As the lads fell out when they could drink no more,
> Then back to the WAAFERY walking up the big hill,
> And into the Cookhouse to eat of our fill.
> We stoked up the fires with scuttles of coke,
> Then off to Ablutions to have a good soak.
> On with best blues and our faces to fuss –
> We go back DOWN the hill, this time ON A BUS,
> Provided especially by the powers that be,
> For a Bonfire with a HITLER effigy.
> The Cheers that rang out as that guy burned,
> (Relaxation for Aircrew was very well earned).
> A Dance in the Hangar with the Palais Glide,
> The Tango, Jitterbug and the Jive,
> The weave of the Conga – ALL IN LINE,
> The laughter, the shouting and the wine,
> Then transport back to complete our day,
> When we went back home to 'HIT THE HAY'.

(Courtesy of D. Summerhayes)

Celebrations for VE Day on 8 May 1945 in one of the hangars at RAF Tempsford. (Courtesy of Tom Lowe)

VE Day celebrations at Tempsford on 8 May 1945. (Courtesy of Tom Lowe)

Celebratory drinking during VE celebrations, 8 May 1945. (Courtesy of Tom Lowe)

## Maureen Gurney's Memories

Maureen Gurney of Tempsford recalled how, as a nine-year-old girl, she lived at Manor Farm, Everton, in the 1930s and 1940s. Before the war, grandmother Wisson of Warden Hill Farm used to take her down the hill to Blunham in her white pony and trap. She recalled her grandmother swinging her whip and telling Maureen to hold on for dear life. In what she called the 'inlets' along the road were the painted oval caravans and horses of the gypsies who used to sit on the steps and make pegs, presumably from wood cut from the nearby bushes. Those trips were stopped when construction of the airfield started.

Kirby Laing, the contractor, rented the northern flat and attic, where he lived with his wife Joan. Maureen recalled being treated like their daughter and one day was taken to the Cross Keys in St Neots in Mrs Laing's red MG to meet another of the Laing officials who rented rooms there.

Other wartime lodgers at the farm included Mr Griffiths, the timekeeper on the site, and his wife and four evacuee boys. Her parents were devout Methodists and used to attend the chapel on Everton Heath, where they welcomed any visiting Tempsford personnel. Being teetotal, they and others entertained on Sunday evenings. Mr Gurney had a billiard room, which was quite an attraction for the RAF boys, and an upright piano, around which many a wartime song was sung.

Maureen recalled Tim Gilchrist and his friends but was particularly struck by the gorgeous Ron Sharpe. He was one of the Lysander pilots who, one day, brought her and her sister Christine bottles of French perfume, said to have been bought in Paris. Christine worked in the munitions factory in Papworth and had to catch the bus every morning with some of the other young women in the village. Maureen still recalls Christine waiting by the pub in her snood on cold mornings.

As Maureen's room was in the attic, her window overlooked the airfield to the west and also the corner of the road by the Thornton Arms. It was a matter of much amusement to her to be woken up by the chatter of a gang of Irish labourers who, having left the pub, lined up against the fence and urinated before wending their way down the hill to their accommodation.

Maureen's father was an air-raid warden and was often out in the evenings. She recalled her mother making milky cocoa most nights and father taking a cup across the road to Brian, one of the armed guards on duty at the barrier at the top of the hill. He had an iron fire pot which kept him warm during the cold evenings. Maureen's father knew from Brian which nights the flights were on, but Maureen could tell when she saw carloads of men from Hasells Hall, all dressed up in their blue RAF uniforms, being driven past the barrier down the hill.

Another story Maureen told was of meeting Jim Cousins and his mates, a group of soldiers just returned from Dunkirk. She was surprised that they were so exhausted that they slept in the pig yard all day before moving across to Woodbury Park. She wasn't certain but it was possible Jim was part of a contingent supervising the POW camp on the estate. She recalled being chased while on her bike by an Italian who wore British army fatigues but with a huge circle cut out of the back, over which a yellow cloth had been sown.

Her father, like Mr Bettles, was a 'swill man'. He had a pass allowing him to go down onto the base and collect the slops from the NAAFI for his pigs. Sometimes, on her father's return, Maureen was told to open the cans carefully as inside there was a wrapped-up slab of butter or something. Her Aunt Hilda worked there.

She also got to meet Padre Edwards, and after him Padre Eric Richardson. Although there was a chapel on the airfield, every three weeks the padre would call in at the Methodist chapel on Everton Heath and occasionally at their house on Sunday evenings. In fact, she got to know him so well that, when Maureen got married, he came and officiated the ceremony at the Biggleswade Trinity Methodist church.

Maureen got to know some of the Tempsford WAAFs. She recalled meeting Joyce Underwood, who used to visit Maureen's mother at Manor Farm. One day, Joyce told Maureen that she was going to get married and showed Maureen her engagement ring. It later transpired that Joyce's husband was a bigamist with another wife elsewhere. There was also the story of a local girl who was being consoled by Maureen's mother after her RAF fiancé jilted her.

After the war, Maureen lived in Pasture Close, near Letchworth golf club, where she became friends with Andrée, a beautiful and very wealthy French neighbour who was married to Captain Turner, one of the bosses of Irvings' parachute-making factory in Letchworth. She told Maureen that she was from a very wealthy family in France before the war and that her diamond ring was worth £36,000. On discovering that Andrée had a hatred for green peppers, it came out that, during the war, she joined the Resistance and was dropped by parachute into occupied France. Tempsford was never mentioned. On one occasion, she had to hide in the rafters above a churchyard lychgate. Being on the run from the Gestapo, she had to survive for several days on only green peppers. Whether they were responsible for a perforated stomach was not mentioned, but she told Maureen that the family who hid and her friend arranged with the local doctor for her to be given a blood transfusion, and that she was attached to to her donor for two days.

## Dorothy Pickard and her Dog Ming

In October 1942, Wing Commander Charles Pickard, DSO Bar, DFC, one of the most famous and charismatic pilots of the war, replaced Group Captain Edward Fielden as Commander of 161 Squadron. He was a giant, blond Yorkshireman known as 'Pick' to his friends and, being a married man, rented White Wood Cottage, a large bungalow on the edge of Woodbury Park, just a few miles from the airfield. He moved in with his wife Dorothy, two horses and Ming, his Old English sheepdog. Ming went with him everywhere. Alexander Hamilton, in his book *Wings of Night*, narrates some of Pick's exploits. During one of his missions, Dorothy was woken up at 1.30 a.m. by Ming pulling the sheets off the bed. The big sheepdog had done this before when Pick had had to make a forced landing, so she was apprehensive. Hamilton related how:

> She opened the front door to allow the dog the use of the garden, bitterly cold and covered in snow. Ming walked outside but made no effort to spend the proverbial penny. The dog looked up to the sky, to the right and to the left and, of a sudden, Dorothy knew that Pick was in trouble. Covered in her shaggy great coat, Ming did not seem to feel the effect of the cold. The dog remained outside in the cold, constantly looking up at the sky, to the right and to the left. No words of coaxing on the part of Dorothy would induce Ming to come into the house. She remained outside as Dorothy closed the door against the weather and returned to the lounge to make up the fire, and wait out the night, fearful and in trepidation.
>
> Outside in the snow and the cold, Ming continued to look to the sky while Dorothy made the odd call to the ops room for word of 'O for Orange'. Oddly enough, it was more than three years before when Pick and his crew had force landed in the sea, in a Wellington, also under the code name of 'O for Orange'. The code name was growing ominous and monotonous. For obvious reasons there was no news of the Hudson over France and Dorothy had no alternative to leaving Ming out in the cold as the dog persisted in her refusal to come into the house. With a heart of lead, Dorothy waited up most of the night, sitting by the fire, hoping for the best but anticipating the worst.
>
> It was a long and bitter night until precisely half past five in the morning. Shortly after the half hour struck on the clock, Dorothy heard a constant and loud scratching on the door. In a state of great trauma Dorothy moved to the door not knowing what to expect. Ming looked up at Dorothy as the door was opened, wagged her short tail, and swept past Dorothy towards the fireplace. Curling up in front of the fire, Ming was sound asleep in a matter of minutes, and Dorothy retired at once to bed. Now that Ming had returned and was sound asleep in the lounge by the fire, Dorothy knew that Pick was somehow, somewhere, on his way back. Shortly before 8 a.m. Dorothy was again awakened by Ming. Between Pick, the baby and the dog, Dorothy's hours were growing more irregular. She opened the door as Ming scurried out. Approaching the end of the runway a Hudson hove into sight. Dorothy watched out long enough to read the identification letters. They read 'O'. Pick was back.

This particular operation carried out successfully in the most adverse conditions, bogged down for four hours, hitting the tree on take-off and finally limping back to England without the fighter protection asked for, brought in its wake the third DSO to be awarded to Charles Pickard.

James 'Waggie' Wagland, the last of Tempsford's station commanders, married Molly Cleevely, an attractive WAAF who was in charge of his map store at Tempsford. Flight Sergeant Witt of 161 Squadron recalled a story about a Norwegian friend of his who, on a flight to Norway, gave him directions as to which valley to fly up and exactly where to land. The agent returned with his girlfriend who, once back at Tempsford, arranged their marriage in a local church. Someone must have got wind of her presence and Witt said that a message was sent to the Station Commander enquiring about an unidentified alien on the base. As she was then in another plane on her way back to Norway with her new husband, he was honest in replying that there was no one fitting that description on the base.

## Further Stories

Murray Peden, a Canadian pilot, told me that he and his crew paid £42 between them for a little 1937 Ford, about £1,224 at today's prices. It got all seven of them to Tempsford and many of the nearby pubs. On a level road and with the wind behind them, it took about a mile and a half (2.5 km) to work up to her maximum speed of 50 miles (80 km) per hour. When all seven went out for a drive, two of them had to push a little at first 'to help the straining power plant break the vehicle's stubborn inertia'. One lunchtime the Met man told them that a slow-moving front, trailing rain, cloud and ice, was scheduled to move in, so that night's ops were cancelled. Luck had it that two Wren friends they had met in London rang with a message for him and his friend J. B., saying they had 36 hours' leave. They were ready to leave London by train and were expected at Bedford station in an hour and a half if they were available.

We assured them that we were most assuredly available, and would shortly be departing for the railway station in our private limousine to meet and transport them to the Bridge Hotel, Bedford's finest, prior to squiring them on a private tour, the likes of which they could never hope to match.

About half an hour later we had secured permission to leave the station until noon the following day. Then we went over to the NCO's billets, commandeered the crew car, and set off for the impressive old private home – a mansion really – that the Air Force had taken over for the officers' living quarters. It was our intention to spruce up, trade our battledress for our very best serge, and just generally dazzle the hell out of the two Wrens with our splendid appearance and limousine.

The mansion was situated about a mile and half away on the crest of a gently rising ridge, a magnificent location from a purely aesthetic point of view. We headed for it happily, our only concern being that we had not ourselves very much time and would have to change and freshen up smartly. The last half-mile of our path was on the rising grade. It was so far from being a steep grade that the thought of it presenting any difficulty never even crossed my mind until we tackled it and the engine began bucking.

I was forced to change down quickly to keep from stalling. In ten seconds I had to change down again … and yet again. It became apparent that we were not going to make it. Impatiently I turned about and went back some distance from the base of the grade to take a good run at it. This time we got better than halfway to the top before our faltering power plant gave up the ghost.

(M. Peden, *A Thousand Shall Fall*, 1988)

Despite going back almost to the level crossing and getting up to 50 mph, they still did not reach the crest of the hill. They turned round and headed for Bedford, forgetting about being spruced up. Three miles further on, just out of Sandy, a noticeable tremor developed somewhere around the front end. 'Next thing we know the bloody wheels'll fly off,' Murray said jokingly. No sooner said than done: the left wheel flew off ahead of them into a farmer's field. His friend said that it was the most coincidental event he'd ever experienced. Pushing the car into the side of the road, they hitched a lift in an American weapons carrier all the way to Bedford. The car was not there when they came back. It was never seen again. However, luck had it that the girls' train had been delayed.

At the hotel we encountered as a receptionist an abrasive old harridan with a sense of humour like Madam Defarge's, obviously determined to make the most of the power she presently had to treat people so rudely with impunity. I restrained myself with difficulty from asking if she had started her career as one of John Bunyan's jailers, since she looked ancient and bitchy enough to qualify … Pandering to her appetite for power by allowing her to abuse us for another three or four minutes, we eventually pried one double room out of her, but one was the limit. The Chesterfield wasn't very comfortable.

Wendy King told me how in June 1944, as a second-year PE student in Bedford during the war, she and five of her friends used to meet up with a crew from 138 Squadron. The men were in their early twenties and seriously impressed the girls by leapfrogging over a postbox in front of the eighty-year-old college principal and then asking for permission to take out six of her students. They told the girls that they had told the 'old matriarch' that they were on 'ops'. Greatly pleasing the girls, she agreed. One of the pilots, twenty-year-old F/Lt John Kidd of 138 Squadron, had a 'little old banger' and used to drive Wendy round the country lanes. She recalled ending up seeing a show put on in the hall at Cotton End village primary school. Sometimes, John flew his Halifax over the college grounds and 'gave its wings a wiggle'. Wendy only knew John and his crew for a month. On the night of 18/19 July, their Halifax LL364 never returned. His twin brother Geoff turned up to see her one day shortly afterwards and told her the news.

In Freddie Clark's book *Agents by Moonlight*, he said that the Halifax was seen by the reception committee of Dick 89 to collide with an American B-24 Liberator piloted by Lt D. A. Michelson, USAAF, of the 801st Bomb Group, Harrington. Neither crew survived. There were eight in the American crew. Kidd and his crew were buried at Marigny l'Eglise, which is 15 kilometres south of Avallon in the Yonne. Geoff Kidd returned successfully from Shipwright 9 and, when he next met Wendy, told her that he knew John was not coming back as he had seen all his kit and belongings on the floor by his bunk.

Losing loved ones and not knowing exactly what happened is one of the common experiences of women involved with Tempsford crews. One particularly poignant story was sent to me describing how a Polish woman eventually located the crash site of her fiancé.

Mariusz A. Wodzicki was due to be married in September 1939. A fortnight beforehand, he was called up to serve with the Polish Air Force. Zanet, his fiancée, never saw him again. She had dreams of him though, standing beside a large crashed aeroplane. After the war she married but always wondered what had happened to him. She and her husband made enquiries and eventually found that Mariusz joined 138 Squadron at Tempsford, flying on missions to France, Holland and other countries. His most demanding and dangerous were the 13–14-hour return trips to Warsaw. These missions to drop Polish agents and supply weapons, ammunitions, explosives and large sums of money to the resistance tended to be during autumn and winter as the shorter hours of daylight meant there was less danger of being spotted.

On 29 October 1942, Halifax W7773 pilot F. Zaremba took Captain Wodzicki, five other crew and three Polish agents on one such mission. They did not make the DZ and were hit by German night fighters. Probably the wings, steering mechanism and wireless got damaged. Knowing they would never make it back to Tempsford, the pilot tried to escape to the nearest coast and belly land in a snow-filled mountain pass between Helleren and Refsland in southern Norway.

More than forty years later, Zanet and her husband went on a highly emotional trek to find the crash site. They had been to Tempsford to see where Mariusz had taken off and then went to Norway. Just to give one a feeling of what it must be like discovering the site where a loved one lost their life, an extract from her husband's letter is included:

The roads were difficult, one way and winding through rough terrain until we came to a sign pointing to Helleren. From this point on it was only a dirt road and a twenty minute drive, the road ended at the farmer's complex of houses, barns and other structures. It was already late afternoon and was turning cold and windy with a light drizzle.

Our young friend went by himself to the min building and entered the house. He told us later that he asked for permission to see the sight of the crash. The older farmer was not in favor but later his son-in-law came and gave us permission, after we told him we had come from the U.S.A. and my wife was previously the fiancée of the leader of the plane.

We headed out on a dirt road by foot, because the older farmer made four barriers, so that a person could not trespass by car. After a long walk around a large lake and steep climb, the road ended. My wife was completely exhausted and could not continue. She was so close to the place where her fiancé had fatally crashed and could not go on, even with her great desire to see and be at the place where he went down.

We left my wife with Wenche and her daughter Siri under a large protecting boulder from the wind and rain and I, Svein and his boy Roy went on. Roy Kenneth ran to the top of each hill and mountain, only to give a disappointing sign. After the first large lake, another huge lake followed. The rough terrain consisted of big stones, wild bushes and knee-deep grass and also quick flowing mountain creeks. I thought we would never make it. Then came a barbed wire fence from the lake up to the top of a small mountain. We had to pry open the wires and slide through ripping our clothes.

After a long climb in this wild, muddy terrain, we noticed the beginning of a third lake, where a high stone wall bordered the lake, so the only way was to go around on the right side over the big hills. On top of them Roy signalled that he had spotted the site of the plane crash.

We kept moving, now faster (here I probably lost one camera) and finally after long hours we arrived at the site. The debris of the crash was strewn from the high wall for about a hundred feet toward the lake. For over forty years probably the most attractive and important pieces were taken and the only big pieces we noticed were close to the lake. A big chunk from the main body of the plane was on the right side of a huge boulder and an engine was submerged in the water near the edge of the lake. Most parts had a silver shine and other parts showed military paint from the outside of the surface of a war plane. We did not notice any burn marks from a big explosion or fire. Naturally, after such a long time, this could have been washed away. We made some Polaroid pictures and 8 mm super movies from the scene. Unfortunately it started to get dark quickly.

(Personal memoirs, courtesy of Roger Tobbell, Inkberrow)

After interviewing local people, they discovered that ten Polish prisoners of war were marched to the crash site. Three or four survivors were executed and all the bodies were carried down the mountain and buried secretly, along with ten executed English soldiers, at Brusand, by the coast. The latter had been captured when two Horsa gliders crashed into the mountainside in a failed attempt to attack the German's heavy water plant at Telemark.

## The Royal Visit to Tempsford

The skill, daring and enterprise of the Tempsford station brought special visits from the top brass of the SOE, the Government and the Air Ministry. Winston Churchill, the Prime Minister, is said to have flown out of the airfield on a secret mission to Ireland. It was jokingly said that he had left his initials on some of the doors! Sir Archibald Sinclair, Secretary of State for Air, also visited, and on 9 November 1943 there was a royal visit by King George VI and Queen Elizabeth. The *Bedfordshire Times & Standard* included an article on the occasion a few days later.

### King and Queen Visit RAF Station

When a short train drew into a quiet little countryside station in Bedfordshire on Tuesday afternoon few people in the neighbourhood knew that two of the passengers were the King and Queen, who had arrived to pay an unofficial visit to an RAF station near by. The news of this Royal visit, however, had spread among some of the villagers, and a small group of onlookers, mostly women and children, had waited patiently

Queen Elizabeth greeting the American and Canadian pilots at RAF Tempsford on 9 November 1943. (Harrington Aviation Museum)

at the level-crossing gates in order to catch a glimpse of Their Majesties. There was excited chatter among the spectators when they heard the approach of the Royal train, and heads were eagerly craned as it slowly came to a standstill alongside the platform.

While senior officers from the RAF and officials, including the Deputy Chief Constable of the County, stood smartly to attention, the RAF Station Commander was the first to greet Their Majesties as they stepped on to the platform. The King was wearing the uniform of Air Marshal, and the Queen was charmingly attired in an Air Force blue ensemble and fur.

Wing-Commander J.E. Pelly-Fry, D.S.O., the bomber 'ace' recently appointed temporary equerry to the King and Lady Delia Peel accompanied Their Majesties. The station bridge obscured the view of the people at the level-crossing gate, but after a few moments the King and Queen came into sight, and children who were returning home from school stood spellbound upon recognizing the smiling visitors. Spontaneously the small crowd burst into cheer and waved. A mother picked up her little daughter, and the Queen had an especially sweet smile for the child.

At the end of the platform Their Majesties, who looked the picture of health and who were obviously in cheerful spirits, were introduced to the Station Commander's wife and little child, and they chatted for a minute or two. Afterwards the Queen, with characteristic grace and charm, waved an acknowledgement to a group of women and children, and then Their Majesties walked over the railway crossing to a saloon car that was waiting to take them to their destination.

Understandably, the article made no mention of the importance of the airfield or the purpose of the visit. Clark mentioned the royals being met at Sandy station by AVM R. Harrison, AOC No. 3 Group, G/Capt E. H. Fielden, W/Cdr J. Corby and Commander Willis, RN, the Chief Constable of Bedfordshire. An account of the visit was included in Major Kempthorne's history of the airfield. He was one of the liaison officers at Tempsford.

The King and Queen undertook a very thorough inspection of the Airfield, and amongst other interests, manifested considerable anxiety to acquire a sound appreciation of all those appurtenances which form the equipment of Agents being despatched, i.e., 'striptease clothing', methods of jumping, arms, rations &c &c.

(TNA CAB102/650 W. M. Kempholme, *History of the SOE, RAF Station Tempsford*)

One of the senior members of staff at Gaynes Hall told his son how he was driven to the airfield for the royal visit. He was especially amused to observe the Queen closely inspecting a display of the Q gadgets – specially made explosive devices designed to look like wine bottles, rocks, logs and stuffed rats and mice – that were sent to the Resistance. She was so excited by the potentially explosive horse droppings that she rushed over to get her husband to come and have a look.

## Relieving the Tension

It was particularly demoralising if agents had taken off and then had to be returned to Tempsford Airfield. Missions had to be aborted if the reception committee didn't turn up, didn't flash the correct recognition letter, or if the visibility in the landing area was too bad. The postponing of the mission meant that agents needed temporary accommodation in one of the nearby 'safe houses'. Some were accommodated close to the airfield at Hassels Hall, near Sandy, others at Gaynes Hall. From here WAAF or FANY drivers would take over, arriving on the evening the agents were to be flown out, collecting them and driving them in blacked out cars through the highways and byways to Gibraltar Farm. It was essential they weren't able to identify which airfield they flew from.

Queen Elizabeth chatting to the WAAF Captain after inspecting the women on the royal visit to Tempsford, 9 November 1943. (K. A. Merrick in Freddie Clark's *Agents by Moonlight*)

While the agents waited at these holding stations, the FANY's job was to help relieve the tension. Music in particular helped. Playing the piano and listening to the wireless or to records on the gramophone was relaxing. Sue Ryder noted that:

Several of the Bods enjoyed playing the piano and the works of Chopin and Bartok were particularly loved. We learnt the Bods' folk dances and songs, especially the Czech and Polish ones, and played the haunting melodies of the 1930s and those composed in the Bods' own countries during the war. If I hear any of these tunes now memories come flooding back. I suppose it was all the more poignant as we knew what lay ahead for the Bods and that these occasions might well be their last opportunity on earth to enjoy themselves. I remember too that one group said that the tune 'Jealousy' would be the code used when we knew we could be reunited in Warsaw. It was not the words, but the music they liked. 'All our tomorrows will be Happy Days'; 'Wish me Luck as you wave me Goodbye'; 'Broken Chords' and 'The Gold and Silver Waltz' by Franz Lehar were others I recall. One of the most popular songs they sang was 'Time for us is quickly passing'.

(Ryder, *Child of My Love*)

Given the enormous tension and trauma during the war years, the enjoyment of whatever social life agents were given had a very high priority. The popular music at the time was heard on the wireless or on an HMV (His Master's Voice) wind-up gramophone in the mess. Hit tunes included the recordings of Glen Miller, the Ink Spots and the Andrews Sisters. Drinking was common but most women did not have much spare cash to overindulge. Noor Inayat Khan, one of the female agents, received £350 a year, paid quarterly into her Lloyd's bank account. She is reported to have said, 'I was well off but due to the work I could not spend it.' While many of those involved have forgotten what their wages were, records show that one SOE agent got £35 a month with 6*d* a day 'danger money'.

It is said that there were regular deliveries of beer and spirits from Greene King brewery in Biggleswade. The bars in the officers' and sergeants' messes must have done well. Cards, darts, billiards and table tennis helped while away the hours. Giving nicknames to people was widespread. Whether women in the WAAF with a surname Wright were nicknamed Wilbur or Orville after the pioneers of powered flight is not known, but this was a common practice in the RAF.

One lady told me that during the war she played for St Neots Ladies Hockey Club and twice played a mixed team from the airfield on Everton recreation ground. It was quite an experience, she said. They won one. It was very hush-hush and she recalled having a ham salad tea in the WAAF camp.

Although an early night was often very welcome, alternative stimulation was necessary. Up the hill there was also a canteen for the forces in Everton village hall, which was open every evening as an alternative to the pub. It was run voluntarily by local villagers and was especially popular with those temperate WAAFs who enjoyed going in for a cup of tea and a bun. Inside is a plaque honouring the Czech contribution to the war effort.

In this Village Hall of Everton, men of the 138 Squadron found a 'quiet time' for a cup of tea provided by the local ladies, who ran a canteen for service personnel and so we are honoured to display this memorial to the brave people of Czechoslovakia and the crews of the 138 Squadron. 28th Sept. 1991.

Stuart Black, who was transferred to Tempsford as a fitter in 138 Squadron's maintenance flight in 1942, recalled in his unpublished memoirs that:

Occasionally the NAAFI hall would be used for a concert given by such well-known outfits as the Squadronaires. Max Miller once appeared there and his first part was just typical Miller, but his encore's material, even these days would have had him banned for life. On a similar note we had a fitter, Len Drinkel, who before joining up, had been a Yorkshire stand-up comic. (His son became an actor and I am sure he was one who played a major role in a T.V. series, 'Family at War'.) In a 'Wings for Victory Week' in St Neots he gave his standard club act to the rather sedate St Neots' dignitaries and received a severe rocket in the local press. Following that Fielden sent for him and gave him a good dressing-down for letting down the station!

… One rather special day stands out; it was a Sunday when the padre took about a dozen men and women (who were interested) in a lorry to Cambridge. There we were joined by some Americans to be taken around Trinity [College] by the famous G. M. Trevelyan. We spent some time in the library and even went into his house, the Master's, and saw all the portraits of the Macaulays on the wall alongside the staircase. It must have been in the non-moon period when serviceability was 100%. On other occasional 'stand-downs' I went to Bedford and would row on the river, or go to the cinema and end up in the Corn Exchange for a snack.

A concert band called Silverwings used to give performances in local village halls, which attracted many people from the base. Comedians and drag artists provided alternative entertainment. Black also mentioned that, in the summer of 1942, Wing Commander Ron Hockey had a birthday party for all 138 Squadron personnel in Tempsford village hall. Even his parents were there. Olive Cheverton recalls going to a dance there as her friend Eileen Addison had a friend who had a car. 'Wing Commander Pickard was there. Of course we all did the Congo and the Palais Glide. That was the first and last dance held there. Lots of beer was spilt on the floor in a back room from a barrel of beer which sat on the ground. Quite the night!'

Probably as a consequence of this, Wing Commander Pickard's next big social occasion had to be held elsewhere. As he had theatrical connections, he took all 161 Squadron personnel in lorries to London for 'some sort of celebration which was held in a room in one of the theatres'. On at least one occasion, Silverwings played on the base. An undated programme on the wall of the airfield museum detailing an evening's entertainment shows just how seriously the men and women took their social life.

By kind permission of Gp. Cpt. H. Fielden MVO AFC. Captain Eddie Smith presents 'SILVERWINGS n Odds and Ends' produced and devised by George Iles. Give what you can afford for this programme. Proceeds in aid of the Station Benevolent Fund. The items included:

Hell's Delight with A/C I Iles as Mephisto and L/A/C Dale as Fairy

Impressions by Sergeant Rycroft

L/A/C Harold Harding – Vocalist

Burlesque Sketch, 'Cook House Serenade'

WAAF Cook by A/C Dale and F/Sgt Isherwood

A/C/W Edna Lest – Vocalist

L/A/C Eric Sykes – 'Cheerful Chappie'

A/C Tony Veale and his Uke

Vocal Scena 'Smiling Thro'

| | |
|---|---|
| Maureen, the Bride | WAAF Cpt Perrin |
| Tony, her lover | L/A/C A Ekins |
| John, the Bridegroom | A/C I Iles |
| Vocalist | A/C/W Last |

Sydney Delmonte and his RAF band

Cpl Frank Shiers – Vocalist

GUEST ARTISTE (Sandy's evacuee from Dover) BABY JILL

L/A/C Dale – 'Ever so Lady Like'

Cpl Eddie Smith – Baritone

'ANGELS IN UNIFORM'

| | |
|---|---|
| Florence Nightingale | WAAF Sgt Parfitt |
| Nurse Cavell | ACW C Arnold |
| Red Cross Nurse | ACW Piol |
| N.A.A.F.I Girl | Miss E. Grey |
| Joan of Arc | WAAF Sgt Bird |
| Vocalist | ACW E. List |

'THE KING'

| | |
|---|---|
| Entertainment Officer | F/Lt Jaffe |
| Electrician | F/Sgt Clements |
| Manager and Secretary | Cpl Eddie Smith |
| Stage Manager | L/A/C John Fosbett |
| Producer | A/C/L Geo. Iles |
| Props Manager | A/C Roberts |

Electric Lighting and Effects by The Strand Electrical Co. London

Support the RAF Benevolent Fund      SALVAGE AND SAVE FOR VICTORY

## The Glen Miller Band Performance

Some of those stationed at Tempsford who had transport and money would have cycled or driven over to RAF Steeple Morden, about ten miles away, on Friday 18 August 1944. They went to see the fifty-piece American Supreme Allied Command Band in the large aircraft hangar at 355th Fighter Group. Almost 3,000 people turned up. The USAAF official records of the day capture the event.

> Every supporting girder held a capacity of swing fans. A few bolder ones sacrificed safety for 'look-see' by occupying high positions. The band included Sgt Ray McKinley, a drummer who had led his own band; Sgt Carmen Master, a guitarist who was with the Tommy Dorsey Band. and Sgt Johnny Desmond, a vocalist who was with Gene Krupuk.
>
> There was also a 20-piece string section of ex-soloists and members of the Philadelphia, Boston and Cleveland Symphony Orchestra. The hour-long concert included such classics as Moonlight Serenade, Stardust and Tuxedo Junction, and novelty numbers such as Cow-Cow Boogie. The stage was an innovation of two Air Force airplane trailers parked together on which were seated the 50 musicians. The back centre stage was built up for Ray McKinley and his drums. On McKinley's left was the string section and on his right the brass and reeds and vocal section. After the performance, the orchestra left in five Liberators for another engagement.

Glen Miller and a select group from his band came back the following Saturday to play for more than 400 people attending an officers' dance.

## Entertainment at Local Hostelries

During the war Mr and Mrs Greaves ran the Thornton Arms, the pub at the top of the hill in Everton. It is said that many of the agents drank there, but it was more often frequented by the pilots and crews and those hoping to 'pull' the nearby WAAFs. When some of these regulars hadn't been seen for two to three weeks, the landlady assumed they had been posted. They almost always got back within a month of coming down. The resistance movement got them out through Switzerland, Spain, and Gibraltar. On return, they said such things as 'Oh! We've just swam the Channel' or 'Got a lift'.

Another port of call in Everton was 'Dirty Jimmy's', where pails of beer could be bought. It was in the front room of one of the cottages at the top of the hill. Regulars here had to take their own mugs. Those not wanting alcohol could go to the village hall, but musical evenings were organised at Manor Farm, opposite the Thornton Arms. On the weekends, gangs of Irish labourers used to do a pub crawl from the base to Potton. Local gossip has it that they were very generous on their way back. Mont Bettles recalls having to deliver two-pint bottles to their big canteen on the north side of the road, opposite the entrance to Waterloo (now Fernbury) Farm. They needed a breakfast delivery to help them sober up after a heavy night's drinking.

In Tempsford, Mrs Bass and other local women in the WVS set up a canteen in the Stuart Memorial Hall where, several times a week, the more temperate men could play billiards and take refreshments. Some officers, 'hobnobs' according to the locals, used the Wheatsheaf on the High Street before they flew out. Some of the ground crew used to cycle to the White Hart and the Black Lion on Station Road, Tempsford, both of which are now closed.

In Charles Potten's account of the crash of one of RAF Tempsford's Stirlings, he mentions Eric Homewood saying that when we were at Tempsford we wandered across fields to Sandy, where there was a nice canteen. I don't know who was running it, but it was a lovely place, a nice atmosphere, and I have always remembered it.

Some of the WAAFs found a way to cycle further afield to enjoy the nightlife in Sandy. The most direct route from the airfield was south along the Roman Road, the track that ran along the foot of the Greensand Ridge. Stuart Black was in Hut 15 on Site 7, which was the last site on the way to Sandy. He recalled how 'those of us with bikes, and indeed those who walked, went out along the farm track, riding in the centre through the water where it was solid below. In dry weather there were several ways along the hedges to reach the farm track nearer the railway.'

A popular place for carousing pilots and crews and unattached local women and girls was the 'friendly, oldie worldlier' Red Lion Pub in Sandy town centre. It was a medieval coaching house and was popular with members of the Conservative Club. The landlord, Harry Tinge, was well known in Sandy as chief of the volunteer fire crew. John Charrot said that Harry was 'most tolerant and good natured, particularly when a Polish or Czech crew went missing and glasses would be filled and then swept off the bar in memory of those missing'.

It was demolished after the war and a new Red Lion pub was built on the site. This has since been replaced by Budgens supermarket. However, it was some place to be during the war. Some locals considered it an upper-class pub as it had carpets on the floor! The 'riff-raff' drank elsewhere. Boogie-woogie was often played on the beer-stained piano. According to Jim Peake, a navigator in 138 Squadron:

> It provided us with many happy, often boisterous times, and was our first port of call when ops were cancelled through unsuitable weather conditions. Conditions that didn't deter our gallant crew who cycled on muddy paths, under dripping trees and on wet roads – only the blasted railway crossings delayed us on our way to a refreshing pint or two of 'Greene & Kings'.
>
> (J. Peake, unpublished memoirs, courtesy of Roger Tobbell)

Many of the WAAF and ground crew frequented the Lord Nelson on the Market Square in Sandy, affectionately known as 'Aunt's'. Olive Cheverton and Eileen Addison told of taking their men friends into a back room for a beer or two and calling the landlady 'Auntie'. The ground crew reported it often having the best bitter. There was always someone who knew when and where the Greene King brewery was making its deliveries. Word got round and that pub was well frequented until there was another delivery. When word got out that a pub had a bottle of whisky, it again attracted customers from the base. Other Sandy pubs were the Lord Roberts and Queen's Head.

Gordon Dunning remembered taking a Sandy girlfriend to see *Gone with the Wind* at the Victory cinema. Another popular film was *Yankee Doodle Dandy*. One man reported how Sandy always appeared to be full of American soldiers who drank too much and looked for women. There was a Women's Institute Canteen where they could eat and play darts, and where one was expected to leave one's brevet, the uniform cap, as deposit for a knife, fork and spoon. The Women's Institute served hot cups of tea to any of the

Some of 138 Squadron waiting for a train at Sandy station are provided with tea by the Women's Voluntary Service. (Courtesy of Stan Sicklemore)

troops from a mobile canteen on Sandy station. The hot drinks were very welcome on a cold day.

Elsie Riding, a WAAF stationed in Everton, recalled cycling to Potton to buy some 'lovely bread rolls' at the bake house and buying stamps from an old lady in a tiny post office (a room in the woman's house) so Elsie could send letters to her boyfriend. Phyllis Brown of Pleasant Place, off the Market Square in Sandy, was one of a number of local women who took in laundry for men who rented rooms in the town. They would deliver their folded clothes wrapped up in brown greaseproof paper and tied up with string. On Mondays, the traditional washing day, the clothes would be washed, dried, ironed and folded and rewrapped and tied to be picked up by the servicemen. She also used to deliver the post and one of her stops was up the hill at Hasells Hall. Many of those stationed there would have welcomed any news from home in those difficult times.

St Mary's church in Everton probably had its most cosmopolitan congregation ever on Sundays. Although the base had a non-conformist padre, there is no mention of a chapel. St Sylvester's Mission church, by the crossroads on Gamlingay Great Heath, locally known as the 'Iron Church' because of its corrugated-iron roof, was used as an army chapel as it had been in the Great War. After the services there would have been opportunities for local people to socialise with the village's temporary residents. Bob Miles recalls spending some of his weekly pay of 14 shillings (£0.70) for his role as an armourer with 161 Squadron in Gamlingay Village Institute. (As a Pilot Officer, Geoff Rothwell got 11 shillings (£0.55) a week.) Dances used to be held at the Iron Church and Bob recalls with embarrassment having to apologise to the local girls about standing on their feet with his hobnail boots.

About half an hour's bike ride away to the east, there were dances held in the Old Manor at Potton. One lady recalls being asked by an RAF pilot if he could take her home. He claimed to be the 'proud possessor of an Austin 7'. She declined as she came on a bike. There were also dances held in Wrestlingworth Memorial Hall. Another local lady recalls that one of the Poles at the dance died after crashing his bike at the bottom of Tempsford Hill. Terry Elderton fell off his bike at the level crossing, struck his head on the pavement and died within twenty minutes. One WAAF is said to have died after braking suddenly at the bottom of the hill and going straight over the handlebars. Those not wanting to navigate Everton Hill could venture east to Potton, Gamlingay and Wrestlingworth.

Ian Yuille of Grays, Essex, contacted me about Mary Peake, a Canadian who was buried in a local churchyard. His research showed that she was a driver in the FANY who had been killed on 24 March 1942 when the car she was driving collided with a lorry on the A1 in Eaton Socon, a village a few miles north of Tempsford. While the incident was undocumented, Mary was in all likelihood either delivering one or more agents from Gaynes Hall to the airfield, or returning with them if the flight had been cancelled. She is commemorated on the SOE memorial at St Paul's church, Wilton Place, Knightsbridge, London.

## Grand Victory Ball

At the end of the war, Tempsford's role changed from SOE to transport duties, including picking up British POWs and repatriating foreign POWs. For those who were left and could afford it, a formal celebration was organised in the winter. By the kind permission of Group Captain N. R. Huckle, MVO, the RAF Station Tempsford invited guests to a Grand Victory Ball. It was held on Monday 3 December 1945 at the Corn Exchange in Bedford. Tickets cost eight shillings (£0.40) and there was dancing from 20.00 until 01.00. How many went from the catering staff, WAAFs, FANYs, female agents and local women and girls who were in some way connected with the airfield is unknown.

## The Valençay Memorial

On 6 May 1991, a memorial was unveiled at Valençay on the fiftieth anniversary of the landing of the first French agent to land in France. It was unveiled by André Méric, the Secretary of State for Veteran Affairs, in the presence of Elizabeth, the Queen Mother. The now defunct 64 Baker Street website stated that the memorial was designed by Elizabeth Lucas and entitled 'Spirit of Partnership'.

> Two columns – one black for night, one white for the shining spirit of resistance – enclosing the Moon at the top which represents the conditions under which the SOE and the Resistance operated and agents/logistics dropped, landed or picked up. At the base of the monument floodlights are laid out in the L-shaped pattern used to signal the landing path for Lysander and Hudson pilots who landed their aircraft by moonlight on the fields of France.
>
> (http://www.64-baker-street.org/agents – accessed October 2008)

Pearl Cornioley, one of the forty female agents sent into France and who survived the war, helped raise funds to erect the memorial. It commemorates thirteen very brave women who were involved one way or another with RAF Tempsford, and who lost their lives while working to liberate France. A hundred and nineteen men from the SOE are also listed.

FANY: Denise Bloch, Andrée Borrel, Madeline Damerment, Noor Inayat Khan, Vera Leigh, Yvonne Rudellat, Violette Szabó, Cécile Lefort, Eliane Plewman, Lilian Rolfe

WAAF: Yolande Beekman, Muriel Bych, Diane Rowden

The vast majority of the other female agents have no memorial at all. Their contribution to the war effort has hopefully been rewarded in other ways, but this book will help keep their memories alive for their families, friends and people interested in the human side of war.

# Bibliography

*Books*

Aubenas, J. Van Rokeghem, S. & Vercheral-Vervoort, J. (2006), *Des Femmes dans l'Histoire de Belgique, depuis 1830*, Editions Luc Pire

Aubrac, L. (1993), *Outwitting the Gestapo*, University of Nebraska Press

Basu, S. (2006), *Spy Princess: The Life of Noor Inayat Khan*, Sutton Publishing

*Le Bataillon de Guerrilla de l'Armagnac 158 R.I.*, AITI, 2002

Binney, M. (2002), *The Women who Lived for Danger*, Hodder and Stoughton

Binney, M. (2005), *Secret War Heroes: Men of the Special Operations Executive*, Hodder & Stoughton, London

Body, R. B. (2003), *Taking the Wings of the Morning*, Serendipity

Body, R., Ensminger, T., Kippax, S., Portier, D., Soulier, D. & Tillet, P. (2008), *Tentative of History of In/Exfiltrations into/from France during WWII from 1941 to 1945 (Parachutes, Plane & Sea Landings)*

Bohec, J. (1999), *La Plastiqueuse à bicyclette*, Le Félin

Bowman, M. W. (1988), *The Bedford Triangle – US Undercover Operations from England in World War Two*, Patrick Stephens

Braddon, R. (1956), *Nancy Wake*, Cassell

Buckmaster, M. (1952), *Specially Employed*, Batchworth

Buckmaster, M. (1958), *They Fought Alone*, Odhams Press

Butler, E. (1963), *Amateur Agent*, Harrap

Churchill, P. (1952), *Of Their Own Choice*, Hodder & Stoughton

Churchill, P. (1954), *Duel of Wits*, Hodder & Stoughton

Churchill, P. (1954), *Spirit in the Cage*, Hodder & Stoughton

Clark, F. (1999), *Agents by Moonlight*, Tempus

Collins Weitz, M. (1998), *Sisters of the Resistance*, John Wiley

Cookridge, E. H. (1965), *They Came from the Sky*, Heinemann

Crowdy, T. (2007), *French Resistance Fighters: France's Secret Army*, Osprey Publishing

Crowdy, T. (2008), *SOE Agent: Churchill's Secret Warriors*, Osprey Publishing

De Vomécourt, P. (1959), *An Army of Amateurs*, Doubleday

Escott, B. (1991), *Mission Improbable: A Salute to the RAF Women of SOE in Wartime France*, Sparkford: Patrick Stephens Limited

Faulks, S. (1999), *Charlotte Gray*, Vintage

Fish, R. (1990), *They Flew By Night: Memories of the 801st/492nd Bombardment Group as told to Col. Robert W. Fish*, privately published

Fitzsimons, P. (2002), *Nancy Wake: The Inspiring Story of One of the War's Greatest Heroines*, HarperCollins

Foot, M. R. D. (1999), *SOE: The Special Operations Executive 1940–1946*, Pimlico

Foot, M. R. D. (2001), *SOE in the Low Countries*, St Ermin's Press

Foot, M. R. D. (2004), *SOE in France*, Frank Cass

Fourcade, M. (1973), *Noah's Ark*, George Allen & Unwin

Fraser-Smith, C. (1991), *The Secret War of Charles Fraser-Smith*, Paternoster Press

Griffiths, F. (1981), *Winged Hours*, William Kimber & Co. Ltd

Heidegger, M. (1962), *Being and Time*, Blackwell

Helm, S. (2006), *A Life in Secrets: The Story of Vera Atkins and the Lost Agents of SOE*, Abacus

Heslop, R. (1970), *Xavier*, Hart-Davis

Howarth, P. (1980), *Undercover: The Men and Women of the Special Operations Executive*, Routledge & Kegan Paul

Hudson, S. (2003), *Undercover Operator: An SOE agent's Experiences in France and the Far East*, Pen and Sword

Jones, L. (1990), *A Quiet Courage*, Bantam Press

King, S. (1989), *'Jacqueline': Pioneer Heroine of the Resistance*, Arms and Armour

Kremer, L. (1999), *Women's Holocaust Writing: Memory and Imagination*, Nebraska Press

Kramer, R. (1995), *Flames in the Field*, Michael Joseph

Lynch, D. M. (2007), 'The Labor Branch of the Office of Strategic Services: An Academic Study from a Public History Perspective', MA Thesis, University of Indiana

Mackness, R. (1988), *Oradour: Massacre and Aftermath*, Bloomsbury

Marks, L. (1998), *Between Silk and Cyanide*, The Free Press, New York

Masson, M. (1975), *A Search for Christine Granville*, Hamish Hamilton

McCall, G. (1981), *Flight Most Secret*, William Kimber and Co. Ltd, London

McKenzie, W. (2002) *The Secret History of the SOE*, Little, Brown

Miller, Russell (2002*)*, *Behind the Lines: The Oral History of Special Operations in World War Two*, Jonathan Cape

Minney, R. J. (1956), *Carve Her Name with Pride*, Newnes

Neave, A. (1954), *Little Cyclone*, Hodder & Stoughton

Neave, A. (1969), *Saturday at MI9*, Hodder & Stoughton

Nicholas, E. (1958), *Death Be Not Proud*, Cresset Press

Nicholson, M. (1995), *What Did You Do In The War, Mummy?*, Chatto & Windus

O'Connor, B. (2009), *Return to Belgium*, private publication

O'Connor, B. (2009), *Return to Holland*, Lulu Publishing

Oliver, D. (2005), *Airborne Espionage: International Special Duties Operations in the World Wars*, The History Press

Olsen, O. R. (1952), *Two Eggs on My Plate*, Allen & Unwin

O'Sullivan, D. (1997), 'Dealing With the Devil: The Anglo-Soviet Parachute Agents (Operation "Pickaxe")', *Journal of Intelligence History*, vol. 4, no. 2, Winter 2004, pp. 33–65

O'Sullivan, D. (2010), *Dealing With the Devil: Anglo-Soviet Intelligence During the Second World War*, Peter Lang Publishing, New York

Ottaway, S. (2002), *Violette Szabó*, Pen and Sword

Overton-Fuller, J. (1971), *Noor-un-nisa Inayat Khan (Madeleine)*, East-West Publications Fonds N.V., Rotterdam

Pattinson, J. (2007), *Behind Enemy Lines: Gender, Passing and the Special Operations Executive in the Second World War*, Manchester University Press

Pattinson, J. (2008), '"Turning a Pretty Girl into a Killer": Women, Violence and Clandestine Operations during the Second World War', in Throsby, K. & Alexander, F. (eds) *Gender and Interpersonal Violence*, Palgrave, Macmillan

Pawley, M. (1999), *In Obedience to Instructions: FANY with the SOE in the Med*, Leo Cooper

Peden, M. (1988), *A Thousand Shall Fall*, Stoddart, Toronto

Pearson, J. (2005), *Wolves at the Door: The True Story of America's Greatest Female Spy*, The Lyons Press

Persico, J. E. (1979), *Piercing the Reich: The Penetration of Nazi Germany by American Secret Agents during World War II*, The Viking Press, New York

Poirier, J. (1995), *The Giraffe Has a Long Neck*, Leo Cooper

Potten, C. (1986), *7 x 7 x 90: The Story of a Stirling Bomber and its Crew*, Gandy and Potten

Rake, D. (1968), *Rake's Progress*, Frewin

Rigden, D. (2004), *SOE Syllabus*, Secret History Files

Ringlesbach, D. (2005), *OSS: Stories That Can Now Be Told*, Authorhous

Rochester, D. (1978), *Full Moon to France,* Robert Hale

Rossiter, M. (1985), *Women in the Resistance*, Greenwood Press

Ryder, S. (1986), *Child of My Love*, Collins Harvill

Saward, J. (2006), *The Grand Prix Saboteurs: The Grand Prix Drivers who Became British Secret Agents During World War II*, Morienval Press

Szabó, T. (2007), *Young, Brave and Beautiful: The Missions of Special Operations Executive Agent Lieutenant Violette Szabó, George Cross, Croix de Guerre avec Etoile de Bronze*, Channel Island Publishing

Tickell, J. (1949), *Odette*, Chapman & Hall

Tickell, J. (1956), *Moon Squadrons*, Allan Wingate Ltd

Turner, D., (2006) *Station XII: Aston House – SOE's Secret Centre*, The History Press

Valentine, Ian (2006) *Station 43: Audley End House and SOE's Polish Section*, Sutton Publishing

Verity, H. (1978) *We Landed by Moonlight*, Ian Allan Ltd

Vinen, R. (2006), *The Unfree French: Life under Occupation*, Penguin

Vomécourt, P. de (1961), *An Army of Amateurs*, Doubleday, New York

Walters, A. (1946), *Moondrop to Gascony*, Macmillan

Walters, A. (2009), *Moondrop to Gascony*, Moho Books, Wiltshire

Wake, N. (1985), *The White Mouse: The Autobiography of the Woman the Gestapo Called the White Mouse*, Macmillan, Melbourne

Ward, I. (1955), *F.A.N.Y. Invicta*, Hutchinson & Co.

Willis, S. & Holliss, B. (1987), *Military Airfields in the British Isles 1939–1945*, Enthusiasts Publications

Wynne, J. B. (1961), *No Drums, No Trumpets: The Story of Mary Lindell*, Arthur Baker Ltd

Yarnold, P. (2009), *Wanborough Manor: School for Secret Agents*, Hopfield Publications, Puttenham

## Newspapers and Periodicals

*Baltimore Jewish Times*, Berg, L., 'Story of an Anti-Nazi Spy', 2 June 2006

*Bedfordshire Times and Standard*, 'King and Queen Visit RAF Station', 12 November 1943

*Chambers' Journal*, Buckmaster, M. (1946–47), 'They Went by Parachute'

*Daily Graphic*, 'First British Woman GC: Fought Gun Battle Alone with the Gestapo', 18 December 1946

*Daily Telegraph*, Grice, E., 'Return of the White Mouse', 7 June 1994

*The Economist*, 'Nancy Wake, saboteur and special agent, died on August 7th, aged 98' 13 August 2011

*Guardian*, Foot, M., 'Wartime secret agent and survivor of hard labour at Ravensbrück', 30 October 2010

*Guardian*, 'Nancy Wake obituary', 8 August 2011

*Harrow Times*, Ramos, C., 'From the typewriter to blazing Sten gun', 20 March 2005

*Hunts Post*, Thomas, G., 'Hunts Was a Nerve Centre of Allied Espionage', 23 December 1954

*Independent*, 'Revealed: The story of the spy who led the French Resistance' 1 April 2008

*Independent*, Judd, Terri, 'The scatterbrained spy who helped win the war', 29 October 2010

*Independent*, 'WW2 resistance hero Nancy Wake dies', 8 August 2011

*London Gazette*, Citation for Violette Szabo's GC, 17 December 1946

Pattinson, J. (2006), '"Playing the daft lassie with them": Gender, Captivity and the Special Operations Executive during the Second World War', *European Review of History*, vol. 13, no. 2, pp. 271–92

*The Seattle Times*, 'Nancy Wake Famed WWII Agent', 11 August 2011

*Sun*, 'Nancy's Heroes', 23 August 2010

Rodin, S. 'Mrs Smith: Train-wrecker, spy and Nazi-killer' (1948), held at FANY HQ

*Sunday Express*, Simpson, W., 'WAAF girls parachuted into France', 11 March 1945

*Sunday Express*, Baseden, Y., 'The Tremendous Things that Happened to a Quiet Little English Secretary: Secret Mission', 9 March 1952

*Sunday Times*, 'An MP Paid to Put Paid to Hitler – Before the War', 15 December 1946

*The Times*, Violette Szabo, Yvonne Cormeau and Kay Gimpel's obituaries

*The Trinity Tripod*, Hoffman, A., 'Judith Pearson Delivers a Talk on Spy Virginia Hall', 4 April 2006

## Documents in the National Archives

HS 9/10/2 Personal file, Françoise (aka Françine) Agazarian

HS 9/77/1 Personal file, Lise de Baissac

HS 9/114/2 Personal file, Yolande Beekman

HS 9/165/8 Personal file, Denise Bloch

HS 9/183 Personal file, Andrée Bloch
HS 9/250/2 Personal file, Muriel Byck
HS 9/298/6 Personal file, Blanche Charlet
HS 9/1654 Personal file, Madeleine Damerment
HS 9/457/6 Personal file, Yvonne Fontaine
HS 9/612 Personal file, Christine Granville
HS 9/836/5 Personal file, Noor Inayat Khan
HS 9/910/3 Personal file, Vera Leigh
HS 6/112 Personal file Elaine Madden
HS 9/1089/2 Personal file Eileen Nearne
HS 9/1089/4 Personal file Jacqueline Nearne
HS 9/648/4 Personal file, Odette Sansom
HS 9/1435 Personal file, Violette Szabó
HS 9/339/2 Personal file, Anne-Marie Walters

## Documents in the Imperial War Museum
Vera Atkins 9551/3; 12302/1; 23237/3; 31590/3; 31592/3; 31586/3
Yvonne Baseden 6373/2
Odette Brown 26370/5
Yvonne Cormeau 7385/9; 31572/1
Cecile Pearl Cornioley 8689/2; 10447/3
Jos Gemmeke Mulder 18153/6
Odette Hallowes (Churchill) 9478/3; 31578/3
Hidayat Khan (Inayat's brother) 14991/3
Harry Rée 13064
Elizabeth Small 29894/2; 29894/7

## Document in King's College Library
GB99 KCLMA, *'Never Volunteer' Said My Dad*, Derrick Baynham's undated memoirs

## Films and Television
*Carve Her Name with Pride*, directed by Lewis Gilbert, 1958
*Churchill's Secret Army*, Channel 4, 28 January – 11 February 2000
*Female Agents*, Revolver Films, 2008
*Histoires*, Canvas documentary on Elaine Madden, 17 April 2004
*Moonstrike*, BBC TV series, March 1963
*Now the Story Can Be Told*, RAF film at Hendon Air Museum, 1944
*Odette*, Wilcox-Neale film directed by Herbert Wilcox, 1950
*Secret Agent: The True Story of Violette Szabó*, BBC Midlands documentary by Howard Tuck, 19 September 2002
*Secret Memories*, BBC 2 Timewatch (1997), documentary by Jonathan Lewis
*Wish Me Luck*, London Weekend Television, 1988–89

## *Websites*

http://en.doew.braintrust.at/db_gestapo_4446.html

http://members.iinet.net.au/~gduncan/women.html

http://www.adam-matthew-publications.co.uk/digital_guides/special_operations_executive_series_1_parts_1_to_5/SOE-Summary-of-Operations-in-Western-Europe.aspx

http://www.ajex.org.uk

http://www.bbc.co.uk/ww2peopleswar/stories/55/a6575655.shtml

http://www.bbc.co.uk/ww2peopleswar/stories/17/a4437317.shtml

http://www.bbc.co.uk/ww2peopleswar/stories/53/a9010153.shtml

http://www.bbc.co.uk/ww2peopleswar/stories/66/a4055366.shtml

http://www.bbc.co.uk/ww2peopleswar/stories/09/a8765409.shtml

http://www.bbc.co.uk/ww2peopleswar/timeline/factfiles/nonflash/a6649932.shtm

http://camouflage.osu.edu/leigh.html

http://www.christopherlong.co.uk/pub/rafes.html

http://www.cometeline.org

http://cometeline.blogspot.com/

http://www.conscript-heroes.com/ResistanceTernoisENG.html

http://www.creativeboom.co.uk/leeds/2010/03/17/vera-leigh-soe-secret-agent/

http://www.dailymail.co.uk/femail/article-1274379/School-sabotage-How-arson-bridge-blowing-silent-killing-curriculum-Churchills-school-secret-agents.html?ito=feeds-newsxml#ixzz0nQC16Ggl

http://www.dailymail.co.uk/femail/article-1313039/Charlotte-Gray-revealed-The-Truth-British-Heroine-died-forgotten.htm

http://www.deols-tourisme.fr

http://www.deborahjackson.net/childrensnovels/timemeddlersundercover/specialoperationsexecutive.html;

http://www.destentor.nl/regio/deventer/3514561/NIOD-geinteresseerd-in-brief-Trix-Terwindt.ece

http://en.wikipedia.org/wiki/El%C5%BCbieta_Zawacka

http://en.wikipedia.org.wike/Virginia_Hall

http://entertainment.timesonline.co.uk/tol/arts_and_entertainment/film/article4060466.ece)

http://www.escapelines.com

http://www.fondspascaldecroos.org/uploads/documentenbank/fcc3fab138fbdcecfc01632f1e2f679.pdf

http://www.francaislibres.net/liste/fiche.php?index=96827

http://www.guardian.co.uk/uk/2010/oct/13/eileen-nearne-obituary

http://www.geocities.com/uksteve.geo/blunhistory2.html

http://www.hagalil.com/archiv/2004/07/meisel.htm

http://harpet.free.fr/creation/hist/08_06.jpg

http://harringtonmuseum.org.uk/HistoryTempsford.htm

http://herve.larroque.free.fr/pauline_uk.htm

http://members.iinet.net.au/~gduncan/women.html

http://img.over-blog.com/300x235/2/45/42/71/philippe-8/femmme1.jpg

http://www.informarn.nl/temasholanda/VivirenHolanda/hol040505_resistencia.html

http://www.jewishvirtuallibrary.org/jsource//ww2/sugar2.html

http://www.juppkappius.de

http://www.nigelperrin.com/denisebloch.htm

http://www.nytimes.com/2010/09/22/world/europe/22nearne.html

http://philippepoisson-hotmail.com.over-blog.com/article-alix-d-unienville-agent-du-s-o-e-reporter-hotesse-de-l-air--43696302.html

http://www.plan-sussex-1944.net

http://www.praats.be/zero.htm

http://www.scrapbookpages.com/Natzweiler/SOEagents2.html

http://www.seanet.com/~raines/conflicts.htm

http://www.smithsonianmag.com/history-archaeology/hall.html

http://soe_french.tripod.com

http://www.specialforcesroh.com

http://www.telegraph.co.uk/news/obituaries/military-obituaries/special-forces-obituaries/8009812/Eileen-Nearne.html

http://www.tempsford-squadrons.info/Funniesv2p2.htm

http://www.thememoryproject.com/VeteranAssets/Artifact/Thumb_Large/acw.jpg

http://www.thompsononename.org.uk/pdf/SOE.pdf

http://www.timesonline.co.uk/tol/comment/obituaries/article3752092.ece

http://www.timesonline.co.uk/tol/comment/obituaries/article3686759.ece

http://www.timesonline.co.uk/tol/news/uk/article5887620.ece

http://www.usnews.com/usnews/culture/articles/030127/27heyday.hall.htm

http://www.wartimememories.co.uk/airfieldstempsford.html#Whitford

http://www.ww2awards.com/person/341

http://members.aol.com/HLarroque/pauline.htm

http://www.plan-sussex-1944.net/anglais/pdf/infiltrations_into_france.pdf

http://www.buchenwald-dora.fr/4documentation/rp2/2res/3hist/06/03/02his.htm

http://philippepoisson-hotmail.com.over-blog.com/article--jeanne-bohec-la-plastiqueuse-a-bicyclette--38321016.html

http://www.adam-matthew-publications.co.uk/digital_guides/special_operations_executive_series_1_parts_1_to_5/SOE-Summary-of-Operations-in-Western-Europe.aspx

http://www.historynet.com/amy-elizabeth-thorpe-wwiis-mata-hari.htm